BY GERALD T. DUNNE

Monetary Decisions of the Supreme Court
Justice Joseph Story and the Rise of the Supreme Court
Hugo Black and the Judicial Revolution

Hugo Black
AND THE Judicial
Revolution.

by Gerald T. Dunne

Simon and Schuster
NEW YORK

Designed by Irving Perkins
Manufactured in the United States of America

1 2 3 4 5 6 7 8 9 10

Library of Congress Cataloging in Publication Data
Dunne, Gerald T
Hugo Black and the judicial revolution.
Bibliography: p.
1. Black, Hugo LaFayette, 1886–1971. 2. Judges—
United States—Biography. I. Title.
KF8745.B55D86   347'.73'2634 [B]   76–44363
ISBN 0-671-22341-0

Permission to reprint from the following is gratefully acknowledged:

"Justice Hugo Black and Robert Jackson: The Great Feud," from *St. Louis University Law Journal*, XIX, no. 4, pp. 465–87, Summer 1975, copyright © 1975 by St. Louis University School of Law. Reprinted by permission of *St. Louis University Law Journal*.

"Justice Hugo Black and the Brown Decision: A Speculative Inquiry," from *Missouri Law Review*, XXXIX, copyright © 1974 by The Curators of the University of Missouri. Reprinted by permission of *Missouri Law Review*.

"New Year Letter," from *Collected Longer Poems*, by W. H. Auden, copyright © 1969 by W. H. Auden. Reprinted by permission of Random House, Inc.

Hugo Black's letter of July 9, 1925. Reprinted by permission of Hugo L. Black, Jr.

*To the memory
of my father and my mother
Patrick J. Dunne
Anne J. Dunne*

Contents

11

12   *Contents*

14   *Contents*

Foreword

This book is in many ways a sequel to *Justice Joseph Story and the Rise of the Supreme Court* and continues an effort to write institutional history in the idiom of personal biography. The parallels between Joseph Story and Hugo Black are obvious enough—an accession to the bench under something of a portent, a seemingly brief jurisprudential ascendancy and a judicial sunset marked by disagreement and dissent. Beyond this there seemed far more divergence than continuity, although I was some time in glimpsing the continuity and I am concerned whether I have set it down here successfully.

More than that, I am concerned with my success in encasing within a few hundred pages the complex, mercurial spirit that was Hugo Black. So let me set down here the one characteristic that might have fallen through the interstices of the printed word —this man's extraordinary ability to make people love him. It made up for so many other things that emerged in uncovering the less attractive side of his steel-hard personality.

I glimpsed this bright side of Black, refracted, so to speak, in a cluster of warm attractive people who helped me with this book. Foremost was Elizabeth Black, a lady of radiance and charm. I must also record my obligation to Mr. Justice Douglas, whose towering record in the law will one of these days get the chronicle it deserves. A debt is also owed to Jerome Cooper of the Birmingham bar, whom I called "Buddy," almost by compulsion. Finally, there is Diane Kemelman, a lady who never knew Black, but whose shining, intrepid spirit is lineal to his own, and whose counsel and encouragement were indispensable.

Justice demands that I add the names here of Carol Ann (Mrs. Robert) Wagman, whose secretarial skills and lively and perceptive insights were unfailingly responsive to my outrageous typing requirements and undecipherable handwriting, Virginia V. Hamilton, my guide and fellow searcher in the past, and Franz Steinberg, M.D., who brought me back from the edge of the shadow. Needless to say, without the sustained support of my wife and children during a difficult period of recovery and rehabilitation, this effort never would have seen the light of day.

GERALD T. DUNNE

St. Louis, Mo.
December 15, 1975

A warmth throughout the universe
That each for better or for worse
Must carry round with him through life
A judge, a landscape, and a wife.
—W. H. AUDEN, "New Year Letter"

The kind of things you sweated for when you were twenty and thirty, and forty, they get a little dim and you start to compromise . . . Now I don't think Hugo Black ever lost it.

—JAMES M. LANDIS

Tennis and Television

The Camera's Eye

On September 20, 1968, Eric Sevareid and Martin Agronsky called at 619 South Lee Street, Alexandria, Virginia. Six nineteen was a pleasant Colonial house in the older part of the city, lying some twenty minutes across the Potomac from Washington, D.C. For over twenty-five years it had been the residence of Hugo La Fayette Black, senior member of the Supreme Court, and the well-known commentators had come to tape an interview with the Justice for subsequent telecast. Actually, they arrived as something of a rear guard; several days previously a CBS camera crew had been busy photographing the eighty-two-year-old Black playing his still vigorous game of tennis and working around the yard.

Mr. Justice Black no longer chased the baseline shots, but his legs were trim, his wind good, and particularly arresting, as the camera close-ups showed, were his strong, black-haired hands and thick wrists. The camera also strikingly captured the way his five-foot-eight frame still showed the trim line that had gone so well with his uniform of World War I and had even come

19

through the thick-shouldered, double-breasted blue serge that he wore as a freshman Senator in the Coolidge administration or the lumpy white Palm Beach that became *de rigueur* for that body in the days of Franklin D. Roosevelt. However, the camera crew particularly outdid the interviewers in capturing the spirit of the subject with their shots of Black on the tennis court, for the style of the Justice's play was not without a larger significance.

Black had been a Justice for a long time—in fact, a few more years and he would set a record—and he had been playing tennis longer yet. Obviously, the same enormous drive and vitality that underlay the sport also underlay the tenure. But work and play had an even more intimate connection; it was no accident that tennis—chosen long ago over the essentially self-competitive golf—was Black's game. As in his equally aggressive bridge, an adversary was indispensable. "Hugo liked to win," an in-law later recalled, "whether the arena was a political campaign, a courtroom, the Senate floor, the tennis court, or the Supreme Court Conference Room." And the view of a judicial colleague, far less congenially reminiscent, came out to the same effect: "You can't just disagree with him. You've got to go to war with him. . . ."[1]

Unlike the great majority of compulsive winners, however, the necessity of putting someone down formed perhaps the smallest element in the zest for confrontation. To be sure, that dedication to the adversary principle was the very stuff of life for Hugo Black, and it involved an overfull measure of intellectual pride. "He did not like to admit that he was wrong," his in-law's recollection went on, "and he seldom did. . . . I admit to occasions when I found his intellectual stubbornness a source of personal exasperation. . . ." And many years before, his eight-year-old daughter said to Justice Frankfurter ("with fierce intensity"), "I wish you would vote against Daddy, because he always has to have his way." The stubbornness ran to any number of things, both great and small—his reasons for joining the Ku Klux Klan, missing a turn-off on a Washington cloverleaf, holding fast to a point of constitutional law. But Black could also be the most surprised man in the world that a sense of hostility could survive a clash of adversary opinion. ("There is no earthly reason," he once wrote a correspondent, "why you and I should think less of one another because we happen to disagree. Disagreements are the life of progress.") And a Harvard law professor once suggested the basis of it all—an intensity of moral commitment, the focus of an unwavering vision, the drive of an immense prowess.[2]

Remarkably enough, commitment, vision and prowess did not in this case produce austerity and aloofness. Rather, even more singular than Black's brand of good winning was the way he persistently exhibited in his personal life the democracy he asserted as a political theory. Almost incredibly he managed to be the dedicated social reformer who not only loved humanity at large but also seemed to find something attractive in almost every representative of humankind who crossed his path at close hand. Particularly revealing was his habit of occasionally lunching in the Supreme Court cafeteria and pushing his tray down the line to take the nearest convenient seat, perhaps with the stenographers, perhaps with the young law clerks, perhaps with some tourists from Idaho. And virtually everyone who had the slightest acquaintance with him referred to him as "Hugo." But they called him that behind his back, for even in his politicking days in Alabama it would have taken a brave man to slap him on the back and loudly proclaim him a good ol' boy. Perhaps the respected aloofness was the radiation of a gamecock pugnacity that instinctively phrased compliments in a *machismo* idiom ("This was a man!") and also surfaced—so his own son said—in jealous conviction that every man in the world was looking at his wife and an unworthy uncertainty "that she wasn't looking back."[3]

And even more remarkable than the anomalies of the good winner and the practicing egalitarian was the way in which the outgoing geniality was shot through with a touch of detachment whereby the Justice was, in the most literal sense of the words, a lonely man. Not coincidence, but choice, had him by himself at virtually every critical turning point of his long career. Back in 1926 he had stood as just another figure in the crowd watching the news of his first election to the Senate being flashed in the newfangled electric lights on a Birmingham newspaper building. ("There are times that are so important in a man's life that he wants to be alone . . . that night of the election—of tremendous import to me—I wanted to be alone.") A decade later, he was eating lunch by himself in the Senate dining room when his nomination to the Supreme Court was going to Capitol Hill. And shortly thereafter he had taken the pair of oaths required for the Court before the Secretary of the Senate and a single clerk, but without the presence of one friend or one member of his family.[4]

Little wonder, then, in view of this blend of characteristics, that Black's stamp was on American law from its most workaday forms to the highest reaches of constitutional interpretation. It was the stamp of his tennis games. For if the clash of encounter, which Black loved on the tennis court, made him prefer juries to judges and legislatures to courts as affording the wider arenas of contest, he was even more insistent that the battle go forward under rules that were simple, precise, predictable, and applicable to both sides of the net. For him the glistening perpendiculars of the tennis court—where a flash of chalk dust would show even the closest shot in or out—typified almost everything the law should be. And contrariwise he had strong ideas on what the law should not be, particularly as to judges with authority to raise the net or extend the baseline under the impression of applying eternal verities.

But Justice Black would go with juries and judges just so far. Binding them and binding the democratic process itself was the great letter of the law that had been drawn from the constitutional text during his three decades on the Court in a great judicial revolution that had been very much his own—up to a point. Part of that movement seemed almost a counterrevolution, for it had sharply constrained the historic powers of judges to punish for contempt or overturn jury verdicts. And far beyond such workaday matters, there had also been demolished the judicial veto previously imposed on economic legislation in the name of a transcendental constitutional protectorate over the rights of property.

Over those years the judges had changed Black too, and within his own constitutional vision there evolved a view of what judicial authority should be—all the more intense, perhaps, because of the very narrowness of focus—he used judicial review he had once despised, and its attendant authority, to produce those fruits of the judicial revolution that were peculiarly his: a Bill of Rights binding the states to the same substantial degree as it did the nation; a First Amendment shielding preachers and pornographers alike; a right to a lawyer in any criminal trial on American soil; and an electoral calculus of one man, one vote.

Abraham Lincoln noted, however, that revolutions do not run backward, and thus the forces of change that Black had set in motion inexorably passed the bounds he had proposed for their measure and limit. Ironically enough, the vigorous protests that he had raised fifty years earlier over what he saw as a constitutionally unwarranted judicial protectorate were heard once more over what he saw as a judicial *hubris* undertaking to extend the protectorate on a scale and to subjects without precedent in history or sanction in the constitutional text.

In protest or in ascendancy, however, Black was a man to be reckoned with. Those areas of the judicial revolution that were his own had been brought from dissent into ruling case law almost by sheer force of his will. But, quite apart from this extraordinary achievement, he would have to be accounted a towering figure of his times had he passed out of public life after his ten years in the Senate, without spending a day on the Supreme Court. For he had been a New Dealer before the term was coined, and his impress in one way or another was on most of the organic statutes of the Roosevelt administration. More than this, his had been the single-handed and tactically decisive thrust that shifted the center of gravity of the New Deal itself from relief and recovery toward more fundamental reform. And, in a still larger context, he had reshaped the media of American government and politics by transforming the congressional hearing from an exhumation of past facts into an apparatus for profoundly influencing the course of current events.

But most remarkable of all was the way in which Black had done all these things, always the solitaire and seldom playing the hierarchical game by its rules. And it was little wonder that, for all his extraordinary self-possession, he looked back with a touch of astonishment at the long journey that had brought him from a frontier farmhouse in the hills of Clay County, Alabama, to the seats of the mighty. There were along the way any number of people who were astonished too, most of all, those who thought they had him in their pocket or at least appraised and predicted. Remarkable both for their own diversity and for the ubiquity of their common delusion, the latter groups included at various times the Ku Klux Klan, Alabama's Bourbon ascendancy, the Senate inner circle, the nuclear New Dealers, and the postwar intellectual establishment. It also included some Justices on the Supreme Court who had been his colleagues and coadjutors in the great judicial revolution. But through it all, Black had gone his own way, unbossed and unmanipulated, to reach the peak of his career by being both the intellectual leader of the Court on which he sat and the great dissenter from much of the jurisprudence he had helped bring to pass.

Paradox, however, was nothing new for him; contradiction had been the dominant note of both his legislative and his judicial life. When Black went on the Court in 1937, Max Lerner observed as his most fascinating characteristic the way the new Justice embodied a whole bundle of them. Black had risen to national prominence by using, in several senses, the Ku Klux Klan as part of the classic double formula—first, rousing the boobs while denouncing the interests; and second, effecting a postelection rapprochement with the initial targets of denunciation. Both parts had been performed almost as a set piece. Black ran his first race as the populist critic of the Alabama Power Company and the ascendancy of the Bankhead family. Before the next congressional contest was over, he had become not only the establishment ally but the foremost spokesman for a Bankhead's right to that family's Senate seat. Then, his own reelection secured, and under the shattering impact of the Great Depression, he undid the formula in a countermarch not only back to his original populism, but well beyond it, to earn the label of the ultraradical of the Senate. And a full generation later there were those who saw something of the same turnabout pattern in his judicial career with the great discontinuities of the 1960s seeming to turn him from iconoclast to outraged traditionalist.[5]

The television interviewers accordingly had a fascinating subject to work with, and more than that, one with a sixth sense for both the visual image and the spoken word. Even at eighty, Black could galvanize a Supreme Court session with a summation of some dry-as-dust technicality whenever he "spoke out in that marvelous voice that must have been one of the keys to his great success with juries in his younger days." No doubt a great impresario had been lost in him, for much of his record could be seen as a natural line of development of the arts he had mastered in the folk theater of the Southern courtroom.[6]

Certainly it was a logical extension, when he passed from jury summations and appellate advocacy to become an accomplished radio speaker in the era of Franklin Roosevelt and Father Coughlin. More than this, he had not only mastered but also shaped the new media. For what Franklin Roosevelt had done with the presidential press conference and the fireside chat Black did with the congressional hearing. For here he made his contribution to the media of government and politics by a brilliant orchestration of almost virtuoso techniques that others could only copy—the knack for the headline phrase, the ratable distribution of bombshell stories between morning and evening papers, the leverage afforded by legislative powers of inquiry, attachment and contempt, and above all, the possibilities of each witness for comedy or villainy. Here Senator Black turned the very power of a hostile press against itself, and developed a new and extraconstitutional apparatus of congressional authority, and indeed did such an extraordinary job that Justice Black one day would help cut the apparatus back to size.

Given such background and talent in its subject, it should have been no surprise that the program turned out to be enormously popular. In fact, as telecast and retelecast, "Justice Black and the Bill of Rights" made media history, for nothing like it had ever been undertaken before. Or almost never.

The Judge as Folk Hero

There was a precedent of sorts. Back in 1931 a nationwide radio broadcast had featured another senior Associate Justice of the Supreme Court, when Oliver Wendell Holmes sent his greeting to the country upon the occasion of his ninetieth birthday. Like Black, Holmes spoke from his study rather than from a studio, and in further coincidence, each program occupied prime time in the evening and was reported front page center in the next morning's *New York Times*. And, quite apart from the popular tribute implicit in coast-to-coast programs, each of the Justices could look to other items of extracurial acclaim. Thanks to *The Magnificent Yankee*, Holmes was the only member of the Supreme Court to be the hero of a Broadway play and a movie as well. Black could hardly match this, but he had appeared in color at the summit of American iconography, the cover of *Time*. Taken together, these varying indicia suggested that the two Justices were united in one of the rarest of American accomplishments—the judge who becomes something of a folk hero in his own time.

Perhaps the popular acclaim itself attested a collective flash of insight into the fundamental affinity between men who seemed so very different and yet may have been as much alike at the root as any two members of the Supreme Court have ever been. On the surface, of course, the Brahmin-born Holmes appeared to be about as contrasting an American type as it was possible to find from the self-taught "plain country fellow" (as Black described himself). For if Black was a hillbilly, he came of that special breed that Arthur Schlesinger categorized as "the hillbilly raised to the highest level, preternaturally swift and sure in intelligence, ruthless in action, and grandiose in vision." Like Holmes, he was a voracious reader, insatiably curious about the uses of the past and at the same time clinically perceptive in appraising, not only their limitations, but also traditional recognition of what the past supposedly was.[7]

And doubtless this willingness to see the unclothed emperor threw something of a bridge across the differing channels of vision in which each of the two men saw and wrote about the world and the law. For, to Black, things came through in sharp lines and clear contrasts. ("I read 'no law abridging' to mean *no law abridging.*") Holmes, on the other hand, saw everything—or almost everything—as a shade of gray and line drawing as the heart of the judicial process. ("That is the question in pretty much everything worth arguing in the law. . . . Day and night, youth and age, are only types.") Different perceptions spilled over into differences in style. Forty passages in Bartlett's *Familiar Quotations* attested that what Holmes wrote was elegant, epigrammatic, at once hauntingly memorable and exasperatingly obscure. In contrast, Bartlett carried but one quotation from a Black opinion, and a number of his critics constantly deplored the hyperbole of his writing. But there were others who found that Black's prose, for all its lack of conscious style, held a distinctive and effective lucidity; and perhaps, for better or for worse, it resembled nothing quite so much as the tough, springy, splintery pine of his native Alabama hills.[8]

But for all the different styles, and doubtless part of the cause of general popularity, both Black and Holmes could make law intelligible to laymen, and the instinct to do so was a manifestation of a common intensity and drive to effect real results in a real world. Here, in particular, the comments that *The Nation* ("irrepressible intellectual zest and unflagging enthusiasm for life") and *The New Republic* ("the refusal to make his private scheme of thought the measure of the State's well being") had for Holmes in 1931 could well have been applied to Black in 1968. But beyond this may have lain a deeper level of unity in the form of a kind of reverent agnosticism that was the last vestige of an intense religious inheritance. (The theology faded, Edmund Wilson noted of Holmes, but the habits of mind hung on.) For each man manifested in his own way an amalgam of hard-bitten realism and mystic vision that in turn resulted in an array of coincidental nutshell words separately coined for either —existentialist, positivist, idealist, romantic, judicial activist, progressive, nationalist, patriot and so on. And here the pair had yet another thing in common. For in each case, the nutshell word, while catching a touch of the man, also fell badly short of encasing the whole.[9]

About a year after the Holmes birthday broadcast, H. L. Mencken proposed resolving the paradox by presenting a view that saw the Yankee from Olympus not as one man, but as two. (Curiously enough, Max Lerner caught much the same vision but apparently never elaborated on it.) On three days out of four, Mencken suggested, Holmes should be seen as the soldier—precise, pedantic, unimaginative, even harsh—who was delighted to help his fellow citizens go to hell if such were their wish. Then on the fourth day, Mencken went on, Holmes would become the seer and the sage who urged the selfsame citizens not to hell but to the very stars. A few years later, Mencken also had a few words for newly appointed Mr. Justice Black, whom he promptly dismissed as a cracker demagogue, and his judgment was unquestionably reflected as a general sense of distrust of the judge who had come to the bench as the wild man of the Senate, the grand inquisitor of congressional investigations, and—as belatedly unmasked after he had taken his Supreme Court oath— as a onetime member of the Ku Klux Klan.[10]

But Mencken should not have been so quick to disparage Hugo Black. Within a few years, Black was to provide in even greater measure the very test that Mencken had proposed as the index of Holmes's complexity—a range of opinions that ran from the loftiest sentiments of freedom to ratification of sternest constraint.

On Lincoln's Birthday 1940, Black spoke for a unanimous bench in *Chambers v. Florida* ("courts stand against any winds that blow for those which might otherwise suffer because they are helpless, weak, outnumbered") and reversed a death sentence based on the coerced confessions of four black tenant farmers. On reading the opinion, Franklin Roosevelt observed that the

detractors of the press—obviously including Mr. Mencken—
owed a very special apology to Justice Black; Charles Beard, in
The Republic, went even further and prophesied that *Chambers*
would ring with power as long as liberty and justice were cherished in the United States. Yet not too long after *Chambers,*
Black also wrote *Korematsu v. United States* ("hardships are a
part of war and war is an aggregation of hardships") and put his
stamp of approval on what his dissenting colleagues bitterly
called the concentration-camp incarceration of over one hundred
thousand American citizens and their relatives, solely on the
basis of their race.[11]

If Mencken was right and the polarities of opinion demand
that Holmes be viewed as two men, then the void between *Chambers* and *Korematsu*—vaster than anything separating opinions
Holmes ever wrote—suggests that Black be seen as at least four.
For Black could expound the Bill of Rights with the same fire,
faith and categorical literalism that a fundamentalist preacher
might reserve for a favorite passage of Scripture. Paradoxically,
and to the almost apoplectic distress of his friend and antagonist
Justice Frankfurter, he could be the self-taught freethinker dismissing a venerable tradition of the law with a stroke of his
judicial pen. In still another plane of encounter, he could be his
father's son, whose outraged country-storekeeper reaction to
lunch-counter sit-ins resembled nothing quite so much as those of
his old friend and sometime small businessman, Harry Truman.
("If anyone came to my store and tried to stop business, I'd
throw him out.") And, finally, as was once to be noted far more
in sorrow than in anger by the American Jewish Congress, he
could be the dedicated public prosecutor ("crime, horrid crimes,
are with us") where his concern that a criminal trial be a fair
fight largely obscured his corresponding insistence that it be a
hard one—to the death, if need be.[12]

Accordingly, this extraordinary cluster of characteristics made
Black, as it made Holmes before him, a controversial, fascinating, and (in the most literal sense of the word) popular figure.
Like Holmes, he had something of a double constituency. One
encompassed the intellectuals—the academics, the philosophers

and the pundits both in the law and out of it—and the other involved a more broadly based affection, a kind of warm and uncritical adoption—half as father figure and half as revered uncle—that American public opinion occasionally bestows on a man of green old age, strongly held views, and a disposition to scorn repose and thrive on disputation. "I have an opinion on all subjects," Andrew Jackson, perhaps the first such figure, once wrote, "and when that opinion is formed I persue it *publickly* regardless of who goes with me."[13]

Few judges achieve this adoption, however, and the parallel success of Holmes and Black suggests at least three other elements in those who do. Obviously it helps to be a strongminded dissenter. It also helps to have a lively turn of phrase. (Perhaps the venerable Holmes best caught this quality in his bristlingly good-humored comment on an unfounded newspaper report of his retirement—that no sonofabitch was going to paragraph *him* off the bench.) But it also helps to have some idiosyncratic *panache,* irrelevant to the law but especially appealing to human interest. For Holmes, it was his bristling cavalryman's mustachios; and for Black, as millions of television viewers saw, it was a dog-eared copy of the United States Constitution carried in his right coat pocket.[14]

Media and Messages

Yet, for all their coincidences, the Holmes and Black programs also had their profound differences. Most obvious was the way in which television surpassed the older medium of radio in impact and immediacy. Here an illuminating detail as to the changing requirements of the eye and the ear was suggested by the issue in 1931 as to whether Justice Holmes would so much as pose for prebroadcast photographs. (He did.) But even more illuminating as to the way things had changed in the ensuing thirty-seven years was the content. The radio broadcast was essentially a recollection of the past; the television production came through as an intense combination of a dialogue in the present with a foreview of things to come.

The Holmes program was a conventional testimonial ("Holmes, 90, Greets Nation by Radio; Lauded by Hughes") wherein three speeches of tribute were climaxed by the brief but moving reflections of the venerable Justice. Holmes was at his best as he noted that the riders in the race did not stop short of the goal ("There is a little finishing canter") and then quoted an ancient Roman poet ("Death plucks my ear and says, Live—I am coming"). Nonetheless, for all the Holmes style, the whole affair was the product of the typographic age, a kind of set piece, which might have been presented in print with equal, perhaps greater, effectiveness.[15]

Even more striking in retrospect was its almost antiseptic insulation from the crises of the contemporary world. Nothing was said about the contemporary moral dilemma as to whether the "noble experiment" of national Prohibition should continue. Not a single reference suggested that there was so much as one black person in the United States. Nothing was said about widespread interrogation under torture colloquially known as the "third degree." There was not a hint of the widespread sickening apprehension that the current economic trouble and its massive unemployment involved a collapse of a type never experienced before. There was nothing about current political scenes wherein the opposition Democrats were assailing the wasteful spending and cryptosocialism of President Herbert Hoover. And nothing was said—understandably enough—of the running criticism of the Supreme Court. The criticism came from a variety of quarters, and two sources in the Capitol Building itself—the aged Oliver Wendell Holmes on the Supreme Court and young Hugo Black in the Senate—suggested how Holmes's colleagues on the Court had badly confused their private economic and social predilections with the commands of the constitutional text.

But the television program, as the headlines of 1968 vividly attested ("Black Believes Warren Phrase Slowed Integration"), was cut from an entirely different cloth. Here the participants were completely engrossed in the nation's current concerns, and particularly with those difficulties where exorcising the racist sins of the spirit—even with all deliberate speed—made the earlier concerns with Prohibition seem a simple business indeed. For Black's headlined reference concerned the 1954 *Brown* decision outlawing segregation in public schools, and his comment on the chosen tactic of deliberate speed was not quite a confession of error, but at least an admission of the possibility that the Court's caution could have been badly self-defeating. In further contrast to the detachment of the Holmes broadcast of 1931 was the way in which the Black program focused on current political events, the turbulence attending the recently concluded Democratic Convention receiving special comment and attention. ("I don't know what they were doing . . ." said Justice Black of the youthful demonstrators. "Daley says they did so-and-so, while the other side says they're just a group of nice young idealists singing sweet songs of mercy and love.") Particularly relevant was the way in which the telecast mirrored the manner in which the Court had become a storm center of American life.[16]

That Justice Black was on the airwaves at all showed that at eighty-two his capacity for unpredictability continued undiminished. For three decades he had been a model of judicial taciturnity. When he first took his seat on the Court he had made a brief comment on his onetime Klan membership, and the terse firmness of its concluding words ("When this statement is ended, my discussion of the subject is closed") indicated what his standard would be. A decade later he did speak out, only to reiterate that standard—"I haven't made a statement of any kind to the press since coming up here. I don't expect to make any now." To be sure, he had not been completely silent—a convention here, a law-review dinner there—but he had held his peace to such a degree that a few months before the broadcast, his colleague, cousin and great intellectual antagonist, Justice Harlan, hailed his taciturnity on the great events of the time as especially exemplary. And then without a word of consultation with Harlan or any other member of the Court, Black broke that silence in a manner and on a scale without precedent in history.[17]

Motives were not hard to find. A few months before the telecast, the Gallup Poll showed public hostility to the Court outweighed public favor, and by a ratio of 3 to 2. Ironically enough, very little of that hostility concerned the one-man-one-vote reapportionment decisions in which Justice Black had pioneered in dissent, and that Chief Justice Warren had proclaimed as the most important work of his judicial government. But enormously unpopular was the decision banishing voluntary prayer from the public schools. Indeed it was here that Black himself capped a complex series of opinions in the area of church and state by an uncharacteristically devious footnote, which attempted to temper the breathtaking secularization of the major premise. ("There is, of course, nothing in the decision . . . that is inconsistent with the fact that school children . . . are officially encouraged to express love of our country . . . by singing officially espoused anthems which include the composer's profession of faith in a Supreme Being. . . .") Unfortunately, however, there were those who chose to believe the text rather than the footnote, and a presidential candidate brought down the house at a Junior Chamber of Commerce convention by deploring the banishment of "America" from the school song repertoire because it contained the word *God*.[18]

Closely related was a widespread resentment that saw a *de facto* constitutional sanctuary extended to every form of obscenity at the very time Scripture in public places had been reduced to outlawry. Here a not unconnected pretelecast datum also included the failure of the Senate to confirm Justice Abe Fortas as Chief Justice of the United States in a milieu whose format had included a showing of *Flaming Creatures* as an index of material accorded First Amendment protection by the nominee. The forty-minute film received an even wider endorsement by being featured as the stellar attraction of the Abe Fortas Film Festival of the Yale Law School. It was no laughing matter whatever to Mr. Justice Black, and he felt obviously prompted to emphasize that the new permissiveness and the noisome horror of Times Square were not the consequence of a judicial predilection for pornography—"I don't like it. I don't use it. I never have; I've always detested it."[19]

But even more frequently and forcefully presented in the new antipathy to the Court was the spiraling crime rate in which the colloquialism "mugging" had replaced "third degree" as a verbal artifact of crime and punishment. Here Judge Warren Burger of the Court of Appeals, while decrying the acrimonious and irrational criticism of the Supreme Court, nonetheless pointed out that the District of Columbia had more homicides than Britain, and he suggested that the framework of deterrence and punishment was doing neither. Public opinion agreed. The Harris Poll showed, in addition to the general unpopularity of the Court, 70 percent of its respondents believing that crime had been encouraged by judicial decision.

Obviously, much of what Black had to say came in response to these concerns:

> SEVAREID: Mr. Justice . . . so much of the public clamor about the Court is based on this notion that its decisions . . . have aided criminals . . .
> BLACK: Well, the Court didn't do it.
> SEVAREID: The Court didn't do it?
> BLACK: No. The Constitution-makers did it. They were the ones who put in no man should be compelled to convict himself. . . . And so, when they say the Court did it, that's just a little wrong. The Constitution did it.[20]

In fact, parts of his comment sounded remarkably like a specific rebuttal to certain speeches in Congress accompanying the passage of the significantly labeled Omnibus Crime Control and Safe Streets Act of 1968. And other parts seemed responsive to what was being said in the current presidential campaign wherein two presidential candidates seemed to be running every bit as much against the Supreme Court as against Hubert Humphrey. Richard Nixon had a standard passage which his hearers seemed to find self-evident:

A cab driver has been brutally murdered and the man that confessed the crime was let off because of a Supreme Court decision. An old woman had been brutally murdered and robbed, and the man who confessed the crime was let off because of the Supreme Court decision. And an old man had been beaten and clubbed to death, and the man who committed the crime was let off when he was on a spending spree in Las Vegas after he confessed, because of a Supreme Court decision.

And I say, my friends, that some of our Courts and some of their decisions in the light of that record have gone too far in weakening the peace forces as against the criminal forces of this country.

And George Wallace was even briefer and more to the point both in private conversation ("the Supreme Court . . . it's a sorry, lousy, no-account outfit") and public address:

If you walk out of this hotel tonight and someone knocks you on the head, he'll be out of jail before you're out of the hospital, and on Monday morning, they'll try the policeman instead of the criminal.[21]

But, in startling contrast to 1931, transcending religion and crime, and lying beneath and around everything else, was the mode in which race had become the omnipresent reality of American life. Suggested by the very headlines of the interview, pressing in on every side and shrouded in an occult and ambiguous vocabulary was a complex reaction and counterreaction to the *Brown* decision of 1954. *Brown* itself now lay far behind, an almost forgotten springtime of naïve and simplistic euphoria. Already it had lost the referendum in which those most concerned had voted with their feet.[22]

No longer did petitions in the federal courts speak of compelled exclusion; rather, now pleadings talked in terms of flight, exodus, and proposed recapture as the American dilemma passed into even more intractable and insoluble forms. One aspect was to be compressed in a smoldering reaction against busing and the use of other people's children for social engineering. The other horn of the dilemma was strikingly shown when, shortly before the telecast, a young N.A.A.C.P. lawyer published —and was promptly fired for—a *New York Times* article under the headline "Nine Men in Black Who Think White." ("One step forward, one step back, then sideways, sideways.")[23]

Indeed such was the intricate web of religion, crime, race and politics that even the time lapse between taping and telecast was not without its own implications. It was not until almost a month after the 1968 presidential election that the CBS News Special "Justice Black and the Bill of Rights" went over the airwaves. And here might be hypothesized any number of things, ranging from a delicate defusing of equal-time requirements of the fairness doctrine to sensitive survival instincts of a regulated industry.

In view of this mix of factors, both obvious and arcane, the opening comments of the program seemed legalistically appropriate, for, in his glottal, half-swallowing way, Sevareid noted the lack of precedent for a sitting Justice to undertake a running discussion of the law, the Constitution, and the Supreme Court. Curiously, the commentator did not repeat the customary phrase that the program would be spontaneous and unrehearsed. In fact, he implied something of the contrary with a roundabout indication that the one subject that would *not* come up was Justice Black's onetime membership in the Ku Klux Klan.

Certainly there was much to be said for avoiding the topic. Even sixty minutes was far too short for the range of relevant material to be covered, and there was nothing in Black's public life to suggest that the principles of the Klan were in any way relevant to it. Beyond this, common decency asserted its own statute of limitation against taxing an old man with something almost half a century behind him. And, finally, Justice Black had already gone into the subject; the telecast was not quite as novel as Sevareid had suggested, and the precedent was not the Holmes broadcast either. Thirty-one years, almost to the day, before the taping, and speaking from a residence in a Washington suburb rather than a studio, Mr. Justice Black had addressed the nation coast-to-coast and in the process had given some of his views on the Constitution and the Supreme Court. But there the coincidence seemed to end, for the forbidden topic of the telecast of 1968 had been the central theme of the broadcast of 1937.

But perhaps the coincidence did not end there. The broadcast, shaped by Black with a tone and content at variance from the counsels of conventional wisdom—including possibly no less than the purported advice of Franklin Roosevelt—had been an extraordinarily successful application of the media of politics. And a decade later when the same conventional wisdom had foredoomed the election of Harry Truman, ex-Senator Black had predicted his old colleague's victory on the basis of a presidential speech at the Democratic convention. And with such experience and such insights into the workings of that mysterious force called public opinion, Mr. Justice Black surely had every reason to believe that a properly prepared and presented case—even on behalf of the Supreme Court—might carry to a favorable judgment.

And had the telecast gone out before the 1968 election, instead of after it, things might have been decidedly different.

Part One

The Big Broadcast

CHAPTER ONE

The Naming of a Justice

Two Nocturnes

The 1937 broadcast had featured Black solo and, in this respect, stood a world away as well as a generation apart from the relaxed and genial interchange between the respected guest of honor of 1968 and the immensely respectful interviewers. Even on the telecast, however, there had been a few subtly tense exchanges, and one had the feeling that, had the program been *Meet the Press,* the Justice would not have gotten off so easily. The brushes notwithstanding, however, the television interrogators differed very much from the interviewers—or, more precisely, the would-be interviewers—of 1937. For the earlier group had hounded him abroad, had sought him out relentlessly at home, and were lying in wait on the evening of October 1, 1937, when the newly appointed Justice Black had arrived for his first broadcast at the Chevy Chase residence of Claude Hamilton, Jr. Unlike the television taping of 1968, the previous broadcast had been arranged, not as a concession to years or to prominence, but as a stratagem of security. "Absolute secrecy,"

41

gravely reported *The New York Times,* "surrounded not only
the nature of the speech, but also the preparations."[1]

But the security turned out to be something less than absolute.
The press surrounded the Hamilton house in strength; and, in
addition, a large crowd was in attendance. In consequence, the
owner and Justice Black were obliged to drive through the alley
to the backyard garage ("dodged up a back alley," reported
Life) and enter the house through the cellar door. (Mrs. Black,
handsome in an evening gown, had arrived earlier.) Between the
garage and the house an alert photographer had caught the new
Justice in a most unflattering picture—hat over eyes, a slouching
stride, and carrying two packs of Chesterfields. Even better than
the picture, the cigarettes were an acute index of the tension
Black was under. He had been a three-and-a-half-pack-a-day
smoker up to his entry into the Senate a decade earlier, and since
then an unlighted Red Dot cigar had been his only form of to-
bacco indulgence. Black had every reason for solace and release
in cigarettes, for the broadcast point seemed the most macabre of
locales. Outside the Hamilton house the smoke of the magnesium
flares of the newsreel cameras plumed up in the autumn air and
inside Black looked out unbelievingly at the crowd from an up-
stairs bedroom window. ("How could all those people be interested in what I have to say?") But he quickly collected himself
and went to the first floor to face a battery of six microphones
and fifteen announcers and technicians.[2]

In contradistinction to what he had to say and prophetic of the
telecast many years later, the eye of the camera caught the heart
of the matter, and this time the backyard photograph compressed
a fall from the height of personal and political triumph to the
razor edge of ruin and disgrace. For it was barely six weeks
earlier—although it must have seemed to the Justice almost a
lifetime—that he had made another nocturnal visit. The earlier
call had been made to the White House itself, and then he had
accepted Franklin Roosevelt's initial appointment to the Supreme Court. All in all, the visit involved an evening very different from the one in Chevy Chase.

The Nomination

The White House visit was not without some dramatic elements of its own. Most obvious perhaps was the contrast between the patroon-descended President and the senior Senator from Alabama. To be sure, Black was not without a quality lineage of his own, but in terms of the hard experience of life, he was not too far removed from the hardscrabble farmers his country-storekeeper father had served in the Alabama back country. Yet between Hugo Black and Franklin Roosevelt there was really more affinity than contrast, for the President and the Senator were as one in a quick, almost biological, turn of intelligence.

But the person Black really resembled was the President's wife. Like Eleanor Roosevelt, Black was a personal Puritan, unconcerned with appearances but intent on realities, and a dedicated and purposeful champion of the underdog who had taken up that role by deliberate intellectual and moral choice. Like Mrs. Roosevelt, he was hard as nails underneath an effortless urbanity; unlike Mrs. Roosevelt, who was constantly held back by the constraints attending the First Lady, Senator Black had many occasions during the ten preceding years in the Senate to display his steel. "Black, if he chooses," wrote William Allen White from Emporia, Kansas, "can snarl and snap and show his teeth." Over-all, however, the steel came wrapped in silk. Compact, trim, looking younger than his fifty-one years, Black in 1937 remained what *The New York Times* called him on his first election to the Senate in 1926, "a bundle of energy, physically and mentally." Some Washington observers subsequently sensed another strain, and Felix Frankfurter saw something of an Ishmaelite who expected "every hand to be raised against him, and therefore [tends] to be unwarrantedly suspicious when nothing but friendliness is intended."[3]

Yet, if there was a touch of the Ishmaelite, Black was singularly free of that ongoing felinity that persistently beset Franklin Roosevelt and made the President, in a moment of rare insight, confess that he seemed to enjoy hurting the people he liked the most. And the feline mood appeared to be very much with the President in his meeting with Black on the sultry evening of August 11, 1937. For some minutes he dallied through a round of meaningless badinage with his forewarned visitor even though he had a poor subject for teasing. The Senator waited in cool self-possession until the President tired of his cat-and-mouse game and came to the point by abruptly exhibiting a Supreme Court nomination form, which lacked only the nominee's name. Roosevelt asked if he might supply the omission with his visitor's; a brief discussion as to Black's value to the administration in legislative versus judicial capacities ended in the obvious answer. The President accordingly printed "Hugo L. Black of Alabama" on the designated line where the upper- and lower-case letters strikingly contrasted with his earlier entries in bold slanting script.

Almost a century earlier another New York President had executed such a form from an Alabamian, and Franklin Roosevelt thereby did for Hugo Black of Birmingham what Martin Van Buren had done for John McKinley of Florence. Roosevelt's fondness for history notwithstanding, anticipation of the near-term future, not recollection of the distant past, was uppermost in the President's mind as he sealed the completed nomination form in an envelope for delivery to Capitol Hill the next day. The nomination was tremendously and gratifyingly important. Strategically, it was the first step in his great design to cut down the Supreme Court from superlegislature to tribunal of law, and quite apart from the grand strategy of the act, the *Schadenfreude* of execution had assumed an importance almost equal to that of the goal itself.

For, if the President enjoyed hurting those he loved, he delighted in hurting those he hated, and a rare opportunity for maximum feasible discomfiture of his enemies was afforded by his first Supreme Court nomination. At the largest level, the enemies' list included all those who had opposed F.D.R. in the last election or at any other time. Formally, this included the Republican opposition, now broken badly as a political force, but also the business community, which had shaped itself into a solid phalanx against the New Deal. Surfacing as a half-structured opposition, particularly in Congress, were the increasingly disaffected Democrats. And, seemingly repentant and turned about, but still unforgiven by the President, was the Supreme Court.

The new member of the Court, however, had to have other requirements than discomfiting the incumbent justices, and a mock advertisement set them out. One was relative youth, a necessity of consistency given the presidential strictures on the age of those incumbents. Another was Southern origins, thanks to the long nonrepresentation of the Deep South on the Supreme Court. Above all was Senate confirmability by a body that had persistently shown its independence and before which the administration simply could not risk another defeat.

Hence, a list of probables published by the *Literary Digest* in late May—perhaps as a consequence of deliberately misleading leaks—was suspect on its face. It was headed by the aged Attorney General. It lacked a Southern name. Its other designees ran the whole scale of the possibilities of confirmation—Assistant Attorney General Robert Jackson, J. Warren Madden of the National Labor Relations Board, James M. Landis of the National Labor Relations Board, Donald Richberg sometimes of the NRA, Lloyd Garrison of the University of Wisconsin, and the thirty-nine-year-old William O. Douglas, of the SEC.[4]

In this context of feint and maneuver the name of Hugo Black came almost tailor-made. To conservatives at large, he had been the prime demagogue of the Senate ever since he proposed a thirty-hour week in early 1932, and the president of the AFL seconded his suggestion and called for a general strike to give it effect. To the business community, thanks to his special Senate investigating committee, he was viewed with a fear and loathing (comparable only to that which the national intellectual community, some two decades later, reserved for Senator Joseph R. McCarthy) as a consequence of his midnight summonses, dragnet seizures of correspondence, and the sharpest of cross-examination of prominent executives. And to the Senate and

Supreme Court, those special presidential targets, there was an even more arresting potential for exacerbated sensibilities.

The congressional situation was particularly apposite. Ever since the beginning of the new Seventy-fifth Congress in January of 1937, the Senate had seemed especially zealous in maintaining its historic tradition of checkmating Presidents, and even appeared to be succeeding the Supreme Court as a major roadblock against New Deal policy. The impasse was an extraordinary and ironic turn of affairs. The President's landslide victory in November 1936 appeared to have insured the hegemony of the New Deal in all three branches of the federal government. For top-heavy congressional majorities came in on the presidential coattails, and within months of the election the Supreme Court had come through with a turnabout decision that clearly showed that it too had read the returns.

Yet despite the fact that almost every Democrat in Congress owed his seat in some measure to Franklin Roosevelt, it was the Seventy-fifth Congress that had balked the President more than any other he had ever dealt with, and the United States Senate served in the role of particular villain. Certainly the President had suffered his most spectacular defeats in the upper chamber. Painfully prominent was the failure of the Supreme Court enlargement, or packing, plan, which would have permitted the President to appoint a new Justice for every incumbent over seventy and by which six additional seats on the Court would have nullified once and for all the overhang of judicial veto. The proposal had produced nothing save a bruising intraparty battle (for the Republicans stayed discreetly silent), and was said to have actually taken the life of the majority leader, Senator Joseph T. Robinson of Arkansas. And this debacle—congressional relations actually got worse for the presidential intervention in the election of Alben W. Barkley to succeed Robinson as Senate majority leader; Barkley won by only one vote—almost caused another party rebellion and left the Roosevelt stock at an all-time low with a large number of Democratic Senators.

But his stock was as high as ever with Senator Black, who here, as elsewhere, seemed a conspicuous exception to any rule.

All through the turbulent spring and summer of 1937, Black had been the faithful and formidable legislative champion. One particularly conspicuous front was the administration's minimum-wage proposal. Here the very name of the bill, Black-Connery, combined with the Supreme Court's belated validation of constitutionality that spring, and the endorsement of both party platforms the preceding fall, suggested how quickly the controversial could become almost commonplace. Not that the proposal was quite that commonplace, for Black laid his career on the line to sponsor the measure and anticipated the fight of his life in the Alabama Democratic primary of 1938.

But nowhere had his allegiance been more conspicuously displayed than on the Court plan, a controversy also calculated to increase his electoral problems in Alabama. Here he had been supremely faithful and highly visible as he spoke on the floor and off the floor, in private conversation, and on coast-to-coast radio in favor of the presidential proposal. And when the final roll was called on the wreckage of the plan, he was numbered among the twenty Democrats who had stood by the President until the bitter end.

Unlike most of that twenty, Black was no coattail rider. In fact, his antipathy toward judicial review long antedated anything Franklin Roosevelt had to say. Nor had his entente with the President always been a particularly cordial one. During the bitter in-fighting that racked the patchwork Roosevelt coalition during the historic Hundred Days of 1933, it was Black who turned the conservative flank by suddenly pushing his thirty-hour bill through the Senate and almost through the House as well. His effort forced an alarmed Franklin Roosevelt to bring out the NRA as an aborting and defensive countermeasure. ("My notebook," recalled presidential adviser Raymond Moley, "contains Roosevelt's reaction to the Black bill under the category of 'Threats.' ")[5]

Ironically enough, it was the Supreme Court's veto of the NRA as part and parcel of its more general obstructive effort that did much to cement the rapprochement of Black and Roosevelt. And in any event the NRA experiment, never quite the

monopoly shelter Black had feared, was itself a matrix of much
further New Deal legislation, all bearing Black's stamp. Certainly by 1937 the controversies of four years before seemed
ancient history. In the interim Black had continued another line
of rapport to the administration by a role he wore with distinction before Herbert Hoover left Washington, and this was the
virtual archetype of the senatorial grand inquisitor. Black had
shown himself a real genius for using the investigating committee, whether the end was, in his words, "pitiless exposure" for its
own sake, or whether it pursued the more specific targets—all
remote from fact-finding—of breaking a legislative impasse, of
countering a whispering campaign, or of serving as a sounding
board to offset the opposition's total control of the press in ex-
ploiting the key issue of a presidential campaign.[6]

In the long hot summer of 1935, during a lobbying investigation, he had seized the files of the telegraph companies to investigate utility-company propaganda, had mercilessly harried their
executives, and had generally conditioned public opinion for
comprehensive and systematic regulation of corporate power in
this area. In the spring of 1936, when the Democrats were short
of funds, bereft of newspaper support and plagued by defections,
Black's investigation exposed the Liberty League as the mask of
reaction and plutocracy and, so, provided a key element in the
overwhelming electoral victory that followed. As apostate New
Dealer Raymond Moley noted in his *Literary Digest* column,
Black was truly F.D.R.'s terrible swift sword (" . . . inquisitional
faculties . . . held in readiness as a threat to all and sundry
critics of administration policy"). And he had other legislative
skills. He had been a formidable antilynching filibusterer. More
recently, in the aftermath of the Court-plan fiasco, those skills
had been deployed for the presidential cause in the areas of public power and public health, where bitter Senate rebuffs not only
had soured Roosevelt but had so shaken the Democratic majority—still smarting over the majority-leader controversy—that a
special "harmony" party had been staged at the Willard Hotel.[7]

It was a spectacular affair. A live pigeon was released to circle
the diners as a symbol of party harmony, and even the ice cream

was shaped in the form of a dove. The President did his part, so some cynics said, by staying away. A photographer snapped the group, and Black, by this time indirectly apprised of his selection as the presidential nominee to the Supreme Court, looked like the proverbial cat that swallowed the canary. With the single exception of Senator Minton, the presidential emissary in the matter and his future colleague on the Supreme Court, he was the only man present who knew that he had been tapped as the successor to recently retired Justice Willis Van Devanter. It was just as well, for any such news would have made a number of the participating Senators choke on their White Rock and bourbon.

For six weeks the search for Van Devanter's successor had been going forward in secret. Attorney General Homer S. Cummings had served as the solitary presidential instrument to narrow the field of choice, and not even Jim Farley or Felix Frankfurter was privy to the quest. Roosevelt was delighted to use the uncertain timing of selection to goad the Senate as a prelude to his final revenge, and he did so with the bland suggestion of a recess appointment, thereby presenting the upper house with the grim alternatives of forgoing its traditional summer recess or, upon its return, facing the constitutionally perplexing *fait accompli* of a sitting nominee.

The heat and the abrasive nonaccomplishment of the session had rubbed nerves to the breaking point, and all members of Congress were anxious to be off and away. The last roadblock to adjournment had been seemingly cleared with the shelving of an antilynch bill and with it the threat of a filibuster (which would have included the formidable skills of Senator Black). Suddenly departure plans seemed thwarted by a suggestion in Attorney General Cummings' announcement that all candidates for the Supreme Court would be given a close FBI screening. The President accordingly had the delight of seeing the tormented Senate kick against his goad. "All during last June and July," Senator Henry F. Ashurst recalled of the early summer malaise, "the Senate testily and sourly demanded that the Chief Executive make haste and send us his nominee for Associate Justice of the Supreme Court."[8]

Even the Senate might have known in some measure what was coming, for a *Literary Digest* mock advertisement—seeking a young, Southern New Dealer—merely set out the obvious. Yet the ad had omitted one key element and this was to give the Senate a nominee it might gag over but where it had no choice but to swallow. And there was a precedent of sorts. A half century earlier, Grover Cleveland, bruised and battered by the Senate over the tariff question and facing fresh controversy over a Supreme Court vacancy, brilliantly resolved the second problem by giving the upper house back the name of one of its own, Edward Douglass White of Louisiana. Whether the President in 1937 knew of his predecessor's earlier *riposte,* he followed it in fact. By early August and despite announcements to the contrary, his list of eligibles had narrowed to three—Black, Senator Sherman Minton of Indiana, and Solicitor General Stanley Reed of Kentucky.

The tincture of revenge placed the two Senators at the top of the list. In terms of discomfiture of the Supreme Court, both had been long-time critics of the Court and ardent supporters of its packing. And while both had been articulate and aggressive in debate, Minton's remarks had been personalized to a degree that even he suggested to the President that someone else might be a better colleague for the incumbent Justices.

The indicated unwillingness of Minton and considerations of Senate displeasure tipped the scales to Black. For, while there was no doubt that the Senators would confirm a colleague, Black would have unquestionably won the unpopularity contest in any secret poll of the upper house. Nor was it solely a matter of character or personality. Rather, in a chamber that prided itself on institutional gregariousness and the traditions of the club, Black, after ten years' service, remained the loner, the reader, the man of a few close friends and a number of casual enemies. In some respects he seemed a throwback to Charles Sumner of Massachusetts—a razor tongue in debate, an utter indifference to getting along by going along, and an instinct for safeguarding his political base. Ironically enough, however, it took another maverick to say what many of the Senators thought—". . . it is not pleasant for me to oppose the nomination of any man . . . whom I have met day in and day out for these past ten years . . . [but] I say that judging him by disposition, he ought not to be made a member of the Supreme Court"—and California's Hiram W. Johnson would fit his vote to his words, but few others would. For Franklin Roosevelt had accurately appraised his man and his man's colleagues when he gleefully let James A. Farley in on the secret—"And they'll have to take him too."[9]

Spots on the Ermine

Chief Justice Charles Evans Hughes and his colleagues on the Court preserved their judicial decorum upon the announcement of the name of their new colleague; but on and off Capitol Hill, although the Senate's approval seemed virtually certain, an extended debate on the merits and limitations of the nominee commenced. Indeed it began with the announcement itself, for, as a few Senators gathered around Black's desk with congratulations and Henry Ashurst moved that the Senate follow its "immemorial" tradition and confirm one of its own forthwith, Hiram W. Johnson rose to refuse the necessary unanimity of consent. And for the first time since the nomination to the Court of Mississippi's Lucius Quintus Cincinnatus Lamar back in 1888, the name of an incumbent Senator or a former Senator went to committee for consideration.

Even before it arrived there, a cross-purposed exchange of views got under way. Senator Burton K. Wheeler praised Black's technical competence, while the *New York Herald Tribune* deplored it. William Green and John L. Lewis briefly laid aside their bitter quarrel within the labor movement to commend the President. Representative Nat Patton, who had been speared in a Black investigation, said that he would not take an appeal to the Supreme Court "with *him* there." Representative Bertrand H. Snell somewhat ambiguously said the appointment spoke for itself. Senator King, in an equally elliptic reference to the recent Court-packing plan, asserted the country was fortunate that the President did not have six vacancies to fill.[10]

But, quite apart from statements on the record, rumors began flying and suggested that the President's desire to exploit his barb by maximum secretiveness might well have been, in the British phrase, too clever by half. It never had occurred to Roosevelt (as the President later conceded) to bring up any such matter in his evening meeting with Black; and, notwithstanding the Attorney General's announcement, no FBI investigation had been undertaken. Yet, had Jim Farley or any of the other old party hands been consulted, they would have told the President what *Time* immediately reported—that, in addition to having been a Klan-supported candidate in prior elections (as were perhaps a third of the Senate), the nominee was something more. *Time* did not say what; rather, it footnoted the current quip of the cocktail parties that the new Justice need not buy but only dye his robes.[11]

Despite emerging press comment, the Klan connection did not come up in initial subcommittee consideration. What did surface at the behest of Warren R. Austin, Senator from Vermont and future U.N. ambassador, was the possible application of Section 6 of Article I of the Constitution, which forbade a member of Congress during the time for which he was elected—in Black's case until January 3, 1939—to be appointed to any office under the authority of the United States, either created or whose "Emoluments" were "encreased" during such time. One proposed application of the clause was essentially pettifoggery—that since Justice Van Devanter, by retiring rather than resigning, technically remained a member of the Court, it was his successor who took the newly created office. Yet virtually all who advanced this proposition conceded that Congress could clear up the whole matter with a single sentence specifying that it was the retiring Justice who took the new post. More substantially, however, and beyond legislative repair was the parallel disqualification presented by the "Emoluments" provision.

The purpose of the ban was clear, but its mechanics were curiously convoluted. In the fifty-fifth Federalist Paper, James

Madison noted that its goal was to prevent the appointive power from becoming a "fund of corruption," and in the seventy-sixth, Alexander Hamilton traced its historic lineage to the venality of the House of Commons. Even though both initial commentators had indicated that the partial, rather than total, disqualification of legislators to offices or salaries they had a hand in instituting probably sufficed to meet the potential evil, there were other perceptions. In his classic *Commentaries on the Constitution,* however, Justice Joseph Story, who had seen the Jacksonian spoils system in operation, deeply regretted that the prohibition had not been made absolute.

More importantly, Story insisted that the coverage reached every species of compensation or pecuniary profit, and the application to retirement pay, while still obscure in the emerging pattern of collective bargaining, had been underscored in recent congressional treatment of judicial salaries. Here was emphasized the distinction between the stipend of a judge who remained a member, albeit a retired member, of the federal judiciary, and that of one who had left it by resignation. The difference was crucial; it amounted to the difference between a judicial salary armored against reduction by the Constitution itself and a pension that might be diminished or even cut off for any reason sufficient to Congress.

The difference, moreover, had been given a particularly sharp emphasis a few years back, when the stipend of the aged, infirm —and resigned—Oliver Wendell Holmes had been cut in half by the Economy Act of 1932. Ironically, the status of former Justice Holmes varied from that of his colleagues in the lower courts. While Supreme Court Justices might resign after ten years' service and draw a pension based on terminal salary, the lower federal-court judges had the option to retire—and stay judges at full pay—after a like time in service and, moreover, under ruling constitutional doctrine, that full pay could not even be taxed.

This arbitrary differentiation within the federal judiciary had been widely discussed, and in fact it had been rumored that several aging members of the Supreme Court were willing to leave the bench if some provision might be made to avoid a repetition of the treatment of Justice Holmes. By yet another irony, it was just such a judicial retirement provision authored by Congressman Hatton W. Sumners of Texas—an opponent of Roosevelt's Court-packing plan—which ultimately provided the occasion for the President's first appointment. Introduced in the early days of the Seventy-second Congress, the progress of the measure had been overshadowed by the Court-packing controversy. Its purpose, however, was plainly demonstrated when in both houses of Congress the case of Justice Holmes was discussed at length.

The bill passed the Senate on February 27, 1937, Black's fifty-first birthday. Obviously he had not the faintest idea he was giving himself a birthday present as he cast his vote for the measure. Yet in a few short months, the legislation would personally mean to him the difference between $20,000 a year for life, certain, and $20,000 a year for life at the demonstrably uncertain bounty of Congress. In fact, within the tax framework that Mr. Justice Black would do so much to change, the change of pension status from a forfeitable to a nonforfeitable character was to constitute, *mutatis mutandis,* a substantial item of taxable income made within the context of corporate compensation. In fact, so clear was the status of such a change that a substantial cash payment to the Bureau of Internal Revenue based on the actuarial value of the assured income was to be required from the beneficiary in the year his rights became nonforfeitable, unless the arrangement was made pursuant to a qualified pension plan.

The Confirmation

The "Emoluments" argument left the majority of the subcommittee unimpressed, and it exerted no greater effect when the full committee met on Monday, August 16. After a reportedly stormy session the parent group favorably reported the nomination by a 13-to-4 vote. The following day, however, the constitutional question was given an airing in the Senate debate and was sufficient to influence the negative votes of Senators Johnson and Borah. There was, however, vigorous opposition on the point, with Senator Ashurst acidly inquiring whether the Justice's spacious offices in the new ten-million-dollar Supreme Court Building did not also constitute an "Emolument."

As indicated, there was another Senator to be heard from on the basic question of eligibility, William E. Borah, sometimes known as the Lion of Idaho, who had succeeded to the mantle of Daniel Webster and John C. Calhoun as the Senate's oracle on constitutional law. Like Black he was a maverick, and unlike Black he was an impulsive one. The combination of friendship, integrity, impulsiveness and erudition led him into several painful entanglements during the Black debate. Most obvious was his successive quotation of Black as categorically denying and then not categorically denying past Klan membership. And on the appointment itself, his votes were cast in what some observers saw as irreconcilable contradiction—to favorably report the nomination to the floor, not to send the nomination back to committee, and against confirmation itself—but a contradiction that Borah doubtless regarded as consistency personified. And, characteristically, Borah was not troubled at all on the emoluments issue, but was very much concerned on a point that almost everyone else regarded as insubstantial.

Borah's position epitomized the rugged and unpredictable independence that characterized his whole public life. From the very first he insisted that Black was constitutionally disqualified for appointment to the Court: "Now, the only thing that troubles me is whether or not there is a vacancy. But very few people seem to agree with me. In fact, before Black's nomination came up, practically no one agreed with me. That does not change my views. . . ."[12]

But on the issue of whether the nominee was personally fit for the Court, the Senator from Idaho was on the other side of the question, and he rousingly responded to one of Black's detractors:

I do not regard Black as a "New Deal Lunatic." Bear in mind that Black voted to strike out the entire National Recovery Act, the very basis of "New Dealism." . . . And bear in mind also that the New Deal wages-and-hours bill . . . was rewritten by his committee under his influence. While in my opinion it is not a desirable bill, yet it is far saner and wiser than when he took hold of it.

Besides . . . if Black is not appointed, who will be? Some names have been suggested which would indeed make a man shiver.[13]

And much the same sort of left-handed tribute came from Walter White, Executive Secretary of the National Association for the Advancement of Colored People. He and Black had gotten to know each other during the Senator's tenure as chairman of the Senate Committee on Labor and Education, and an extraordinary reciprocal respect bridged the gulf that separated them. White later wrote that Black seemed an "advance guard of the new South he had dreamed of,"[14] and he often jested about running against Black in Alabama to insure the latter's political triumph. The two had a deep conversation on the day Black's nomination was announced, Black asserting that he would indeed measure up. Obviously predisposed to support the nomination, White nonetheless felt institutionally obliged to fire off a telegram requesting an open hearing on Black's suitability for appointment, but coupled his public apprehension with private expression of confidence.

But there were others who were reportedly playing a far more Machiavellian game. One was Senator Edward R. Burke of Nebraska, an anti-Roosevelt Democrat. Burke had absolute proof of Black's Klan associations—or so one newspaperman privately alleged—and mounted a deliberately bumbling and inept attack, whose real aim was to draw a Black denial, with a view to the far more devastating triumph in a postconfirmation exposure. Another maneuver came out of the forthcoming elections in New York City, in which Senator Royal S. Copeland was a mayoral candidate. Copeland pressed the Klan issue particu-

larly hard, even though he himself had allegedly been the beneficiary of Klan support some years back.

Black was in a painful dilemma. The prize within his own
grasp, the judgment of the President, indeed the national position
of the administration, were increasingly threatened by an episode
out of the dead and seemingly buried past. Explanation was
utterly out of the question in any event, but particularly for a
man of such temperament. And while his position of silent
audacity was not without inconsistency—for Senator Black had
himself insisted that a nominee traduced by an adverse allegation
had a duty to come forward and speak up before the Senate
could proceed further—he carried it off. Indeed he carried it off
so well that three decades after the confirmation controversy he
could with obvious honesty protest perplexity over "what all the
fuss was about" on a matter which, he insisted, was common
knowledge at the time.[15]

Yet, during the six-hour debate that raged on August 17,
1937, the knowledge was not quite that common, and the nominee showed no disposition to extend it as he waited off the floor
in the office of the Secretary of the Senate. Not that he had been
completely silent. When his name was before the Judiciary Committee, a group of friendly colleagues sought clarification led
by—so a prominent newspaper editor privately wrote a Harvard
professor—"a Senator whose identity I mustn't hint at, but
whom I will call Senator B---h of the state of Idaho." They got an
answer in which Black told the whole story, but with lawyerlike
caution—that he was not now a Klansman, but any Senator
concerned about former membership should vote against him.
Disclosure could scarcely have been more candid—"without
actually saying so," the editor went on, "he let the committee
understand that he had been a member." To any lawyer, indeed
to any politician, the delicate nuance should have been obvious.
But it was not. The headstrong and impulsive Borah heard what
he wanted to hear, took the floor to pay Black a moving personal
tribute, and thereby demonstrated why the imperfect tense was
so named; "We know that Senator Black has said in private

conversation, not since this matter came up but at other times, that he was not a member of the Klan and there is no evidence to the effect that he is. What is there to examine? . . . [If] I knew that a man was a member of a secret association organized to spread racial antipathy and religious intolerance . . . I would certainly vote against him. . . ."[16]

But Borah, who voted in committee to send Black's name to the floor (even though he would ultimately vote against it there), did more than speak on the Klan issue, although speech was important. In his customary rhetoric he reiterated his defense in private correspondence. ("I do not know of a single iota of evidence to the effect that Black was a Ku Kluxer. He has denied positively that he was, and denied it long before this appointment came up. One has to have some evidence of a thing before he can permit it to control his vote.") There was no doubt that the Borah endorsements on and off the floor were tremendously influential. "There is Borah's statement," Professor Frankfurter triumphantly wrote the President, "saying that the Senate knows Black has several times, long before the present matter came up, denied that he was a member of the Klan. Incidentally, I have seen the private letter from Borah in which he speaks very warmly of Black's character and ability. . . ." And the *Chicago Times,* one of the few papers to back the nominee, summed it all up in a triumphant headline, "Enemies Fail to Prove Black a Klansman."[17]

It was a long, long afternoon. The drama was not all on the Senate floor. Mrs. Black, black linen suit and wide hat, provided a note of beauty in the family gallery. She had some company:

> And in the senators' private gallery sat an unusual number of men. Well-dressed men, leaning far over their seats, listening with hardset faces to the debate. They were the lobbyists, representing the numerous interests on whose toes Black had stepped in his investigations and who wanted to beat him because of his economic views. It was their fight that a number of Senators in the pit below were making. But of course during all the hypocritical debate, not a word was breathed about that.[18]

There had been some other issues, particularly Black's use of the investigative subpoena, and the really critical vote came on the unsuccessful motion to return his name to committee for further examination. The proposal could muster only fifteen votes, and the actual confirmation that quickly followed, by 63 to 16, seemed almost anticlimactic.

Typifying the senatorial anguish that the presidential ploy had so successfully produced was the case of South Carolina's Ellison D. ("Cotton Ed") Smith, whose flamboyant racism had been exemplified in a famous walkout from the Democratic Convention as a Negro minister rose to give the invocation. ("My God," Smith had said, "he's as black as melted midnight." The minister, however, had the better of the exchange: "Brother Smith needs more prayer.") But now as the roll was called on Black, Cotton Ed who had initially " 'Goddamned' the nomination all over the place" at the moment of truth stood indecisive and inarticulate in the doorway, half on and half off the Senate floor, and voted only "present" as Franklin Roosevelt's bitter cup was pressed to his lips.[19]

Was Black culpable? Opinions varied. Perhaps the best verdict for the virtually compulsive silence was best expressed by the father of a future President who well understood the press of a tight spot. Black himself was predictably adamant that any fault lay with Roosevelt ("F.D. must have known, but he didn't ask me.") "The President," Harold L. Ickes wrote in his diary after a White House conversation, "when he appointed him [Black], had no knowledge of this, and it apparently never occurred to him to ask." F.D.R. said much the same thing to Joseph P. Kennedy when the newly appointed ambassador came by en route to Britain, but roared with laughter at Kennedy's earthy explanation: "If Marlene Dietrich invited you to make love to her, would you say you were no good at making love?"[20]

CHAPTER TWO

In the Court of Public Opinion

In Brief Ascendancy

Two days later, Black was back at the White House, now in broad daylight and this time for lunch. Once again the President had a piece of paper to exhibit—this time the commission of an Associate Justice of the Supreme Court, duly signed by the host, countersigned by Secretary of State Cordell Hull, and doubtless delivered with an appropriate Rooseveltian flourish. Black left with the precious document encased in a cardboard cylinder and nonchalantly carried under his arm. To the reporters clustered around the White House gate, he said that he had not decided when or from whom he would take his judicial oath, but thought he might do so on that day or perhaps the next and would resign from the Senate at the same time. True to his word he returned to the Senate Office Building and with a nice state's-rights touch tendered his resignation personally to the Governor of Alabama, Bibb Graves, by a letter whose style suggested a one-draft dictation—"On account of the fact that the President of the United States has appointed me . . ."[1]

It was a remarkable ceremony. The governor had flown from

Montgomery shortly after Black's nomination, had gone to the Senate and was accompanied by his wife, Dixie Bibb Graves. There was more to the journey than personal or even local sentiment, though there was an abundance of that. Graves and Black had risen together, each first winning office in the election of 1926. And they had formed a loose alliance in progressivism. ("The first Alabama governor," Black later recalled, "who was not a tool for corporations.") Indeed Graves, a Yale graduate, had turned in a remarkable record, raising corporate taxes and pouring a vastly increased flood of spending into education and public health. He and Black had been far more than fellow candidates; they had been fellow Klansmen—the governor being the onetime Excellent Cyclops of his hometown—and they had been co-laureates at a monster Klan rally held to celebrate the 1926 victory. At that time they both received solid gold "passports" in the Klan and were thereafter assertedly known in knowledgeable Alabama circles as "the Gold-Dust Twins."[2]

Eleven years, almost to the day, after that rally, the twins met once more in the Senate Office Building with the governor now accepting the Justice-designate's resignation; and immediately appointing his own wife to succeed to the vacant Senate seat. There was a singularly ironic element here, however, for the governor's action was not a cynical act of uxorial spoilsmanship; rather it was a tactical effort to buy time in a boiling Alabama political situation, where his and Black's records had produced a conservative reaction that threatened to engulf them both. In fact, the 100,000 Alabama voters delinquent in their poll taxes, and thereby ineligible for the next election, were thought to be made up largely of Graves-Black supporters, and some observers felt this was a critical factor in Black's decision to prefer the Court to another battle at the polls.

In any event, Black's decision to leave politics required only one more action to give it effect, and that was taken care of toward the close of the day. Late that afternoon, in the chambers of the Secretary of the Senate, he was sworn into judicial office by the Secretary of the Senate, Edwin Halsey. Most offices, whether President or postman, need only one oath. Two, however, were required for the Supreme Court. One was the affirmation of allegiance demanded of anyone as a prerequisite for drawing a salary from the public Treasury. The other was the judicial oath to administer justice without regard to persons and do equal right to poor and rich. Customarily, a new justice was sworn in in a two-step process, taking the first oath in private, usually before his colleagues, and the second in open court just prior to taking his seat on the first day of judicial service.

While unusual, the procedure in Black's case was not unprecedented. Chief Justice Taft, for example, had also taken a "double-barreled" oath. More remarkable was the clandestine nature of the proceeding. Only Black, Halsey and the financial clerk of the Senate, Charles Pace (to act as notary), were present. Otherwise, no one, not even Mrs. Black, was there. The haste, of course, could be put down to the fact that the Court was in recess, and delay in the formalities would have meant a corresponding delay in receiving the first installment of the $20,000 salary, double Black's senatorial pay; and perhaps it was necessitated by an impending departure on a European tour. Moreover, the expedition was completely in keeping with the do-it-now dispatch that Black's energy brought to bear on everything. But there could have been other reasons for haste—"them" getting an injunction against his taking his judicial seat. His friends depreciated the possibility, but he was adamant. ("I told them they didn't know that crowd, and I knew them better than they did.")[3]

And what he had to fear from a temporary restraining order was that special knowledge of the Senate's leading investigator that the most hidden facts may come out under a determined search, and perhaps private information that such a search was already under way. Not that investigating the investigator was new. Some years before, the utility companies had undertaken a secret, clumsy and fruitless countereffort to "get something" on their tormentor. But the confirmation controversy was something else again and virtually guaranteed that Black's Klan association would sooner or later come to light.

Manifestly, had it done so before the vote on August 17, the nominee never would have won the Senate confirmation. Indeed, had it done so before he left the White House on August 19, it is improbable that he would have carried his precious cardboard cylinder away with him. Indeed, the truly interesting question is whether the President would have ever delivered the document, had the facts surfaced. Hence, with the clock ticking away, there was every incentive to complete the formalities and put on the constitutional armor of his new position.

If these were Black's forebodings, there was a real touch of the dramatic in the two journeys that followed. The new Justice and his wife sailed from New York on a luxury liner at approximately the same time Ray Sprigle of the *Pittsburgh Post Gazette* headed south with a reporter's instinct not unlike Black's inquisitorial sense, ironically enough—and an ample expense account. Unlike the utility investigators, he had a touch of Black's luck; an extraordinary stroke of good fortune enabled Sprigle to penetrate both the ritualistic secrecy of the hooded order and the far more formidable cultural barrier facing any inquisitive Yankee.

It had not been easy going. The engrained suspicion and hostility still prevailed. ("I just got promoted on a WPA job and I reckon maybe Roosevelt wouldn't like me going round and making affidavits about a Supreme Court justice.") Nonetheless, Sprigle came up with two documents which could neither be ignored or denied. One was Black's resignation from the Klan, written entirely in his own hand and establishing his membership beyond any possible doubt. The other was an actual transcript of a subsequent Klan meeting called to celebrate Black's first senatorial victory and replete with evidence that the resignation was a charade.[4]

Documents on the Klan connection were nothing new. In fact a facsimile of the "golden passport" had been the subject of front-page newspaper publication during Black's second Senate race. But the "passport"—unsolicited, *ex parte* and self-serving—was almost beneath contempt as hard evidence of anything. But the resignation and the transcript were something else again.

Where Sprigle got them remains a mystery. One hypothesis

makes the source James Esdale, onetime Grand Dragon of the Alabama Klan, whose disbarment shortly before Sprigle's investigation supposedly left him vulnerable to the blandishments of the reporter's expense account. But another possibility indicated by a comment of the *Post Gazette*'s publisher (that the lead came from a "Southern friend of a friend") is that Black's betrayer was a high member of the Alabama establishment who could well have gathered the documents as ammunition for the upcoming senatorial campaign and then released them as a last act of vengeance against the New Deal Senator in particular and his colleagues in reform in general. But irrespective of source, the documents were extremely damaging.[5]

For there the prospective Senator acknowledged his obligation to the order and confirmed the implication that the real thrust of Black's holographic message lay not in its body but in its cabalistic close, "Yours I.T.S.U.B.," meaning, in Klan parlance, "In the sacred unfailing bond." And that the sacred secret bond remained unfailing was suggested by the transcript's caption, "Klansman Black," which preceded all his remarks, as well as the title "Klansman," by which he was unfailingly addressed. Indeed both old and new titles were deftly linked in a solid-gold Grand Passport, presentation of which was the high point of the rally and which stated in the present tense "that the bearer, Kl. Senator Hugo L. Black, is a citizen of the Invisible Empire."[6]

The Unmasking

The copyrighted Sprigle story had been arranged to break on Monday, September 13, and on the preceding Friday, *The New York Times* tried to contact Black in Paris, where he had been staying for a few days. It was a sickening development in what had been a memorable trip. In London, Black made a point of looking up Harold J. Laski, visiting Toynbee Hall, and scouring the bookstalls for some volumes of Grote's *History of Aristotle* and Thucydides' *Peloponnesian War*. Paris perhaps was even better. The Blacks stayed at the Georges Cinq and indeed were lunching as guests of honor with Ambassador and Mrs. Bullitt at a Chantilly château just before the *Times*'s inquiry came. Black declined all comment ("Silent in Paris," said the *Times*); and suddenly the chase was on, with the grand inquisitor now transformed to quarry. It was an extraordinary reversal, and doubtless there was great rejoicing among utility executives throughout the United States who once had blanched to hear Black summon reporters to hearings—"Tell the boys of the press to come in; the show is about to begin"—and now exulted that the boys had another show to attend.[7]

After he had been pursued and run to earth in London, Black's hotel announced that he was "permanently out" after its distinguished guest had bitterly complained of his lack of privacy. And not without reason, for an enterprising INS man rapped at his door early one morning as the "tired and haggard" Justice declined to make a statement and snapped: "I do not read the newspapers. I don't want to read them." Thereafter the room was guarded by what one periodical petulantly called "stalwart hotel lackeys." Yet even this security had its limits. The Blacks were cornered at a performance of *Victoria Regina,* and then once again in the darkened hotel corridor, where Mrs. Black was badly frightened by a stranger who suddenly came stepping out of the shadows. (The stranger was James "Scotty" Reston, and Black never forgave him for it.)[8]

Understandably these experiences steeled his will and sharpened his instincts to make his isolation from the press complete, and one London paper sought its story by telephoning the Imperial Wizard of the whole Klan, Hiram Wesley Evans, at national headquarters in faraway Atlanta. ("No ma'am, Mr. Black don' belong. He ain't no Klansman. Why he don' even sympathize as far as I know.") Evans had vacillated remarkably since Black's name had been placed in nomination. When informed of Senator Copeland's charge that Black was a member, he announced that he was hoeing his own row and that he didn't care "a dern" about either one of them. At the time of the exposure, in response to a *Times* interview, he said he could not recall whether or not Black had been a member, noting that a million and a half men had joined the Klan in the year of Black's asserted affiliation. By early October, however, he was to find some praise for the new Justice—"He has a judicial mind. He'll make a great judge on the bench."[9]

But in September, Black showed up poorly enough with the shoe on the other foot. ("I have been hounded by you fellows ever since I left home . . . I know what you want. You simply want to ask the questions so you can write: 'Black refused to answer.'") As Max Lerner sympathetically noted, he had been caught at a tremendous tactical disadvantage. Anything he might have said would have been compressed by the cable to the mere admission that he had indeed been a member of the Klan. Hence, his only course was to hold his silence against the time he could reply dramatically and hard, and after a feint at an Irish trip, the Blacks sailed aboard a slow mail steamer bound for Norfolk.[10]

Manifestly, the Justice needed both isolation and time to think, for the news had exploded on the domestic scene like a bombshell. Given what *Newsweek* called his "ambition, tenacity, and self-confidence," there was never any real question that he would yield under fire. Yet, while reaction split by and large along party lines, a significant proportion of the New Deal's heterogeneous coalition was demanding his head, and the number of recanting Senators ("Senate is Sorry, President is Angry, and the Justice is Silent") confirmed the obvious assumption that Black never would have been confirmed had the news come out earlier. Senator Burke, looking like the cat that ate the canary, fired off a cable to the Justice and announced "All I wanted to do was to get Mr. Black before the Committee."[11]

Outweighing the recantations, however, were old friends who stood by him in the hour of trial. The liberal press shifted its belief that he was never a Klansman to the position that he had not been one for a long time, and *The Nation* carried an article "Who Exposed Black?" suggesting that the exposure was really the work of a New York private detective and darkly noting the death in a fall beneath a railroad car of one of Sprigle's informants. In the Senate, George W. Norris, kept from the confirmation fight by illness, more than made up for his first absence with an insistence that Black was being subjected to criticism "because he is a liberal, because he wants to bring the Supreme Court closer to the people—not because he is a Klansman." Black's onetime opponent and later colleague Senator John Bankhead, as much of a Klan foe as a successful Alabama politician could be at the height of Klan popularity ("They were as thick as bumblebees wherever I went"), introduced, and had printed as a Senate Document, some testimonials to Black's basic decency and fair-mindedness coming from witnesses with a variety of associations—the Assyrian Club, the Italian-American Progressive Association, the Mobile Council of the Knights of Columbus, and Tuskegee Institute. And Borah specifically absolved Black of misleading him on the Klan issue: "I am quite sure he denied it in my presence. Knowing him as I do, I simply cannot believe that he would lie about it."[12]

Indeed the Lion of Idaho had some explaining to do; one of his correspondents noted that "no man did more to accomplish Black's confirmation." The venerable Charles Culp Burlingham, patriarch of the American bar—for whom the confirmation episode would long rankle but who would change his view of Black one day—dissected the categorical statement that Black was not a Klansman into its equally permissible implications touching the moment of assertion or any time in the past. And Grenville Clark observed that Borah had given a virtual certification that the accusations were beneath serious notice.[13]

While refusing to recant his earlier statements, Borah did yield considerable ground, but his bristling response to an impertinent questioner suggested that even at bay, the Lion was not to be baited: "I am not a member of the Ku Klux Klan, neither am I taking suggestions from intellectual prostitutes." But he no longer spoke in terms of an iota of evidence but instead conceded his knowledge of Black's membership ("I had an impression that he probably had been") and submitted personal observation that the long past was truly dead: "I served with him eleven years in the Senate, and I never heard or saw anything upon his part that indicated racial or religious prejudice."

And an extraordinary development occurred in New York. Al

Smith, now in bitter estrangement from the administration, had been scheduled to give what was billed as an anti-Black speech. Perhaps the memories of 1928 carried a momentum of their own, for when Smith took the podium he said not a single word about the Black controversy, but instead devoted his remarks to—of all things—taxation.[14]

But the critical element in the entire complex of circumstances was the President himself. "To say that the White House was stunned is putting it mildly," wrote columnist Robert Allen, and Roosevelt's obvious concern appeared in a terse "No comment" delivered by his son and secretary, James Roosevelt. In a subsequent press conference the presidential reaction seemed to move from shock to wariness; some of his more arch nuances implied that Black had deceived him on the Klan issue, and his mode of comment was extraordinarily uncharacteristic:

> THE PRESIDENT: . . . Get out your pens. (Reading) I only know what I read in the newspapers. I know that stories are appearing serially—not seriously, I said "serially"—and their publication is not complete. Mr. Justice Black is in Europe where, undoubtedly, he cannot get the full text of these articles until such time as he returns, there is no further comment to be made.
>
> Q: Returning to the appointment of former Senator Black, had you received any information from any source as to his Klan membership?
>
> THE PRESIDENT: No.
>
> Q: May we ask, if it turns out that he is a member—
>
> THE PRESIDENT: That is an "if" question.
>
>   .   .   .
>
> Q: To get back to the Black situation, did the Senate discharge its full responsibility?
>
> THE PRESIDENT (Reading): . . . until such time as he returns, there is no further comment to be made.
>
> Q: That seems to be a hint that there may be a further statement when he returns.
>
> THE PRESIDENT: No, don't write yourself out on a limb.[15]

The press immediately seized on the exchange as a not-so-subtle presidential hint to Black to explain ("Bid for Black to speak seen"), and notwithstanding his unusual form of commentary, the reporters generally agreed that over-all, little in Roosevelt's attitude seemed to show either anger or chagrin. More significantly, before the week was out the President moved from defense to attack by renewing his assault on the Supreme Court with a speech that demanded that the Constitution work for the people now rather than "wait while the law catches up with life."[16]

The speech came on Friday, September 17, and was a major policy address delivered at the base of the Washington Monument in commemoration of the 150th anniversary of the Constitution. The Washington press corps duly noted that Alabama's Governor Bibb Graves was seated next to the President, along with his wife, now the junior Senator from Alabama. The seating order held a critical significance for Graves also had been identified as a Klansman in the Sprigle disclosures, but unlike Black the governor had never formally resigned. ("When you quit paying dues, you quit belonging.") And hard on the heels of the speech came the most important development of all—the President's decision that the Washington scene was calm enough to let him make a scheduled Western tour that would keep him away until early October. Needless to say, it would also have him a continent away from the capital when Mr. Justice Black returned to it. The press misinterpreted the gesture ("F.D.R. Takes Run-out Powder on Black Sheet"); the President was not abandoning his nominee, but merely keeping his options open. At this point he had done all he could; the rest was up to Black.[17]

Broadcast I

The Blacks landed at Norfolk on September 30, the Justice obviously refreshed, cheerful and composed. "A flotilla of lighters, filled with reporters" had met his ship, but hardly as a welcoming delegation. Ray Sprigle was among them, but so was Max Lerner, who stayed for breakfast. That the sea voyage had restored Black's charm was indicated by the comment of a fellow passenger. Mrs. Thomas R. Crumley, wife of the president of Jersey Central Power and Light, announced to the reporters: "My husband will cut my allowance when he hears this, but I think Justice Black is swell." Yet even though utility executives' wives might be converted, the press itself was another thing again. The Justice firmly declined to say anything and did so in terms that were hardly flattering to the waiting journalists: "When I have any statement to make . . . I will make it in such a way that I cannot be misquoted and that the nation can hear." The obvious implication was a radio broadcast, and well it should be, for the spoken word rather than the written one was Black's natural *metier*. Indeed in this respect he was one of the new breed to whom the electronic political process came almost as second nature. In American affairs Franklin Roosevelt had made the fireside chat a domestic institution, and over the water in a pathological context, the rise of Adolf Hitler was in its way also a phenomenon of radio.[18]

Washington rumor had Black in touch by the older medium of telephone with the President in Seattle, a possibility given considerable substance by the vigorous White House denial of any such communication. In any event, Black quickly dropped from public gaze as he headed for the Alexandria farmhouse of Clifford J. Durr, husband of his wife's sister, and then Assistant General Counsel for the Reconstruction Finance Corporation, to prepare for the biggest speech of his life. It was more than a broadcast debate, even nationwide, for some New Deal cause. It was far more than a Senate oration. It was much more than a campaign address. Rather, the only proper comparison was a criminal trial, and Black was there in two capacities: he was the lawyer making a jury summation; he was the defendant at the bar.

To be sure, he had much going for him. Foremost was the commission to the Supreme Court, signed, sealed and delivered, and forfeitable only for high crimes and misdemeanors *in futuro*.

Even on the constitutional issue of emoluments, the only assault on his office could come via a most unlikely suit in a mandamus proceeding filed by the Attorney General in the Supreme Court of the District of Columbia. Equally important, his record during his Senate career was unimpeachable. He had helped carry Alabama for Alfred E. Smith in the bitter 1928 campaign. His had been the critical influence in ousting from public life Senator J. Thomas Heflin, his one time colleague and the nation's foremost Catholic-baiter. Ironically, much of what he said—of all places, in his antilynching filibuster—was absolutely true: "I would be the last, Mr. President, to be pleading against a measure which I believe would accomplish the purpose of raising the standard of the underprivileged in America, whatever might be their color, their race, or their creed. I have tried to demonstrate since I became a member of the Senate that the greatest purpose of my life is, by my service here, to bring about a nearer approach to social and economic justice. I have gone much further than have many of my colleagues from my own section of the nation. . . ."[19]

Nonetheless, the fact remained that he had been taken, if not *in flagrante delicto,* then close to it. At the age of thirty-seven, a veteran, a lawyer and a mature and purposeful adult, he had raised his right hand to heaven, had placed his left over his heart, and had solemnly taken the Klan oath, paying his ten dollars in dues, of which six was for his white robe. (Indeed his judicial gown had cost ninety dollars, which gave a certain point to the cocktail-party jape.) Moreover, his last-known participation in the Klan's liturgy showed both those rubrics at their most noisome without the slightest remonstrance on his part and, moreover, suggested that his relationship to the order was both covert and continuing.

Given these circumstances, the old maxim of the courtroom applied with special vigor—if weak on the law, argue the facts; if weak on the facts, argue the law; if weak on both, assail the other side. This, essentially, was the thrust of the address that Black brought with him to the residence studio on the evening of October 1. Three networks had given him thirty minutes of prime time, but he needed only eleven. His tactics followed the courtroom injunction not to talk too long; rather, make the unavoidable admission as quickly as possible and get off the air with a minimum of explanation.

In retrospect, most clinical analysts taking account of the tenor of the times thought it was a very good address. And indeed it was—a crisp, lawyerlike product stamped with Black's style; on its face it refuted James A. Farley's hearsay that the real author was Claude A. Hamilton, owner of the broadcast residence and an RFC attorney. Farley's statement was doubly surprising. It took nothing away from young Mr. Hamilton—who subsequently went on to a distinguished career at the New York bar and a senior partnership in a Wall Street law firm—that Black's pride of craft would not entrust him, or anyone else for that matter, with the biggest speech of all. This Farley should have known, but even more surprising was Farley's naming Thomas G. Corcoran, inner New Deal counselor, as the source of the statement.[20]

For Corcoran had actually looked in on Black—secreted in offices of the Reconstruction Finance Corporation—and had seen the new Justice at work on the address. Black and his in-law, Clifford Durr, were nonplussed as to whether Corcoran came as an emissary of the President or simply on his own initiative. In either capacity, his counsel was unwelcome, for what he had to propose was "abject repentance and a plea for forgiveness, accompanied by an indictment of the Klan and a repudiation of its members, past and present." Corcoran's asserted recollection ran somewhat to the contrary with the interim draft being an unapologetic and half-defiant assertion of the Klan membership as an obligation to friends.[21]

Perhaps the Corcoran visit was providential if it did nothing else than excise the combativeness that could come to Black almost as second nature. Indeed as things turned out, apologies and defiance could have been equally fatal. In retrospect the final draft contained only one serious flaw, and that a product of some subsequently developing nuances of language. This was Black's assertion that some of his best friends were Catholics and Jews, even though (somewhat unusual for Birmingham of the twenties and thirties) some of them actually *were* Catholics and Jews— ". . . in my case it was true."[22]

Over-all, it was a crisp and workmanlike effort. The beginning was a hint of innocent surprise at the "planned and concerted attack" during his recent absence on vacation and the assertion that this attack was "calculated to create racial and religious hatred." From here it was easy to work into the touch of hyperbole, outlining the potential of this hatred to revive the turbulence of the twenties, infect political life, bankrupt many businesses, punish professional men, and, in general, to set neighbor at war with neighbor. Accordingly, Black went on to do his part "in averting such a catastrophe"; he was breaking with precedent and making the speech. He then got down to the business at hand in a series of staccato sentences that conceded the undeniable and not a whit more:

> I did join the Klan. I later resigned. I have never rejoined. I have never considered and I do not now consider the unsolicited card . . . as a membership of any kind in the Ku Klux Klan, I never used it. I did not even keep it.
>
> Before becoming a Senator I dropped the Klan. I have had nothing to do with it since that time.

From this point he briefly reviewed his public and private life, passed to a characteristic *defi* ("With this statement my discussion of the subject is closed") and then, after noting that official conduct must always receive close scrutiny, said goodnight.[23]

Someone later made a count—108 lines of attack, 10 of admission, and 94 of defense and explanation. Over-all, the eleven-minute performance was a smooth one, with a minimum of flaws —at one point in the broadcast, there came a loud hum as the household Frigidaire cut in; at another, one of the Hamilton children could be heard calling from the top of the stairs; and at the close, one of the small assemblage of guests broke out in a brief burst of solitary applause as Black lit up a Chesterfield.

The next day's comments were basically predictable. His old friends stood by him; his avowed enemies were conspicuously

outraged. Press comment, as on his nomination, was almost
wholly critical. There were some arresting data at the margins.
Hiram Wesley Evans in a neat turn of phrase called the speech
renunciation without denunciation. Raymond Moley rejoined
that the Imperial Wizard had coined a definition of hypocrisy
worthy of immortality. And Black's blandness on the point set
off an almost distinct controversy. Norman Thomas, bristling at
the suggestion of Black's defenders that the Birmingham Klan
was really something of a service club ("I rise to the defense of
Rotary"), wrote a slashing letter regretting the absence of anything in the address approaching censure of the masked brotherhood and deploring Black's lack of candor during the Senate
debate. And, on the ambiguity of Black's stance, a counterpart
condemnation was also enunciated by Senator Josiah W. Bailey
of North Carolina, whose political philosophy was about as different from that of Norman Thomas as it was possible to be:

> He confesses that he was a member of the Klan and ad-
> mits that he stood silent when the impression was being
> made in the Senate . . . that he was not . . . He con-
> fesses that he joined the Klan, but he repudiates its prin-
> ciples . . . He claimed that he resigned, but . . . I have
> always understood . . . one gets out of the Klan only by
> banishment. . . .[24]

At the moment, however, Black's delicately grafted neutrality
of position occupied front stage center, and many of his supporters reflected Corcoran's position in regretting that he had not
said at least a few words of censure. No one had really expected
him to denounce the Klan or Imperial Wizard Evans in the profane rhetoric of Huey Long (" . . . that Imperial bastard . . .
when I call him a sonofabitch, I am not using profanity but
referring to the circumstances of his birth"), but some mild condemnation had been hoped for.[25]

Yet the address, even as it stood in uncontrite finality, showed
that the country was making some progress. Certainly, an even
half-apologetic admission of Klan membership compared quite
favorably with Grant's counterpart explanation for the Know

Nothings almost a century earlier; and in a more recent context it stood poles apart from the bravado assertion of Klan membership made by the only other member of the Supreme Court to hold it. For Hugo Black and Edward Douglass White had more in common than being Southern Senators whose nominations to the high court were undertaken with an eye to their Senate colleagues' automatic approval. They were also at one in their admitted membership in organizations that successively called themselves the Ku Klux Klan; White not only had belonged to the earlier growth, but proudly told the promoter of the movie *The Birth of a Nation* that "I was a member of the Klan, sir . . . Through many a dark night I walked my sentinel's beat through the ugliest streets of New Orleans with my rifle on my shoulder."[26]

The Verdict

The critical reaction to what Black said or did not say, however, rested in that elusive and unpredictable force called public opinion, and a reading of over-all response of all the people who heard him. As things turned out, he had the largest audience since the abdication speech of Edward VIII. The critical appraisal, however, came from a man who assertedly had not heard him at all. On this point the White House was adamant, although the explanations of the presidential staff could be reconciled only with difficulty. One version was that there was no radio in the touring car in which the President was entering Fort Lewis on the far-distant Pacific Coast at the time of the speech. A second was that the radio in the car was not working. A third said the radio was indeed working but had been drowned out by the military band and the salute of twenty-one guns.

In any event, however, upon his return to Washington, the President told Jim Farley that Black's address was "a grand job" and that it "did the trick." Farley, his eyes ahead on the next election, was not quite so optimistic, but nonetheless thought that Black had done the best he could. The President's view,

however, was the one which obviously counted and for a number
of reason. "His hunches . . . ," wrote a contemporary political
observer, "are backed by an almost uncanny knowledge of the
state of the American mind at a particular time and on particular
issues. He is generally right about what the American people will
take and when and how much they will take. . . . He is sensitive to the public as some people are sensitive to weather." And
more than that, once the initial shock had passed, the Klan controversy presented the President with precisely the sort of situation he faced with relish. For just a few months earlier, Senator
Ashurst had noted in his diary the extraordinary faith of the man
he referred to as Eff Dee "in his own capacity as a helmsman to
steer the Ship of State in what he believes off-shoals directions.
[He] frequently disdains to consult map, chart or compass, and
prefers to adjust himself into the situation as it arises and to
shape policy as and when they develop."[27]

The President responded to the Black crisis accordingly. His
first moves—the anti-Court speech following the Klan disclosures and the seat of honor given there to ex-Klansman Graves—
had been essentially tactical probes testing the terrain. The critical maneuver came during the return from the Coast on a Chicago stopover designed to secure a particularly sensitive and
restive component of the New Deal coalition, the blue-collar
ethnics. ("Out here there is considerable anti-Black feeling
among Catholics," reported Irving Brant from St. Louis.) The
President had an answer for that in the form of a long luncheon
with George William Cardinal Mundelein followed by a tour of
the city in which New Dealer Bishop Bernard Sheil was a highly
visible motoring companion in the presidential limousine.[28]

Secretary Ickes had been apprehensive about the luncheon
engagement, feeling that it would only exacerbate existing religious tensions. Nonetheless, he must have been enormously
pleased with what Roosevelt reported upon his return. For the
Cardinal, speaking with either the innocence of a dove or the
guile of a serpent, asserted that on matters of race, religion, or
parochial schools, there was no judge he would rather face than
Black. ("He will bend over backwards to be fair.")[29]

Roosevelt's Chicago stopover also included a major foreign-policy address in which the President sharply broke with the isolationist past and called for a quarantine of international aggressors. Arthur Krock reported that the passage—which had been interpolated at the suggestion of Harold Ickes without the knowledge of the State Department professionals—"panicked the diplomatic bureaucracy." Columnist George Sokolsky, however, insisted that the interpolation had been made and the course of history changed in order to divert public attention from the Black controversy. And, as captured documents showed after the close of World War II, so did the German ambassador to the United States, Hans Dieckhoff.[30]

The latter conclusion undoubtedly drew on something of a long bow. Nonetheless, subsequent events suggested that the President had not lost that deft touch in the subtle interplay that went on between him and the state of public opinion. Unquestionably, Roosevelt was far too modest in implying that Black's radio remarks "did the trick," for he obviously gave the trick a helping hand. But in any event, he was right; the Gallup poll, which shortly after the Klan disclosure showed a majority sentiment in favor of Black's resignation from the bench, swung round quite the other way after the big broadcast and indicated that a majority favored Black's remaining on the bench.

There remained, however, the tactics for coping with the last reverberations of the storm during the few days that remained before the opening of the Supreme Court for the 1937–1938 term. A strict embargo was placed on the press, with the job of enforcement given to Black's newly appointed clerk, Jerome "Buddy" Cooper, of the Birmingham bar. Cooper enforced the constraint with some reluctance against Max Lerner, who now fared no better than the lowest cub, but perhaps the job otherwise was not without its satisfactions. For Cooper himself had been the subject of cynical newspaper comment over Black's appointment of a Jew, a Catholic and a Negro respectively as his clerk, secretary and messenger. Yet if the appointments were intended as a theatrical ploy, the Justice had been setting the stage for a long time. He had known Cooper's father from his own university days as a fellow member of the Masonic Lodge in Tuscaloosa. And in fact so deep was the family friendship that Cooper's father had half-prophesied his son's appointment the moment that of Black was announced. ("Maybe he'll take you with him.")[31]

And thus both Justice and clerk began the process of acquaintance in an environment where the welcoming tones reflected the sentiments of the latest Gallup poll. The frequently dissenting Justice Stone, who as Coolidge's Attorney General had once retained lawyer Black for a special assignment, renewed acquaintance with him, offering help and a veiled admonition: "Despite all criticisms . . . the Court is a great tribunal . . . and the preservation of most of its traditions is worthy of our best efforts." Far more significant was the attitude of Chief Justice Hughes, whose bearded and Olympian aloofness masked a sagacity capable of beating Franklin Roosevelt at his own game. There was a truly exquisite irony here, for Black had opposed Hughes's confirmation just seven years before; it was part of "the most savage assault ever made upon a nominee for Chief Justice of the United States," Senator Ashurst noted. But if the President had hoped to insert this as the last barb, the effort miscarried. The Chief Justice was fidelity itself to the principle of returning good for evil; on the morning of October 5, 1937, he welcomed Black to his first day as a sitting Justice of the Court "with all the courtesy and cordiality that could have been bestowed upon the most distinguished jurist in the land."[32]

One final hurdle remained. A potential personality clash loomed with James Clark McReynolds whom two decades had transformed from Wilson's trust-busting Attorney General to the most irately reactionary member of the federal bench. He showed signs of extending to his new colleague the especial exasperation he reserved for cigarette smoke, law reviews, women lawyers and Franklin Roosevelt—"The man is really mad is he not? Do you think he'll have to be committed?" But McReynolds reckoned without the determined geniality which had carried Alabama against overwhelming odds, and he was soon to experience that geniality at first hand.

On Justice Black's instruction, law clerk Cooper was to plot the hour and minute of McReynolds' daily arrival at the Court until the moment was reduced to predictability. Shortly thereafter, and by seeming happenstance, one morning as the venerable Tennessean arrived at the floor of his chambers, the elevator door opened to reveal his newest colleague, hand outstretched and flashing a "Clay County smile," announcing in the broadest of Alabama accents: "Gud mawnin', Mr. Justice *McReynolds!*" And the older man's grumpy reserve dissolved like frost beneath a spring sun.[33]

And that was as it should be, for underneath it all Black and "Old Mac" were made of much the same steel. Their antitrust views were remarkably alike. Someone said that Old Mac's model of business competition was a fight to the death in a dark Tennessee cabin. Nor was Black's too far away. Indeed, in the Supreme Court photograph, the two looked like father and son.

More difficult to neutralize than Justice McReynolds were the separate motions that two New England lawyers had filed in their individual capacities as members of the Supreme Court bar and as members of the public, seeking to raise the "emoluments" issue and thereby challenge Black's right to his seat. Perhaps it was for this reason that Black did not undertake the customary repetition of the judicial oath in open court but instead mounted the bench without ceremony. Yet here again the Chief Justice's handling of the challenge was not without its significant aspects. One petitioner, Patrick Kelly, of Boston, attempted to raise the point during the presentation of candidates for admission to the Court's bar and was publicly rebuked for violating the Court's announced order of business. The other, Arthur Leavitt, of New Haven, was sharply pressed by Hughes as to the conformance of his motion with the rules of the Court. ("Yes, it has been duly printed.")[34]

Not that compliance with either the announced order of business or the rules did much good. One week later, both petitions were dismissed, not on the merits but by reason of the lack of standing of the petitioners to raise the issue. Usually such a disposition was merely recorded by the clerk in the reports without comment or explanation. This time, however, the Chief Justice departed from precedent by orally announcing the result from the bench. Unfortunately, the record did not show that Black had disqualified himself from consideration of the issue and thereby permitted his critics to assert that he had begun his judicial career by sitting on his own qualifications to sit.[35]

There were other criticisms, but there were some tributes too, and prophetic ones at that. Out in St. Louis, Irving Brant shared honors with Walter White in forecast as he wrote an editorial predicting that the new Justice would become the Court's foremost champion of civil rights, only to see it suppressed in favor of one attacking Black as a Klansman. (There was a happy ending here, Brant recalled, for the publisher permitted "a eulogy of Black at the first demonstration of his true position.") From Wichita, Kansas, Henry Ware Allen echoed what Borah had to say as he wrote *The New York Times* and suggested that Black's anti-NRA stand showed a fundamental c.nservatism, which had gone unnoticed. And in the Senate itself, Josiah Bailey of North Carolina, not quite his enemy but never his friend, proposed the best foreview of all—that Black would "read the Constitution to find out what it means and not what he wishes it to mean or he thinks people wish it to mean."[36]

Bailey had marked him well in appraising those characteristics which Black, unbought, unbossed and unmanipulated, had shown in his Senate years and most particularly in the last thirty days. That Hugo Black, playing the game of politics in his own way, had come to the threshold of the Supreme Court was itself a virtual miracle. That he had passed over the threshold was an even greater one given the elements at work—had Senator Burke revealed his proof during the Senate debate, had the Klan affiliation leaked out otherwise than the way it did, or had the characteristics of nonforfeitable pensions been fully explored. And others were even more imponderable—had Black panicked in the first hours following disclosure, had the President reacted otherwise than as he did, indeed, had Cardinal Mundelein reacted otherwise than as *he* did, things might have been very different.

But things were not very different, and before the month of October 1937 was out, the Blacks had moved from their crowded white bungalow in the District of Columbia to Alexandria. And one broadcast lay behind and another lay ahead.

Part Two

The
Alabama Years

CHAPTER THREE

The Upland Beginnings

The Men of Clay County

A few months before the telecast, Justice Black recalled that perhaps no one who knew him as a boy thought he would get beyond the confines of the small rural county where he was born. He was certainly wrong on that count, for reports of his tenacity and drive, even in boyhood, clearly forecast that he would make his mark well beyond the place of his birth. But his further reminiscent estimate—that the closing years of the nineteenth century in that small rural county made for a particularly hard time in a particularly hard place—was formidably correct. In fact a full generation later, a laconic first line on a campaign flyer— "Born on a Farm in Clay County"—sufficed of itself to be a patent of origins that were indisputably humble and hardscrabble. Almost a half century later, the name still served as an index, as Mr. Justice Black described a new law clerk from Harvard "tops in his class though he came from a God-forsaken place—worse than Clay County."[1]

Situated in the heart of the scrubby-pine hill country of east-central Alabama, Clay County lies thirty miles from the Georgia line and a hundred north of the Gulf. The last census of the nineteenth century counted 15,765 residents, 14,601 of them white. Like the line on the handbill, the terse double statistic was also intensely meaningful, for it epitomized that county's critical differentiation from the rich down-state country, where an inverted racial ratio and a fertile, loam earth doubly justified the name of black belt. The interplay of soil and name, however, ran quite the other way in Clay County, whose lines had been drawn just following the Civil War (indeed, the day after Alabama had rejected the Fourteenth Amendment) and which had been named for Henry Clay, the great compromiser.

But the name was doubtless a matter of hope rather than expectation. Even before the Civil War and right up to Secession itself, that red-soil region had persistently kicked against the goad of political domination by the slave-owning white minority to the south. Ironically enough, emancipation changed things very little. Rather the unwitting role an exploited black majority played in the continuation of that domination—first by manipulated franchise and later by mere numerical representation in legislative allocation—gave a deep tincture of racism to the successive waves of protest that swept northern Alabama in the post-Civil War years.

The protests had a variety of labels, including greenbackism and Bryanism, but as characteristic as any was that first Populist trumpet call that went out from Clay County's seat, Ashland, in 1892 and demanded the formation of the People's Party of Alabama. It was sounded by a now-forgotten politician named Joseph Manning, whose contemporary statewide nickname, "the Clay County evangelist," amply attested to both the fundamentalist fervor and geographic epicenter of the new dispensation. And it was in lineal descent of this tradition, which mingled concern and racism, protest and reform, that two other sons of Clay County went out from it to be heard throughout the nation and indeed around the world. Between the pair lay an extraordinary and star-crossed relationship wherein common elements ran their course on separating lines of development.[2]

Fittingly, the dramatic high point was commemorated in a reference coming in the middle 1920s, emphasizing the thin red soil that both had left many years before:

> Klansmen, I should say that this is a case of where Clay County meets Clay County. (Applause)
>
> You know, I don't think Alabama ever thought much of Clay County, probably; we never did think much of it. But first we got a Wizard from over there, and that didn't seem to do them much good. You know, a whole lot of people didn't think that was much of an honor, to have a Wizard coming from their community, so we tried again and we got a United States Senator from over there. So now I think Clay County will be on the map hereafter. (Applause)[3]

The commentary came at something of a high-water mark, even though the relationship had a long time to run thereafter. Both men were fated to survive to an advanced old age, and in the course of the lives ahead, some threads were to be strongly twisted by the fates. One of the two was to rise to the pinnacle of international honor and fame, the other was to live out his time in disgraced obscurity on the charity of friends. And in the twin courses of rise and fall the thread of the fates had one specially tangled twist whereby one man was to sit in judgment on the other in the highest tribunal of the nation.[4]

But the relationship ran far back as well, with the father of the Imperial Wizard serving as the teacher of the Senator and Justice in the public school of Ashland. ("I received instructions from that teacher as the teacher of my early boyhood. Some of the most pleasant memories of my life cluster around Judge Evans. Some of the greatest inspirations of my life I received from your father.") Remarkably enough, at its beginning the association also seemed destined to be brief, for the Wizard's family left Ashland for Texas not too long after the Blacks had moved into the county seat from the out-country. Yet the red-soil politics figured even here, for the father of the future Wizard had moved up from teaching to a probate judgeship, only to be turned out of office and forced to seek new horizons when the Populists swept the county elections in 1892.[5]

The Family Roots

Not that the incoming family of the future Senator had much to do with the political displacement of that of the future Wizard; on the contrary, general-store keeper William La Fayette Black had little sympathy with the Populist cause. He was a familiar-enough rural type, secret drinker, rack-renting landlord, and usurious moneylender (rates running to 50 percent) as well as a merchant, but still far more a victim than an instrument of the system in which he found himself. A veteran of the Confederate Army, which he had joined at fourteen, he had taken to store-keeping in the Clay County out-country after the war and in 1889 moved both store and family to the county seat in an effort to combine enlarged commercial horizons with expanded educational opportunity for his seven surviving children. He did well enough in this effort, with his boys entering medicine, teaching and the law, in addition to the one who eventually took over the store. The work ethic of his strict Baptist household, where (despite secret drinking) liquor was forbidden and even coffee suspect, was evident in the stiffly posed, Sunday-best family photograph taken on the Ashland front porch around 1892. Two members of the family stand out conspicuously in the American Gothic setting. One is the thin, dark, intense mother. The other is the small, diffident boy, five or six years old, standing between her and her husband.

The boy was the last of her eight children, and he had been born at Harlan, some ten miles away. Harlan was no town, but rather a Post Office designation for the complex of the country store, farmhouse, and tenant cabins that William La Fayette Black owned there. The wife, Martha Toland Black, was the postmistress of the place, and there is a tradition that her eldest daughter, Ora, had been reading Victor Hugo while the mother was carrying her eighth child. "The name Hugh was in my family," Black later reminisced, "Hugo had been used by one Toland. My sister had been reading Victor Hugo. Hugo Toland had been an actor with Lillian Russell, who was really something back then." Accordingly, the author's last name was duly joined to the father's middle one to provide French first and middle names for the boy who was born on February 27, 1886.[6]

In any event, Martha Toland Black not only had a touch of intellectual distinction, but a social edge as well. The quality-descended Tolands were generally ranked higher than the thoroughly respectable Blacks, and by common estimate Martha Toland did not exactly go up in the world in marrying the son of a country storekeeper who carried on in his father's occupation.

But for those who thought these things important, there was vindication in the youngest son. Though dead for a third of a century, she was very much in his thoughts when he took the bench to begin a career on the Supreme Court. ("I am very proud and grateful for this moment. There is one person I wish had lived to see it. My mother.") Fittingly, a third of a century after that, her name led all the rest in the slim volume, *A Constitutional Faith,* which the son intended as his juridical testament; he dedicated it to her.[7]

But if Martha Toland Black was her son's first educator, and the father of the future Imperial Wizard of the Ku Klux Klan one of the first, there were others. Many years later, Justice Black wrote with obvious affection about the "half-public, half-private" college, Ashland Academy, of which his father was a trustee and where the ambitious listing of the curriculum—literature, rhetoric, logic, Latin, Greek, chemistry, astonomy and higher mathematics—made its diplomas sought not only by Clay Countians but "by boarding students who came from other parts of Alabama." Doubtless the availability of the Academy had in part underlain William Black's decision to move from Harlan to Ashland, and its existence also underlined the slender resources of higher education in the state—a situation that would finally be turned around under a Klan-elected governor. Meanwhile, Black moved up to its opportunities, which were abruptly ended toward, but not at, the end of scheduled instruction. While young Hugo Black was not exactly "expelled" from the Academy, a remonstrance with an overbearing teacher did result in scholar and school parting company forever.[8]

The incident also indicates the emergence of the steel that was not particularly apparent in the shy five-year-old in the family photograph. Other childhood stories tell of zest and energy coming out in cotton-picking and typesetting chores and doubtless annealing the softness that the bookishness might otherwise produce. But perhaps there was another strain in the process, at once an introduction to vicarious combat and a special form of education in itself. In addition to its academy, Ashland also held the county courthouse, and from the age of six Black attended every trial he could. ("I cannot remember the time when I did not want to be a lawyer.")

Inheritance too may have been at work, for his maternal uncle was a distinguished California attorney, and the Toland connections in the law went back to Thomas Addis Emmet and the golden days of the Irish bar. Ironically, maternal counsel and admiration for a physician brother combined to set his steps on a false start, and in the fall of 1903 Black entered Birmingham Medical College. Here he covered two academic years in one; but experience, which included a summer's apprenticeship serving his brother, apparently drained all desire to follow the healing arts, and in the summer of 1904 the eighteen-year-old Black left for the University of Alabama. ("I just decided I wanted to be a lawyer more than I did a doctor.") It was the first decisive turn in what he would later call the "long journey from the frontier farmhouse in the hills of Clay County to the United States Supreme Court." Even as he set out he did not know his feet were already set on the path of the law. But he did vividly remember the effort in covering the hundred miles—as the crow flew—to Tuscaloosa on the west. For the Justice who would see Americans walk on the moon began this long journey with a twenty-mile buggy ride to Goodwater, took the Central of Georgia to Birmingham and made the rest of the trip by Alabama Great Southern.[9]

Tuscaloosa Interlude

Thirty years or more after Black first made the trip, Carl Carmer's *Stars Fell on Alabama* vividly described the almost physical sense of encounter that attends the first sight of Tuscaloosa's verdancy after a journey beginning in the northern Alabama hills. And many years after that, the same vividness attended the venerable Justice Black's recollection of his first view of the same university town, so different from the red dust and rural poverty of Clay County. ("I can now see in my mind's eye some of those beautiful old houses with their large columns, indisputable marks of the old South. . . . The most vivid recollections of Tuscaloosa's beauty, however, that now rush in upon me relate to the beautiful, large, spreading oaks that lined each side of University Avenue.") Visual pleasure, however, was followed by academic shock. Black was denied regular admission to the sophomore class, notwithstanding his Ashland Academy education, and the denial was confirmed by no less than the president of the university, a former member of the Academy faculty.[10]

The law school, however, was willing to take him as he stood, and he accordingly enrolled there. The school was limited in both physical and instructional resources. ("The Law School classrooms, as I recall, could certainly not be called the choicest classrooms at the University.") Moreover, the faculty consisted of a pair of professors, and the style of instruction for the two-year course was by text rather than the new-fangled case book. Yet, for all the deficiencies, Black's recollection was generosity itself, and he commended his old professors in an idiom characteristic of his evolved judicial philosophy. ("They taught us, as I recall, that legislators, not judges, should make the law.")[11]

One of the two-member faculty frequently told people in Black's presence that he never had a student who made greater progress—adding with an enigmatic smile the further statement that Black had the farther to go. Other distinctions were more clear-cut. In addition to being one of seven members of the class to achieve average grades of 94 or better, Black was a class officer in both years, and the University Yearbook, the *Corolla,* contained successive references to his urbanity and tenacity.

In May 1906 he received the University's LL.B. degree, and many decades later both an honorary doctorate in law and an earned Phi Beta Kappa key. In 1906 the first order of business was to come back to Ashland and begin his practice, for his diploma automatically admitted him to the bar "at the age of twenty years with the disabilities of non-age removed." Yet the fates had prescribed that Clay County was not for him, no matter how hard he tried to make it so. In September 1907 the building containing his office and library burned. Without friends or influence, but with the resources of his youthful vigor—he was then twenty-one—and the Damascene blade of his mind, Black headed north and west to the city that was to be the nearest thing he ever had to a home town—Birmingham.[12]

The Forge of Vulcan

Surmounted by a statue of Vulcan, Birmingham lies in a valley atop a rich mineral dome, where the smoke and clangor of the steel mills seem to be the lame god's forge expanded to gigantic dimensions. It was a new city. Someone has noted that the word *Southern* implies a legacy going back to Calhoun and slavery, but Birmingham had no such historic roots. Rather it was founded six years after Appomattox.

But if it had no organic past, it was not without ancestral elements. Here the brutality of the new industrialism seemed to be crossed with older plantation repression, to make a world that had the worst features of both. For most whites it was a sweltering, raw, brutal place; and doubtless the hardness of life gave a special attraction to the consolations of religion. The town had one church for every seven hundred inhabitants and regularly led the nation in some other statistics—illiteracy, venereal disease—and its homicide rate made it known as the murder capital of the world. "Practically every reporter on our staff," recalled a veteran of the *Birmingham News,* "had been an eyewitness to at least one gun duel."[13]

Birmingham was really two cities inhabited by hermetically separate communities that feared and hated each other. Bad as life was for the whites, for the submergent black underclass it was incomparably worse. How much worse might be best suggested a half century later by Martin Luther King's famous letter from the Birmingham jail and a Sunday morning murder of the innocents that would combine to give a searing meaning to the long-time black name for the town, "Bombingham." But, doubtless, young Hugo Black took all of this as much for granted as the polluted air he breathed when he arrived for his second and final stay in the town in September 1907.

With him came a change for the worse in the economic climate and the beginning of a long encounter with the darkest side of American capitalism—unemployment, industrial warfare, absentee ownership, regional exploitation, corporate bureaucracy —which would hammer out his ideas as surely as the forge of Vulcan hammered out the artifacts of war. For, other than the accident of geography, Black had no association with the Populist tradition. Indeed, his father's anti-Bryanism in the great test of faith afforded by the election of 1896 was the strongest indication to the contrary. But if he had little connection with radical agrarian reform, he did have a sustained firsthand encounter with the hard problems of an industrial society. It was little different from the experience he would have gotten in Akron or Pittsburgh.

The year before Black came to Birmingham, John W. "Bet-you-a-Million" Gates predicted that within twenty years Birmingham would contain a million people and be the largest city in America. Gates was wrong. In a matter of months the backwash of the Panic of 1907 rolled over the town like a tidal wave and produced one of the shaping events of Black's life. The event itself occurred within weeks of his arrival, a thousand miles away; and doubtless years passed before Black so much as heard of it—the banker's meeting in the library of J. P. Morgan on the night of November 2, 1907, which decided the fate of the Tennessee Coal Iron and Railroad Company—popularly known in Birmingham as the T.C.I., the largest owner of coal and iron properties in the area—by formally integrating it into the corporate empire of United States Steel Company.

The consequence was to make the company the dominant force in Birmingham's life. The local activities of national competitors were abandoned, and the new owner moved to press its cost and production advantages to the fullest. But this was not the only development linking Birmingham to the vast national aggregates of corporate power. All through the nineties and the first decade of the new century, the trunk-line railroads that served the town were increasingly merged and consolidated, and in the same year of 1907 that saw Hugo Black's arrival and U.S. Steel's acquisition of the town's largest enterprise, the Alabama Power Company was organized. The newborn utility and the newcomer lawyer were fated to have a long and tangled relationship. Alabama Power was to be one of the lawyer's favorite targets when he ran for the Senate and when he spoke from the Senate floor. And characteristic of the way in which the firsthand encounters of his personal and political life were to recur in his legislative and judicial career, Senator Black was to serve as one of the principal surgeons in the dismemberment of its holding-company concentrate Commonwealth and Southern.

At the time of his arrival in Birmingham, however, the future Senator met the industrial system in the form of unemployment and general stagnation as the impact of the Panic of 1907 verified the Birmingham proverb "Hard times come here first and stay longest" and made the usually difficult business of getting started in the law even more formidable. Black shared a rented room with three other men, moved between rented desks in law offices, and investigated applicants at fifty cents a head for a mail-order insurance company.[14]

His professional career in Birmingham began with a suit whose subject matter, a convict lease, exemplified a cross-fertilization of the old slavery and the new industrialization. Well-known before the Civil War, the leasing system received an expansive development with the foundation of the coal-and-iron economy. Theoretically, the system seemed a reformer's dream, for it provided convicts with economically useful work instead of idle incarceration with wages paid upon release.

In practice, everything worked out quite the other way. The mine stockades were stifling in summer, cold and damp in winter, and ridden with tuberculosis. Flogging was frequent, and torture common. More than that, the system was perverted in both supply and release. To keep up an assured source of laborers, the Birmingham sheriff's office used decoy crap games at which the players were literally scooped up and auctioned off. And on the discharge side, there was a continuing temptation to the leasing employers to hold a man past his release date.

And one steel company did exactly this in keeping a black convict named Willie Norton twenty-two days longer than his sentence. Usually a victim bore his exploitation without remonstrance, simply for want of remedy. Norton, however, sought out Hugo Black, who, in the appropriate devotion to a first case, poured all his energy and talent into briefs and argument and turned aside the pretrial motions of William Grubb, a leading local lawyer and future federal judge. "Billy," prophetically announced the trial judge, "I don't think you are going to scare this young fellow or talk him out of it." Nor did he, as Black pressed on victoriously to a verdict of $150 and a first fee of $37.50.[15]

But matters did not always end so triumphantly. The economic backwash of the panic produced a fresh pressure in the Birmingham mines, and this in turn provoked an organizing effort by the United Mine Workers. After a series of stealthy and clandestine meetings, twenty thousand miners struck in 1908. A measure of the miners' scanty resources and the essential hopelessness of their cause was their use of the legal services of the young newcomer from Clay County. Between the leased convicts and strikebreakers on one hand, and a showdown test of sheer physical power and appeals to racism on the other, the strike was finally broken, with Tom Lewis, the national president of the U.M.W., coming to Birmingham to sign the articles of surrender. Any number of repressive arrangements grew out of the surrender, including the special house lease of the company town.

("Lessor may at any time forbid ingress and egress over the adjoining premises of Lessor to any and all persons other than Lessee and the members of his family living with him.") Yet, if the miners lost the battle, there was a longer war ahead, and in their long struggle the young lawyer of 1908 would have much to say about many things ranging from labor relations in general to company towns in particular. ("Justice Black talked quite a bit about his personal knowledge of 'company towns.' He had seen them in Alabama and described them in great detail.")[16]

And in getting to the point where he would have much to say about many things, Black's Birmingham years would exemplify Tocqueville's point that in the United States the profession of law offers an almost unique ladder to the poor but able men to rise in a mode unparalleled in other cultures. From the debacle of the U.M.W. strike his fortunes steadily mounted, and the progression was effected without Black turning his back on his original clientele. On the contrary, his association with the labor movement and its membership deepened and broadened both to his advantage and to theirs; the contracts and trust won in institutional associations led naturally to referrals in litigation growing out of the carnage of industrial accidents and thence to damage suits generally.

It was a field of law that fell in admirably with his talents. Notwithstanding its bad press, the so-called damage-suit law is a profession within a profession and has its own high claims to honor. All too often it is the last call to justice of those maimed in body and disadvantaged in mind. Its practitioners show their own special characteristics—the quick, catlike intelligence to sift the crucial from the incidental, a superb forensic sense of the courtroom, the cool courage of bargaining where miscalculation can entail total forfeit for counsel and client alike. And it frequently involves seemingly compulsive gregariousness with a wide variety of activity—political, fraternal, religious—supplying *de facto* the advertising that the canon of legal ethics forbids *de jure*. Black's lodge activities in the Masons (which he had joined in Harlan), the Knights of Pythias and the Odd Fellows, as well as his ecclesiastical service with the First Baptist Church, where he was to teach an adult Sunday-school class for twenty years, fell into this category. These associations and his other obvious talents combined to win him appointment as police judge when the City of Birmingham came under a reform administration in 1911.

First Judgeship

As in damage-suit law, the police court institutionally and Black's police-court experience in particular have been the subject of particularly patronizing comment. Yet, for better or for worse, that court is the one American tribunal that truly serves as the index for Lord Acton's comment that the treatment of the unfortunate is the critical test for any social order. For the police bench is very much the Supreme Court of the poor. The wrong man can make it an overpowering instrument of oppression. The right man can do much to soften its institutional infirmities. And in Black's case the police-court appointment provided the first manifestation of what was admiringly called "his sure instinct for the core of the case . . . his fertile legal imagination . . . and the ability to devise ways—new ways if need be—of serving his conception of it . . . the largest good."[17]

There was the case of Thomas Sherman, white and a future staffer of the *St. Louis Post-Dispatch,* who would proudly recall that he had been charged with "Sunday gaming" before a future Supreme Court Justice—guilty and fined ten dollars in a brisk, no-nonsense fashion. There was Mose Roden, black, charged with assaulting a loan shark's agent—case dismissed, the court observing that 300 percent interest was punishment enough. There was the couple, white, charged with kissing in the public park—guilty, with a five-dollar fine to the man, a one-dollar fine to the girl, the court observing that the kiss should be worth that much more to him.

The judgeship provided several dimensions of development quite above and apart from encounter with a particular set of manipulative techniques in the law itself. One was yet another

manifestation of that ongoing drive forecast by the description of
the appointing authority of the new judge ("quick, enterprising,
smart") and the mode in which the new incumbent demonstrated
quickness, enterprise and intelligence—advancing the convening
time to the unheard-of hour of 8:30 A.M. Doubtless also there
was an impetus to his ultimately flowering reformer's sense, especially in the vision of reducing crime by reducing the conditions
of its necessitous occurrence.[18]

But most of all there was that instinct for media that was
reflected in the usual press stories about goings-on within the
police court. For here was duly reported the noteworthy decisions of the judge and also items suggesting a prickly independence, which time might soften but never would destroy. One
datum came in the nicknames—variously "Old Ego," "Hugo-to-
Hell" Black and "Hugo-all-the-way" Black—given the judge.
Another afforded after its fashion a perverse tribute, in a duly
printed comment that vividly attested contemporary community
standards and the unusual judge as well ("When a nigger suc-
ceeds of convincing Judge Black of his innocence despite the
testimony of the arresting police officers, he is going some.")[19]

The police judgeship, as such judgeships usually are, was but
part-time employment and permitted virtually full-scale professional activity otherwise. Black reduced its constraints still further by a vigorous disposition to keep pending cases moving
along. Remarkably enough, even though his judgeship represented the consolidation of several courts, he was successful and
left its docket cleared and current when he stepped down from
the bench in 1912. His action, however, was only a pause in, not
an end to, local public service. In December 1914 he was elected
county solicitor, which was the title held by the public prosecutor
of Jefferson County.

The energy and vigor, conspicuously shown in police court
and private practice alike, surfaced once again in the prosecutor's office. Here again the first target was the overblown
docket, itself corrupt fruit of the convict-lease system. For it was
the practice of the state to pay maintenance and costs against a

prisoner's subsequent work-off on the rolls of a leasing contractor, and this had both swollen enormously the lists of pending charges—three thousand cases were pending when he took office —and delayed the trials in like proportion. Black, however, set matters to rights with a sustained and driving effort, which almost overshadowed his handling of the regular business of the office. Dismissing five hundred of the charges out of hand, he swept like a whirlwind through the remainder as he and his two assistants tried twelve of the capital cases in the first week alone. And then came the affair of the Bessemer jail, itself the hallmark of the many sharp and unpredictable turns which lay ahead. There were many Bessemer jails in the country, in the South, and doubtless in the Birmingham area. But there were few prosecutors like Hugo Black. Without a shred of foreseeable political gain and at some obvious, if imponderable, disadvantage to his own career, he moved against the jail after his attention had been arrested by the assembly-line stream of confessions that came from it. The technique of interrogation was simplicity itself, with the prisoners, usually black, being mercilessly beaten until they confessed to whatever charge had been lodged against them.

For a variety of reasons, including basic decency—but also a contempt for the forensic attitude that preferred a plea of guilty to a trial on the facts or saw a confession as the ultimate pleading if trial were joined—Black acted on his own and in an area of doubtful jurisdiction. His first effort involved directing a grand-jury investigation into the outrageous condition. He subsequently undertook to argue the issue before a special citizen's group. But as in the coal strike, nothing substantive came of his effort at the time. Yet in terms of the years ahead, the incident could not have been said to lack consequences. Perhaps the mere act of exposure accomplished something. And over a half century later, the millions of Americans who observed Black's reading of passages from his great opinion in *Chambers v. Florida,* condemning confessions *incommunicado,* were really witnessing the closing part of a process of development that had begun long before, at the Bessemer jail.[20]

American Legion and Junior League

The abortive character of the Bessemer investigation doubtless contributed to Black's decision to resign from office before the expiration of his elected term. There appeared to be other reasons, including a jurisdictional clash with yet another prosecutor, called the circuit solicitor, in a case that went all the way to the Supreme Court of Alabama and that Black lost. A few weeks after the decision the United States entered World War I, and the combination of events turned out to be decisive, as Black gave up his office and joined the Army. The decision could be variously viewed, perhaps the least important or perhaps the most important decision of his life.

Its purely military aspects can be noted merely to be laid aside, for perhaps the high point in terms of honorific recognition came in Black's cadet days when a Rome (Georgia) waitress, mistaking his apprentice bars for those of an officer, addressed him as "Captain." She was premature and conservative. After a year of service, all stateside, the addressee was discharged as a major of artillery, and returning to Birmingham he quickly took over where he had left off. In terms of experience it would appear that the only consequence of military service was the broadening of "joining" activities afforded by his eligibility for the American Legion.

But a more far-reaching consequence came when he not only associated with members of the newly formed American Legion but married one, a Navy veteran, who was still wearing her Yeomanette uniform when they met at a country club dance. The other veteran was Josephine Foster, a Presbyterian minister's daughter, who, after a year at Sweetbriar, had gone to Barnard and from there had joined the Navy at the outbreak of the war.

It was far from a whirlwind courtship. The Yeomanette and the artillery officer were separated by sixteen years, and neither had been in any haste to marry, however local folkways might endorse the idea. And the subtle and mutual nonconformance here suggested something of a deeper alienation held in common. Black's maverick strain was the more obvious. For, notwithstanding his ultraconventional behavior at the most elementary level—bustling, teetotaling, celibate, in court all day, at a different lodge meeting every night, and at his Bible class bright and early every Sunday morning—there was also the labor-union–damage-suit law practice, the Bessemer-investigation reputation, and general outspokenness during the postwar Red Scare, which added to the nickname of Hugo-to-Hell that of "young Bolshevik."[21]

More complex, perhaps deeper, was the alienation of the girl he married. Again, the surface seemed conventional enough—fine Southern ancestors, Sweetbriar, Junior League, and a father who was a successful insurance man. Yet even at this threshold of encounter some elements suggested themselves; the prosperous father had left the Presbyterian ministry rather than submit to fundamentalist dogmatism, and the daughter had left Sweetbriar for the wider horizons of New York as soon as her freshman year was over. Moreover, through it all she exhibited a deep and questing artistic sense, touched occasionally by a tinge of what Southern gentility called melancholia.

The two covert rebels were married conventionally enough in a modish ceremony in the living room of the bride's fashionable home in 1921. Interestingly, the groom had lived nearby although proximity did not result in meeting. Rather, the neighboring address was characteristic of his combination of aloofness and sociability, for he preferred a room in a family home to one of the newfangled apartments that he had tried shortly before his army service. The transition from the four-in-a-bed rooming house was index enough of the groom's social mobility. Another lay in the composition of the wedding party. Only one of the groom's family, and that an in-law, was present; his father and mother had died long before, and the survivors of the eight children had scattered.

So, the wedding evidenced a remarkable match in many ways, not the least of which lay in its organizational nuances. Not only did both groom and bride belong to the American Legion, but

the bride was one of the few Legionnaires who held a membership in the Junior League as well. There was another dimension,
however, to her marriage to the man from Clay County—every
subsequent reference to Josephine Foster Black made especial
mention of her charm and gentleness, her taste and style. And
there were some who thought they saw in a far more subtle mode
that fierce independence of spirit that sustained and reinforced
the same strain in her husband. And to the extent that a man's
career depends on the happenstance of encounter, undoubtedly
that of Hugo Black—and the consequent loss of a police-court
nickname—was profoundly shaped by a meeting at a country-
club dance.

The Master Advocate

In that remarkable study *The Lawyers,* Martin Mayer lists
Birmingham among the cities where law practice tends to proceed in a pronounced partnership form. Here Black conformed
to local custom as he went through a string of easily formed,
easily dissolved professional associations. One of them would be
the triggering cause of the bitterest feuds ever to rack the Supreme Court. But, in tandem or solo, his practice flourished. As
his living quarters changed for the better, so did his professional
offices, each passing year, and his legal skills while running a
broad spectrum of subjects crystallized in those areas which draw
heavily upon forensic ability. Here his reputation as a trial lawyer mounted, and also as an appellate advocate, as his cases went
up to the Alabama Supreme Court. There were some aspects
here that would in time bear fruit. One was the differing standards of the state and federal courts, not only to different roles of
law to be applied to the same set of facts, but to the enormous
power of the trial judge under the federal system—to comment
on evidence, to take a case from the jury, to cite for contempt.
Another not insignificant factor was the virtual absence of corporate representation in his practice. "Hugo felt it would mean
sacrificing his convictions," his father-in-law recalled. "If you

accepted a retainer, you had to think the way the corporation that hired you did. Hugo couldn't stand that."[22]

But it was his fairly minor criminal practice that provided his most celebrated case, involving a homicide, which occurred exactly sixteen years prior to the day Franklin Roosevelt tendered the Supreme Court appointment. On August 15, 1921, the Reverend Edwin R. Stephenson, well-known as the marrying parson of the Birmingham Courthouse, shot and killed Father James E. Coyle on the front porch of St. Paul's rectory. The forensic evidence seemed damning; the bullet had gone through the priest's head on a course that indicated that he had been shot while sitting, rather than (as the defense claimed) in rising to attack his assailant. Nonetheless, by certain Birmingham standards, there seemed provocation enough, sitting or rising. Stephenson's daughter, a convert to Catholicism, had been married by Father Coyle to Pedro Gussman, a dark and curly-haired Puerto Rican.

The charge was second-degree murder, the plea self-defense, and the jury was out four and a half hours before returning a not-guilty verdict. A round of handshakes followed the verdict, but any number of Birmingham Catholics bitterly insisted then and insisted sixteen years later that defense attorney Black's exploitation of racial and religious prejudice, rather than the evidence, produced the verdict. Nor were Catholics alone in their criticism. A former governor, a Presbyterian, insisted that life had now become cheaper and less secure in Alabama and deplored "murder . . . justified on account of the religious creed of the victim."[23]

And reports of the trial did indicate that the comments of Black's detractors were not without substance. There was Black's exhibiting an earlier photograph of Gussman—"I just wanted the jury to see this picture taken before the witness had his hair worked on." There was his arranging the courtroom lighting to accentuate Gussman's dark complexion. There was his comment on the religion of the Catholic witnesses for the prosecution— "brothers in falsehood as well as faith." There was his summation of his client's action as a reaction to proselytizing—("The homes of Birmingham cannot be touched. If that brings disgrace, God hasten the disgrace.")[24]

As long as the adversary system of justice obtains, a defense lawyer's obligation is to work for the acquittal of his client. There are limits, to be sure, but perhaps Black's adroit exploitation of local bigotry was not too far distant from a contemporary maneuver in faraway New York, where the great mouthpiece Michael Fallon (born, coincidentally enough, within a few days of Black) was arranging to have *his* client drop a rosary at a suitably climactic moment in the proceedings. There was, however, one possible difference between Birmingham and New York. In the Southern city the scales may well have been unequal at the start thanks to the ascendancy of a new and growing organization that had appropriated the name and the terrorist tactics of the old Ku Klux Klan. Not only had the new Klan raised a substantial defense fund for Stephenson but the prosecution was incredibly inept—the principal evidence was not introduced when it was admissible, and the tactical defense of Hugo Black kept it out thereafter. More than this, the foreman of the jury was a Klansman, and the Chief of Police—who testified for the defense—was a Klan officer. From the vista of over half a century another onetime Klan figure looked back: "Hugo didn't have much trouble winning that verdict."[25] Perhaps the only wonder was that the jury was out four hours.

CHAPTER FOUR

The Road to the Senate

The Righteous Kingdom

A touch of obscurity will forever enshroud a part of Black's long journey from the hills of Clay County to the United States Supreme Court: the part that he made with an undetermined measure of commitment through the land of the Invisible Empire. For the insight it affords both on the traveler and on the trip, it has a significance out of proportion to its actual character. Black indicated that the eleven minutes he gave it in the broadcast of 1937 was all he would ever have to say, and for a variety of reasons others who knew the story or something approaching the story were also silent.[1]

But Black's stiff-necked pride could not simply leave matters at the eleven minutes of the broadcast and the drive of the tennis court produced over the years a sequence of explanations as complex as the man himself. Characteristically, he never uttered a word of regret and, as late as 1956, regarded his joining as at least an open question—"Whether I'd join if I had it to do over again, I'm not sure"—and in any event the Klan was an insignificant part of his life. ("I went to three or four meetings. Then

105

I joined the Moose. The speeches I could have made . . . to the
A.C.L.U., and they'd have liked it.")[2]

He also gave more structured and extended interviews. Two
came thirty years apart (the latter was for posthumous publication) and there was a remarkable unity to them. One was in
1937 to Max Lerner, who said really all there was to say: "That
a man like Black should have come to join the Klan is one of
those facts monstrously hard to grasp until you approach it not
as a moral problem, but simply as a piece of political behavior."
More importantly, however, Lerner also sketched the larger context of that behavior where analysis is indispensable as a prelude
to understanding of the act itself. And here he noted the carry-
over of the wartime sense of national unity and purpose; the
widespread bewilderment and anger over the collapse of legal
and social constraints; the overwhelming desire for the tranquil
world of yesteryear; the growing inadequacies, if not breakdown,
of the older forms of religion.[3]

One form of the reaction came in the sudden, indeed virtually
overnight, extension to national dimensions of the prohibition of
the manufacture and sale of intoxicating liquor. The concept of
such repression was old enough, but the speed of its imposition
was another thing again. The critical change came after the turn
of the century. By 1906 thirty states had local-option laws; and
in the next year (the one in which Black came to Birmingham),
Oklahoma provided a new facet as it entered the Union with a
prohibition clause in its constitution. Total state prohibition was
the prelude to a final surge of triumph that came in tandem with
the wartime years. Not only did state after state enact such statutes, but indicative of the accelerating moralization in the
national mood, compulsory temperance, which was not so much
as mentioned in the two major platforms of 1916, was written
into the national Constitution itself by 1920.

The Prohibition movement had always had something of a
particularly Southern tincture and thereby called to much in
Black's heritage and experience. Liquor was forbidden, and even
tea and coffee were suspect, in his Baptist father's house. The
attitudes so begun were given an especial engraining during his

boyhood, when an older brother, supposedly under the influence of whiskey, drowned in a buggy accident. Nor did Birmingham serve to change the Clay County channel of vision. Indeed the squalor and distress attending liquor traffic provoked an especial severity in punishments from his police-court bench visited upon those who maintained or even patronized "blind tigers" or bottle clubs maintained in violation of the municipal ordinance.

Alabama's statewide ban on liquor in 1915 enlarged his prosecutorial activities accordingly. In one effort he went to the Supreme Court of Alabama to obtain an injunction banishing outstate newspapers with liquor advertising from the Birmingham newsstands. In terms of the prosecutor's future philosophy, there seemed not to be one word in the controversy about the freedom of the press provided under the First Amendment. Yet the claims of the future did not go totally ignored, for the local judge who had refused the writ did so because of his doubt of the compatibility of the state statute with that very commerce clause of the national Constitution that both Senator and Justice Black would so powerfully construe.[4]

And yet another proceeding, which was not a foreshadowing of the search-and-seizure controversies that lay ahead in the Senate and on the Supreme Court, came in the so-called Girard cases, wherein Black served as special state prosecutor in the summer of 1916. The episode took its name from the small town just across the Chattahoochee River from Georgia, where thousands of gallons of illegal liquor had been both concealed in buildings and still more in barrels placed in the river itself and secured by ropes attached to the Alabama shore. The evidence had been seized without specific search warrant, and the point became critical when special prosecutor Black ordered its destruction upon the defendants' failing to appear for trial and was upheld (one of his old law teachers dissenting) when the issue reached the Supreme Court of Alabama.[5]

Doubtless it was credentials such as these that prompted the redoubtable Mabel Walker Willebrandt, Assistant Attorney General of the United States, to recruit Black for temporary service with her "flying squadron," that special strike force charged with Prohibition prosecutions in those cases where considerations of politics or efficiency suggested that the local United States attorney be bypassed. For in late 1923 both conditions seemed more than present in an array of indictments that came out of Mobile, Alabama. Some 117 prominent citizens of that city were charged with conspiracy to bribe that very officer, and the defendants in turn insisted that *he* had attempted to bribe *them*. The United States Attorney accordingly stepped aside on his own motion, and Attorney Hugo Black of the Birmingham bar was selected to present the government's case.[6]

The retainer was quite consistent with Attorney General Harlan Fiske Stone's professed desire to get the best possible man for the squadron, preferably Republican, but Democratic if necessary. In this case he got a superb prosecutor who not only was rising to a professional peak but, as a certificated Democrat, was twice as effective as the best Republican ever could have been in a state where Republican officials were still regarded as the agents of an occupying power. Black tried the case with characteristic vigor and, after dropping some of the defendants in midtrial, pursued the remainder through the spring of 1924. At the end of May, the jury came back with a "guilty" verdict, which not only operated as a great triumph for the righteous kingdom of Prohibition but yielded the previously unknown federal prosecutor a degree of fame throughout all of Alabama.

Beneath its triumphal aspects, the Mobile prosecutions did contain a few curious elements. Thus, Assistant Attorney General Willebrandt's recruitment for her squadron must necessarily be considered in the light of her delicate relations with the Republican National Committee, the emerging presidential aspirations of Al Smith of New York, and the possibility of impaling the Democrats on the barbs of rum and Romanism. Conversely, the Willebrandt recruitment was matched by the anomalous willingness of Birmingham's busiest damage-suit attorney to take on a difficult and lengthy prosecution two hundred miles from his home and practice, to do so at his own expense, and to go to Washington to press the offer. And considerable financial sacrifice was involved, in terms of forgone retainers. Black's practice was rising to the $40,000 it would bring in for a half-year's work in 1925, and its fruits were manifest in a pleasant home on fashionable Altamont Road and a membership in the Birmingham Country Club.

The Invisible Empire

Attorney General Stone, however, would have none of gratuitous service, and he insisted that his special prosecutor receive the regular, if modest, stipend for effort. Nonetheless the prosecutor's willingness to work so far afield from the warm home and family on Altamont Road—for the Blacks now included two-year-old Hugo junior—and for free at that, involves yet another puzzling element. Here may have been the fine hand of another Birmingham lawyer, who had known the future Chief Justice Stone even before the future Justice Black did. The lawyer was James Esdale, an alumnus of Auburn and the Alabama Law School, who in 1911 and 1912 had taken his first year of law at Columbia University. There his engaging talents had assertedly been displayed in convincing Nicholas Murray Butler that he was a poor Southern boy worthy of a partial scholarship and in persuading Dean Harlan Stone that he deserved a better grade in criminal law than that originally given.* In Birmingham the same talents had been exerted with great success on behalf of the Benevolent and Protective Order of the Elks (James A. Farley starting out the same way), but were subsequently put to work in the interest of the Ku Klux Klan. In fact, as the Girard trials were carrying Black from local to statewide prominence in public affairs, Esdale was undergoing a corresponding rise by moving up in the goblin hierarchy from Cyclops of Birmingham's Robert E. Lee Klavern #1 to Grand Dragon of all Alabama.

* (Author's note) I was skeptical enough of Mr. Esdale's story about his criminal-law grade to check the subjects Harlan Stone taught at Columbia, and on looking into Mason's biography I found that Stone did indeed teach an occasional course in criminal law. Moreover, Professor Louis Lusky advises me that Stone did teach criminal law during the period when Mr. Esdale was enrolled.

It would say too much to call Black and Esdale friends, but they were not without a certain similarity of temperament. Not only did they share a brisk and vital energy and an ambition scaled to a like dimension, but each seemed to have a lively appreciation of what the other could do for his own plans. Hence, Esdale's blandishments must have included at least a hint of what a vigorous statewide organization could mean for a man interested in getting on in the world. (In fact, Esdale thought Black's design for success was keyed to becoming general counsel for United States Steel.) Doubtless, Esdale left unsaid the assistance that such an ally, when risen to power, could be for his own plans within the Invisible Empire.

The new organization bore the same name as the one carried by the post-Civil War terrorists, and as James Cash noted in *The Mind of the South,* the repetition was no accident, but rather a significant projection of the past into the present, "a meaningful witness of the continuity of Southern sentiment." Hence, in a very real sense it was the original Ku Klux Klan that had been reconstituted atop Stone Mountain outside Atlanta by W. J. Simmons, Alabama-born dentist. Shortly thereafter, it came to Birmingham, where the soil for Esdale's salesmanship had been well prepared by a local group called the True Americans, who had carried the municipal elections of 1921 and then swept all Catholics (save two policemen) from the city payroll. But the True Americans had no real chance for long-run success against the national organization from Atlanta.[7]

Part of their downfall was obviously due to the transfer of the Esdale organizational talents from the Elks to the new arrival. But even more important was the new thrust that came from the Klan's national headquarters in Atlanta at the beginning of 1923, when Dr. Simmons was toppled from office. Leading the *putsch* was the other man from Clay County, Hiram Evans, who had left a Dallas dental career to become National Kligriff, or secretary, of the brotherhood. The inside revolution had its external counterpart in a proceeding in the (Atlanta) Fulton County Superior Court that wrested fiscal control from the incumbent leadership under charges of gross mismanagement and personal enrichment. But there was more than merely a change of command; there also was a fundamental change of direction.

Many years later the character of that change in direction was underscored by a letter written in defense of Black and defending also "the regime of Dr. W. J. Simmons, the original founder of the Ku Klux Klan, which was founded on the basis of a Christian mecca to help, protect, develop, educate and support women, underprivileged children, the unprotected widow and orphan." But that was not the Klan of Hiram Evans. Rather, the Clay-County-born dentist, showing one of those phenomenal late-blooming capacities for executive organization and direction, had indeed turned the organization completely around. Now a tightly knit administrative checkrein descended upon the once loose infrastructure. The cabalistic array of Dragons and Cyclops found themselves subject to Imperial Wizard Hiram Wesley Evans' paper bureaucracy, which ran from serially numbered executive orders to a requirement that a verbatim transcript of proceedings at all important meetings be made by an official court reporter. And most important of all, the order went forth that the Klan should lose its largely working-class coloration with the intensive recruitment of members from professional and managerial ranks.[8]

The crushing of the unions had given the Klan an almost ready-made workingman base, but a receptive soil also lay in the managerial echelon. Years later a Black in-law would write of the undercurrent of Populist resentment among the Birmingham upper-middle class of the conditions its members were required to defend—absentee ownership, basing points, discriminatory freight rates—and "the general sense that the South was the colony of financially well-heeled outsiders." In terms of professional memberships, moreover, nothing succeeded like success, as Black himself noted in an interview published after his death—"I was trying a lot of cases against corporations, jury cases, and I found out that all the corporation lawyers were in the Klan. A lot of jurors were too, so I figured I'd better be even-up."[9]

While Black suggested jury considerations as his main reason, there could well have been another. Looking back from the perspective of half a century, Senator John Sparkman recalled the intensity with which the Klan had tried to recruit him, not once but twice. One invitation came while he was still a senior at the University of Alabama Law School; again he was solicited when he opened his law office in Huntsville. And while Sparkman successfully resisted both ploys, he also remembered another circumstance of the times operating to shake the will of any man considering running for office in a statewide election—the knowledge that the Klan controlled the voting machinery in virtually every Alabama county.[10]

James Cash subsequently reflected that the Klan was not another tin-pot fraternal order, but rather an authentic folk movement, and unquestionably Evans' thrust provided the means that fortified the body of common whites with what Cash called the blood of the upper orders—great industrialists maintaining contact through the membership of underlings, small businessmen coming in by the swarm along with planters and landowning farmers generally, and even the politicians whether "maverick, demagogue or hierarch" forced to traffic with the Klan in some way.

Consequently, the Klan was able to sum up

> within itself, with precise completeness and exactness, the whole body of the fears and hates of the time . . . eventually spreading far beyond the borders of Dixie. It was . . . at once anti-Negro, anti-Alien, anti-Catholic, anti-Jew, anti-Darwin, anti-Modern, anti-Liberal, Fundamentalist, vastly Moral, militantly Protestant. And . . . it brought them all into focus . . . with the ancient Southern pattern of high romantic histrionics, violence, and mass coercion of the scapegoat and the heretic.[11]

Perhaps. As in so many things, the indictment includes a sharpened hindsight shaped by, among other things, the Caliban racist state. But the Klan was no Third Reich, even potentially, and this notwithstanding the endemic violence and racism then pervading American society. It was at once far more complex and far more simple. It was a safe haven for the insecure, a perpetual Halloween for the drab of life, a link to the past, to the alienated, and in all these things it combined "chameleonlike" morality, vigilantism and sadism. And the latter, a dark and sinister underside, obviously gave Black pause as his personal apologia via Max Lerner over a decade later showed:

> He was from the very beginning a "joiner." Even before he was of age, he had put in his application for the Knights of Pythias and the Masons. He had a youthful fervor for secret societies. Somewhere around 1920 he was approached to join the Klan. He pleaded lack of time; he was then Grand Chancellor of the Knights of Pythias and an officer of his Masonic lodge. He was skeptical of the Klan's exclusion of Jews (the Masons admitted them), anxious to know the character of its members, suspicious that they might take the law into their own hands. The matter was dropped, but soon a close friend approached Black again, and this time overcame his objections. But it was not until two years later that Black attended a meeting and paid dues. He went to very few meetings, and when he spoke it was to warn against lawlessness and religious intolerance.[12]

Thirty years later, the posthumously published *New York Times* interview disclosed who was the friend and what was the friend's reasons. It was Herman Beck, a Birmingham merchant, in whose home Black had lived prior to his marriage and whom he named as his executor on going off to World War I—"a Jew, my closest friend . . . said they needed good people in the Klan. He couldn't be in it, of course, but he wanted me to be in it to keep down the extremists. . . ."[13]

For Black there never were simple, lineal explanations. To the plea of Beck, there was added what Black had called "the real reason" for joining—to get one up with all the corporation lawyers in the mechanics of jury selection. To this there was added yet another blandishment, perhaps the instrument of formal recruitment: "an old law partner got me to join." There were still others: "Practically everyone belonged. The preachers, et cetera, were all for it. The name Klan is magic down there. Thad Stevens and his Reconstruction have never been forgotten."[14]

Curiously, he was not explicit on what obviously was another factor in his decision, the fact that ninety percent of Birmingham's union members were also involved with the Klan. And these were the very people—literally, his clientele—with whom his influence would be the greatest, certainly in terms of restraint of violence, flogging and kidnapping. ("I told 'em . . . that if I saw any illegality going on . . . I'd turn 'em in to the grand jury.")[15] His words would come with far greater effect (indeed almost as an insider) than would the counsel of a member of the Birmingham establishment against which the Klan itself was a symptom of protest.

Whatever his tangle of motives, he joined Robert E. Lee Klavern No. 1 at dusk on September 11, 1923. It was hardly a secret act. With him were 1,750 other initiates, and the ceremonies took place before 25,000 spectators. That he went through with it came as something of a surprise, for he had indicated otherwise: "I said I'll pay an initiation fee, sign up, but not be initiated." Despite his words, he went through with it in a ceremony that itself involved a singular development.[16]

The End of an Era

That the county solicitor who exposed the operation of the Bessemer jail should join the Klan was an anomaly almost as marked as the busy lawyer volunteering to prosecute a case in a distant city for free. The improbable events not only were given a certain plausibility but were put in a coherent pattern by a third circumstance—the unstable Senate seat of Oscar Underwood.

Like Black, Underwood was a lawyer who, barely out of his teens, had come to Birmingham to seek his fortune. There the resemblance ended. Born in Louisville, Underwood had been educated at the University of Virginia, where he had been president of the Jefferson Society, the school's highest honor, and to

an outstanding education he had added natural attributes of
character, candor and personal charm. He had been elected to
the House of Representatives in 1894, and as Democratic majority leader in the Wilson administration, he had been responsible
for much significant legislation, including the tariff that bore his
name and the first modern income tax. In 1914 he went to the
Senate, where he again rose to the post of majority leader, and
became the first Southerner in post-Civil War history to seriously contend for the Presidency. In fact, he had jousted with
Wilson for the Democratic nomination prior to the election of
1912; but his name won a place in the history of American party
politics when it led the roll call of the states ("Alabama casts
twenty-fo' votes for Oscar W. Underwood") through 103 separate ballots at the deadlocked Democratic convention of 1924.

In a sense the deadlock aptly symbolized the impasse to which
his own particular Jeffersonian philosophy had led him. Underwood was already suspect in many parts of the Democratic party,
where his second marriage to the daughter of a wealthy indus-
trialist, his close friendship with President Harding, and his
seemingly arcadian detachment from the problems of the postwar age seemed to range him increasingly in a conservative
camp. And the problems of that age included not only the Ku
Klux Klan, but the difficulties that had brought it into being.

Specifically, however, the convention deadlock derived from a
proposal to denounce the Ku Klux Klan by name, which lost by
one vote, and in the process shattered beyond repair both Underwood's presidential ambitions and the unity of the party. Indeed
such was the course of events that Al Smith assertedly offered his
own supporters if Underwood could obtain the support of just
two more Southern states. Ironically enough, it was at this point
that his anti-Klan stand was his undoing, doubtless as a consequence of events that had occurred just a little more than a year
earlier.

For it was on October 23, 1923, that Underwood had undertaken to do himself what he subsequently urged on the Democratic national convention: he denounced the Klan by name and
did so in the Klan stronghold of Houston. There was a remark-

able sequel. One day later, and a hundred miles to the north of Dallas, Imperial Wizard Hiram Evans denounced everything Underwood stood for, in a rousing speech before a vast audience on Klan Day at the Texas State Fair. (Indicative of the Klan's mixed roots, he also included a call for an insured program of medical aid not unlike the future Medicare.) But Evans had come to Dallas prepared to give a very different speech than the one he delivered, and it would have endorsed Underwood for the Presidency. Indeed, Evans subsequently observed that the nomination would have been Underwood's "had he just simply 'set' "—a classic political epitaph—but, as one of his friends observed, "Oscar won't demagogue, not even a little."[17]

Oscar had refused to "demagogue" on Prohibition, which he fought directly on the floor of the Senate and indirectly in opposing Alabama's ratification of the Eighteenth Amendment. He likewise refused to "demagogue" on the Ku Klux Klan. He soon had his answers. While the convention was still in session, a monster Klan rally was held in Birmingham with forty thousand people gathering to watch the initiation of four thousand new candidates. Just a few months later, seven thousand more Klansmen were inducted in the city; this time the ceremony included Underwood's burial in effigy as a coffin bearing his name was interred through a trap door in the speaker's platform. The significance soon became apparent. Before the year was out, the man who in spring had overwhelmingly swept the state Democratic primary in his quest for the Presidency found himself challenged for his Senate seat; a contender, John H. Bankhead, filed against him, and the Alabama papers proclaimed that the senatorial race was on. Ironically, the father of the challenger had nominated Underwood for the Presidency at the Democratic convention of 1912.

The Double Election

Thereafter the aspirants came on, "thick as bumblebees," as the Alabama saying had it. By spring of 1925, Thomas E. Kilby, a onetime governor said he would run for the Underwood seat, and shortly thereafter so did James J. Mayfield, a former justice of the state Supreme Court and a sometime Underwood supporter. In early June, Hugo Black, now thirty-nine, and virtually unknown, made his declaration; and on July 1, Senator Underwood announced his retirement from politics at the close of his current Senate term.

Black had some preliminaries to take care of. On July 9, he submitted his handwritten resignation from the Ku Klux Klan—"effective from this date on. Yours I.T.S.U.B." The cabalistic close assertedly stood for "Yours in the sacred unfailing bond," and years later it would raise questions about the good faith of the severance. At the moment, however, its efficacy seemed to run quite the other way, for the Klan had its own Hatch Act, and Klansmen were supposed to be more kingmakers than kings.[18]

Moreover, James Esdale, now Grand Dragon of the Alabama Klan, aspired to be king-maker par excellence, with his alumnus of Robert E. Lee Klavern #1 and fellow member of the Birmingham bar as his subject. Almost a half century later, Esdale recalled how he had planned to expose his aspirant to his 148 Klaverns and 80,000 Klansmen. The opening ploy was a speaking tour, to be undertaken in advance of the formal campaign; the Klaverns were to be the forums, the Klansmen the audience, and the topics (which assertedly included an attack on political Catholicism) general rather than political. Nor was it an especially covert operation, for a decade later, in an article on Black, the *Birmingham Post* would recall Esdale "escorting him about the state." Still, some security was required, and instructions accordingly were supposed to include a programmed response to any ingenuous inquiry about the candidate's Klan membership. ("Say 'That reminds me of a story,' and keep talking until you get out of there.")[19]

Indeed in a singular linkage of the Esdale effort and his own senatorial aspirations, there had been a Klan rally in the courthouse square at Ashland on the night before Black made what was formally his keynote address. But the event transcended its

Klan connections. Rather, the talk touched history in its attack on the Alabama establishment and its candidate, John H. Bankhead. That establishment had changed very little since the turn of the century. Certainly it was far from the political machine, in the Tammany sense, that its opponents called it. But its vague and diffused coalition—courthouse politicians, the county office-holders, the industrial lobbyists, the down-state planters so appropriately labeled the Bourbons—was remarkable in its persistent ability to both attack and defend ensemble in behalf of its ragtag community of interests.

Hence, the keynote speech was most significant in being delivered on the very spot where the call for the formation of the people's party of Alabama had gone forth many years before. The old-time Populists would have been very pleased at what they heard. One part concerned the uses for the dam at Muscle Shoals, begun as part of the preparedness program prior to World War I and still unfinished. The other dealt with the Alabama Power Company and the Bankhead ascendancy. Black managed to unite proposals and targets in a series of interrelated propositions.

On the issue of the dam—a controversy which would dominate his political life for so many of the years to follow—he favored completion under a plan that would stress fertilizer production under either public or private ownership rather than transfer of the structure or its production of power to a private utility. Accordingly he joined his proposal on Muscle Shoals with a thrust at the Alabama Power Company and followed with another passage whose similes linked the utility with the man he saw as his major opponent:

> The electric lights of Mr. Bankhead's vision do not shine far enough. They do not light my way. The vision I see shines from the sunlight of justice to all and special favors to none. In that vision, none stand in the electric spotlight of favor or cower in the darkness and obscurity of denied opportunity.[20]

Within a week, however, he would have to be rewriting the speech, for the calculus that had marked out John Bankhead as his principal opponent was enormously complicated by the belated entry of Lycurgus Breckenridge Musgrove into the race. Musgrove posed far more of a problem to Black than he did to his fellow townsman Bankhead; not only was the new entrant rich, progressive, dry, and well known (having run a vigorous race against Oscar Underwood six years back), but in an arcane sequence of maneuver and intrigue, he entered the current contest with the blessing of the national headquarters of the Ku Klux Klan.

That blessing was far from a guarantee of success, for already Evans' work in shoring up the organizational infrastructure was producing its own countervailing force. As one perceptive observer noted, the Klan's very source of discipline, fear and strength—the hierarchical principal that all power should originate in the Wizard and move downward from him—had already produced two perverse consequences. One lay in its exploitation by the ambitious and power-hungry through manipulations that had little to do with law enforcement, Americanism or morality. The other was growing resentment by the rank and file of dictation from on high "about the making of policy, the endorsement of politicians, and the choice of their leaders."[21]

Moreover, in attempting to impose his will from Atlanta, Evans faced the classic problem of the centralized commander contending with localized insurgencies. Here Alabama was but one salient on a far-flung battle line running from Florida to Oregon. And all along that line Evans had his difficulties. In Indiana he was forced to obtain an injunction to restrain a breakaway local group from using the Klan name. In Texas, his candidate for governor was pressed hard by Miriam "Ma" Ferguson running under the motto "Better a Bonnet than a Hood." In Louisiana, his alliance with the Fuqua forces was unstable, and he had already sensed the steel of a young red-neck named Huey Long, whose guarded neutrality toward him would one day turn to outright hostility against "that Imperial Bastard."

But endorsement was still important, and Evans was able to transfer a patina of official approval to Musgrove. The Bankheads fighting to extend their ascendancy saw what they thought were their minor opponents of Black and Musgrove in respective characterizations of "one radical and a Ku Klux." Rank-and-file perception, however, was another thing again, and the inner struggle was to see that it blended rather than differentiated the Bankhead characterizations. Through it all, Black persisted as "the" Klan candidate, notwithstanding a bewildering series of seemingly official circulars granting and revising the official endorsements, an emissary from Atlanta who threatened to suppress the Robert E. Lee Klavern #1, and a hotly disputed version of a discussion between Esdale and Musgrove of an exchange of $125,000 for endorsement by the state Klan.[22]

The campaign within the campaign was duly reported front page center with speculation as to the degree to which defections to Colonel Musgrove were taking away Judge Black's Klan following. And in its own way, the inner struggle critically affected the outer one. For the larger contest, notwithstanding the five-man field, was seen at the outset as a two-man fight between former Governor Kilby and John Bankhead, the Senator's son. But it proceeded in the folk-theater tradition of old-time Southern politics—fragmented, kaleidoscopic, and highly personalized—the issues, roads and fertilizer, were increasingly overshadowed by a cross-accusation of violations of the Corrupt Practices Act, estimates of net worth and campaign spending, and demeaning comment on opponents' background and fitness for office. The subject matter of debate was one virtually tailored for an underdog, and Black skillfully escalated the initial side thrusts at his damage-suit practice into a major confrontation with the front-runners.

Moreover, he was able to do so within media ideally suited to his message. In addition to being the least-known candidate, he also began as the least-reported one, and even his newspaper advertising ("Paid for by himself") contrasted with the swollen committee listings of his opponents. But he did not depend on the papers to reach his constituency. Instead, he once more resorted to the spoken word and the face-to-face encounter as, repeating his Klavern tour of a few months earlier, he wore out two automobiles in ceaselessly crossing and recrossing the state, shaking hands and speaking in courthouse squares, service-club meetings, and the innumerable church, civic and fraternal gatherings. And in the closing days of the campaign, perhaps in a final surge for the indispensable Klan vote or perhaps as an indication of a stance in a future power struggle, he replaced John Bankhead and the Alabama Power Company with Al Smith for his target.

On August 10, 1926, the results came in and showed that Black had won both referenda. In the formal election operating under the complex Alabama dual-choice system, he piled up a surprising 72,000, or 32 percent, of the first-place votes. These, combined with 12,000 second-place indications, gave him the Democratic nomination without the need of a run-off. Bankhead, Mayfield, Musgrove trailed him in that order, and former Governor Kilby was a surprising fifth. In the informal Klan referendum between local autonomy and central control, he seemed to have done even better, and observers noted that Black's number of first-place votes stood remarkably close to the number of Klansmen in the state. Grand Dragon Esdale, whose own position within the order's power structure had hung in the balance, was jubilant, and exultingly he told a reporter, "We licked 'em clean in the election, and I've got 150,000 men who will scratch Al Smith's name if they put him up for President next year."[23]

The Great Klorero

Victorious along with Black was Bibb Graves, sometime paid Klan lecturer and Cyclops of his home town, Montgomery. A Yale graduate, Graves had sought the nomination for the governorship, and throughout the campaign there had been no dispute whatever on his possession of the Klan endorsement at both national and state levels. His triumph, together with that of Black, could be seen as a public vindication of the order, and manifestly the time had come to heal whatever wounds remained after the bitter senatorial campaign.

The occasion of the healing was the fourth annual Klorero of the entire Birmingham Klan, held on September 2 at the Robert E. Lee Klavern #1 on South Twentieth Street. To help pour oil on the waters, Imperial Wizard Evans duly made his pilgrimage from national headquarters in Atlanta, and pursuant to his administrative rules, a stenographic transcript was made of the proceedings by A. B. Hale, official court reporter for Jefferson County.

The meeting opened "in regular Kloranic form" with Grand Dragon Esdale presiding, and nine Catholic children from the Klan orphanage being led across the stage as Judge Virginia Mayfield of the Jefferson County Juvenile Court explained to the applauding audience that "before we get through they will be Protestants." Next introduced was Imperial Legal Adviser William E. Zumbrum, of Washington, D.C., with an explanation that despite the name, he was a native-born Midwestern American, and Zumbrum spoke of the recent senatorial contest: "You have given us a man named Black who wears white—do you get that, boys?—to occupy a seat in the Senate." Either the reporter was negligent or the "boys" did not, for the sally was one of the few points where a pleasantry was not followed by "(applause)." But the lapse was more than repaired when "(Laughter and applause)" greeted the reference to the governor-elect's work as Excellent Cyclops in Montgomery, "where the Jews have had a foreclosure sale . . . the Catholics are on the run, and the Negroes are in hiding." And at this point Dr. A. D. Ellis of Tuscaloosa awarded the solid-gold passports to the two electoral victors—"They are good as long as you are good." The passports were ambiguity itself, in part (reflecting the Klan's labor-union connections) something in the nature of a withdrawal card, in part (reflecting a Masonic matrix) something of an advanced degree and unsolicited honorary membership, and in part perhaps what they said they were—a message from the Grand Klan of Alabama to all Exalted Cyclops that the bearer was a citizen of the Invisible Empire entitled to unmolested passage and fervent fellowship.[24]

Bibb Graves responded in a rousing address, which began with a vigorous attack on Al Smith and the recent Catholic Eucharistic Congress and closed with a pledge of a better Alabama for all the citizens of that state. Then it was Black's turn, and he matched Evans' olive branch with some postelection hokum of his own from the Wizard—"Some of the greatest inspirations of my life I received from your father." He then passed from Evans' family to Evans' enemies as, perhaps repeating some passages from the Catholicism talk of the Klavern circuit, he took due and darkling notice of the Mexican government's current efforts to enforce its ultrasecular constitution—"I hope it never becomes necessary here." And then, acknowledging his debt to the Klan in a characteristically paradoxical change of pace, which strongly contrasted with the remarks of Governor-elect Graves, he told the unlikely audience: "The thing I like about this organization is not the burning of the crosses, it is not attempting to regulate anybody—I don't know, some may do that —but, my friends, I see a bigger vision . . . the principles of human liberty."[25]

Doubtless the peroration was simply the spontaneous restatement of irenicism he had been seeking to impose from within upon his fellow members of Robert E. Lee Klavern #1. Or perhaps it was a covert response to the Imperial Wizard that he was his own man. For Evans had made a point, possibly in trying to salvage some laurels in defeat, of how he had brought down one United States Senator who might have had the Presidency by going along. ("Let me tell you a little bit about this Underwood thing.")[26]

In any event, the dialogue, if such it was, turned out to be unnecessary, for the great Klorero was said to have been Black's last Klan meeting, and the next time Black and Evans were to come into significant contact, it was Black who would be dominant. Meanwhile, there was still the November general election to be faced, but in solidly Democratic Alabama that was the merest of formalities. Shortly thereafter the Blacks sold their house on Altamont, transferred their voting address to the Foster residence, and left for Washington. Alabama's Senator-elect had turned forty, and his wife was twenty-eight, by far and away the youngest of the Senate wives.

In Washington, Oscar Underwood, in the best tradition of the Southern gentleman and good loser, introduced his successor around and took him to the White House to meet President Coolidge. The record does not show whether the successor attended the Gridiron Dinner, at which Underwood was an honored guest along with another former public figure now deemed emeritus, Charles Evans Hughes. Indeed, the honor of journalists was appropriate, for on retirement Underwood turned to letters himself, returning, not to Alabama, but to a showplace Virginia estate near Mount Vernon. The man who had reportedly declined a seat on the Supreme Court from Warren G. Harding and who had been ousted from public life by Hugo La Fayette Black wrote a loftily Augustan political testament, which he appropriately entitled *The Shifting Sands of Party Politics.*

Part Three

Senator Black

CHAPTER FIVE

The Apprentice Years

The Education of a Senator

The Seventieth Congress convened on December 5, 1927, and in the Senate chamber at noon the Senators-elect came forward, alphabetically and in fours, to take the oath from Vice-President Charles G. Dawes. First up were Barkley, Bingham, Black and Blaine, each accompanied by the incumbent colleague from his state. Down the aisle with Black came Thomas L. "Tom-Tom" Heflin of Mobile, perhaps the most energetic Catholic baiter in the history of the upper house, and a politician who was once summarized by the *San Francisco Bulletin* as "a notorious blatherskite [and] high-hatted, long-coated windbag." And this he was.

But he was a good deal more like the Klan and Prohibition; he was, in his twisted way, an authentic voice of protest in a time badly out of joint. And, in the conglomerate fiefdom of personalities that was Alabama politics, he was a real power. There was little love lost between himself and Black, who had defeated his brother in the early race for the office of county solicitor back in 1912, but the complex realities of the latter decade made for a

127

realistic rapport between the two Alabama senators. "The K.K.K. stuck to Black . . . all over the state. . . . It is in every way best for you in a political way that Black won," Heflin's brother wrote after the Democratic primary. Nonetheless Black walked an uneasy postelection tightrope, for he and Heflin were about as temperamentally dissimilar as men could be.[1]

Indeed the new Congress was scarcely under way when the basic antipathy showed itself as Heflin denounced the new Democratic leader, Senator Joseph T. Robinson of Arkansas, as a sycophant of Catholic power and sought his ouster. The effort was repulsed 38 to 1 by the Democratic caucus, and in a significant manifestation of the caution that would serve him well when confronted with crisis, the new Senator Black abstained from voting at all.

But the fact that he also stood aloof from his senior Senator was revealing, for in four years Black would lead Heflin's successor down the Senate aisle, and he would perhaps be more responsible for the change than any other man. Moreover the change in colleagues would be something of an index of the change in himself. For a transformation was about to take place, and it was well under way when, in mid-January of 1929, Heflin sought to displace the minority leader. By that time the Blacks had been in Washington for almost two years. His formal senatorial term had not begun until March 4, 1927, and under the old lame-duck provision of the Constitution the new Congress did not even meet until December.

The press of official duties was light, for Capitol Hill between sessions was manned by a skeleton staff and, like the dowdy and provincial city of which it was a part, went into virtual somnambulance. Black had given up his law practice, stopped tennis on doctor's orders, cut his smoking from three packs a day to nothing in adjusting to an income drop from $40,000 to $10,000, and was doubtless coiled like two steel springs. He accordingly made the Library of Congress his postgraduate school and undertook a reading program with the same energetic zest that had cleaned the Birmingham dockets and shaken every available hand on the campaign trail.

Little in his life had previously suggested any authentic intellectual dimension. The one sustained exposure experience should have given him—the King James Scripture encountered through twenty years of Sunday-school teaching—appeared to leave minimal impress, and this even though the Bible in the Senate of the late twenties remained the most widely used repository of quotation. If anything, the urbane skepticism of Edward Gibbon's *Decline and Fall of the Roman Empire,* which he had read aloud in his Birmingham rooming house, seemed closer to his ethos than Scripture ever had been.

Now, however, he struck out in what was to be a lifelong effort, beginning with *The Wealth of Nations* and moving on to other works in economics, politics and government as one book suggested another. His reading list early included a heavy concentration on the Founding Fathers with Franklin, Hamilton, Adams and Jefferson, thereby resembling the reading list of Andrew Johnson, who was also a latecomer to such matters (and in Johnson's case to literacy itself). But Black also took in an extended classical dimension—Plutarch, Suetonius, Seneca, Cicero—to the degree that Washington gossip was to report his copy of Livy as the most underlined and marginally noted in the capital. And in a tincture of prophecy, he included on his reading list general literature on the Supreme Court.

In their separate ways, both the reading program and the removal to Washington manifested something of the same hint of alienation that came through again and again in both the Blacks. Certainly they could not seem to get out of Birmingham fast enough. At a time when Senators spent as much time under their family roofs and practicing law in their home towns as they did in the capital, Black had neither. Shortly after the election the Blacks sold the house on Altamont Road and transferred their voting addresses to the Foster home. Likewise closed out was the law office in the First National Bank Building. There were obviously regrets at their leaving, as one Junior Leaguer lapsed into artless verse to mark Josephine's departure—"Yesterday, I passed where once you lived, my dear, and passing, looked the other way." Nor was their new home so very different from the one they had left. In fact, the pleasant white home on Washington's Cathedral Avenue was perhaps a cut below Altamont in both style and size for the growing family, which now included, in addition to Hugo junior, Sterling Foster, who was born the year of the senatorial election. To be sure, Washington had its wide boulevards and public buildings, but what style it had otherwise came from the embassies and those local socialites known as cave dwellers, thanks to their Massachusetts Avenue habitat. For the city was unquestionably the dullest and most philistine of the world's capitals. And there were other reminders of Birmingham. One was the summer's sweltering heat. Another was recollected by Justice Douglas: "Forty years ago in Washington, D.C., a black who was found after the sun set in the northwest section of the District on or above Chevy Chase circle was arrested, though his only 'crime' was waiting for a bus to take him home after caddying at a plush golf course in the environs."[2]

The Freshman Speeches

Intellectual assertiveness was not Black's dominant characteristic in the early Senate years. On the contrary, he appeared to rigorously observe his own initial injunction that he intended "to occupy an inconspicuous place in the Senate" during his apprenticeship, and with two exceptions he did so during the first session of the Seventieth Congress. Both were carry-overs from his campaign. One concerned Muscle Shoals, a complex of dams and nitrate plants on the Tennessee River in extreme northwestern Alabama, which had begun in the preparedness phase of the Wilson administration and still remained unfinished. Black had campaigned on a proposed dedication of the complex to the production of nitrate, an obvious boon to the thin red soil of Clay County and the other Southern farms whose use of fertilizer far exceeded the natural average. ("Cotton is a voracious plant," said Cash, "and to grow it [on most Southern land] would require fertilizer, and in increasing amounts.")[3]

Whether this was done by sale or lease, and to Henry Ford

(who had made an offer) or another corporation, was a matter of indifference to Black. On the other hand, veteran Senator George W. Norris saw the dams as the core of a public-power complex and the disposition to private interests as an unconscionable subsidy to business. Given this difference, Black and Norris must have disliked each other at first sight, for the Nebraska liberal's gentle but rocklike integrity was a world apart from the rapierlike temperament of the Alabamian. But the difference held a character very different from that separating Black and Heflin. Rather, association with Norris brought a close personal friendship and a reciprocal modification of position. Black retreated from his rhetoric ("the farmers are asking for the bread of nitrate and they get the stone of power . . .") and the overcapacity of the Southern utilities, and Norris enlarged his proposal to include fertilizer manufacture. The coalition, however, was unavailing, for the proposal at the end of the session fell, perhaps appropriately, under the pocket veto of the silent President.[4]

George Norris was part of that group of progressive mavericks in the Senate to which Black was increasingly drawn, thanks to his reading program and enlarging horizons. The group largely lay outside his own party—the "radical Republicans," Senator Ashurst called them, for in addition to Norris the group included William E. Borah, Robert M. La Follette, Jr., and Bronson M. Cutting. Senator George H. Moses had given them another label, the sons of the wild jackass. For, while an occasional exception had to be made in both partisan and sectional terms, the Senate into which Black had come contained not two parties but four. In addition to the Norris component, however labeled, the Republicans contained its orthodox Old Guard, while the Democrats were bifurcated between North and South.[5]

And indeed it was a fellow Democrat, William C. Bruce—a border-state (Maryland) Senator, but a Northern partisan, especially in his anti-Prohibition sentiments—who occasioned Black's other freshman speech. This one came on as an apparently spontaneous rebuttal, for Bruce had been taunting the Deep South for voting dry and drinking wet. In what turned out to be a two-day exchange, Black took the floor in an uncharacteristic but extended peroration to Dixie, and Bruce's counterthrusts came uncomfortably close to home. The Father Coyle homicide came up, with Bruce showing that he was mixed up on some facts but accurate enough on others:

> MR. BRUCE: . . . I have heard it said that the junior Senator from Alabama owes his seat in the Senate to the Ku Klux Klan vote.
>
> MR. BLACK: If the Senator will let me reply to that, that statement, like the others he made, is absolutely untrue. I got all the Ku Klux votes I could get—
>
> MR. BRUCE: Yes—
>
> MR. BLACK: And all the Catholic votes I could get, and all the Jew votes I could get, and all the Baptist votes I could get, and all the others, and I have no apology to make for it, and I am here representing them.
>
> MR. BRUCE: I understood you were ready to resort to any expedient to get them.
>
> MR. BLACK: I am sorry I cannot state exactly what I thought about that statement, and so I suppose the best thing is to let it go.
>
> MR. BRUCE: I think so. I think you show to better advantage when you keep your seat than when you rise to your feet.[6]

The exchange at that point veered off in another direction, but the uncharacteristic yielding of the Senator from Alabama suggested that there were subjects on which he had a remarkable sensitivity. Obviously the Klan was already looking much different to him and mere mention must have occasioned an apprehension as to who now had his manuscript resignation.

The Razor's Edge

"Good Tom," wrote H. L. Mencken of Senator Heflin in April 1928, ". . . faces a very trying situation. If he carries his struggle against the Vatican to the floor of the Houston Convention, and is there put to rout, he will be in difficulties indeed. For he must then either swallow Al [Smith] and so desert the Bible, or lead a bolt and so commit mayhem upon the Democratic party. In either case, he'll be sure to get a dreadful beating for it later on." And, but for the accident of term, the dilemma could have been Black's.[7]

Heflin failed at Houston, and Al Smith, wet and Catholic, became the Democratic nominee for President. (Indeed, on the night of the nomination Mabel Willebrandt raided every speakeasy on Broadway.) Black was not at Houston, although as a United States Senator he could have had a place in the delegation if he wished. Perhaps he should have attended, for there were those who saw the convention's action as fatal to his own political fortunes. ("Hugo's ruined," commented his brother when the party's nominee was chosen.) Black himself indicated as much, for little more than a year earlier he and Heflin had together gone to Montgomery to insure the selection of an anti-Smith delegation, and their efforts had been overwhelmingly vindicated in the spring elections that followed.[8]

At the time of Smith's selection, however, he was conveniently far away in Wisconsin at another convention, that of one of his innumerable fraternal orders. And while he had made his views clear beforehand that Smith's nomination would disrupt the party, he wired a newspaper after the party's choice that Smith's views generally were "a clarion call to progressive democracy." That was about all the endorsement the nominee was going to get from him.[9]

But in contrast to his senior colleague, Black's position was enthusiasm personified. For Heflin touched the core of every article of personal belief as he vigorously called on the God of White Supremacy against the false god of Roman social equality, over his brother's frantic plea, "Don't say you will not vote for Smith." He broke the sacred Reconstruction covenant and spoke the unspeakable words: "So help me God, I will vote against Al Smith if they read me out of the Democratic Party and drive me from every Senate committee."[10]

And with these words he managed to immerse himself in the

same racist quicksand that had swallowed up Oscar Underwood's career. Not that the declaration attached him to an articulate champion of racial equality. (Democratic campaign propaganda, however, did have it that candidate Hoover once danced with the postmistress of all-black Mound Bayou, Mississippi.) But it was the breaking of the front of the white Democratic phalanx that local consensus made the ultimate line of defense for the existing way of life and was symbolized in the rampant rooster and legend "White Supremacy" at the head of the Democratic ticket.

There were others who bolted in the other direction. George Norris, notwithstanding the essentially Protestant, rural and Prohibitionist cast of Nebraska, left the Republican party, to support Al Smith. Hugo Black did not bolt, but neither was his voice loud. "Why do we not hear from Hugo Black in this campaign?" wrote a reader of one Birmingham newspaper. "How about Senator Black?" echoed a letter to another. Yet, the only time Hugo Black spoke out in Birmingham in the autumn of 1928 was to call for support of the Community Chest. Indeed, even though he was a member of the Senate Democratic campaign committee, he was not seen at a public breakfast when Josephus Daniels came to town seeking support of the national ticket.[11]

Surprisingly, the loyalists did manage to surmount the issues of religion and Prohibition as they carried the state for Smith by fewer than 7,000 votes. It was not much of a triumph, but it came when other components of the once Solid South were defecting for the first time. And it was a hard campaign. ("Do you want to wake up some morning," Carl Carmer recorded as a swatch of campaign argument, "and find a dago priest in the White House a-givin' orders to white folks? Do you know what he plans to do right here in Alabama—he's goin' to give Alabama over to be ruled by a nigger Cardinal.")[12]

Black's cautious maneuvering did not go unnoticed; the *Montgomery Advertiser* linked his name with Heflin and Governor Graves as three men who were so tightly in the grip of the Ku Klux Klan that they could not bring themselves to "discharge their plain duty to the Democratic party." The judgment was much too harsh. Black did discharge his plain duty to the Democratic party. ("I backed Al Smith in '28, but it was hard. He was encouraging violations of Prohibition. That may be O.K. when you're a private citizen, but not when you're in government.") But for the party, the hero of the election was Theodore Bilbo who came over from Mississippi to stump Alabama for Smith.[13]

All in all it was quite a race. The Alabama Women's League for White Supremacy did its part. So did the Democratic propagandists who told and retold the story of how Hoover, as Secretary of Commerce, had desegregated the Bureau of the Census. The 122 Negro delegates to the Republican Convention were contrasted with the Democratic gathering where "not a single black face" appeared. Despite the denials of the devoutly Baptist and nondancing Mrs. Booze, the story of her alleged waltz with Herbert Hoover was accorded much prominence. And Bilbo had a line which he used with great effectiveness: "As to religion, I don't think either Smith or Hoover has enough to alarm anybody."[14]

Countermarch

The narrowness of its margin of victory obviously intensified the determination of the Alabama establishment to abort as summarily as possible the broadly based white opposition that had emerged in the 1928 election. Their tactic was to deny reentry into the white phalanx to the leaders—but not to the followers—of the movement that had sallied out from its protective ranks to vote against Smith. Formally, the exclusion appeared as an oath, exacted as a condition of entry into future Democratic contests, that the aspirant had supported the party ticket in 1928. In view of Heflin's public vow that he would do exactly the opposite, the measure ruled the senior Senator out on its very face, and there were those, Hugo Black included, who feared that it was capable of more refined separations from the party ticket.

The exclusionist proposal was not adopted without considerable misgivings. John Bankhead, its presumptive beneficiary, reflected that if Heflin could not be bested in a contest confined to Democratic voters, it was highly unlikely that he could be in one open to all comers. Black came out in flat opposition. While he had beaten the establishment two elections back, there was no guarantee that that upset could be repeated in the contest of 1932, which drew nearer with each passing day; and the possibility of a midstream change of electoral rules boded him very little good.

His position was not based on any sudden postelection rapprochement with Heflin, in relation to whom he still tacked and veered with manifest wariness. Their joint service was a remarkable mosaic. Black had matched his abstention on the proposed Robinson ouster by inserting in the *Congressional Record* a florid tribute to his senior colleague that Dr. F. J. Thomas had pronounced at a mammoth Masonic meeting in Chicago—"Like David of old . . . against an insidious, powerful, and dangerous foe." And after that he had voted for Heflin's proposal to end the Navy tradition of flying the cross-inscribed church pennant (presumably an arcane Roman symbol) over the national colors, and for a Heflin bill to cut off federal funds for Howard University.[15]

But in terms of long-run implications the pattern of emerging differences far outweighed elements of rapport, and something of a preview was suggested by measures over which the two Senators parted company. A significant fission came on a resolution by Senator Thomas J. Walsh that he use on the power trust the techniques developed in the Teapot Dome investigation. Appropriately, Hugo Black, who was fated to become the inquisitorial scourge of that industry, voted for the proposal. Contrariwise, Heflin opposed—some said because of reluctance to advance the Catholic Walsh's political fortunes.

More meaningful yet was the split that surfaced in the debate over a pornography-and-sedition amendment during the legislative voyage of the Smoot-Hawley tariff. On the tariff itself, Black stood in the Alabama free-trade tradition that Oscar Underwood had championed. But he did so with two exceptions. One was an effort to obtain a protectionist duty for Clay County's graphite. The other was to oppose the peremptory ban that the sponsoring Senator Reed Smoot had proposed on seditious and salacious publications of foreign origin. The exclusion proposal had attracted attention as far afield as Ogden Nash ("Smite smut, Smoot"), and within the Senate one of the radical Republicans suggested that the operative power involved be given to the courts rather than to customs inspectors.

The suggestion for judicial administration received the enthusiastic support of the junior Senator from Alabama, and his extensive remarks ranged from a comparison of the relative obscenity of American and foreign books ("Oh, I have some that were printed in this country which would shock the morals of a man who has not been in church for forty years") to an exhibition of the fruits of his reading program in references to Jefferson, Voltaire, Locke, and the burning of the Alexandrian library. Remarkably enough, the selfsame question was to come up for constitutional review during Black's sunset days on the Supreme Court, and it was to find his libertarian views ranged in opposition to the views of a majority of his colleagues on the bench just as four decades earlier they differed from those of the senior Senator from Alabama. For Thomas Heflin was not about to be put off with references to the Song of Songs and similar Biblical passages—"The Sermon on the Mount is not barred by the provision . . . I do not propose that any amendment shall pass if I can prevent it that will permit this country to become the dumping ground of all the unfit literature on earth."[16]

In the short run, however, as 1929 passed into 1930, community rather than confrontation characterized the relations of the two Alabama Senators. Thus, Black spoke of his "anxiety" over the primary exclusion rule, which he increasingly saw aimed at him. More than this, his sometime partner and professional confidant, Crampton Harris, argued before the Supreme Court of Alabama on Heflin's behalf the precise point that Black was urging in both public statement and private correspondence: that a political party simply could not have two classes of membership, one eligible to vote and the other eligible to run. But the Court declared itself without jurisdiction in a purely partisan selection process (a general doctrine that Justice Black would one day have a hand in changing), and with Tom Heflin cast into outer darkness, John Bankhead easily won the truncated contest.[17]

Black kept his own counsel during the primary itself and cast a truly secret ballot for a virtual unknown who ran at the last minute against John Bankhead and the Alabama Power Company. The general election, however, forced his hand. In a sense it had already been forced by his covert orthodoxy of two years earlier. Indeed there was little escaping the Bankhead reminders that the regular ticket of 1928 had been supported by himself and Governor Bibb Graves, "both recognized as K.K.K. sympathizers." But if his support was forced by memories of 1928 it was forthcoming in the same way—not a word for the party candidate by name, but strong, if late, words for the party itself and for its bringing "the sunlight of peace, happiness and security to the white men and women of Alabama."[18]

There was a swirl of crosscurrents underlying that enunciated position. One supporter had written Black that Heflin was up against "the men who opposed you four years ago and who will very likely oppose you again in 1932." And this obvious set of circumstances yielded the conclusion, sometimes admiring and sometimes critical, that the junior Senator "had made a trade" with the establishment, trading his endorsement in the present for its support within two years. Certainly the immediate exchange was worth it, for on November 4, 1930, the Democratic general ticket, which had won the state by fewer than 7,000 votes two years earlier, now rolled in victory with over 50,000. It was a smashing defeat for both Klan and Anti-Saloon League alike. James Esdale resigned as Alabama's Grand Dragon, and Tom Heflin headed back to the last session of the Seventy-first Congress, where Senator Ashurst nostalgically entered a political epitaph in his dairy:

> Of all the Lame Ducks in this session who will soon no
> longer be englamoured with the oratory and destitute of
> a toga, none is more dejected than the orator, Senator

Tom Heflin of Alabama. In support of the Ku Klux Klan, he "talked" himself out of the Senate. He has no private income and has been away from the bar so long he has no law practice to return to.[19]

The somber note on the state of Heflin's material fortunes had held a new meaning ever since the fall of 1929 and the beginnings of the general economic retreat that was soon to become a rout. Indeed, Heflin's fall from political favor was itself merely an index of the collapse of the Klan and Prohibition as front-line political forces, and these had declined as a consequence of the widening economic downturn. Indeed it was that very downturn and the limited market for ex-Senators that in part prompted Heflin to file a complaint and seek to bar John Bankhead from the Senate both on the exclusionist primary device and by reason of allegedly widespread voting frauds in the election itself. The move made the breach between Heflin and Black complete, for the election bargain involved a follow-up not foreseen by its original terms. Now the junior Senator rose to the floor of the upper House to place into the *Congressional Record,* not the praise of Heflin's fellow Masons, but rather the condemnation of the Alabama legislature deploring his "very poor sportsmanship" in not abiding by the result of the contest.[20]

Heflin formally left Congress with the ending of the lame-duck session on March 4, 1931, and on the following December 7, Black led John Bankhead, his old opponent, down the center aisle of the Senate to take the oath of office. Bankhead, however, was seated only provisionally, and he spent his early service under a cloud, for the investigation and disposition of Heflin's charges continued for well over a year. At the three-quarter mark of that interim, Black filed for reelection, duly submitting the affidavit that he had supported his initial target of denunciation at the 1930 election, and in like contrast, his second campaign for the Senate differed from the first about as much as one political effort could differ from another. This time he did not attempt to visit every county of Alabama and shake every available hand. Nor did he talk about Alabama Power, electric lights, and Mr. Bankhead's vision. Instead he campaigned from the Senate floor, and his *de facto* platform was the right of John Bankhead to retain his Senate seat, uninvestigated by the federal government.

And he did so in the best states'-rights tradition, sounding like a cross between Jefferson Davis and John C. Calhoun—"I deny the right of the Federal Government to go down to Alabama, sir, and tell the people who shall vote and who shall not vote . . . I am opposed body, mind, and spirit to any additional step which gives the Federal Government the right to go into any State."

And Heflin also ran from the Senate floor, where, even though no longer a Senator, he had been given the right to speak. He used his rare privilege vigorously enough, denouncing his "one-time friend," whom he persisted in calling the junior Senator from Alabama (even though Black was no longer any such thing) as he vigorously rang the changes against the utilities ("Every Alabama Power attorney in the state but two were strong partisans of Mr. Bankhead") and the fundamental equity of his own case. ("Did they read Senator Norris out of his party?") But it was love's labor lost. If Senator Robinson had been seeking revenge for the attempted ouster of five years earlier, he more than had it as he held his Democrats in line for Bankhead without a single defection. Only a scattering of Republicans, including George Norris, voted for Bankhead's ouster, and it was defeated 65 to 18. "Ex-Senator Heflin," noted Henry Ashurst in his dairy, "stunned by the result, slowly walked out of the Senate."[21]

Reelection

Black's defense of Bankhead, while serving in large measure as his campaign for renomination, required a measure of supplementary efforts, and midway in the first session of the Seventy-second Congress he returned home to joust with the four contestants who had filed against him. Again it was a five-man race, and once again former Governor Kilby was in the lists against him. But there were also changes, largely depression-wrought. Now Klan support was no longer sought but spurned, and the former governor attested to the new order of things as he released, with no visible effect one way or the other, a copy of the Grand Passport which had been awarded Black back in 1926. How much water had gone under the bridge in four years and the low estate to which the Klan had fallen was indicated by still another circumstance—the rumor that a candidate for office had arranged for a fiery cross to be burned in front of his house.

Much of the steam had gone out of the Prohibition issue as well, and it was difficult to believe that only four years earlier Senator Ashurst could have written that "neither Flood Control, Farm Relief, Tax Reductions, Merchant Marine, Muscle Shoals, Boulder Dam, nor all these issues rolled into one arouses such interest now as does the liquor question." But here too public concern had waned to a distinctly subsidiary level, and Black maneuvered with characteristic skill.[22]

One consequence of the proscriptions following the 1928 experience had been the repeal of the first- and second-choice nomination statute. Thus, Black's hairbreadth failure to win an absolute majority in the May primary (in which Franklin Roosevelt swept to victory as the presidential choice) forced him into a showdown run-off with the former governor, who smote him hip and thigh—Black was the "arch-deserter" of the party in 1928; his silence in the first primary had attracted unwarranted dry support; and Black "would double-cross the Ku Klux Klan too, except for the fact that he is a life member of that order."[23]

But all to no avail. Black at the eleventh hour defused the Prohibition issue by proposing a referendum on the point, while averring his own teetotaling position. The thrust was decisive. While some members of the establishment supported Kilby (as did Heflin), the combination of its support plus the Prohibition maneuver, plus incumbency, gave Black a 29,000 majority, by which Kilby was sunk without trace.

Indeed it was a world turned upside down as the attacker of the Bankhead ascendancy in 1926 won reelection in 1932 in the role of its defender. But still more convolutions lay ahead.

In Black's second campaign perhaps the only element that had sparked overtones of character were the allegations of nepotism attending the employment of his wife as a temporary secretary in his office. In other times there was little mileage in the charge, for it was a deeply engrained custom on Capitol Hill, but it broke the Southern taboo of traducing a lady. Moreover, in this case it traduced a lady who had learned her stenography as a volunteer Yeomanette in World War I and was a member of the American Legion.

But these were not other times. Rather it was a period when a rising share-the-work movement attested the rising public concern with growing unemployment and the sickening apprehension that the current economic downturn might be something quite different from anything the United States had ever experienced before. For not only did the number of people out of work steadily mount, but those employed only part time grew correspondingly. In Black's Birmingham, a quarter of the usual wage earners had no job at all and most of the remainder were on a partial work week. Manifestations of social distress accordingly multiplied, and with it the character and function of proposed governmental response.

With it multiplied the opportunities and perhaps the necessity for Black to play that role for which he was so admirably fitted, the opposition gadfly. In part his hostility had doubtless been sparked by the Hoover veto of the Norris Muscle Shoals bill. Unlike his predecessor, the President did not kill the measure in silence. Instead, in what was called a veto of unparalleled ferocity, he summarily ended what was the principal object and product of the Norris-Black rapport—"it is the destruction of equality of opportunity amongst our own people; it is the negation of the ideals on which our civilization is based."[24]

But the hostility was also grounded in general antipathy, and here Black harassed the beset administration as a trial lawyer presented with a hostile and inarticulate witness. Thus, the administration's opposition to relief and its stand in favor of private charity brought a waspish comparison of Hoover's differing standards for the starving Russians of the early twenties and the starving Americans of a decade later. Along the same line he contrasted the public subsidies to massive industries and the stinted efforts to individuals. Indeed an anti-Hoover response seemed almost guaranteed on almost every public question—the Hoover Farm Board, the moratorium proposals, intervention in Nicaragua—and not without reason did Herbert Hoover remember him as a "rabid New Dealer." Fortunately for future relationships on the Supreme Court, Black let his negative vote rather than any words constitute his unsuccessful opposition to Hoover's nomination of Charles Evans Hughes for the Chief Justiceship of the United States. But if he were on the losing side on Hughes, he was among the victors when the Senate—indeed his vote was decisive in the 41–39 total—responded to an AFL-NAACP coalition and rejected the allegedly anti-Negro and anti-labor Judge John J. Parker for advancement to the high bench.[25]

One remarkable aspect of Black's vote on Parker (which cleared the way for unanimous Senate endorsement of one Owen J. Roberts) lay in his silence when the Senate considered and passed the law stripping the federal courts of the very instrument of judgment—injunctions issued, usually against employees, in labor disputes—which had been the root cause of the nominee's rejection. Obviously his silence on what eventually became the Norris-LaGuardia Act was due to that delicate sense of maneuver by which he attempted to negotiate the treacherous waters where Heflin had been swallowed up and the consequent prudence of minimizing his prolabor views. And doubtless the same delicate sense of survival, particularly given the contemporaneous states'-rights ultraism he was taking in the Heflin-Bankhead contest, accounted for his opposition to the La Follette-Costigan bill, which proposed an unprecedented federal relief expenditure of $375,000,000. Almost incredibly, Black stood shoulder to shoulder with the Hoover administration in opposing the proposal, with his own position ostensibly based on the proposition that state rather than federal authority should control allocation of the funds involved.

But others saw his motives differently. Reporter Paul Y. Anderson, later his ardent supporter, bitterly wrote that Black exhibited "a hysterical reaction to the relief plan, which might feed Negroes as well as whites, and gave an exhibition which brought a blush to the face of Tom Heflin lurking in the rear of the chamber." And indeed the performance was doubtless given because the challenger *was* lurking in the rear of the chamber, and indicative of the changing times was Heflin's willingness to fish in troubled waters and to condemn Black's performance as "a cruel act."[26]

Countermarch Again

Yet as the other events of 1932 unfolded, particularly after the critical Democratic primaries of May and June, it became apparent that Black's seeming rapport with the establishment was every bit as much a marriage of convenience as had been the association with the Klan six years earlier. Even before the primaries he had become identified with a group of activists pushing for a vast public-works program to the degree that Justice Brandeis singled him out by name as a member of a Senate opposition "very well led and has proved very effective." And in a sense, so did President Hoover, who excluded him from relief discussions. And this basic attitude toward unfolding events became unmistakable. In the month following the last primary when the bonus marchers were ousted from the national capital Black became the only Senator to speak out against the paramilitary action. And while he once again did not attend the Democratic National Convention in the following month, he promptly pledged his support to Franklin D. Roosevelt when that other past master of maneuver received the party's nomination for the Presidency. "Keep in touch with Farley," the nominee wired him. And keep in touch with Farley he did, as he spent much of the 1932 campaign outside his native state speaking for the national ticket.[27]

As that ticket was carrying the entire country, he rode with it to almost effortless victory in Alabama and an overwhelming majority there. Now there was one final rite to be attended—the last lame-duck session of Congress, an anomaly soon to be ended by constitutional amendment sponsored by his friend George Norris. And indeed the passing of former ways of doing things could not have come with greater symbolism, for the old order was breaking down fast as a new administration of unknown ideas marked time to take over.

In the *entr'acte* came the last lame-duck session, or as one historian graphically labeled it, the interregnum of despair. During it the Senate Finance Committee held some hearings on what might be done to solve the ever-deepening depression. Before the Committee came a parade of witnesses from the national establishment—Bernard Baruch, Wilsonian Secretary of the Treasury David F. Houston, Paul Block of Block Papers, Nicholas Murray Butler, Charles E. Mitchell of New York's National City Bank— all reiterating the conventional wisdom: "Balance the budget." (Indeed, Franklin Roosevelt had said the same thing on the campaign trail.) Yet there were a few heretics. One was Hugo L. Black who took the floor of the Senate to challenge that conventional wisdom as expounded by Mr. Mitchell "about the manner in which the balancing of the Budget would bring about prosperity." But he did more than this. In a countermarch to and through the populism of his 1926 campaign, he brought in a bill to require a maximum 30-hour week in all industries.[28]

William Green, the usually placid president of the usually conservative American Federation of Labor came to Washington to testify for the Black bill and bluntly told the Senators that if the proposal were not enacted into law by the usual legislative process, labor would compel that result "by universal strike." Senator Black had a question for Mr. Green, "Which would be class war, practically?" The response of the president of the AFL was crystal clear: "Whatever it would be, it would be that . . . That is the only language that a lot of employers ever understand— the language of force."[29]

And as far as the record shows, Senator Black neither demurred nor dissented at this point.

CHAPTER SIX

Senator Black: The Master

Deus ex Machina

Among the hundreds of telegrams that poured into Hyde Park for the President-elect on the last day of February 1933 was one urging that no person connected with companies receiving subsidies through mail contracts be appointed Assistant Secretary of the Navy or Commerce or Assistant Postmaster General. It was signed "Hugo L. Black." Some member of the Roosevelt staff noted "U.S. Senate" alongside the telegraphic signature and "File Supple." at the top. And that seemed to be that. Yet the telegram had a few characteristics worth noting. The tone, while deferential enough, was hardly that of some importuning favor seeker. More than this, the content involved the inquisitorial activity by which the sender would make his name well known both inside and outside the new administration and render marginal identification unnecessary.[1]

Yet even with the penciled addendum and assuming that the President-elect saw the wire at all, there was a reasonable doubt whether he could visualize the sender in any meaningful sense. Perhaps he recalled a brief meeting with Senator Black when he had swung north through the future TVA complex at Muscle Shoals on the return from a postelection vacation at Warm Springs, Georgia. But he had a host of other things on his mind as he headed for Washington, and the state of the new administration's policy response to the deepening national crisis was the state of fierce contention among the oddly assorted band of lawyers, politicians and academics who took the B & O down from the New Jersey ferry to Washington shortly thereafter. Foremost was the financial debacle with its swarms of closing banks which would virtually monopolize the exacerbated discussions with the outgoing administration and stood to hold the first priority in legislative business. And closely behind that came the current farm difficulties. Indeed, at the very time when William Green was calling for a general strike to impose Black's 30-hour week upon the nation, Edward O'Neal, president of the Farm Bureau and Black's fellow Alabamian, was using another congressional hearing to predict revolution in the countryside within twelve months if something were not done for the farmer.

Ironically, however, it was the cities that remained quiet in the face of William Green's call to class war; revolution, however, was actually abroad in much of the countryside where the processes of foreclosure law had been halted by shotgun-carrying bands of farmers. And the squealing wheel—still politically dominant if economically secondary—got the grease, and this even though the heart of the national difficulty lay in the industrial heartlands. Indeed, action here earned not only urgency but priority, for as Hugh S. Johnson vigorously argued aboard the New Deal special from the experience of government-controlled industry in the War Industries Board of World War I, the real crisis was unemployment, and an increase in farm prices without a corresponding recovery in industrial effort could be catastrophic. And so, manifestly, Senator Black saw things much the same way. Yet as the new administration settled into the seats of power, industrial unemployment seemed to be seen in terms of effect rather than cause, with direct remedial action being accorded a distinctly secondary priority.

It was a dizzying time at both ends of Pennsylvania Avenue,

and to get attention and action in either the White House or on Capitol Hill called for considerable effort. "President Roosevelt during the special session," Senator Ashurst wrote in his diary, "sent Congress so many messages that one grew dizzy. Before we could analyze one message from the White House, swiftly upon that message would come another and yet another . . ." But that was a game at which any number could play. On March 10, a message traveled in the reverse direction as Senator Black advised the White House that the unemployed could not be put to work without shorter working periods, announced his intention to offer a bill to that effect, and requested the President to include such "imperatively necessary" legislation in his relief message.[2]

The President did not. He ignored the implied threat, and Black brought his 30-hour bill to the floor on April 3. He narrowly won a critical pass of arms in beating off an administration thrust to substantially modify the proposal and then easily carried the day by a 53–30 vote on April 6. The bill had solid labor support, but much more. Indicative of the general core of national concern was the action of Michigan's Senator Arthur H. Vandenberg, who, after conferring with some industrial constituents, threw his weight behind the Black measure.

But if Vandenberg was cooperative, Franklin Roosevelt definitely was not. "My notebook," recalled presidential adviser Raymond Moley, "contains Roosevelt's reaction to the Black bill under the category of 'Threats.' " For the proposal brought the administration to the moment of truth. "Remember," Moley went on, recalling the early New Deal Days, "Roosevelt was a very conservative President. . . . Most of the reforms that were put through might have been agreeable to Hoover if he had the power to put them over." And Moley's roll call of leading figures of the first New Deal would indicate a powerful coalition of the same mind—Cordell Hull, William H. Woodin, Dean G. Acheson, Lewis Douglas and, though he was too modest to include his own name, Moley himself. And certainly Roosevelt's record as governor of New York indicated that he was no revolutionary.[3]

Nonetheless, revolution was exactly what Washington pundit

Ernest K. Lindley saw boiling up from the bottom in the way Black's bill sailed through the Senate and threatened to do in the House. Along somewhat the same line, William Green no longer spoke in the idiom of the forthcoming class struggle, but his prior comments obviously colored his current ones as he hailed the Senate action. But the President did not think so. Instead he muttered darkly of flexibility and straitjackets, newspapers and dairies, and "the rhythm of the cow." And Secretary of Labor Frances Perkins, who hastened to the House hearings to sabotage the Black bill under the guise of concerned agreement, in subsequent recollection unconsciously caught the tension between the inner New Deal circle and the outside upstart: "How this idea [of a 30-hour work week] came to Senator Black, a lawyer from Birmingham, I do not know."[4]

To the pressure of the Black bill was added a rising demand for the public-works program that Roosevelt had spurned during the budget-balancing rhetoric of his campaign, and the President, resentful, beset and concerned, gave ground. Almost in passing he told Moley to organize some of the administration staff and to come up with a counterplan of sorts. Moley in turn, and quite by accident, bumped into Hugh S. Johnson in the lobby of the Carleton Hotel and in a roundabout direction, the issue for which Johnson had contended on the B & O inaugural train was now dominant, thanks to the Senator from Alabama. After terrific infighting within the administration, its substitute measure was ready by mid-May. Called the National Industrial Recovery Act, it was a two-part measure. Part I provided for intraindustry cooperation, fair competition, exemption from antitrust laws—all of which was assertedly broad enough to provide a ceiling on hours—and an unprecedented Section 7 (a) guaranteed labor the right to organize. Part II was a $3.3 billion public-works program. The whole bill was to be in effect for two years.

But the antitrust exemption was not what Black had contemplated at all, and he was lying in wait when the NRA bill came to the Senate after its easy passage in the House. Showing more faith in the resiliency of the private-enterprise market system than some of its professed defenders did, and flying his panache of the adversary principle, he teamed up with his old progressive allies, William E. Borah and Burton K. Wheeler, to hammer the antitrust exemption and the rule-making power of industry:

> This bill, if it shall pass and become law, will transfer the lawmaking power of this nation, insofar as control of industry is concerned, from Congress to the trade associations. This is exactly what has happened in Italy.

Three decades later he remembered the hot Senate contest: "I fought [Roosevelt's] NRA," he told his interviewers on a television program. "I said it was unconstitutional on the Senate floor." It was not quite that simple—in a typical pattern of complexity, Black voted against Title I, for the bill, and—after the bill returned from conference—against the conference report. Remarkably enough (as a prescient writer for *The New York Times* noted at the time of his accession to the bench), the very objections he voiced on the floor of the Senate were those with which the Nine Old Men were to shoot the law down, a rare show of unanimity.[5]

Yet the historical perspective of Franklin Roosevelt afforded perhaps the better and more enduring judgment. While Madame Perkins subsequently recalled that the President's mind was as innocent as a child's of anything approaching the NRA upon his arrival in Washington, Roosevelt not only was unstinting in his praise but indicated that Black had had a hand in the idea all the time. "History," the President hopefully noted, "probably will record the National Industrial Recovery Act as the most important and far-reaching legislation ever enacted by the American Congress." And certainly the statute came close. Section 7(a) was the matrix of the Wagner Act on labor relations. The authorization for work limitation served a like function for Black's own minimum-wage bill. But far more than this, the basic ecology of the government and business were fundamentally and permanently changed.[6]

Accordingly, it was both characteristic and appropriate that, at Frances Perkins' behest, Roosevelt should write the man who had started the whole thing with a commendation of "Dear Hugo" for molding public opinion through "commendable and praiseworthy work . . . in behalf of the limitations of hours for labor . . . which made it possible to include this subject in the NRA act."[7]

The Grand Inquisitor I

The telegram that Black dispatched on the eve of Roosevelt's departure for Washington grew out of a discovery made in the waning days of the lame-duck Congress; its consequence was not only to make his name almost a household word but to bring a new dimension to one of the classic instruments of congressional power, the investigation.

Examples of that extraconstitutional instrument went back almost to the beginning of the Republic, but the development of the real potential of such parliamentary inquisition, raising it almost to a level of legislation, was itself a consequence of the typographic age and the rise of mass media. The critical point of inflection came with the congressional committee on the executive conduct of the Civil War; the protoclassical type of twentieth-century development emerged in Senator Walsh's investigation of the Teapot Dome scandal. And still another mutational leap was to come at the hands of Senator Black, who differed from the man whom Raymond Clapper called "patient, plodding" Thomas Walsh about as much as an aircraft did from a locomotive.[8]

Perhaps foremost was his trial-lawyer instinct—itself really a sense of theater—which seized on the mode in which the distinctive procedures of the congressional committee might be exploited. For here an appropriately gifted man could be both judge and prosecutor—examining, cross-examining, leading, passing on evidence, indulging in asides, demanding some replies and ruling others out of order, and doing so with all the tricks of the trial lawyer's trade—the gentle and seeming non sequiturs leading to the hidden deadfall, the supposedly bomb-shell document held portentously in the hand, the sure feeling for lies, inconsistencies and evasions.

But beyond this were other talents that Black brought to bear: the phenomenal memory, the ear nicely tuned to facts (as Justice Douglas was to call it), the possibilities afforded by income-tax returns ("Special Senate committee—held up by reason refusal request examine income tax returns . . . important see President"), and the instruments, new and old, of his new forum. One was the mode in which the ancient writ of *subpoena ad testificandum* could be turned into a warrant of arrest and a witness roused from his bed at midnight or taken from beind his desk for immediate interrogation in a congressional hearing room. More important was the technique of making the nation at large members of the hearing-room audience. ("Tell the boys of the press to come in. The show is about to begin.")[9]

Indeed, such was the way in which Black had transformed the venerable instrument of legislative fact-finding in an instinctive grasp of the new media of politics, that Postmaster General James A. Farley could tell his Republican predecessor in office that Black's investigations not only were political in nature but were those of a "publicity hound." The epithet provided a signally appropriate note, for the two old-fashioned politicians could reach across a partisan gulf and Farley could sympathize with a Republican target of Senator Black's inquisitorial zeal.[10]

The spark that had ignited the controversy in question was Black's discovery in the waning hours of the Hoover administration of Postmaster General Walter F. Brown's plan to award a ten-year, ten-million-dollar contract for the steamship transport of the United States mails. It touched a particularly sensitive nerve, for the subsidized shipping industry had long been a target of his wrath. Back in the first year of his first term he had taken the floor of the Senate to denounce the waste of the U.S. Shipping Board and to place a statutory snaffle on certain expenditures. Again, he served something of an apprenticeship in a lobby inquiry under Senator Thaddeus H. Caraway. But the Coolidge-Hoover ascendancy generally left little ambit for his investigations. The end of Republican administration, however, radically changed this aspect of his fortunes, and the turn of the tide placed him in the chairmanship of a special Senate subcommittee charged to investigate this very side of maritime affairs. He responded with perhaps the most thorough analyses of American merchant shipping ever undertaken.[11]

The long-run result was the Merchant Marine Act of 1936, a quietly successful statute whose investigatory base has been far overshadowed by the more dramatic sequel of airmail subsidies. The occasion of Black's airmail investigation was a journalist's tip (itself an index of his rapport with the working press) of the corruptive mode in which public subsidy had been grafted (in several senses) on a regulated industry. Black turned out to be something of the hidden, or not so hidden, villain of the piece as the administration moved to enforce its will by canceling outstanding contracts with the airlines and turning the job over to the appallingly unprepared Army Air Corps. For the latter move came to pass—or so *Time* Magazine asserted—on Black's advice, with the President acting against his better judgment.

Postmaster General Farley loyally canceled the existing airmail contracts at the President's behest, and the job of flying the mails was given to the Army Air Corps. It was a job foreign to Air Corps's mission and skills, and moreover was thrust upon the military flyers at a time when the weather was the worst. The consequence was a series of crashes that provoked widespread public indignation, in part genuine and in part the contrived response of a frustrated opposition being given its first real opportunity to hit back at the popular President. Nor did the lesser participants go unnoticed as *Time* combined its report on pilot deaths on the wintry mountains and plains with a note on how Black "badgered" onetime Postmaster Brown in the "snug and warm" hearing room and Farley gave a speech on administration air policy in "balmy Savannah."[12]

Time had still more to write about when Black used his *subpoena duces tecum* in ordering a Washington attorney to surrender his professional files on his airline clients. And it was quite a story, for the attorney, in the short run and perhaps in the long also, beat the grand inquisitor at his own game. While ostensibly awaiting his client's permission to make the disclosure, he in fact permitted them to remove what correspondence they wished. Thereafter, when he refused to appear and denied the committee's power to make him, Black had him arrested and brought before the bar of the Senate. There the investigator served as prosecutor in the trial for contempt of the Senate, a trial that eventuated in a ten-day jail sentence, all duly appealed and ultimately confirmed by the Supreme Court, in an opinion by Justice Brandeis. Perhaps he could not be said to have resisted in vain, for the pilot fatalities overshadowed the disclosed subsidies; and as the winter of 1933–34 drew to its close, the *status quo ante* was largely restored in a face-saving arrangement with the private carriers.[13]

Grand Inquisitor II

Nor was the effort a loss for Black. Indeed, before the year was out, the investigatory blade that he had brought to a keen edge in the airmail hearings was employed with magistral effect in securing the passage of the Public Utility Holding Company Act of 1935. That Black's development was proceeding along other lines was indicated by the recollection of Charles Beard of an initially nameless table companion at a small Washington dinner party in the early months of 1934. The subject was a man who "had read widely in history . . . had made scholarly excursions on his own account, was eager to get to the bottom of things, and dealt in a most judicial temper with all the dissents and objections I filed with him." It was, of course, the senior Senator from Alabama, and Beard saw him at his best in the milieu that the Blacks preferred in protocol-conscious Washington—small gatherings, interesting people, good talk.[14]

But the general public caught a very distinct picture in the holding-company struggle, and it served as a microcosm for the whole New Deal effort. Certainly the utilities epitomized American capitalism at its worst—monopoloid in their very nature, politically corruptive almost as a matter of institutional survival, exploitative, malorganized, cross-purposed in both operation and financial structure. And all these elements seemed to focus around the holding company. For here the leverage of control by one corporation through the stock ownership of others was frequently, indeed characteristically, built up in a jackstraw heap that had little resemblance to considerations of operating service, territorial need, or functional finance. What it produced was a rambling nationwide half-system, whose pressures might be felt from Muscle Shoals, Alabama, to Passamaquoddy, Maine, and whose critical points of control were held by a group of corporate executives, both small in number and highly insulated from political, institutional and market-place control.

And while the holding-company system had accomplished its own revolution in the mobilization of capital and the construction of facilities, such were its sins that it represented the one force in American business against which the unremitting hostility of virtually all parts of the heterogeneous Roosevelt coalition was summed up in Vice-President John N. Garner's draconian judgment that holding companies could not be permitted to go on as before.

The only real division, and it was not much of one, came on whether the reform should be accomplished by regulation of the status quo or by abolition of all holding companies that could not justify their existence. It was not much of a division, and the majority sentiment was summed up by Senator Black: "I have no more sympathy in the attempt to regulate them than to regulate a rattlesnake." And given his long vendetta with the Alabama Power Company, there was no doubt he spoke the truth. In fact, he was automatically listed in support of the Wheeler-Rayburn bill introduced into the new Seventy-third Congress at the beginning of 1935, with the avowed purpose of passing a "death sentence" on every holding company that could not justify its existence.[15]

Under the leadership of the rising and attractive Wendell Willkie, the utilities rallied and counterattacked in an extensive appeal to public opinion and a call for that opinion to make itself felt; and make itself felt it did, with a flood tide of seeming grass-roots response ranging from protest against the ruination of small investors to apocalyptic predictions of the end of the enterprise system. And it left its mark in the legislative passage of the bill, for the Senate cleared the death sentence by a single vote and the House virtually eviscerated the provision.

But the very vigor of the effort brought a countering response as both the House and the Senate authorized investigations of lobbying activity. Black, chairman of the Senate group, moved promptly. An early bag was lobbyist Philip Gadsden, chairman of the Committee of Public Utility Executives, who was seized in his office one morning and hustled before the Black committee to testify without warning or preparation on the recent utility propaganda campaign. It was as Gadsden took the stand that the affable committee chairman issued his famous summons for the boys of the press to come in to "the show." And during the interrogation, the Black investigators searched the lobbyist's files and papers down to matters of childhood itself.

Mr. Gadsden thought it was an outrage, and so did Arthur Krock of *The New York Times.* That was about the extent of the protest, for public opinion seemed to side with Black's assertion that he was within the precedents set by earlier Senate investigators and that in any event the ends justified the means. For Mr. Gadsden's admission that his clients had spent over $300,000 to fight the bill aborted adverse reaction to the committee's summary procedure. And much to the same effect was the case of an advertising man—roused from his bed at midnight and produced before the committee the following morning—who admittedly had initiated the widely circulated rumor that the President was insane.

Black's methods were, in part at least, prompted by an apprehension that he was contending not only with avowed foes but with dissembling friends. The other lobbying investigation too, that of Chairman John J. O'Connor's House Rules Committee, was in the field that summer. Suspicions had already been sparked when O'Connor's brother was retained by a utility company, and they were confirmed when utility magnate Howard C. Hopson chose to evade Black's net and instead appear in secret before O'Connor's committee. Served with a Senate subpoena at the door of the House hearing room (and after a distressing jurisdictional squabble in which the Rules Committee overruled its own chairman), Hopson had a very different time of it the next day before the open and press-crowded proceedings of Senator Black. In a relentless and grueling *tour de force* in which the investigating committee's chairman made particularly effective use of supposedly bombshell documents conspicuously exhibited but never used, Hopson was figuratively skinned alive as he stumbled from pillar to post in a litany of damaging admissions. (One sympathetic spectator in the hearing room wept for him—Mrs. Hugo Black.) And Black thus filled in one element of the jigsaw puzzle whose other critical piece he had earlier supplied—the exposure of the seeming grass-roots avalanche of protest as a vast tissue of unauthorized signatures. Here he had another star witness, Elmer the Western Union delivery boy, whose precocious and bucolic musings were the saving of many a poor news day.

And not content with taking his case to the court of public opinion through the hearing room, Black also drove it home with a radio address excoriating the "high-powered, deceptive, telegram-fixing, letter-framing, Washington-visiting five-million-dollar lobby." Indeed, after Chairman Black had finished his thrust, the only surprising element was the depth of resistance in the House of Representatives, where some concessions were required to pass the death sentence, and Raymond Clapper predicted that its presence in the law was "another notch in the gun of Senator Black."[16]

The Grand Inquisitor III

Black's holding-company *tour de force* was observed with appreciation by the master of the new political media, and Harold Ickes recorded the President's view as to how Black differed from other legislative inquisitors in appraising the options in a Senate tax investigation still to come:

One [plan was] to name a perfectly respectable Senator as chairman, one who stood pretty well in public opinion and then to name as chief investigator a man of the same type . . . the other plan was to make Senator Black chairman of the investigating committee and give him a vigorous, aggressive chief investigator.[17]

And yet, at once ironically and characteristically, Black began 1936 at odds with both the President and the Senate leadership on a tax bill ("the only person who can stop Black . . . is yourself," Alben Barkley told Roosevelt), and he maneuvered to attach a special levy on undistributed profits to the pending exaction. Indeed, Roosevelt had already felt another touch of his steel the preceding summer, when a judicial vacancy emerged on the federal district court of Alabama. Curiously, the vacancy occasioned Esdale's last conversation with Black in a vain effort to obtain the Senator's support for the position. Black had another man for the office, and he might have been thinking of Tom Heflin as he made his wishes stick: "Mr. President, I am for David J. Davis, first, last and always. He is the best man. In fact, I'm going to say something I never thought I'd say. If you don't make this appointment, I'm going to fight you on the floor of the Senate, and if necessary, I'll even bolt the Democratic party."[18]

But the approaching presidential election prompted ranks to close, and confrontation started early, with the American Liberty League firing the opening gun in a monster dinner at the Mayflower Hotel. The featured speaker was the Democratic nominee of 1928, Al Smith, and his remarks were duly reported in a press whose sentiments lay overwhelmingly with the opposition. But now, notwithstanding the safe passage of the holding-company act, the administration once more wheeled out the Black investigating committee, and it responded with a second round of effort. ("The Democratic National Committee's first 'battle order,' " Jim Farley recalled, "was to ignore the Republican party and concentrate fire on the Liberty League.") One set of salvos went against the Liberty League and its ringingly named, if narrowly based, affiliates—the Farmers Independence Council, the Southern Committee to Defend America, and the

Sentinels of the Republic. Another opened up once more on the lobbying effort of the preceding summer.[19]

Black's counteroffensive against the Liberty League was highly successful with the organization shown to be a chain of fronts backed by the same small nuclear core of contributors. The second look at the lobbying thrust was something else again. It began with *de facto* cooperation by the FCC and a demand that Western Union furnish all copies of wires sent during the time of the congressional consideration of the holding-company bill, an estimated five million or so; and the very sweep of the request brought a countering effort—a Chicago law firm obtained an injunction that prohibited the wholesale surrender of communications passing between Western Union and its clients. And at this point, however, the Black luck held, for William Randolph Hearst joined the controversy.

For Hearst sought judicial aid to restrain, not an *en masse* and indiscriminate turnover of correspondence, but the surrender of a single and precisely identified wire. The effort miscarried; not only did the courts decline the remedy but a Congressman under attack by Hearst read the very wire into the *Congressional Record* on the floor of the House, and Black ostentatiously withdrew the subpoena. But Hearst was not deterred; he returned to the struggle seeking to enjoin the surrender of wires passing between himself and his editors.

Chairman Black gladly joined the battle giving to claims of freedom of the press the same short shrift that he had previously given assertions of the attorney-client relationship. ("Unwillingness to answer questions, often under the unwise advice of lawyers, makes it necessary . . . to examine personal files and papers.") Armed with a $10,000 grant from the Senate's housekeeping funds—the House, still petulant over the Hopson episode, declined to concur in a more conventional appropriation—Black brought Crampton Harris up from Birmingham to fight the Hearst suit through to a final judgment in the Circuit Court of Appeals for the District of Columbia.[20]

And Harris won it; the Court declared itself without power to control a coordinate branch of the government. It nonetheless

160 *Hugo Black and the Judicial Revolution*

rebuked both Senator and FCC for acting as they did—"without authority of law and contrary to the very act under which the commission was constituted"—and the opinion would later plague Black when the Senate debated his confirmation. Nonetheless Black had emerged as Franklin Roosevelt's light cavalry of strike and devastation.[21]

CHAPTER SEVEN

To the Threshold

The Past and the Present

As noted earlier, one nineteenth-century Senator whom Black resembled in several arresting particulars was Charles Sumner of Massachusetts. Both men had remarkable tenacity and will. Both seemed to take an almost perverse pride in being the professional outsider with a studied unconcern for the Senate's clubby tradition. And both had almost a sixth sense in tending their power base in the home state.

Black, certainly during his Senate days, would have rejected the analogy, for he had formed a hostile estimate of his counterpart largely through the medium of Claude Bowers' popular Reconstruction history, *The Tragic Era*. And to be sure, there were striking differences as well as striking similarities. Even though neither played the usual political game and each went his own way as his own man, Black had a knack for inside maneuver that Sumner always lacked. Indeed, as the episode of the district judgeship showed, Black could make his point like a Tammany leader. And not only as to judgeships—"To C[ordell] H[ull]," went a terse White House memo on a diplomatic appointment, "Hugh G. Grant to Albania. Hugo Black wants it."[1]

And in a larger dimension were the differing balances struck between principle and pragmatism. Much of Black's liberalism, unlike Sumner's, necessarily had its context far away from home, and characteristic was his position regarding the Scottsboro case and his tart answer to the Northern college girls who had come to seek his intervention—that they might find appropriate injustices to be righted in their own regions. Yet here perhaps he was more sinned against than sinning in view of the charade whereby the White House routinely forwarded to him the protests that it had received.

And on a distinct but related point there remains the question of his mutational development of the congressional inquiry under the ethic that the end justifies the means, the discovery the techniques. For here the question remains, notwithstanding strong insistence to the contrary, whether the congressional inquiries that followed World War II were qualitatively different from those that had taken place earlier. Professor Schlesinger's arguments for the defense must be noted—that, while Black's methods were brutal, he questioned the motives of a few and the patriotism of none. Neither did he drag in innocent persons, indulge in promiscuous character assassination or concern himself with what people thought. Yet Walter Lippmann also had a view of the matter as he observed the general public approval that attended Black's pursuit of the generally unpopular lobbyists and suggested that the real question was against whom and what the apparatus devised by Senator Black would be turned next. And there were those who would have seen his answer as prophetic: "I do not know. But I do know that when lawlessness is approved for supposedly good ends, it will be used even more viciously for bad ones."[2]

And Black and Sumner had yet another thing in common. Both had some harsh things to say about the Supreme Court from the Senate floor.

The Court Critic

Black was in the news in another mode as the year 1936 began. This came when, in the case of *Butler v. United States,* the Supreme Court vetoed the procession tax of the Agricultural Adjustment program. The decision was handed down on January 3, by the narrowest of majorities. It was also noteworthy for the insistence of Justice Roberts, writing for the ruling bloc of five, that all they did was lay the statute alongside the Constitution and see if one squared with the other. The press sought out the senior Senator from Alabama for a terse and headline-worthy comment. They got it. "This means," asserted the Senator, "that 120,000,000 people are ruled by five men."[3]

The role of critic of the Supreme Court in particular and the federal judiciary in general was not a new one. Almost since his first days in the Senate he had been a continuing critic of what he saw as the judicial overreaching of Congress, the powers of the states, and the rights of the people. Indeed, he committed the ultimate heresy, questioning the very power of the Court to invalidate statutes at all and to do so through judges appointed for life. ("If I had my way, the Constitution of the United States would be amended so as to provide that the federal judges should be elected, because I believe in a democracy, and I believe in the election of judges by the people themselves. . . . Whose government is this?")[4]

And even before this he had emphatically registered his disagreement with the Blackstonian canon of the bloodless and automaton judge who carries the law in his breast and squares documents one alongside the other, when he voted, unavailingly in one case and successfully in the other, against President Hoover's nominations of Charles Evans Hughes and John J. Parker to the Supreme Court of the United States on the ground that their background had shaped their views.

Indeed, in the very part of the year Black was calling for direct election of federal judges—ironically, part of his opposition to an antilynching law was the enlargement of federal judicial jurisdiction—the power of that group was demonstrated very close to home in several particulars when District Judge W. I. Grubb of Birmingham, acting at the behest of a preferred stockholder of the Alabama Power Company, enjoined the sale of electric power by the Tennessee Valley Authority.

The judge had been the adversary counsel in Black's first case, and it was singularly appropriate that he should once more appear on the opposite side of controversy where so many points coalesced. Most obvious was the continuing controversy on regional economic development. After successive vetoes by Presidents Coolidge and Hoover, this had now been seemingly settled by the Tennessee Valley Authority Act, which, as passed in the historic Hundred Days, combined Norris' vision of public power, Black's interest in fertilized soil, and a great deal more. Yet little more than one hundred days after the plan was under way, passed by Congress and approved by a President, a single federal district judge, by a scratch of his pen, stopped it dead in its tracks.

Nor was Judge Grubb alone. In 1935–36 over 1,600 injunctions forbade government officials from carrying out duties that had been enjoined by a statute. And this Black found intolerable. At the time of Judge Grubb's decision he earnestly predicted the forthcoming Supreme Court reversal. Meanwhile, it stayed stalled on dead center as the process of appeal played itself out.

Black's response was to assert the historic control of Congress over the business of the Supreme Court. On March 6, 1935, he introduced a bill to eliminate consideration of challenged legislation by the intermediate federal appellate tribunals and send the controversies directly to the Supreme Court. Chief Justice Hughes and two colleagues appeared in opposition, and the bill never left the Senate Judiciary Committee. Up in Cambridge, Massachusetts, Professor Felix Frankfurter noted that the real issue was the Supreme Court's control of its docket by hearing precisely the cases it chose to hear and no other.[5]

And the mode in which the Chief Justice bested the Senator from Alabama aptly symbolized the manner in which his Court had asserted its supremacy over both government and nation. The TVA survived judicial review, and so did administration monetary policy, which had been challenged in the gold-clause cases. But otherwise, commencing with the October 1935 term of the Court, the fundamental statutes of the New Deal seemed to start falling like tenpins.

But more than the national power was challenged. In *Morehead v. Tipaldo* in early 1936, the Court undertook to strike down state minimum-wage legislation as well and thereby invalidate local efforts to deal with economic difficulty.[6]

Black saw *Tipaldo* as the last straw, creating a no man's land in which neither state nor national government was competent to act. With the outbreak of the sit-down strikes in 1937, he asserted that the Court thereby left the workers recourse only "to the bayonet and the gun." In mid-1936, however, a more obvious remedy was suggesting itself, and this lay in changing both the structure and the function of the federal judiciary itself. As his direct-appeal bill indicated, Black had no inhibition about changing accepted ways of doing things. Indeed even in the Hoover administration he had been an enthusiastic if discreet supporter of George Norris' successful fight to abolish the injunctive powers of the federal courts in labor disputes. Again when his investigative efforts were challenged in the Supreme Court of the District of Columbia, he took to the Senate floor to deliver a don't-tread-on-me warning—". . . if any judge ever issued an injunction to prevent the delivery of papers which are sought by this body . . . Congress should immediately enact legislation taking away that jurisdiction. . . ."[7]

The Turn in the Road

Black's travels in the summer of 1936 exemplified his political dilemma. With an obvious eye on his own political fortunes two years hence—Franklin Roosevelt had no problems, with cotton selling at twelve cents a pound, with Alabama's vote in the impending Presidential contest—Black stumped sixty-one of the state's sixty-seven counties. But that fall, as a member of the Democratic campaign committee, he traveled Missouri, Illinois

and Indiana, whose votes for the President's reelection were not
nearly so assured.

Indeed the transformation from maverick to establishmen-
tarian seemed completed when he not only went that June as a
delegate to his first Democratic Convention, but served as a member of its platform committee. It was an unusual establishment
that he was joining and one still in the process of becoming such.
Yet Franklin Roosevelt's grand design for a larger and enduring
coalition beyond the traditional party limits was already becoming apparent. And here Black's inclusion, as the only Southerner
and at the President's behest, in one of its elements, the Progressive National Committee of old Bull Moosers, mugwump intellectuals, and dissident Republicans, which met in semisecret
conclave in Chicago in mid-September, held an especial significance. And so his inclusion in the score of advisers who fore-
gathered with the President at Hyde Park at the end of that
month. But perhaps the best measure of all was the way in which
Franklin Roosevelt tailored his speeches in the closing days of
the campaign in response to the suggestions of Hugo Black from
the field.

The very dimensions of the Roosevelt landslide prompted reflections on the momentum that could carry well through the
next election. The victorious President was talking about the
type of party and country he wanted to leave his successor in
January 1941, and down in Birmingham the *Weekly Call,* a
labor paper, suggested the state's senior Senator as the logical
man for the legacy.

Indeed, Franklin Roosevelt himself had stated the problem,
recalling how he had added Black to the Progressive Committee—"They say that the Democratic Party can't be liberal because of the South. But things are moving. . . ." Calculating the
pace and the elements in the movement, however, called for an
exquisitely tuned calculus alongside which the problems of
Underwood and Heflin in prior elections were relatively simplistic. Black was aware that his third race for the Senate shaped up
as "the toughest primary fight of my life" and probably both his
goal and his strategy were shaped up early.[8]

In this respect it was singularly ironical that his part in the Southern filibuster against the antilynching legislation of 1935 was intended to secure his home base and suggest his own revolutionary line of departure from the politics that made such efforts necessary. Similarly motivated was his waffling on the famous Scottsboro case. On that issue the White House deadpan and half-cynically sent him copies of protests that poured in from the country and around the world. But whatever else Black was, he was no racist. Such was "his superiority of intellect and character," wrote Walter White of the N.A.A.C.P., "over most his colleagues from the South . . . that he seemed to be an advance guard of the new South we had dreamed of. . . ."[9]

Still the advance guard could not get out too far ahead of the troops, and Black took the floor of the Senate in an erudite *tour de force* that combined attacks on the federal judiciary, disquisitions on legal history, and constitutional exegesis. Completely absent was the racist demagoguery which had characterized the filibustering efforts of so many of his Southern colleagues under like circumstances. And perhaps equally noteworthy was the fact that Senator Black seemed not only to take his stand, but to burn his bridges in favor of new industrialism where the organized trade-unionism, rather than twelve-cent cotton, would be the dominant Alabama political force.

And indeed within days of his antilynching filibuster of 1935 he was once again offering his 30-hour proposal and insisting that the flaws that had just doomed the NRA before the Supreme Court were absent from his bill. For the time it was to no avail, as the majority leader managed to keep the measure from the Senate floor. Yet the setback was temporary. With the convening of the new Seventy-fifth Congress, top-heavy with Democrats in both houses, thanks to Roosevelt's smashing victory at the polls, Black once more introduced his favorite measure. Moreover, he was in a singular position to do something about it, for he had now assumed the chairmanship of the Senate Committee on Labor and Education.

To take the new post he had to give up his seat on the Judiciary Committee. That seemed a favorable exchange for Black and even for the New Deal; but it may have been a decisive factor in the defeat of President Roosevelt's plan for curbing the Supreme Court's power to annul his legislative program, for it was the Judiciary Committee that would pass on or hold up any legislation affecting the Court.

Indeed, hand in hand with his 30-hour bill, Black also reintroduced his priority-appeals measure into the new Congress and wrote the President about making the Supreme Court more responsive by having it sit in divisions adding two Justices to its bench. Nine days later, Roosevelt wrote back that he and Black seemed to have been thinking "along the same or else parallel lines." For the day before the letter was written, Roosevelt had unveiled his own Court reform measure, the appointment of one new Justice for each incumbent over seventy years old. Presented largely in terms of improving efficiency, the proposal would give the administration six appointments, thereby ending the narrow margins of 5 to 4 and 6 to 3 by which administration measures had been invalidated. It was also too clever by half.[10]

By the fortunes of congressional maneuver, including that of Black's fellow Alabamian, Speaker William B. Bankhead, consideration of the Court bill opened in the Senate, and here Black was to prove one of its most vigorous and articulate champions. He immediately spoke up for the proposal upon announcement ("I favor the plan"), and shortly thereafter went into a variety of forums to present the administration's case—the Mutual Broadcasting System, a rally in Carnegie Hall, a Town Hall debate in Washington.[11]

Unhappily for the administration, these were all the wrong places. The place that Black was critically needed in was the Senate Judiciary Committee, where the Court bill was being slowly netted and strangled, with no one of his competence to defend it, as the forces of astonishingly diverse constituents coalesced to deliver the final blow. There were those who saw the hand of Chief Justice Hughes in all of the opposition, including the event which all agreed was the critical turning point—the bombshell *West Coast v. Parrish* of March 29, when the Supreme Court by a single vote sustained state minimum-wage legislation and thereby reversed the position it had taken only the preceding spring.[12]

A second, related blow came on May 18: Justice Willis Van Devanter retired pursuant to a recent act giving members of the Supreme Court the same vested rights as other judges, and the Senate Judiciary Committee reported the Court bill with an adverse vote of 10 to 8—six Democrats, responding to a variety of pressures, in opposition to the President—urged that the bill "do not pass." The Van Devanter retirement strengthened the opposition by proving what Senator Ashurst had urged in suggesting that Roosevelt go slow: "Father Time with his scythe is on your side. Anno domini is your invincible ally." It also complicated the President's task, for he had virtually promised his first Supreme Court vacancy to his majority leader, Senator Robinson of Arkansas, whom he did not fully trust. Indeed, in referring to the Southern Senator, Roosevelt made no bones of the matter. ("One of the things that I am proud of is that I made men like Joe Robinson . . . swallow me hook, line, and sinker.")[13]

Hence, the President gave ground in a new compromise, which would permit him to appoint one new Justice per year for each seventy-five-year-old who stayed on the bench. Robinson responded with a heroic effort to pass the compromise and thus achieve the Supreme Court's bench—his own life's ambition. But he dropped dead on the morning of July 14, and with him fell the last hopes of the Court plan. On July 22 it was ignominiously sent back to committee to die; only twenty Democrats—including Senator Black of Alabama—voted to stand by the President and keep the measure alive.

Of Wages and Hours

Even though Black was not where he would have been most effective—the Judiciary Committee—in supporting the President's Court bill, he was prominent enough in both debate on the Senate floor and in strategy consultation at the White House. And yet, ironically, his participation in these efforts was limited by another consequence of the *West Coast Hotel* decision in the obvious green light it afforded to federal wage-and-hour legislation. Indeed, Black did not need *West Coast Hotel;* the very day the Supreme Court outlawed the NRA, he was writing the President that "believing further that Congressional action regulating hours and wages is vital to the nation, I hope you will accomplish that purpose by supporting the . . . Thirty Hour Week bill. This bill is not at variance with the judgment of the Supreme Court. . . ."[14]

Within weeks of that decision, however, an administration bill was drafted by Thomas G. Corcoran and Benjamin V. Cohen for concurrent introduction into the House and Senate. Even here the intellectual patronage of the inner circle remained, however, and a great to-do was made of a newly discovered constitutional justification for the statute. "The clause 'affecting interstate commerce' was thought to be a new approach," Secretary Perkins wrote in May 1937—as if Senator Black had never once in years past articulated his soaring view of the national commerce power as a plenary base of federal jurisdiction over all matters affected by it.[15]

But bygones were bygones, and the Black-Connery bill (named in part for the cosponsoring Congressman from Massachusetts) reflected the process of accommodation and compromise. It fixed neither hours nor wages but instead authorized a five-man board to do so within a designated range for specific industries. "Unfair" goods—including those produced by child labor—were banned from interstate commerce.

Hence, throughout the summer Black's support for the Court bill was diverted to the wage-and-hour measure as he presided over joint Senate-House labor committee hearings to speed the progress of hearing witnesses and substantially rewriting the Corcoran-Cohen product. ("While in my opinion," wrote Senator Borah, "it is not a desirable bill yet, it is far saner and wiser than when he took hold of it.") Under Black, the discretion of the board was restricted, the minimum wage fixed at forty cents an hour, and the week for "hours worked"—a phrase that would yield a bitter harvest for Justice Black—set at forty.[16]

Throughout July, Black led the debate in the Senate in a preview of what would be coming from the Supreme Court—although no one yet knew it—the concern for the losers ("I speak for little men and women . . ."), the ear nicely tuned to facts ("Here is another voucher, 4 days, wages $2.68. That figures up . . . to about 8 cents an hour"), the taste for history. And more significantly, he led the fight against an opposition composed substantially of his fellow Southerners, whose concern ran from the most extreme of economic reaction to a sophisticated and genuine concern that regional cost differentials were for the South to close the gap separating it from the rest of the nation, particularly, as Congressman Sam Hobbs of Alabama suggested, "the tariff-protected and freight-not-favored East."[17]

Nowhere was this substantial consensus of opposition more insistent than in the response welling up from Alabama. For Congressman Hobbs also said the Black bill would drive Southern businessmen between the plow handles "looking at the east end of a west-bound mule." Yet even this prospect was not without its brighter aspects as the Southern Pine Association took full-page ads to warn that passage of the Black bill would raise the price of field labor to three dollars a day.[18]

The local press was widely hostile, not only on the merits of the bill but also on the general record, where Black was vulnerable for his New Dealing ways as well as for his recent defense of the sit-down strikers. J. P. Mitchell, of the *Wiregrass Farmer*, recalled other aspects and suggested what the 1938 campaign would be like: "He likes to conduct inquisitions and hold up to disgrace men who have the temerity to question the wisdom of some aspects of the revolution. He is particularly good at opening other people's mail. . . ."[19]

But local pressure was to no avail and in an adroit thrust Black countered with some Southern *bravura* of his own: "I subscribe to the doctrine that a man who is born in Alabama and who can do as much work as a man born . . . in New England is entitled to the same pay if he does the same work." Throughout five days of bitter debate—explaining, thrusting, parrying through a seemingly interminable series of votes—Black was the

172   *Hugo Black and the Judicial Revolution*

superb parliamentarian as he brought the measure home to victory on July 31. Coming nine days after the ignominious end of the Court bill, the action was an especially significant New Deal victory. In fact, although few realized it, the measure was to be the last significant administration triumph in the Senate in the first session of the Seventy-fifth Congress.[20]

The Might-Have-Been's

Or perhaps it might be accounted the next-to-last, for in seventeen more days the upper house, after another debate, was to confirm the senior Senator from Alabama as an Associate Justice of the United States Supreme Court. And while both votes were also triumphs for Hugo Black, a moment's speculation would suggest other triumphs had Franklin Roosevelt's choice for the Court fallen elsewhere. Certainly Black would have been returned in triumph to the Senate in the 1938 election, for Lister Hill ran as a virtual surrogate and won handily.

And from this point, his stunning victory and his superseniority in the Senate power structure could well have combined with Roosevelt's announced intention (expressed in the Progressive movement of 1936) to remold the Democratic party to make Black the vice-presidential nomination in 1940. Even in more ordinary circumstances, his Southern antecedents and liberal temper would have been virtually made to order. (Indeed his fellow Alabamian, Speaker William Bankhead, making a formidable bid for the office at the 1940 convention, was actually leading at the conclusion of the roll call, until the large states changed their votes under administration pressure.)

Hence, the speculation is permissible, indeed imperative, that Black's demur to F.D.R.'s offer of a Court appointment ("Mr. President, are you sure that I'll be more useful in the Court than in the Senate?") was based on an insight that he stood as good a chance as any man in the Democratic party to move to the other side of the presidential desk.[21]

The possibilities of the future were strikingly compressed in a profane exchange outside a Birmingham office building as the senior Senator bustled by: "Look at the little sonofabitch. He thinks he's goin' to be President of the United States." "You know, the little sonofabitch just might."[22]

Part Four

Mr. Justice:
Part One

CHAPTER EIGHT

Opening Curtain

The Double Deception

The new Justice began conventionally enough, notwithstanding some variation from the norm: his first judicial act seemed to pass on the motions that challenged his fitness to pass on anything. This was in sharp contrast with his legislative abstention when his own confirmation came before the Senate. Aside from this, however, he maintained the silence he thought befitting an initiate; he did not ask his first questions from the bench until mid-December, and even these came well after he had read his first opinion early in the preceding month.

In terms of sequence, his opinion was the first read by any Justice at the 1937–38 term, and the extraordinary favor thus shown by Chief Justice Hughes was duly noted in the press. Actually, the Chief Justice had granted a double favor in the assignment. *Federal Trade Commission v. Standard Education* was neither complex nor subtle nor productive of division within the Court. Rather, what was at issue was the sales tactics of an encyclopedia publisher who falsely told prospects that thanks to their personal prominence and consequent advertising value, they had been chosen to receive encyclopedia sets. Such sets, the ploy went on, would be provided free if a ten-year loose-leaf extension service was ordered at the same time. The FTC had ordered the publisher to cease and desist from these representations, but the Court of Appeals for the Second Circuit through the great Learned Hand suppressed the order dealing with assertedly free books. ("We cannot take seriously the suggestion that a man who is buying a set of books and a ten-year's extension service will be fatuous enough to be misled by the mere statement that the first are given away, and he is paying only for the second.") Junior Justice Black (perhaps on the strength of memories of the Birmingham police bench concerning purchaser gullibility and drummer guile) spoke for a unanimous Court and reinstated the original order on grounds that must have been particularly dear to the former Senator's heart—that Congress had provided that findings of the FTC, if supported by appropriate evidence, were dispositive, and that this was the case here.[1]

Yet, over the long pull, Black's evolved judicial philosophy would fall remarkably close to that of the man whom he overruled in his first judicial opinion. More than this, his ultimate turnabout would involve a far more striking line of departure than the first bombshell dissents that contrasted so strikingly with the conventional neophyte silence when that brief period of initiation had passed. Three of those dissents had particularly captured the notice of the profession and, while involving widely differing subject matter, were nonetheless framed around the central attack upon the towering superstructures erected on the most modest of constitutional bases.

Most widely noted was Black's solitary protest in *Connecticut General Life Insurance Co. v. California,* all duly subheadlined in *The New York Times*—"Is Only Justice Ever to Hold Corporation Is Not a Person under the Due Process Clause." Drawing most attention was his equally lone and impatient attack on the Talmudic doctrinal maze that had encrusted federal judicial reexamination of state utility regulation. ("I believe Indiana has the right to regulate the price of water in Indianapolis free from interference by the Federal courts.") His third protest came in another case up from the Hoosier state, in which a teacher convinced every Justice save one that an Indiana statute had unconstitutionally abrogated her right of tenure. But she did not convince Black, who saw the basic issue quite the other way. ("This reversal unconstitutionally limits the right of Indiana to control Indiana's public schools.")[2]

Remarkably enough, the bombshell trilogy was particularly infirm as a portent of things to come, and in still further irony, the one issue that Black was to regard as his foremost judicial hallmark—incorporation of the Bill of Rights into the Fourteenth Amendment and thereby a mechanism of constraint on state power—saw him aligned with Justice Benjamin N. Cardozo's denial of that precise point in the double-jeopardy contest of *Palko v. Connecticut*. Indeed, if anything, the trilogy in many respects was far more a mirror of the past.[3]

This was particularly true of his insistence of corporate vulnerability to hostile state action, and its character as a reprise to what he had to say in his antilynching filibuster. For here he had read the Fourteenth Amendment on the Senate floor and tendentiously inquired: "Did any member hear the word 'corporation' . . . ? He did not. The word 'corporation' does not appear in the Fourteenth Amendment." Mercifully, Mencken ("I can see little in Black except a Cracker demagogue. The idea that he is a mastermind is complete nonsense") did not link up the filibuster preview when in a characteristically scathing passage he visited his ridicule upon the *Connecticut General* dissent:

> It seems to me that Hugo Black's view of the 14th Amendment is completely cuckoo. Carried to its logical conclusion, it holds that persons organized into corporations have no human rights whatsoever. I see no essential difference between them and other persons. If I have rights as a private man, I have the same rights as a stockholder.[4]

Black would come around to something approaching this position in fact if not in rhetoric. Likewise, in a tortured maze of valuation and utility rate making ("When such things come up," wrote Justice Holmes, "I want to sit down and cry or tell them to ask Brandeis"), his doctrinaire flourish would be tempered to admit federal judicial intervention this side of patent confiscation. But, most remarkable of all and in explicit contradiction to what he had to say in the teacher tenure case, the great judicial revolution of which he was a part would take as its very foundation stone the categorical constitutional proposition that a state did not have a right to run its school system as it saw fit.[5]

And the past, rather than the future, was very close at hand in any number of other things. Doubtless his peripheral involvement and comment in the Scottsboro case prompted his self-disqualification when Heywood Patterson, now lodged as one of the main attractions of the Birmingham jail ("That Patterson, he's mean") sought to have his fourth conviction for rape reexamined by the Court, which had previously set aside two of them. And just on the other side of North Capitol Avenue, the Seventy-fifth Congress had been called into unusual autumnal session by a President anxious to get on with his mangled legislative program. It grappled with a number of unfinished items that in a sense were Hugo Black's unfinished business too.[6]

One concerned the great problem of race in America, and here the customary Southern filibuster against antilynching legislation had to go forward without his formidable talents. Yet, though gone, he was not forgotten. His successor in office, Senator Dixie Bibb Graves, read into the *Congressional Record* the selfsame five-hour speech that Black had delivered during the successful 1935 defense. More than this, during the heat of the debate Senator Tom Connally flourished a copy of the bill at its sponsors and predicted that as a member of the Supreme Court, their former colleague would assuredly hold the measure unconstitutional.

The new Justice was spared that duty, for the filibuster ran the usual course and aborted any chance the bill had for passage. There were, however, some items of legislative business that were enacted successfully. One was the lineal descendant of the 30-hour measure that Black had proposed in the depths of the Depression and Franklin Roosevelt signed into law on June 16, 1938, under the title of the Fair Labor Standards Act. The publishers of the *United States Code Annotated* had their own ideas about labeling, and they duly cross-indexed the new statute as the Black-Connery Law.

Constancy and Change

The new order of things that Justice Hugo Black had brought to the Supreme Court was conspicuously apparent in the remarkable number of state statutes that had survived judicial scrutiny at his first term. Yet the truly significant beginnings of that new order lay in two obscure opinions that were handed down on April 25, 1938. One reversed a judgment obtained for a trespassing pedestrian who had been injured by a swinging boxcar door while along the Erie Railroad right-of-way near McKeesport, Pennsylvania. The other upheld the conviction of the Carolene Products Company for shipping Milnut, a milk and coconut-oil product, in interstate commerce. And the new Justice had a remarkable association with each.[7]

To the extent to which public notice was taken of the two cases at all, notice was taken of *Erie Railroad,* and not without reason. Justice Stone said it was the most important opinion that had been handed down since he was on the Court, and in a letter to President Roosevelt, Professor Frankfurter of the Harvard Law School explained why:

> I certainly didn't expect to live to see the day when the Court would announce, as they did on Monday, that it itself had usurped power for nearly a hundred years. And think not a single New York paper—at least none that I saw—having a nose for the significance of such a decision. How fluid it all makes the Constitution.[8]

The problem was as old as the Republic and almost inevitable when two sets of courts sat in one territory over common controversies. The specific root was the statute whereby the First Congress told the federal tribunals to follow "the laws of the several states . . . in cases where they apply." In a way the instruction was worse than none at all. There was the threshold problem of whether "laws" included precedents set by state judicial decisions as well as the statutes passed by state legislatures. But far more difficult was the problem of when such "laws," whether statutory or decisional, applied at all.[9]

Back in 1842, in the great case of *Swift v. Tyson,* Justice Joseph Story responded to both questions. Laws, he said, did not include state decisions but only state statutes. More importantly, he went on to provide that the only cases where such laws applied were those involving real estate or some comparable parochial and immobile subject matter and certainly not to interstate or international commercial transactions. In the latter instances, Story insisted, national courts would make their own rules of decision on the basis of the logic of the common-law tradition.[10]

And thus one legacy of *Swift v. Tyson* was to make the legal rights of a trespasser on a railroad right-of-way in Pennsylvania dependent on what train hit him and therefore upon the court in which he sued. A Pennsylvania court would grant him damages only on a showing that he had been deliberately injured. But if he were hurt by the train of an outstate corporation, he could invoke that jurisdiction which the Constitution granted the federal courts in controversies between citizens of different states and the engrafted doctrine that a corporation could be so classified. More to the point, he could also invoke the judge-made federal rule that required that he be safeguarded from negligent injuries as well as deliberate ones.

But lying beneath *Swift v. Tyson* and all its progeny, including the double standard for right-of-way injuries, was a view of the law wherefrom the men who wrote the Constitution saw it—or more precisely, felt it—as a metaphysical reality whose objective existence was every bit as authentic as the Van Allen belt. It was, as Justice Story's citations of Cicero's stoic certainties attested, the inherited intellectual capital of an ancient consensus. It was also a capital that was far away. Even at the height of its American judicial ascendancy, there were those who insisted that in the very nature of things, the law could not be, in Justice Holmes's famous words, "a brooding omnipresence in the sky," but rather the articulate and identifiable voice of some sovereign here on earth. And this in turn was succeeded by the even more revolutionary view that saw law merely as the apparatus for the attainment, consciously or otherwise, of a predetermined result under a façade of an objective quest under neutral principles.[11]

And thus in the *Erie Railroad* case at the 1937–38 term of the Supreme Court, the venerable Justice Brandeis engrossed the newer views upon the constitutional text when he insisted that under existing law the legal standard of care for a trespasser on a railroad right-of-way in Pennsylvania was not set in heaven but was laid down by the Pennsylvania itself. Mr. Tompkins' lawsuit accordingly went back for disposition in the same mode as would have transpired had he sued in a Pennsylvania court in the first place.

But well before April 25, 1938, the Court had been long at work trimming and pruning at what had been thought to be the excesses of *Swift v. Tyson.* A passage from an opinion handed down in the closing days of 1937 conceded that the case "has been much criticized, and the tendency of the decisions . . . has been to limit it somewhat strictly." The limitation itself was part of the classic common-law process whereby the most radical changes were brought to pass in the long run by almost imperceptible changes in the short. And the effort to preserve the continuity, coherence and integrity in the "law" was after its fashion almost as much a tribute to Cicero's metaphysics as *Swift v. Tyson* itself.[12]

The bombshell trilogy of dissents had shown Black's antipathy toward the exercise of federal judicial authority as a continuing censor of state legislative authority. *Swift v. Tyson* did much the same thing toward that authority in terms of its relationship state decisions. But beneath each was hostility to the constitutional framework that permitted judges to roam unchecked in the vast domains of public policy and impose their private ideas in terms of constitutional doctrine. There also was, as he disclosed much later, an experimental element in his doctrine—the damage suits that he lost in the federal court in Birmingham and which he would have won in the Alabama courthouse just down the street.

Hence, what might well be viewed as the most important of the opinions Black delivered in his first term was that which came down on St. Valentine's Day of 1938 in *New York Life Insurance Company v. Gamer.* It involved a Montana insurance controversy that turned on the presumption against suicide. It was in some ways a subtle and complex issue involving the wavering line that separates substantive from procedural law. To the new Justice, however, the issue was crystal clear, and no more complicated than the duty of a federal court to come to the same conclusion as its state counterpart in the trial of an ordinary lawsuit.[13]

Moreover, of all Black's opinions in that first term, his *Gamer* dissent could be read as foremost, both for itself and as the overture to *Swift v. Tyson.* For here was overturned, as Felix Frankfurter pointed out, not so much a precedent as a way of looking at the law. The plane of the earlier vision had been phrased by Benjamin Cardozo as the vision of law in a "Platonic or ideal existence." And just a few years later Hugo Black explicitly indicated what he thought of that vision in insisting that with *Erie Railroad* "legal realism replaces legal fictionalism." But while *Erie Railroad* ended one mode in which the miracle, mystery, and authority of American law found its constitutional sanction, the mystique itself was not abolished. Rather it was merely transferred to another framework of reference, as the companion case of April 25 abundantly showed.[14]

The Fourth Footnote

If *Erie Railroad* came to destroy, *Carolene Products* remained to fulfill. The second case came out of the Federal Filled Milk Act of 1913, a statute whose major sponsor appeared to be the American Guernsey Association, and one that banned from interstate commerce as adulterated and unfit for human consumption any skimmed-milk product fortified by vegetable fats. Senator Oscar Underwood, bereft of any knowledge of cholesterol but insisting that existing food and drug legislation was capable of dealing with asserted abuses, denounced the statute as a raid by special-interest groups upon the purses of the poor. A quarter century later much of his argument was picked up by the Carolene Products Company, who insisted that Congress could not by applying opprobrious epithets to an innocent product and making a legislative finding that was contrary to fact ban that product from commerce and ruin the business that produced it.

Underwood's successor had already spoken to that exact point, however. Back in 1935 Senator Black had insisted that the constitutionality of a congressional statute banning anything from interstate commerce could not be determined "by the harmfulness of the product alone." He went on to admit that legitimate and desirable products might be so excluded. Justice Stone did not put the matter quite so bluntly in upholding the Filled Milk Act. He did agree with Black that the power of Congress over interstate commerce was subject to no restraint save that set out in the Constitution itself and that the Fifth Amendment banning deprivation of property without due process of law did not operate as any such restraint. Then in an arresting assertion, marked "THIRD," which was not at all necessary to his decision, Stone went on to observe that

> regulatory legislation affecting ordinary commercial transactions is not to be pronounced unconstitutional unless in the light of the facts made known or generally assumed it is of such a character as to preclude the assumption that it rests on some rational basis within the knowledge and experience of the legislators.

But this was not all. Having formally surrendered the constitutional weaponry with which the Court had exercised its economic censorship over national economic legislation, Stone went on to assert the far more soaring claim to the guardianship of the nation's political processes and a special judicial protectorate of what he called discrete and insular minorities.[15]

To be sure, he made the point in the mode that Felix Frankfurter later was to assail as constitutional amendment by footnote. Moreover, this particular footnote—the famous Number 4—was written with such disclaiming turgidity as to almost defy both grammatical and logical analysis:

> There may be a narrower scope for operation of the pre-sumption of constitutionality when the legislation appears on its face to be within a specific prohibition of the Con-stitution, such as those of the first ten amendments, which are deemed equally specific when held to be embraced within the Fourteenth.
>
> It is unnecessary to consider now whether legislation which restricts those political processes which can ordi-narily be expected to bring about repeal of undesirable legislation, is to be subjected to more exacting judicial scrutiny under the general prohibitions of the Fourteenth Amendment than are most other types of legislation. . . .
>
> Nor need we inquire whether similar considerations into the review of statutes directed at particular religious . . . or national . . . or racial minorities . . . whether prej-udice against discrete and insular minorities may be a special condition, which tends seriously to curtail the op-eration of those political processes ordinarily to be relied upon to protect minorities, and which may call for a cor-respondingly more searching judicial inquiry.[16]

For Hugo Black the delicately obscure prose was crystal clear and he indicated what he thought of it in a brief concurring sentence: "Mr. Justice BLACK concurs in the result and in all of the opinion except the part marked 'THIRD.' " Of all Black's solitary disagreements in his first term, the *Carolene Products* was to be the most misleading. For notwithstanding that, Justice Black was to take the incorporation of the Bill of Rights into the Fourteenth Amendment as the polestar of his own judicial phi-losophy, and in the process he was to effect some constitutional amendment by footnotes of his own.[17]

But more than that, the Court at the nadir of its fortunes and notwithstanding the disagreement of its newest member, who seemingly represented the wave of the future, signaled its con-tinuing institutional independence in the very act of coming to terms with the political process, and that transformation was to profoundly affect the philosophy and vision of the newest member.

Trial by Periodical

In early 1938 Washington columnists John O'Donnell and Doris Fleeson reported that some members of the Supreme Court had "hitched up their judicial robes and in dignified fashion were in the process of putting the slug on their colleague Associate Justice Hugo L. Black." Their conclusion drew on two items: a speech of Chief Justice Hughes, and a magazine article whose context had pointed to the anonymous defamation of Associate Justice Stone. And, to be sure, *Time* Magazine had noted some evidence of an initial irritability of the Chief Justice with his most junior colleague not on intellectual grounds, but rather because of the persistent squeaking of Black's courtroom chair. Happily, appropriate repairs were made during the first recess of the term, and the otherwise cordial relationship between the two flourished unabated.[18]

There were, however, logical grounds for seeing Black as the source of another type of concern when, in a speech before the American Law Institute in spring of 1938, the Chief Justice pleaded that a judge should be "able and industrious . . . qualified by training and experience for his office." That Hughes was concerned with practical politics rather than theoretical analysis was beyond doubt. ("My kick against the Chief Justice, in a single word," Felix Frankfurter had written earlier, "is that he has been just as political as the President.") Unquestionably, however, the concern here ran—successfully, as things turned out—to guide the presidential hand in future appointments to the Court. To be sure, the address necessarily implied that the appointment of one maverick was enough, but the denigration of Black, to the extent that it occurred at all, was both incidental and peripheral to a larger motive.[19]

And perhaps something like this was also the case with Justice Stone, whose sleight-of-hand Footnote Number 4 in *Carolene*

Products appropriately symbolized subtlety approaching devi-
ousness. His temperamental differences with Black had already
been apparent, and remarkably they surfaced in areas of judicial
concern, where the two men agreed that change was in order. But
where Stone wished to stretch out the process across a spectrum
wherein black became white through imperceptible changes of
degree, the same exuberant energy that had guided Black from
golf to tennis impelled him to seek doctrinal change forthwith.
Black was all for laying the ax to the root.

Less spectacular than Black's dissents on corporations or rate-
making were two judicial protectorates that the Supreme Court
had raised on its own account in the old dispensation and that
Black regarded as constitutional excrescences and on which
Stone essentially agreed. One concerned the mare's nest of reciprocal immunity that the Court had wrapped around the instruments of state and federal governments in protecting one from
the taxing power of the other. Quite distinct, but still closely
related, was the ongoing veto the Court had passed on local
legislation that it felt bore unfairly upon interstate commerce.

The interplay between Stone and Black followed the same
pattern in the two cases that presented new facets of the old
protectorates. In *Helvering v. Gerhardt,* Stone concluded that the
salary of an employee of the New York Port Authority was subject to the federal income tax thanks to a delicately nuanced
distinction between national and state fiscal authority. Black,
joined by Justice Holmes and Franklin Roosevelt, proposed to
lay all such distinctions to rest by appealing to the letter of the
Sixteenth Amendment and the authority of Congress to tax income from whatever source derived. Again in *South Carolina
Highway Department v. Barnwell Brothers,* Stone upheld a
South Carolina statute limiting the size of trucks—even those in
interstate travel—in an opinion from which he removed one
small but critically significant adverb at Black's behest. For after
the excision the challenged law was validated as "adapted to the
exercise of an acknowledged legislative power," and not as one
"reasonably" adapted.[20]

But there was a darker side to Stone's subtlety, and it appeared in an insecurity that ran some sinister fault line under the Associate Justice's massive granite exterior. Two manifestations in the same month of early 1938 showed his interchange with Black to be going forward. One involved Stone's almost obsessive concern for evidence of the good opinion of the deceased Justice Holmes, and here he brought an unremitting pressure on Harold Laski to comb Holmes's letters for appropriate references. Indeed, such was the pressure that the hapless Laski was reduced to fabricating the alleged comments—"Stone would, I think, make a great Chief Justice"—and Stone in turn tendered Laski the thanks of himself and his children for the testimonial.[21]

The other concerned a living colleague, and for Hugo Black, Stone had some hard things to say: that Roosevelt had appointed him "in a fit of pique"; and that one of Black's dissents "showed the handiwork of someone other than the nominal author." And then he began discussing Black during morning walks with *St. Louis Post-Dispatch* reporter Marquis Childs. The first fruit of the walks came as barbs in which the *Post-Dispatch* began to unveil its "inside view of the Supreme Court" and the concern therein over appointees with "no judicial experience and only a comparatively limited legal experience." Stone was delighted with the article ("just what is needed to educate the public") and had yet another suggestion: "Publish something of the sort in a magazine having a national circulation." The result was Childs's article in the May 1938 *Harper's,* reporting that Black's colleagues supposedly were shocked over "his lack of legal knowledge and experience, deficiencies in background and training."[22]

Stone permitted his secretary to assert that "the Justice will not comment. . . . You may say as coming from his office that he was not the source of the material in the article. . . ." In a like vein Childs asserted a categorical denial in public—"Justice Stone is not a source of material that appeared in the article"— while in private he supposedly said exactly the opposite. Justice Stone never indicated a word of apology, aside from an elliptic indication that he was really interested in Black's improvement; a quarter century later, however, Childs did express regret over his own role in giving widespread currency to the attack.[23]

Indeed, of all parties to the spring uproar in 1938, Black came off far and away the best. Thus, when Irving Brant of the *St. Louis Star-Times* suggested what Justice Stone had really said "did not remotely support" what Marquis Childs had written, Black serenely replied "that I am not disturbed in the slightest about the matter to which you referred." If he were not disturbed, however, some of his admirers were. As stout a supporter as Max Lerner seemingly gave ground in conceding that Black would have to be less of a judicial crusader before he came to maturity as a judge. On the other hand, not all yielded. Writing from the Yale Law School, Walter Hamilton noted that the Supreme Court, "like any savage tribe, demands of its members a reasonable conformity to its folkways." He then submitted a mock indictment of the junior Justice: "Justice Black needs a course in hallowed platitudes. . . . He regards sacred cows as ordinary heifers, finds it impossible to accept verbal symbols as realities, and fails to appreciate the pomp and circumstance of circumlocution, by which the processes of justice are kept decorous."[24]

Black departed for the summer recess as seemingly oblivious to flattery as he was to condemnation. Characteristically he took an armload of summer reading with him, including John Dewey and the modern philosophers. And in its way the selection was not without its own ironic overtones, for the Justice, whose pragmatic opinions had gone from problem to problem rather than from doctrine to doctrine, was already well launched on his own quest for the jurisprudence of certainty.

CHAPTER NINE

The New Deal Court

Changing of the Guard I

The Founding Fathers wrote better than they knew; in providing for one Supreme Court and such inferior courts as Congress might from time to time ordain and establish, they framed an institution that necessarily lags and thereby validates the great germinations in American politics, American government and American law. Indeed, the experience of the great changes instituted under Jefferson, Jackson and Lincoln alike add up to a rule whereby the final and formal ratification of a constitutional revolution by the judicial branch comes to pass only after two full terms of its presidential initiator have run their course. But the administration of Franklin D. Roosevelt presented something of a conflict between the letter and the spirit of the rule. Here the grudging judicial validation of the New Deal might in one mode be seen as the *West Coast Hotel* case, where the Supreme Court by the narrowest of margins upheld state regulation of hours of labor. Handed in only after Roosevelt's landslide reelection and attack on the Court were accomplished facts, the decision left a hanging margin of uncertainty as to its character and permanence. But that doubt was put to rest with the resignations of James Clark McReynolds and Charles Evans Hughes at the beginning of Franklin Roosevelt's third term. These resignations might be said to confirm the rule by their transformation of the Court to a firm—indeed irreversible—New Deal coloration.

Thus, the changing of the guard that began with Black moved forward even before the 1937–38 term of the Supreme Court was completed. With the coming of 1938, Justice George Sutherland resigned and Solicitor General Stanley F. Reed took his place before three weeks were out. On July 9, 1938, Benjamin N. Cardozo died, and the following January the scholar's seat, which had been graced by Story and Holmes as well as Cardozo, passed with singular appropriateness to Professor Felix Frankfurter of the Harvard Law School. Before spring of 1939 was out, Justice Louis D. Brandeis retired at the age of eighty-two, and an extraordinary contrast in age but a remarkable continuity in spirit came with the appointment of William O. Douglas, the forty-one-year-old chairman of the Securities and Exchange Commission. The Douglas appointment marked a critical stage of transformation, and Harold Laski figuratively threw his hat in the air. "One more good resignation," he wrote the President, "(by death or by art is indifferent to me) and it really is 'our' Supreme Court."[1] On February 10, 1940, Michigan's Governor Frank Murphy succeeded Justice Pierce Butler. The appointments of James F. Byrnes and Robert H. Jackson, as a consequence of the Hughes and McReynolds resignations, followed in February 1941. Thus, four years almost to the day after Franklin Roosevelt had sent his abortive judiciary plan to Congress, his triumph was complete, for seven of the nine incumbents on that bench sat there by virtue of his appointment, and this was one more than the plan itself would have given him.

The reconstitution of the Court, for the President a towering and unique event, was to be for Black only the first of a series of turnover transformations. Yet by singular chance throughout virtually all the changes that lay ahead, there would be two careers from the Roosevelt appointments that were fated to lie in a remarkable and parallel course alongside his. One was to be

there as ally, one as antagonist, and both were to stamp an extraordinary impress upon his life, outlook and judicial philosophy.

The Ally

The long-time ally was William Orville Douglas, and while
Black was to have other associates in the work of the Supreme
Court whose attitudes and modes of thought were remarkably
congenial to his own—Frank Murphy, Wiley B. Rutledge, Earl
Warren—nothing could ever quite compare with the long-lasting
philosophical rapport that he was to have with Douglas. Perhaps
their sense of association sprang from their being exiles in the
mode of the famous Joyce play. Certainly each was touched with
a sense of alienation toward both the social order and the conventional wisdom into which they had been born. Certainly both
were indifferent to conventions (albeit in different ways) as well
as to success—or at least to success as defined and measured by
the customary standards. And both were willing to undertake the
lonely and hazardous business of trying to shape, as was well
said, the conscience of a race.

And, in the most literal sense of the word, both were self-made
men, although alongside Douglas' extraordinary background,
Black was at once privileged and provincial. For Douglas, the
son of an itinerant preacher, had been orphaned at an early age
and had been cut down by polio as well. He had soldiered as a
private in the felt-hat army, shocked wheat with the Wobblies,
ridden the rods, and lived in hobo jungles. His opinions could
hold a touch of Steinbeck in writing about "farm laborers in the
West who compete with field hands drifting up from Mexico;
whites who feel the pressure of Orientals. . . ." But there was so
much more than this. He had been also the teacher with class-
room experience ranging from Yakima High to the Yale and
Columbia law schools. He had been the Wall Street lawyer in the
firm of Cravath, DeGersdorff, Swaine and Wood. He had been
picked to head the Securities and Exchange Commission by no

less than Joseph P. Kennedy, who perhaps saw in him the son he really wanted.[2]

And from the first, Black and Douglas took to each other with ideas that seemed to come together in an almost magnetic reinforcement. Even the diversity of experience seemed to dovetail with Black's courtroom years becoming the logical complement to the administrative expertise of Douglas. There was a shared critical concern over corporations, concentration and competition as Douglas carried on the Brandeis tradition in which an encyclopedic knowledge of the apparatus and techniques of finance capitalism went hand in hand with a singular detachment from its *ethos*. But there was more than mere knowledge of facts, for Douglas had the same sure feel for the nuances and necessities of commercial law—perhaps the greatest since Mansfield and Story—although, ironically, he was to get very little credit for it from the corporate and banking bar.

Moreover, Douglas and Black had encountered corporate enterprise with its worse foot forward. ("By God, Felix," Douglas once wrote a future colleague about criticism of the New Deal securities legislation, "I lose my composure at this point, and so would you if you had seen the stark realities I have.") More than this both had glimpsed almost every aspect of American life at its seamiest, and both had seen the ravages of depression at first hand. Finally, each in his own way had picked up a strong libertarian strain which their ongoing association seemed to engrain the more. The over-all consequence was a rapport, perhaps unique in judicial annals, that combined a disposition to let governmental efforts go to great length in the composition of economic problems—with a particular appreciation of the national dimension involved—and an instinct to cry alarm when the secular state placed its hand on political or intellectual processes.[3]

The Antagonist

If in Douglas, Black found a partner who shared his flash of insight, his sense of immediacy, and a feel for the spirit beneath the letter, and the unconcern with consequences that makes up the prophetic half of the law, in Felix Frankfurter he was given one who exemplified the other element, and it was one almost completely absent from his own makeup. For law, like religion, involves a priestly as well as a prophetic element, and Frankfurter was very much the law's priest. He was enormously concerned with its rubrics, its liturgies, and its organic and ongoing integrity. More importantly, this sacerdotal instinct lay below even that long-time and highly visible concern with social reform and individual justice, and the depth of the submergence obscured how fundamentally traditionalist Felix Frankfurter really was. "I am astonished at the extent of my correspondence with him," later wrote old New Dealer Irving Brant. "Between the time of his nomination to the Supreme Court and his confirmation, I was astonished when I read that Boston conservatives were advising their fellow travelers around the country . . . to lay off him. How right they were!"[4]

Ironically enough, Frankfurter had spent most of his pre-Court career in an effort to topple *Swift v. Tyson* from the domain of constitutional law, and it was only in confrontation with Black that his own natural-law conviction really emerged. ("For me . . . Hitler becomes the true prophet if there is no such thing as Law different and apart from the individuals who give it expression.") And in this respect, it is remarkable how much of William Holdsworth's description of an earlier conservative—Edmund Burke, no less—could be applied in his case:

> In an age which was inclined to despise the past and to apply to the solution of its problems its own transient political theories and ideas, Burke was almost the only . . . thinker . . . who saw the present age was the outcome of the past, that the merits and defects of its institutions and its laws could not be appreciated without some reference to their history. . . . This historical sense . . . made him acutely conscious of the difficulty of creating a civilized and ordered society, and impressed upon him a deep and almost mystic reverence for any set of institu-

tions and laws which showed themselves able to master those anarchical forces which are threatening the existence of such a society.[5]

There were other dimensions to the Black-Frankfurter differences. One was a way of looking at things. By his own admission, Frankfurter liked to sit on problems—to mull, twist and worry them. By his own admission he had to brood a lot, even though he was clear about his views. Contrariwise, Black had that turn of intelligence that got to the point of an issue almost in a flash (his onetime law clerk, John P. Frank, said that Black thought faster than any man he ever knew) and then disposed of it. And there was the linguistic gap, when Black made a virtue out of adversity in fitting his writing style to the only language he knew, while Frankfurter's trilingual perceptions emerged in judicial opinions that were crafted arabesques.

But perhaps the greatest difference of all lay in the fact that Black moved up when he went on the Court, but Frankfurter stepped down. Throughout a quarter century before his appointment, Frankfurter had been the Court's chronicler, its analyst, its counselor and, above all, its very special critic. Indeed, when he told the young *Harvard Law Review* editors of their frequent and joyous obligation "to reverse the Supreme Court . . . in an infallible judgment of 165 words," he spoke only half in jest, for here he was really holding up a mirror to what had been his longtime professional face.[6]

But what Professor Frankfurter might say with impunity, Mr. Justice Frankfurter could—or should—not. And exemplifying the difference between the two roles was the extraordinary letter that Professor Frankfurter sent down from Cambridge in early 1938 at the behest of Justice Stone—"Do you know Black well? . . . He needs guidance." Frankfurter did not know Black well ("Black means nothing to me—I have never laid eyes on him," he wrote almost contemporaneously), but he nonetheless proceeded to tell the newly appointed Justice ("in the same spirit . . . were I writing a piece as a professor in the *Harvard Law Review*") how to act as a member of the Supreme Court. And unquestionably insult was especially added to insult in the manifestly spurious *entre nous* about Holmes "and his highbrow way," which probably made Black remember Madame Perkins all over again. Frankfurter's files contain no indication of Black's response, if any, but in any event Frankfurter could never explicitly say as much to Black as a colleague. Nonetheless, spoken or unspoken, the attitude was there, and the didactic bent, carried from campus to court, manifestly exacerbated philosophic differences, which were divisive enough under the best of conditions.[7]

Yet, in a three-quarter truth that contained something of a penultimate irony, a hostile observer has noted that Black and Frankfurter, the two Justices who Roosevelt felt exemplified best the judicial liberalism of his New Deal, were destined to wind up, each in his own fashion, not only in conservative dissent but "literally and figuratively as 'Old Dealers.'" The ultimate irony, however, emerges in the necessity of function of both priest and prophet in the law, and the consequent duality of what Alfred North Whitehead called the reverence for the social symbols and fearlessness in their revision. And in this context Justices Black and Frankfurter may have achieved their especial vindication through that costly but noble tension that each excited in the other.[8]

The Tensions Joined

Ironically, the ultimate and essentially irreconcilable division between Black and Frankfurter went unforeseen at the outset of their joint judicial careers. In fact, Frankfurter's appointment had been urged on an undecided President on the grounds that it would effectively link "Black's economic acumen and Stone's legal philosophy." And certainly at the time some sympathetic buffering seemed in order, to harmonize Stone's cautious progressivism and Black's impatient instincts to wipe the slate clean with a single swipe and begin afresh.[9]

The milieu made for an extraordinary love-hate relationship. Black's cellolike voice, which once coaxed large verdicts from

juries, now ravaged the ears of the Harvard scholar. ("O Democracy, what flapdoodle is delivered in thy name! And not the
less so because it is said in Black's irascible and snarling tone.")
Indeed, Black probably passed over into deliberate deadpan
baiting—"I thought Felix was going to hit me today, he got so
mad. But he'll get over it."[10]

Deep down, Frankfurter did not like William Douglas either,
and without recognizing the mirror he held up to his own cour-
tier's face, he appraised his young colleague "as the most systematic exploiter of flattery I have ever encountered in my whole
life." Like Black, Douglas was disposed to give as good as he
got—"Today at conference I asked you a question . . . An
answer was refused, somewhat insolently. . . . I do register a
protest at your degradation of the conference and its deliber-
ations."[11]

Particularly difficult and divisive were the labor-relations cases
that not only involved sharp challenges to legal tradition, but
threw them up in particularly abrasive form. One facet of the
problem concerned the attitudes and philosophy of the newly
hatched administrative agencies. Another, perhaps more exas-
perating, involved problems of line drawing in the gray issues of
degree that were supplanting the former blacks and whites of
categorical absolutes.

Both facets were involved in the frankly result-oriented judgments of the National Labor Relations Board coming up before
a Supreme Court that was changing but perhaps not changing
fast enough. Indeed, such was the outcome of the first NLRB
appeals before a Court with only a few Roosevelt appointees that
some labor protagonists felt that not only had the Supreme Court
accomplished by construction what employers had failed to win
by amendment, but judicial constraints were themselves serving
as a springboard for further legislative restrictions on the rights
of labor.[12]

Typical in this respect was the undertaking to mediate between old and new, as in Stone's draft effort in *NLRB v. Fainblatt.* Here Stone sought to link the past and present by indicating that permissible local impact of the Wagner Labor Relations

Act was quite different from the intrusion the Court had outlawed in striking down the NRA. Unhappily, the attempted
reconciliation fell between stools. Justice McReynolds' dissent
exploded over "this subversive doctrine," however it was explained. Black, for all his opposition to the NRA on the Senate
floor, nonetheless objected to gratuitous judicial asides and secured the excision of the offending passage: "I am not in accord
with the decision reached in the [NRA] case on this point. . . .
This sentence would in my judgment imply an approval . . . I
do not wish to approve it even by implication."[13]

Along somewhat the same line were the judicial exchanges in
U.S. v. Darby, where Black was able to cast his vote as a Justice
for the statute that he had helped to guide through the Senate as
his last legislative act. Justice Stone wrote the opinion on the
critical constitutional turnabout sweeping away a century and a
half of inhibiting encrustations; it unveiled a soaring view of the
commerce power reaching back to Marshall's prophetic vision.
Senator Black had said much the same thing on the Senate floor,
and Justice Black had left his invisible mark in what the Supreme
Court had to say. For Stone's intermediate draft contained a
ghost-echo of the old-style judicial supremacy in the observation
that the prescribed wage rate was found free from being "unfair
or oppressive." Alert as ever to preserve the legislative prerogative, Black returned to the point he had made in the *Barnwell
Brothers* truck case and found the suggestion constitutionally
unwarranted and impertinent—"so far as the due process clause
of the Fifth Amendment is concerned, I am unable to see its
application to a case coming within the commerce power."[14]

With the offending sentence deleted, Black praised the final
product. Chief Justice Hughes's reactions, however, were considerably different, and they suggested why the opinion was written by Stone and not himself. On the final draft, which bore
Black's revision, Hughes cryptically noted, "I will go along with
this." And in correspondence, Justice Stone himself indicated not
only the reason for the Chief Justice's reticence but also that he
shared it: "The truth is that I feel obliged to uphold some laws
which turn my stomach."[15]

The Seeds of Change

As Black's Scottsboro position had indicated, racial injustice was far more intractable than economic malfunction and seemingly beyond the power of political accommodation. More than this, it was an integral and reciprocally reinforcing part of the other inequities of American life. For while the minorities who had been the historic losers in that process were, by definition, discrete and insular, their disabilities were reinforcing.

Two events, diverse in setting and topic, but close at hand in point of time, were to show it clearly. Less than a month after *Carolene Products* and his dissenting concurrence, he spoke for the Court in *Johnson v. Zerbst,* in which a federal convict sought to gain his freedom, not through the customary appeal from sentence, but in an application for habeas corpus.[16]

The great writ was available for one imprisoned by a court that had no jurisdiction to do so, and here the necessary condition was asserted on the fact that the accused had been tried without a lawyer to defend his cause. This absence, it was asserted, violated the Sixth Amendment's guarantee that in all criminal trials the accused should enjoy the right "to have the Assistance of Counsel for his defense." And if this was true, it followed that the failure to comply with the literal constitutional injunction made the sentence of the trial court rest on force rather than on law.

The suggestion ran against the grain of much of the legal tradition for jurisdiction—the right to decide a case wrongly was about as fundamental a thing as there was in the law. That jurisdiction, having once attached, could be lost as a result of irregularities was in its way an astonishing legal heresy, both in its fundamental concept and in its disruptive consequences to the settled doctrine that mistakes and miscarriages be corrected by orderly appeal rather than by an extraordinary writ.

Yet, following one of the trials of Tom Mooney, the Supreme Court had opened the door a crack to suggest that there were some developments so unfair, some procedures so fundamental, as to go to the heart of jurisdiction itself. *A fortiori*, the Zerbst proceeding presented an even stronger case. Just how such an appeal was to be taken—especially within stated limitations of time—without counsel, whose absence in the first place caused the whole problem, posed an almost insoluble problem. Almost but not quite, for it came as almost second nature for Black to combine the very difficulty with an appeal to the literal language of the constitutional text. He did not grant the requested writ, but he did send the case back for a hearing on whether the defendant had competently and intelligently waived his right to counsel at the original trial.

It was a decision that perhaps constituted as much a fountain-head of Black's juristic thought as anything he had written or would write thereafter, even though it was in many ways not readily consistent with other strands of his thought. The very form of the proceeding exalted, not the legislative, but the judicial prerogative and did so in a juryless proceeding where the court determined both fact and law. Moreover, it did so on a constitutional passage where the original understanding, everyone said, was not that counsel should be supplied but only that his assistance not be blocked.

Yet, it was on the precise point of the effective assistance of counsel (in a capital case to be sure) on which the Court had issued its initial reversal of the convictions in the Scottsboro case, and it was just a few months after *Johnson v. Zerbst* that both the obvious and the subtle interrelationships between that case and the Scottsboro case was suggested by a very special homecoming. The occasion was the meeting of the Southern Conference for Human Welfare, an extraordinary coalition of Southern liberals and radicals. Indeed Mrs. Black's sister, Virginia Foster Durr, was a moving spirit in the coalition, which had come together in part as a consequence of Franklin Roosevelt's envisioned transformation of the Democratic party. The Birmingham meeting presented an extraordinary array of talent—Governor and Mrs. Graves, Mrs. Graves's Senate successor, Lister Hill (whose rousing New Deal victory in that summer's primary left no doubt as to whether Black would have triumphed), Brooks Hayes, Mary

McLeod Bethune, *et al*. It was held at Birmingham's municipal auditorium (the Scottsboro boys were in the Birmingham jail just a short distance away), and Associate Justice Black made a stirring address.

The interconnected concerns of the white liberals in the Birmingham auditorium, the black prisoners in the Birmingham jail, and the Scottsboro case, ensemble, surfaced within four months of the S.C.H.W. Conference, when Black wrote the opinion for a unanimous Court in *Pierre v. Louisiana*, reversing the murder conviction of a Louisiana Negro. Here the Court's action was essentially a reprise of the second Scottsboro appeal, for reversal was based on the patent exclusion of blacks from jury service. Now the tide was running, however, and in the following term Black was again the spokesman, and in *Smith v. Texas* he reached a like result on the basis of a like plea. There was one important difference in that the causal pattern was not so obvious as it had been before. But, in the words of an earlier Justice, Black did not forget as a judge what he knew as a man, and he reasoned backward from result to cause. ("If there has been discrimination, whether accomplished ingeniously or ingenuously, the conviction cannot stand.")[17]

And all of this was appropriately a prelude to what was almost universally regarded as his best effort in the early years, the "sunrise-confessions" case of *Chambers v. Florida,* delivered on Lincoln's Birthday, 1940. Reading in a slow, solemn voice and doing so as the spokesman of a unanimous Court, Black reversed the murder convictions of four "ignorant, young colored tenant farmers"; he found that they had undergone "protracted interrogation by State officers and other white citizens in a fourth-floor jail room, where as prisoners they were without friends, advisers or counselors." The circumstances, Black concluded, were calculated "to break the strongest nerves and the stoutest resistance."[18]

The opinion, we are told by one of his former law clerks, was "not easy" for him and was reached "after great internal struggles." Perhaps his difficulties, in part at least, rested upon the explicit jury findings of an absence of physical brutality and a voluntary character to the confessions themselves. In fact, he had voted against the Supreme Court's taking the case in the first place. But his ear for facts stressed the duration and the isolation of the questioning—five days on the fourth floor of the Dade County Court House (three decades later, on the CBS telecast, he remembered it as "three nights on the seventh floor")—and those facts may well have stirred the recollection of other facts, perhaps even of the Bessemer jail, and the necessity of having "friends, advisers, and counselors" if justice is to be done.[19]

The reception of the opinion was almost unanimously enthusiastic, and a typical enthusiast was the *Catholic World,* which had called his appointment "a first-class calamity." Now it spoke no longer in the idiom of calamity but of compliment—" . . . direct, sweeping, and brilliantly written. . . ." Charles Beard, the Justice's sometime dinner companion, noted in his *Republic* that the opinion would "ring with power as long as liberty and justice are cherished in our country." And at his press conference, President Roosevelt suggested that the newspapers owed an apology to Mr. Justice Black.[20]

Yet there remained somewhat ungracious notes in the outpouring of congratulations, and one came from Wendell Willkie

> . . . it was a good opinion. It was an opinion rendered on behalf of four men who were poor and weak. But the protection of the weak will not by itself entitle Mr. Justice Black to the hallmark of liberalism. This protection should extend equally to the strong and rich. It was only two or three years before that Mr. Black . . . set as notorious an example of unconstitutional search and seizure as recent American history affords . . . The only reason I am referring to the case here is to indicate once again that due process of law does not mean due process for one group and not another, but for all groups of every kind.[21]

The Fission

In early summer of 1941 Chief Justice Hughes retired under the 1937 statute, and Associate Justice Harlan Fiske Stone took the oath as the new head of the Court before the Commissioner of the Rocky Mountain National Park. The low-keyed inaugural appropriately typified that continuity of symbol that Stone saw as the Court's essential function but was now harder to come by with the easy decisions over and the far more difficult questions of degree still to come.

What was surfacing now were fundamental differences not only of outlook and philosophy, but of personality and temperament. As Herman Pritchett has noted, the plight of the Court was the plight of the New Deal. American liberalism was exhausted as an instrumental philosophy, and the ideas that had exploded at the turn of the century were now written into law. But still lacking were guides for the future, particularly for a governing coalition whose cross-purposed structure was indicated in the very style of *Hague v. Congress of Industrial Organizations,* where the Court (through the conservative Justice Roberts) upheld by a five-to-two margin the right of the CIO to hold outdoor meetings in Jersey City without permits from the police department.[22]

Perhaps the fact that Roberts' swing had been thus made permanent underlay the *Washington Post's* prediction that "for years to come there would be virtual unanimity on the tribunal," and *United States News's* assurance to the new Chief Justice that he would find "no sharp divergence of opinion among his colleagues." The new Chief Justice thought otherwise. Indeed, he had barely taken his oath when he was reflecting on how he might "mass" the Court into an organization working in unity and harmony, and before the year was out he had changed his metaphor and was writing of his team of "wild horses."[23]

The sharpest goad to the wild horses was the difficult decisions provided by the emerging law of labor relations, where rising unrest and changing law compressed economics and politics, civil rights and civil liberties, administrative law and the judicial function in the most complex of frameworks. And here the easy decisions were over the moment the newly appointed Frank Murphy could speak for a united Court and strike down an Alabama antipicketing statute as violative of free speech.[24]

General principles, as Holmes warned, never solved particular problems, and the abstract proposition that a labor union's communication, as such, could not be constitutionally suppressed did little to assess the contexts in which those communications might be framed. And just as the administrative behavior of the National Labor Relations Board combined with the new techniques of the sit-down strike to force Stone and Hughes to reexamine their judicial validation of New Deal measures, so did the impact of labor violence in the larger context of the judicial process split asunder Black's short-lived rapport with Frankfurter and provide the catalyst for the origins of a judicial philosophy of his own.

The key cases came from two regionally focused labor disputes. One originated in a Chicago vendor system, where small independent entrepreneurs served as intermediaries of and for the dairies and were consequently seen as a threat by the union deliverymen who served a like function. The first skirmish was peaceful enough—an opinion by Black in *Milk Wagon Drivers Union v. Lake Valley Company* that federal statute did not permit a federal district court to forbid the drivers to picket stores supplied by the independents.[25]

But when that picketing became enmeshed in violence and the antipicketing injunction was that of an Illinois court, as was the case in *Milk Wagon Drivers Union v. Meadowmoor Dairies*, the protagonist New Deal justices parted company. Superficially, their differences seemed to lie in factual appraisal; their fundamental difference in premise, however, made the opposing opinions become assertions of nonnegotiable articles of faith. Frankfurter's majority opinion proposed his inner conviction that "the Bill of Rights was the child of the Enlightenment . . . lay[ing] faith in the power of an appeal to reason by all the peaceful means of gaining access to the mind . . . But utterance in a context of violence can . . . become part of an instrument of force."[26]

Black was not convinced.

> It is going a long way to say that because of the acts of [a] few men, six thousand other members of their union

can be denied the right to express their opinion . . .
Even those convicted of crime are not in this country
punished by having their freedom of expression curtailed
except under prison rules . . . and then only for the
duration of the sentence.

But even more important was his assertion of the beginnings of
his own judicial credo:

> I view the guaranties of the First Amendment as the
> foundation upon which our government rests and without
> which it could not continue to endure as conceived and
> planned. Freedom to speak and to write about public
> questions is as important as is the heart to the human
> body. In fact the privilege is the heart of our government.
> If that heart be weakened, the result is debilitation; if it
> be stilled, the result is death.[27]

Difficult as the vendor controversy was, it shriveled alongside
the bitter West Coast longshoremen's strike, and the difficulty of
the legal issues matched the magnitude of the confrontation.
Ironically enough, it involved the contempt citations that California courts had issued against parties on both sides of the dispute. One case, *Times Mirror Co. v. Superior Court of California,* concerned an editorial ("Probation for Gorillas")
admonishing a local judge that he would make "a serious mistake" if he granted probation to certain labor defendants. The
other, *Bridges v. California,* involved a telegram that the well-
known defendant had sent to the Secretary of Labor warning
that attempted enforcement of a state judgment would produce a
strike.[28]

Contempt sentences at the trial level were approved by the
Supreme Court of California, argued at the October 1940 term
without result, and reargued the following year. When the opinions came down, Black was found speaking for himself, Douglas,
Reed, Murphy and Jackson, and striking down contempt citations. It was not an easy opinion, for two obstacles seemingly lay
in his way. One was his *Connecticut General* dissent proposing
that a corporation—presumably even one publishing a news-

paper—be put beyond the pale of the Fourteenth Amendment; the other, closely related to his textual analysis of the amendment itself, involved the difficulty of extending its protection to aliens, of which Mr. Bridges was one.

Concern for consistency, however, vanished before the larger issues, one of which was obviously a deep hostility to unfettered judicial power. Indeed, Black's legislative predilection was evident in his opening thrust that the case came without the benefit of statutory direction by California, and then this point set the stage for the key question as one of fact—that "the substantive evil must be extremely serious and the degree of imminence extremely high." Needless to say, neither element could be found present. But this five-to-four division of the Roosevelt Court was more than a split over an issue of fact. Rather it involved a view of the law itself, and here Black's minor premises suggested some changes pending in the years to come. One was in integration of the First Amendment guarantees of free speech into the constraints the more general text of the Fourteenth laid upon the states. The other was the literalist application to the text, irrespective of what had been the practice of judges since the foundation of the Republic.[29]

The consequence was a sharp limitation of all judges to punish summarily for statements made outside the courtroom. Yet it was a change effected over the vigorous dissent of Justice Frankfurter, who disavowed its calculus completely. Now, in dissent, he bitterly but unavailingly insisted that the Court could not "read into the Fourteenth Amendment the freedom of speech . . . guaranteed by the First Amendment and . . . read out the age-old means employed by the state for securing the calm course of justice." And this was followed by a barbed formulation of a process of balancing soon to become anathema to Black: "Free speech is not so absolute or irrational a conception so as to paralyze the other freedoms of the bill of rights."[30]

The Black-Frankfurter split indicated several things. One was that Franklin Roosevelt had certainly made good his word during the Court fight of 1937 that he would never appoint spineless puppets to the high bench. There was indeed another side to the coin, however. Appropriately it occurred the day after Pearl Harbor, and the bombs that fell on the Pacific Fleet in a way paralleled the explosion that destroyed the fragile New Deal coalition on the Court. There was one difference. The fleet would sail again, but the Roosevelt Court would never be the same.

CHAPTER TEN

Pledges and Allegiances

Nazis and Nisei

In late July 1942, one of the most remarkable proceedings in American legal history took place at the Chester County (Pennsylvania) farm of Justice Owen Roberts. Present were the Justice, his colleague Hugo Black, the Attorney General of the United States, and the Judge Advocate General of the Army. Present also were two Army colonels, and through them eight accused saboteurs currently on trial before a military tribunal where the colonels served as defense counsel. The colonels' "clients" had assertedly been landed by submarine just a few weeks before, promptly apprehended and, pursuant to presidential order, handed over for trial before a commission of—as *Time* noted—"hard-bitten Major General Frank R. McCoy [and] six other boot-tough generals." The order, in effect, demanded that the defendants be promptly executed after a fair trial, and the judiciary was denied any part in these or similar proceedings.[1]

In the latter provision, the proceedings departed sharply from the Articles of War and were otherwise so remarkable that the defense colonels, notwithstanding the presidential order, promptly sought the intervention of the federal judiciary on the theory that existing statutes covered the field of sabotage, that the civil courts themselves were open and functioning to try asserted offenses against them and that at least one of the defendants, as an alleged American citizen, was entitled to be so tried. Nor was their position without some substance. On the contrary, the particular points raised such questions that the Supreme Court went to extraordinary efforts (which included a contrived refusal by Black of a writ of habeas corpus) to resolve the legal question within a limited time frame and provide a result that would assert its jurisdictional prerogative and still avoid a confrontation with the President. The result was a sharp internal struggle, after which the Court, at a specially convened summer session, reluctantly validated the power and jurisdiction of the commission.[2] While the opinion itself was delayed for considerable time, the decision came down on July 31, and a few days later six of the defendants were electrocuted.

The judicial determination that an American citizen might be seized on American soil far from a battlefield, tried in secret, and executed with no appeal save only to presidential clemency not only epitomized the grim Latin maxim that in time of war the law is silent but also served as a prelude in which the plea of necessity and thrust of the times would repeatedly override the plain letter of the Constitution. Indeed, this was graphically underscored in a sequel to the case of the saboteurs. There an old acquaintance of one of them, at the time a naturalized citizen, met the new arrival, took his funds for safekeeping, and notified mutual friends of his presence. Such a face-to-face encounter was the only "overt act" duly seen by the two constitutionally required two witnesses in the subsequent trial for treason.

Black's flintlike judicial stance during World War II rested on a solid intellectual and moral commitment. "And I don't believe in war," he asserted against the Vietnam background of his famous telecast. "We've had only one war that I thoroughly approved. And that was the war against Hitler." He knew something about Hitler too, for his personal library contained a complete, unabridged, annotated edition (1939) of *Mein Kampf* ("heavily marked, personally indexed"). "I read *Mein Kampf* several times. I thought he [Hitler] was brainier than others thought, but as despicable as a man could be." Six months before Pearl Harbor, Secretary Ickes recorded in his diary that Black was "terribly worried about the effect of war on this country."[3]

The law is silent on what character the overt act has to have, and after protracted litigation, the conviction was ultimately set aside on the ground that the witnessed event was itself required to be inherently treasonous. In the litigation Black started to write an opinion on the side of the defendant, but finally swung over to the prosecution's point of view, perhaps on the Lincolnian proposition of saving the Constitution from itself. In any event, by private note he expressed the view that strict interpretation of the constitutional text would require a defendant being "found in the Army of the enemy" before a conviction of guilty could be entered. (Unsympathetic critics agreed that this was exactly what Franklin intended in drafting the particular provision of the constitutional text.) And in a similar severity of attitude he was one of two dissenters from the Court's judgment overturning the conviction of avowed German sympathizers on the ground that the propagandist registration statute did not reach voluntary activity.[4]

But the silence of the law in time of war was singularly illustrated by what it could be silent about. For as Justice Roberts noted in a subsequent proceeding from the West Coast, a native-born American citizen against whom neither proof nor even suspicion attached had far fewer constitutional rights than did naturalized or even alien Germans. Indeed, the key proposition in the saboteurs' case—that a mere assertion of military necessity might permit certain procedural requirements to be dispensed with in difficult trials of unusual crimes—paled before the proposition that citizens might suffer banishment and confiscation without being charged with any crime at all. For this was precisely the situation in the case of the 112,000 Nisei, over 75,000 of them native-born American citizens, who were removed from their homes on the West Coast and sent to "relocation centers" in the mountain states solely on the basis of ethnic ancestry.

The proceedings were first challenged in *Hirabayashi v. United States,* when a University of Washington senior who had violated a curfew regulation—duly published in the *Federal Register*—challenged the constitutional basis of the order itself. The Supreme Court, when the case was finally presented to it, nervously gave ground, rested its rationale on the narrowest possible point, and produced a judgment turning on the "reasonable grounds" of the belief of the commanding general for doing what he did.[5]

But the core of the Nisei transportations came home to rest in *Korematsu v. United States,* where not curfew but relocation itself was put in issue, and it was Black who undertook to write the validating opinion. He made the best of a difficult job, noting at the outset that racial classifications were inherently suspect and embodying in his final product Chief Justice Stone's admonition that "it is not our apprehension . . . which governs but that of the military authorities." In an unusual flourish of solidarity, Felix Frankfurter closed ranks—"I agree entirely with your treatment of *Korematsu,* and I am ready to join in your opinion without the change of a word." Nonetheless his efforts went unregarded as far as three others of his colleagues were concerned. In a singularly formed coalition of liberal and conservative, Justice Roberts denounced the "concentration camp" aspects of the litigation, Justice Murphy the "legalization of racism," and Justice Jackson the forging of a "loaded weapon ready for the hand of any authority who brings forward a plausible claim of urgent need."[6]

The opinion turned out to be the most heavily criticized one that Black ever wrote. Irving Dilliard loyally included it in *One Man's Stand for Freedom,* with the observation that there is one time when Justice Black "will support action by the federal government that normally he would rule out as unconstitutional. That is when the Nation is engaged in war for survival." Others, *The New York Times* noted, "could and did view it as aberrational." But Black did not regard it as aberrational. A decade later he uncompromisingly defended what he did—"The President could have declared martial law. Instead, they took the better way of passing a law to detain them. There's a difference between war and peace. You can't fight a war with the courts in control." And the racial aspects of the case, he insisted, were there only because "a particular race was the threatening invader." Another decade later he was even more adamant:

> I would do precisely the same thing today, in any part of the country. I would probably issue the same order were 1 President. We had a situation where we were at war. People were rightly fearful of the Japanese in Los Angeles, many loyal to the United States, many undoubtedly not, having dual citizenship—lots of them.
>
> They all look alike to a person not a Jap. Had they [the Japanese] attacked our shores you'd have a large number fighting with the Japanese troops. And a lot of innocent Japanese-Americans would have been shot in the panic. Under these circumstances I saw nothing wrong in moving them away from the danger area.*[7]

And doubtless Black's role in the saboteur and Korematsu cases largely determined his position in the closing portion of the criminal prosecution of belligerents, thereby winding up the cycle on the same constitutional note with which it opened—the power of the Court over military commissions. At the close, the petitioner was the Japanese General Yamashita seeking civil review of the judgment of the military commission that had tried

---

* It is noteworthy that, three decades after that decision, Mr. Justice Douglas too reaffirmed his position on *Korematsu:*
> Our Navy was sunk at Pearl Harbor, and no one knew where the Japanese fleet was. We were advised on oral argument that if the Japanese landed troops on our West Coast nothing could stop them west of the Rockies. The military judgment was that, to aid in the prospective defense of the West Coast, the enclaves of Americans of Japanese ancestry should be moved inland, lest the invaders by donning civilian clothes would wreak even more serious havoc on our Western ports. The decisions were extreme and went to the verge of wartime power, and they have been severely criticized. It is easy in retrospect to denounce what was done, as there was no attempted Japanese invasion of our country. . . .[8]

him for war crimes and sentenced him to death. Had the proceeding been before almost any civil court, the character of some evidence that had been admitted and the speed with which the defendant had been forced to conduct his defense would have discredited a judgment of guilty on its face. And this was the point on which the Court came asunder. With characteristic directness, Black put the key issue to the Chief Justice. For Stone had been attempting to carry water on both shoulders by proposing that the issue was only that of jurisdiction, but refusing—perhaps unable to bring himself—to say explicitly that beyond this point the defendant was utterly devoid of constitutional protection. Black objected. Portions of Stone's draft opinion, he insisted to the Chief Justice, "place us in the attitude of defending the commission's action rather than saying it is beyond our powers of review. I hope you will see fit to omit [them]."[9]

And, in large measure, the Chief Justice did. Indeed, to read Mr. Justice Rutledge's bitter dissenting opinion, such were the excisions that, had the commission condemned General Yamashita to be burned at the stake, there was nothing in the views of the majority by which the writ of the Supreme Court would prevent it.[10]

Yet the war was not all silences for the Japanese, whether alien or American. There were stirs and sounds, some from Black's pen and in sharp contrast to *Korematsu*. Thus, in *Ex parte Kamato,* Black removed the ancient common-law disability of bringing suit, which alienage in time of war had traditionally carried with it. And again, in *Duncan v. Kahanamoko,* he struck down the institution of martial law and suppression of civilian courts in Hawaii, but not without bitter irony; the very vigor and loftiness of his views underscored the flimsy basis for the treatment of the West Coast Nisei. Remarkably enough, Black made an especial point of noting that in Hawaii "the dangers apprehended by the military were not sufficiently imminent to cause them to require civilians to evacuate the area or even to evacuate any of the buildings necessary to carry on the business of the courts." Indeed even what he intended as a rhetorical question to clinch his judicial argument stood as the very impeachment of the answer he returned in *Korematsu:* "Have the principles and practices developed during the birth and growth of our political institutions been such . . . that loyal civilians in loyal territory should have their daily conduct governed by military orders substituted for criminal law . . . ?"[11]

Witness to Liberty

Yet, *Korematsu* apart, the record of World War II, compared to previous conflicts, was unprecedented in terms of civil liberties. Experience itself was a good teacher. The Espionage Act, which in World War I had been used with suffocating effect, was remarkably tempered in sanction and application, and the totalitarian systems of the national enemies provided an incentive of sorts. In fact, the totalitarian systems of national allies also provided something of an incentive when, notwithstanding some sharp internal dissension, the Supreme Court made the solemn judicial finding that a long-time Communist was "attached to the principles of the Constitution" and therefore immune from denaturalization. The finding came in a bravura opinion of Justice Murphy, Black concurring, which prompted a sarcastic private note to the author from Justice Frankfurter, noting the failure to list Stalin as a spiritual co-author of the Virginia Statute for Religious Freedom. Virtually by momentum, a similar result was obtained in the case of an admitted Bundist.[12]

But the truly astonishing manifestation of a new libertarian strain crossed with the new judicial activism came when the Court actually reversed itself in midwar by downgrading the veneration required to be accorded to the most sacred of national symbols. The traditional doctrine had been affirmed on the eve of conflict in *Minersville School District v. Gobitis,* when the Court upheld the expulsion from public school of children who refused to join the salute to the flag. Only Associate Justice Stone agreed that dogma of Jehovah's Witnesses on idolatry made their case a matter of constitutional right. On the other hand the privately recorded sentiment of then Chief Justice Hughes epitomized general sentiment to the contrary—"I simply cannot believe that the state has not the power to inculcate this."[13]

Yet in a sense the Witnesses, millenarian and apocalyptic, were also as American as apple pie; they undertook to spread their gospel in the streets and door to door with a hard sell that surpassed the most high-pressure efforts of magazine subscription solicitors or brush vendors. And the inevitable retribution came. One was a tax that the city of Opelika, Alabama, laid upon the privilege of selling books and pamphlets door to door and that the Witnesses challenged as an infringement upon their religious freedoms. As in the flag-salute controversy that preceded, they lost the immediate battle when the Supreme Court ruled against them in mid-1942. But they showed signs of winning their own war, when Black, Douglas and Murphy used the case to announce an unprecedented joint recantation of their position in the initial flag-salute proceeding and belatedly associated themselves with Stone's solitary dissent. (Ironically, back in 1926 it was the *Opelika Daily News* that saw the Black-Graves victory as a triumph of personalities "coupled with certain affiliations which proved to be very formidable attachments.")[14]

If a point of inflection is sought both for Black's judicial development and for the application of the *Carolene Products,* a double one may be seen here. One is the interposition of the federal judicial power against state legislative authority. The other is the mode of the exercise—the incorporation of the First Amendment, which by its own terms is applicable only to congressional action, into the constraints of due process that the Fourteenth Amendment lays upon the states.

The consequence, however, had not arrived as yet, for the recantation meant only a five-to-four division of the Court against the Witnesses' rights. Only one more event was required, however, to turn Stone's initial and solitary dissent into ruling case law by the same margin. This was the resignation of Justice James F. Byrnes to return to active political service as a presidential assistant, and the succession in service of Judge Wiley Rutledge from the Circuit Court of Appeals for the District of Columbia. Byrnes's time on the Court had been much too brief to account for any personalized contribution to its work, and there appeared to have been little love lost between him and Black either there or in their earlier years together in the Senate. Yet, former Senators, familiar with the shortfalls of legislative drafting, can combine in some sentiments, and this Black and Byrnes did, when the latter wrote an opinion—regarded by the dissenters and public at large as outrageous—that read union shakedowns out of a federal racketeering act. ("Justice Black and I knew what the Senate really meant.")[15]

But while Black may have lost an ally in matters of inside knowledge, he gained a coadjutor in his burgeoning libertarian views. The immediate consequences of substitution of Wiley Rutledge for Byrnes on the Court showed itself on the day when Rutledge took his seat and the Court ordered rehearing of the Opelika license case; after reargument it reversed itself by a five-to-four, the new appointee casting the critical turnabout. This also virtually guaranteed a reversal of the initial flag-salute case, and on June 14, 1943, in *West Virginia State Board of Education v. Barnette,* the Court did so. Remarkably, the reversal came at the time when men were dying for the flag from the arctic to jungles and on behalf of petitioners who seemed to have a sixth sense for outraging public opinion by their refusals of military service and abusive polemics. Chief Justice Stone allowed his prophetic dissent to be given legal effect in a reversing opinion written by Justice Jackson, who had also been appointed in the interval between the two controversies. Black entered a concurring opinion appraising the compulsory salute as "more likely to defeat than to secure its high purposes" and also as a "handy implement for disguised religious persecution."[16]

The Chief Justice was delighted with Black's companion effort, praising it for "sincerity and good sense" and for stating "in simple and perfectly understandable form good constitutional law as I understand it." Not all the comments, however, were laudatory ones. Up in New York, Charles C. Burlingham, virtual dean of the American bar, wrote an anonymous letter to the *New York Herald Tribune* denouncing, among other things, Black's turnabout ("One would think that in a case involving the

Bill of Rights, a judge would know his own mind in 1940 as well as in 1943") and in private correspondence with Stone went even further in condemnation—"I have a strong aversion to Black, because he sat silent in the Senate and permitted Borah to state that he had never had anything to do with the Ku Klux Klan."[17]

But the day was coming when Mr. Burlingham would himself be the recanter.

Of Race and Color

Justice Frankfurter not only stood his original ground in the flag-salute reversal but submitted a separate dissent, which began: "One who belongs to one of the most vilified and persecuted minorities in history is not likely to be insensible to the freedoms guaranteed by our Constitution." Two of his colleagues, probably Stone and Reed, waited upon him and pleaded for excision of the passage. Frankfurter granted that they had good reason for wanting it out. But he also insisted he had better reasons for leaving it in.[18]

For even though Frankfurter conceded that he had long departed from the faith of his fathers, his sense of Jewishness made for one of the strongest forces in his nature and doubtless constituted a special element in the constitutional federalism so close to his heart. Indeed, as the flag-salute dissent suggested, it was never too far from the surface.

Sometimes he brought it up—"I am the symbol of the Jew, the 'red,' the 'alien,' " he had responded when questioned on his silence in the Court-packing fight. Sometimes it was thrust upon him, as when he had lost the assignment to write the opinion of the Court outlawing the white primary after two arguments on the issue in *Smith v. Allwright*—"I wonder if you have not overlooked some of the ugly factors of our national life which go to the wisdom of having Mr. Justice Frankfurter act as the voice of the Court," Justice Jackson wrote the Chief Justice. And such were the ugly factors that Stone indeed withdrew the opinion and assigned it to the Kentuckian Reed.[19]

In part *Allwright* was the consequence of the turning point in the war and the Court's immersion in the widespread concern for the shape and character of things to come. Moreover, these concerns struck home with increasing force on a tribunal whose gingerly initial use of its *Carolene Products* power was being validated to pleas to use it and to set to rights those deficiencies in the existing political framework that seemed to be beyond the conventional machinery of redress.

And indeed this was the common thread running not only to *Allwright* but to other decisions of the 1943–44 term that came to grips with matters invested with the overwhelming weight of inertia but also ratified by prior judicial decision. But the primary election was archetypical for years before the Supreme Court ruled it beyond federal reach as long as it was held under partisan rather than state auspices. The result was a device of racial subordination in virtually all the Southern states and on its face a situation seemingly beyond political composition. It was also a device that was crumbling with the passage of time and one that a war fought against a racial totalitarianism could only serve to undermine faster.

Yet, it was a tangle. In 1935, in *Grovey v. Townsend,* the Court unanimously held primary participation a matter of partisan privilege rather than of constitutional right. Six years later when in the split decision of *United States v. Classic,* the Court divided in upholding a conviction growing out of Louisiana voting frauds on the grounds that such a primary violated a right protected by the Constitution. Significantly, however, it was the increasingly libertarian trio of Black, Douglas and Murphy who dissented, not on the substantive merits of the case but rather on the vagueness of the statute involved.[20]

When the specific issue of voter participation was presented, however, the Court acted, although it took two arguments, the affronting withdrawal of the opinion from Frankfurter and a bitter dissent from Justice Roberts. Illustrative of the bitter fis-

sion that lay ahead was Roberts' acid response to the suggestion
that the original primary case had been overruled *"sub silentio"*
in the *Classic* decision. For Roberts, author of *Grovey,* protested that this was not "the manly and frank way" to do things
and, looking at the increasingly frequent reversals, likened Supreme Court decisions to "a restricted railroad ticket, good for
this day and train only."[21]

The Modern Corporation

If the decision banning the white primary suggested a judicial
inclination to do what it could to shape the country's postwar
political institutions, an insurance-rate-making case, *United
States v. Southeastern Underwriters Association* indicated a like
thrust with respect to economic ones. Moreover, it was a line of
departure that bore Black's particular stamp. Indeed, a single-
minded view of the most rigorous application of antitrust legislation constituted perhaps the only legal affinity that Black shared
with the irascible old reactionary, Justice James McReynolds,
whose idea of business competition, it was said, was a fight to the
death in a darkened cabin of his native Tennessee.[22]

And Black's strong devotion to the adversary principle, foreshadowed by his stand on NRA, was luminously underscored by
the hard line he took when otherwise favored institutions crossed
the line into essentially commercial constraints on trade. Thus,
his first antitrust opinion, *Fashion Originators Guild v. FTC,*
found a trade boycott of style pirates illegal, notwithstanding the
enormous provocation involved. Again, in 1943 and despite the
obvious concern he had shown for freedom of the press in the
Times-Mirror contempt proceeding, he almost laughed out of
Court the contention of the Associated Press that its First
Amendment freedoms included immunity from the Sherman
Antitrust Act.[23]

Much the same attitude showed through in the interplay of the
antitrust statutes and developments on the labor front. Here the
Senator who defended the sit-down strikers was the precursor of

the judge who refused to find a proscribed restraint of trade in a sit-down strike accompanied by violence that not only restrained but paralyzed business activity. But once union activity crossed the line to combine with commercial interests and subserve essentially business objectives, what he called the "special exemptions" granted unions no longer obtained, and the antitrust laws applied in their full rigor.[24]

There was another special exemption, however, and this was for the insurance business, thanks to an almost century-old precedent of the Court holding that such activity was not "commerce." As a consequence, the business had passed under an elaborate corpus of state regulation, which permitted, among other things, cooperative rate-making. The investigations by the Temporary National Economic Committee in the later thirties, however, suggested that this state of affairs was regressive and unwholesome. Moreover, the continuity of the enclave of insurance stood as an anomalous exception to the view of an expanding commerce power which was the undergirding of most New Deal legislation—the Wagner Act, the securities statutes, and Senator Black's own wage-hour legislation. ("Economically, in trade and commerce, this Nation is one, indivisible and inseparable, and that today, when the mills of New Jersey may depend on purchasers in South Carolina . . . when cotton grown in Alabama may depend upon purchasers in Wisconsin . . . a national problem must be met by national legislation. I have planted my foot upon that political philosophy. . . .")[25]

This soaring view of the national commerce power and the corresponding conclusion of the thrust of the antitrust legislation framed with the same sweep was reinforced by Black's apprehension of what he assertedly called the devious devices of the great corporations and particularly their implications for the postwar world. ("He knows," Secretary Ickes wrote, "unless we can beat back the economic royalists, we may find ourselves with a fascist crisis of our own.")[26]

Hence Black was singularly deaf to pleas that a more rigorous antitrust enforcement would be upsetting to the economy or that the sudden ending of state insurance regulation would be productive of administrative turmoil. Neither was he moved by the fact that a venerable constitutional landmark would be overturned by less than a full bench. For Justices Reed and Roberts had disqualified themselves with a consequence that Chief Justice Stone found particularly upsetting—"Any number of times . . . I would have been willing to be one of five to overrule a decision, but not one of four.")[27]

Black saw things quite the other way: "We should not decline to decide this case . . . Since Congress has made six members of this Court a quorum, it undoubtedly contemplated that four should render judgments . . . Much as I deplore four-to-three decisions, I am not ready to subscribe to a disposition . . . which would thereafter be cited as a precedent to preclude statutory interpretations by a majority of the Court's quorum." Moreover, rephrasing disposed of the question by making it a matter of statutory construction, which a lesser number of judges might handle, rather than the majority of the Court as customarily required for constitutional matters. But beneath the issue of statute *versus* the Constitution lay a view of the judicial power of the United States, and here it was indicative not only of differing perceptions, but of institutional rupture that the New Dealers Jackson and Frankfurter joined Chief Justice Stone in what almost certainly had been the conservative position of the nonparticipating Justice Roberts.[28]

But that only made three, and Black thereby had a majority of one. In a characteristically tough and tight opinion, he disposed of the whole question with the proposition that Congress had intended to use all of its constitutional power with consequences that swept insurance into the antitrust net. The possible dislocations to the industry were dismissed as exaggerated. To the dissenting Justice Jackson, on the other hand, the "reversal of a long-established doctrine which promises so little of advantage and so much of harm" seemed decisive. Chief Justice Stone, also dissenting, was more doctrinal than pragmatic and sought to distinguish between commerce itself and activities that merely affected it. And in private correspondence he epitomized the whole case: "Unfortunately, Brother Black and his associates take a different view . . ."[29]

Here, however, Congress would have the last word on what it meant. And its exercise of corrective jurisdiction would exact a special price.

CHAPTER ELEVEN

The Great Feud

The Old and the New

Civil wars and family fights, it has been said, make for the bitterest of quarrels, and likewise do the disagreements of men who underneath it all are very much alike. So it was with the United States Supreme Court during the judicialization of the New Deal. The newly reconstituted Court found that with the fading of the common enemy of depression, all pretense of ideological unity dissolved under the solvent of power.

The central factors underlying the new internal bitterness were the portentous consequences of the resurgent judicial power and the hothouse atmosphere of the Court itself. To this was added the frustration of carrying on seemingly inconsequential judicial business in a nation at war, the unresolved internal contradictions of the New Deal, and perhaps most important of all, the fierce intellectual pride of self-made and self-educated men.

All of these factors were involved in *United States v. Southeastern Underwriters Association,* which held the fire-insurance business subject to the constraints of the Sherman Antitrust Act despite venerable precedent to the contrary. The positions of

224

Hugo Black and Robert Jackson typified the rival polarities in *Southeastern Underwriters*. Black argued that the Court's role was not to scrutinize the wisdom of the antitrust legislation, but instead to give congressional language the widest possible scope. Jackson argued for a broader judicial role in construing the legislation to avoid "catapult[ing] Congress into immediate and undivided responsibility for supervision of the nation's insurance businesses." In a four-to-three decision, a majority of the Court supported Black, but Black's victory was short-lived. Later, Congress adopted Jackson's dissent and restored the *status quo ante* with the passage of the McCarran-Ferguson Act, which declared the congressional intent to give the states the primary responsibility for regulating the insurance industry. The Court and Justice Black were thus reversed out of hand.[1]

On the touchy business of divining the congressional will, Jackson scored a second victory over Black in the controversy via the Portal-to-Portal Act of 1947. In *Jewell Ridge Coal Corp. v. Local 6167 U.M.W.*, Black had voted with the majority in holding that the time spent by coal miners traveling underground to and from their places of work—from portal to portal—constituted "work" under the Fair Labor Standards Act and was therefore part of the compensable work week. Jackson dissented on the ground that such a construction of the act would traverse many collectively bargained miners' contracts, a result neither authorized nor intended by Congress. At issue in the portal-to-portal controversy was Black's understanding of the Fair Labor Standards Act, which he himself had authored. Subsequently Congress told Black that he had missed the point, while Jackson had understood. The stage and backdrop were thus set for the bitterest internecine controversy in the Court's history.[2]

The Truman Succession

Perhaps the most remarkable facet of this controversy emerged on a spring or early-summer evening in 1946, on the

White House lawn. The exact day cannot be fixed with precision, but it was one of the earliest warm enough to sit outdoors in the evening. At that time President Harry S. Truman observed to Clark M. Clifford, then a member of the White House staff, that while the current presidential term had considerable time to run, the business of succession should begin receiving attention. In this connection, Mr. Truman reminisced about James Madison's service as Thomas Jefferson's Secretary of State in the years preceding the Madison Presidency. This was an episode that might bear profitable examination, Mr. Truman thought, and he asked Clifford to prepare a memorandum on it.[3]

During the same conversation Mr. Truman also mentioned that there was one man—Associate Justice Robert H. Jackson—whose experience and talents seemed to make him presidential timber. Soon after this episode, however, Jackson, who was in Nuremberg serving as the American prosecutor in the war-crimes trials, sent a cablegram denouncing Hugo Black. The message was received far more in sorrow than anger, but one of its consequences was to end once and for all any further discussion of Robert Jackson as a possible presidential successor.

Dissent and Dissension

The bombshell cablegram had had a long fuse, whose sputtering had been apparent for some years. One portent could be found in the new character of the prose appearing in the reports of the Supreme Court. An obvious indication of the divisions in the Court was the growing volume of dissenting opinions—117 in 1940, 160 in 1941, 176 in 1942, and 194 in 1943. The trend continued into the first judicial day of 1944, when fourteen cases produced double that number of separate opinions. Two of the cases produced five opinions apiece, and in only three was the Court of a single mind. The new wordiness prompted *The New York Times* to observe that the custom of publishing all the opinions of a term in three volumes might no longer obtain.

There was a difference in the quality as well as in the quantity of the Court's opinions. The new judicial style was characterized, noted one distressed observer, as an attack not only on the approach but also on the character of the Justices in disagreement. Pundit Arthur Krock said much the same thing, when he suggested that, in the interest of a democracy at war, the dissenting Justices should disagree in silence or at least eschew personalities.

Yet the fault was not all the dissenters'. Part of the wordiness was also due to the development of the counterdissent, a new type of Supreme Court pronouncement. In the counterdissent, the Justice who wrote the opinion was concerned not so much with the traditional role of explaining the judgment of the Court or, if dissenting, with appealing to the brooding spirit of the law and to the intelligence of a future day. Rather, it was all counterattack, a dissent from dissent, so to speak, in which the writer assailed those in disagreement with the majority, using the new fighting word "gratuitous."

Thus in *FPC v. Hope Natural Gas Co.,* decided on January 3, 1944, Justice Douglas swept away almost at a single stroke the elaborate Talmudic rationale by which the courts had long intervened in utility rate-making. In its place he put the reasoning Justice Black had used in his *McCart v. Indianapolis Water Co.* dissent, wherein Black had urged that the federal courts not "interfere" with the exercise of the states' rate-making authority, unless the rates set by the states were "palpably and grossly unreasonable." In *Hope Natural Gas* it was Justice Frankfurter's turn to dissent on the ground that congressional acquiescence to prior regulatory decisions by the Court should sustain those decisions inasmuch as the "final say under the Constitution lies with the judiciary and not with the legislature." It was an unsuccessful plea, but even in victory Black could not let it pass unnoticed. Writing a special concurring opinion, he protested what he called "a wholly gratuitous assertion as to Constitutional law in the dissent of Mr. Justice Frankfurter."[4]

In a second counterdissent filed on the same day as *Hope Natural Gas,* Black criticized Frankfurter's dissent in *Mercoid Corp. v. Mid-Continent Investment Co.* Frankfurter had decried the "gratuitous innuendos" in the majority opinion that would "embarrass" lower courts and litigants alike. Black responded with a scathing attack on Frankfurter's judicial approach.[5]

Turnabout by Mr. Justice Roberts

A few days later this theme recurred yet another time as the Court considered whether a federal bankruptcy court should fix the fees of attorneys representing a bankrupt estate in the state courts of New York. In a concurring opinion Justice Frankfurter admonished the Court "not to go out of [its] way to embarrass consideration of such delicate questions in the working of our federal system whenever in the future they may call for decision by this Court."[6]

But the most gratuitous affront, certainly as Black saw it, was in the dissent of Justice Roberts in *Mahnich v. Southern Steamship Co.* In that opinion, the last of the Nine Old Men delivered his bitter thrust, not at the obscure point of maritime law under consideration, but at the joint dissent of Black, Murphy and Douglas in the year-old decision of *Jones v. Opelika.* In *Opelika* the three dissenting Justices had disagreed with the majority's approval of municipal fines imposed on Jehovah's Witnesses for unlicensed sales of religious pamphlets. The dissenters also announced, apparently almost as an afterthought, that they had had a change of heart in *Minersville School District v. Gobitis,* which more than three years before *Mahnich v. Southern Steamship Co.,* had upheld a local board of education requirement that all pupils, including Jehovah's Witnesses, must salute the United States flag in daily exercises.[7]

Roberts' *Mahnich* dissent forecast the famous analogy he later made in *Smith v. Allwright* between the Court's constitutional decisions and a restricted railroad ticket—"good for this day and train only"—and deplored the frequent reverses of both longstanding and recent precedent. "The evil resulting from overruling earlier considered decisions . . . [is that] the law becomes not a chart to conduct, but a game of chance." Roberts then sarcastically suggested that the Court "might to some extent obviate the predicament in which the lower courts, the bar, and the public find themselves" by making the *Opelika* dissents a model so that henceforth, the Justices could "make public announcements of a change of views . . . to indicate that they will change their votes on the same question when another case comes before the Court." More startling than Roberts' sarcasm was Frankfurter's joining in the dissent.[8]

There were other indications of the irreparable fission in the New Deal Court. About the same time Roberts was delivering his *Mahnich* philippic with Frankfurter's concurrence, Justice Robert Jackson was saying much the same thing to the American Law Institute, albeit with somewhat better humor.

> Unless the assumption is substantially true that cases will be disposed of by application of known principles and previously disclosed courses of reasoning, our common-law process would become the most intolerable kind of *ex post facto* judicial law making. . . . No lawyer today feels such assurance that a pat case will bring him victory or defeat as lawyers once felt.[9]

Roberts' *Mahnich* dissent and Jackson's A.L.I. observations symbolized an emerging conservative opposition to what was increasingly seen as the "Black Bloc," an ultra–New-Dealing judicial quartet supposedly made up of the putative leader and Justices Douglas, Murphy, and Rutledge. An apparent axis of conservative opposition to the bloc was emerging between Frankfurter and Roberts, notwithstanding the latter's acrimonious criticism of the *Opelika* dissents.

For in criticizing the *Opelika* turnabout, Owen Roberts came close to holding a mirror to his own face, as Frankfurter's comment on Roberts' postelection change of position on minimum wages bitingly showed. "Now with the shift by Roberts," Frankfurter had written Roosevelt, "even a blind man ought to see that the Court is in politics and understand how the Constitution is being judicially construed." Indeed, at the time of Black's appointment, Frankfurter had even used Roberts as an unflattering index of the new Justice's qualifications—"from all this talk

about great legal experience one would suppose that Mc-
Reynolds and . . . Roberts were men of wide culture and
juristic detachment when they got on the Supreme Court."[10]

The New Alliance

Yet Frankfurter was scarcely on the bench before he began a
warm *rapprochement* with his former target. The approach of
the war saw him relaying to the White House Roberts' warm
response on the joy of contrasting the urbane and cultivated
President with the squalid leaders of the totalitarian states. After
the war broke out it was Frankfurter who played the key role in
securing the appointment of Roberts as chairman of the Pearl
Harbor investigation commission. Perhaps the true measure of
their new friendship followed his abrupt resignation from the
Court at the end of the 1945 term, when Roberts gave Frankfurter a long memorandum explaining his own earlier change of
heart in *West Coast Hotel Co. v. Parrish,* the landmark minimum-
wage case. The memorandum was published posthumously along
with a comment by Frankfurter, half in tribute, half in apology— ". . . no man ever served on the Supreme Court with
more scrupulous regard for its moral demands than Mr. Justice
Roberts."[11]

Frankfurter thus managed to get on the public record much
the same sentiment whose excision Black had demanded, in an
uncharacteristic display of spite, from the traditional letter of
farewell given to retiring Justices. Chief Justice Stone had drafted
and circulated the proposed letter upon the embittered Roberts'
announcement of his forthcoming resignation. Significantly,
Roberts quit outright instead of retiring, which would have left
him a pensioned member of the Court. As the price of his signature on the letter, Black had proposed the omission of expressions of regret on the ending of daily association with Roberts,
an understandable position in view of reports that Roberts had
ceased to join the Justices' luncheon on conference days and had

stood aloof from the traditional round-robin handshake before the opening of Court.

Black also struck from the original farewell text Stone's assertion that Roberts had made "fidelity to principle" a guide to his decisions, and then Black sent the expurgated version on to second senior, Stanley Reed, with the explanation that the Chief Justice had had him sign it first to expedite circulation. By that time, however, Felix Frankfurter had learned the whole story and entered the lists with the demand that the unaltered original also make the rounds for consideration. The harried Chief Justice complied, only to have Black withdraw his endorsement from even the truncated version, making it clear that no farewell message whatever would bear his signature. Robert Jackson then joined the battle observing that Stone's first draft was none too cordial and that after the Black deletions, "silence would be charitable."[12]

The upshot of the affair was that Roberts received no letter at all, and the quarreling New Deal Court divided as bitterly on the issue of complimentary phraseology as it ever did on a question of substantive law. Douglas backed Black's position, and Murphy and Rutledge were willing to sign either draft. Frankfurter and Jackson dug in to fight to the end for the original version.

Awards and Testimonials

Something of a similar battle line, with positions reversed, had been drawn just a few months earlier in the context of another type of testimonial. On April 3, 1945, Black received the Thomas Jefferson Award of the Southern Conference for Human Welfare, as the Southerner who had made the greatest contribution to the nation the preceding year. Nine hundred guests and a head table of twenty-four gathered for the occasion at Washington's new Statler Hotel. Senator Barkley presided as toastmaster, and Federal Loan Administrator Fred Vinson, who was the principal speaker, hailed the guest of honor as "a witness and a warrior for the democracy of the common man."[13] Eight other speakers continued in the same vein, including Mrs. Franklin D. Roosevelt, who read a letter from the President so soon to die.

The Conference had come a long way since the Police Commissioner of Birmingham, Alabama, Theophilus Eugene "Bull" Connor had imposed the local segregation ordinance on its gathering seven years earlier. The integrated seating arrangements of 1945 did not go unprotested, for Senator Theodore Bilbo duly raised his voice against them. But his comment did not so much as ruffle the distinguished roster, which included, among many others, Justices Reed, Douglas, Murphy, and Rutledge; conspicuously absent was the remainder of the Court. Justice Roberts stayed away, and Chief Justice Stone had indicated his opinion of such affairs some years before by declining a New England testimonial in his honor when he became Chief Justice —"a judge can never do more than his duty and he ought not to be publicly praised because he has not done less." Justice Jackson's view of the affair was evident from his comments on a similar affair a year earlier, when the Washington Chapter of the National Lawyers' Guild had paid a special tribute to Black. On that occasion, Senator Barkley also served as toastmaster, and two of the testimonial speakers argued cases before the Court shortly thereafter. Jackson had then insisted that had any corporation lawyer given a similar performance before the Nine Old Men "every liberal in the country would have screamed his head off."[14]

It was Felix Frankfurter, however, who gave the idea of the testimonials the most hostile reception. Frankfurter's attitude can be inferred, not from anything he wrote or said, but rather from a passage in a letter from an old friend that he filed and kept. The friend felt secure enough in defamatory assertion to commend the Justice for staying away. "The perfume of public praise from people who ought to know better cannot eliminate the odor of the skunk. Official utterances may fool the public, but there is still no substitute for character."[15]

Portal to Portal

The five-to-four decision of the Supreme Court on the propriety of attending the Black testimonial—a vote of commendation that Black's secure and well-adjusted personality hardly needed ("I hate publicity, and I'm not sure I'd want it even after I'm dead") was accompanied by a like division of the Court on an important judicial matter. The division surfaced concurrently, and its bitterness stood out in a term that was marked throughout by endemic and abrasive division.[16]

An observer present in the Court's conference room during this ongoing confrontation would have seen not only conflict on a perplexing issue of law, but also conflict among personalities. The latter confrontation encompassed not only pride and position, but also profound issues of postwar transition and industrial relations.

In the sharpest focus it concerned the failure of the Fair Labor Standards Act, alias the Black-Connery Law, to deal explicitly with compensation for work-preparatory activity undertaken on an employer's premises for his benefit. Also involved was the question of retroactivity, for an employer decided to pay or not to pay for such effort at his peril. Failure to make payment, if and when due, meant a subsequent settlement at a penalty rate, perhaps with an attorney's fee in addition. No one knew what the total potential employer liability was, but all agreed that nationwide it might run to billions. Moreover, because of tax refunds and cost-plus contracts, the government stood to underwrite a portion of it.

A. MUSCODA LOCAL 123

The basic issues had come before the Court a full year before the Black testimonial dinner in the case of *Tennessee Coal, Iron & Railroad Co. v. Muscoda Local 123*. The case came extremely close to home for Black. The statute had been Black's last hurrah as a Senator. The petitioner was known as T.C.I. in Black's home town of Birmingham, and he must have referred to it that way himself a thousand times. In addition, Local 123 was typical of the trade unions that had provided the bread and butter of Black's law practice—damage suits, workmen's compensation and general labor-union controversy. Crampton Harris, the union's counsel in *Muscoda,* had been Black's sometime law partner in the kaleidoscopic sequence of professional associations that marked his law practice in the pre-Senate years.[17]

A year older than Black, but four years his junior at the Alabama bar, Harris' prelegal and professional education at Emory and the Harvard Law School had extended the time of his admission to the bar beyond that of most of his contemporaries in Birmingham. His career had crossed Black's at some remarkably sensitive points. Harris too had been a Ku Klux Klansman. (Indeed he had been Cyclops of Black's Lee Klavern and had probably recruited Black for the hooded brotherhood.) He had served as defense counsel with Black in the Father Coyle murder trial. In the Heflin controversy, Harris' position was remarkably similar to Black's. And along with Black, Harris was subsequently denounced as a betrayer by Heflin before the United States Senate. Finally, Harris had been brought up from Birmingham to serve as special counsel to Black's Senate investigating committee when the committee had been haled into court by William Randolph Hearst.[18]

Nine years later no one seemed to see anything untoward in Harris' representing the Muscoda local, or in Black's sitting on the case. Certainly there was nothing new about a Supreme Court Justice's hearing a case presented by a onetime law partner or other professional associate; some of the great names of the Court—Story, Holmes, Brandeis and Cardozo among them—had sat under such circumstances. So had Chief Justice Stone, in a gaffe that contributed to the powder train ahead.

Indeed the only noteworthy aspect of *Muscoda* was a hint in Roberts' dissent of the possible applicability of the decision to the then current effort of the United Mine Workers to impose blanket portal-to-portal compensation in coal mining. Otherwise, disagreement turned on the irenic suggestion by Jackson and Frankfurter that the miners' judgment be affirmed on the wholly procedural ground that the sufficiency of the evidence found by two lower courts as to "hours worked" would not be reexamined. Chief Justice Stone stood fast on the general exclusion of travel time from the overtime calculus, so the assignment of the majority opinion passed to Black. He gave it to Justice Murphy, who responded in a soaring view of statutory coverage.

B. JEWELL RIDGE

A year later, a full-blown coal-mining portal-to-portal claim did come before the Court in *Jewell Ridge Coal Corp. v. Local 6167 U.M.W.* It came against a backdrop of nationwide coal strikes, government takeovers, and War Labor Board negotiations, which had been held in abeyance pending decision of the case itself. The difficulty of the case was suggested by the change of positions by the cautious and fair-minded Stanley Reed, who, having initially opted for the exclusionary view of preparatory work, went over to the union side and thereby swung the outcome on a Court that was otherwise divided four to four on the merits. Black once more controlled the writing of the opinion of the Court and it was assigned to Justice Murphy. Jackson, who prior to the Reed turnabout had been scheduled for the role of a majority spokesman, was reduced to that of a dissenter.

Jackson's statement of position, which included a quotation from the *Congressional Record* citing words of Senator Black as authority, contrary to the majority view of the Black-Connery Act, was a product of remarkable ferocity and fire. Predictably enough, Black was outraged when the dissent was circulated. But down it went and with it the pugnacious assertion of the Justice defending on the basis of total context the words he had uttered as a Senator: "The very page from which the dissent quotes negatives the inference. . . . If the dissent does go down as now printed, it will not be a fair representation of the true facts."[19] The substance of the comment was duly incorporated in the majority opinion, where it scarcely neutralized the sting of Jackson's dissent.

The Hand of the Past

As bad as this was, the worst was yet to come, and the unsteady hand of Chief Justice Stone was to contribute its part to the unfolding crisis. Remarkably enough this too involved the Public Utility Holding Company Act of 1935, another New Deal statute in which Senator Black had played a major role. The issue of judicial disqualification was soon to be a flash point thanks to Crampton Harris, but early in the holding-company case the difficulty lay in mustering the statutory quorum of six Justices on a bench that included three former Attorneys General, a onetime Solicitor General, and the former chairman of the Securities and Exchange Commission. Thus, when the appeal from the "death sentence" of the Holding Company Act was carried to the Supreme Court in 1943 by Stone's old law firm, the Chief Justice announced his disqualification on the unspoken assumption that a quorum would be still available to the litigants. But when the situation developed to the contrary, the Chief Justice began to consider reversing his position and requalifying himself.

A further complication developed when additional cases challenging the Holding Company Act appeared on the Court's docket. Justice Roberts raised this problem in conference, suggesting that were the Chief Justice disqualified in one such case, he ought to be disqualified in all. Roberts further announced his intention of circulating a memorandum on the point. The angered Stone in turn directed his clerk to prepare a countermemorandum listing the cases in which Roberts had sat despite the involvement of former clients or partners. (Indeed it was remarkable that the aborted farewell letter got as far as it did.) At that stage in the controversy, Justice Rutledge aptly summed up the whole situation in the following words:

I think it is outrageous for anyone to suggest that there is any valid reason . . . why you should not sit. . . . It is even more outrageous to suggest writing to discuss your action . . . the whole business was purely one of taste, not of law or morals.[20]

Accordingly, on May 8, 1945, Justice Stone announced his requalification in holding-company cases. Stone immediately reaped a bitter harvest for his switch, when the defeated employer in *Jewell Ridge* filed an extraordinary petition for rehearing in the case on the grounds that Black was guilty of a double conflict of interest. The first allegedly lay in his professional association with Crampton Harris, both as a law partner in Birmingham and as the chairman of the Senate committee for which Harris had served as counsel. The second purportedly stemmed from Black's sponsorship of the controversial Fair Labor Standards Act. The petition for rehearing noted, perhaps prompted by Jackson's earlier dissent, that Black had undertaken to construe and interpret as a judge statements he had made as a Senator. And in a more telling point, the petition questioned whether one "so intimately situated in relation to the origin and development of the legislation, and of necessity influenced by many personal recollections, impressions, and predilections *dehors* the record, is in position to judge with appropriate detachment the recorded history, in which he himself was one of the actors."[21]

This suggestion of preexisting intellectual commitment did raise an extremely troublesome point well beyond those crude and simplistic conflicts afforded by former clients and partners. Indeed, it was the most exquisite of ironies that Justice Roberts should be so concerned over Harlan Stone's long past association with his old firm's public-utility clients and oblivious to Justice Black's far more recent statement that he would rather "regulate a rattlesnake than a holding company." Of like stripe was Black's sponsorship of the Wage and Hour Act, for, as a correspondent of Justice Brandeis had asked when Black went on the Court, "How can he be impartial? If necessary in the Supreme Court to vote on his *own* Bill? The Black-Connery Bill."[22]

Yet much the same consideration applied to Justice Murphy, who had helped Black write the minimum-wage plank for the Democratic platform of 1936, and no one suggested that Murphy disqualify himself. In a larger context, the dispute attending the *Jewell Ridge* motion was especially applicable to Justice Frankfurter, who not only had associations with certain frequent litigants before the Court, but occasionally made a point of drawing attention to it.

Indeed, in Black's case, if anything, there may well have operated beneath the threshold of consciousness what Jerome Frank called the most insidious temptation besetting the fair-minded judge—the disposition to lean over backward to be fair. Hence, while one can agree with Sir Edward Coke's canon that no one should be a judge in his own case, that general proposition is not helpful in resolving specific cases. So it was, as Justice Rutledge suggested, that the solution to the conflict-of-interest problem was not to be found in any self-enforcing rule, but only in a judge's judging himself. Historically, it had been the practice on the Court that the judge himself, not his colleagues, would determine whether he should sit on a given case.[23]

When the *Jewell Ridge* motion came up in a stormy conference of June 9, 1945, Black, not unreasonably, thought that precedent should guide the disposition of the Court and be applied as one of those obvious, unspoken rules. Chief Justice Stone, however, proposed that the denial of the motion—which all anticipated—be accompanied by a statement to the effect that the Court as a body never considered questions of disqualification but left the question to the individual Justice. But the mere mention of the subject in the conference carried implications that precipitated a spirited exchange of views, and discussion was postponed for a week, in the hope that tempers would cool. Oblivious to what Rutledge had called "outrageous" in his own case, Stone attempted a neutral disclaimer via an anonymous *per curiam* opinion that would have denied the petition with the comment that "the Court is without authority and does not undertake to pass upon the propriety of the participation, by its members, in the decision of cases brought . . . for review."

But, as in the case of the Roberts letter, he had badly mistaken his man in thinking that Black would go along. "If the *per curiam* goes down in this case . . ." Black tartly responded, "please put the names of the Justices who agree to it, and leave mine out."[24]

Almost incredibly, the Chief Justice made one more effort to clear the hurdle. He proposed a brief statement to the effect that the four Justices in the *Jewell Ridge* minority would not pass upon the propriety of the participation by any other Justice. Some of the Justices were willing to sign, but predictably, Black was adamant and (in Jackson's subsequent words) insisted that any discussion of the subject at all "would mean a declaration of war." The aging Stone collapsed before the threat; Jackson noted later that "at his age he did not want to be in the war." But Jackson was not disposed to give in so easily, noting that "I would not stand for any more of Black's bullying and that, whatever I would otherwise do, I would now have to write my opinion to keep my self-respect in the face of his threat." If being a razor-tongued, forceful opponent meant being a bully, Jackson could be quite a bully himself. In *Jewell Ridge* he made good his threat and wrote his opinion. The strain was telling, and the long-simmering antipathy between Jackson and Black was being transformed—perhaps rationalized—as a debate over concern for the public image of the Court. ("Since the announcement of the mere denial of this petition might be interpreted to rest on any one of several grounds, I consider it appropriate to disclose the limited grounds on which I concur.")[25]

Remarkably, Frankfurter joined in Jackson's *Jewell Ridge* opinion, although he was sufficiently concerned about it to explain his action to Black in a long "Dear Hugo" memorandum, which attempted to explain his position, apparently as much for himself as for Black.

> It happens to be one of my deepest convictions that the world's difficulties are due to no one cause more than to the failure of men to act on that which they believe to be true. I had no share in creating the situation whereby Bob

felt it his duty to make clear the issue of disqualification. But since he had done so, I could withhold joining him only by suppressing my belief in the truth. I do not propose to do that—and that is the sole reason why I join him.[26]

On Monday, June 18, the seething Jackson departed to serve as the American prosecutor of the Nazi war criminals at Nuremberg.

A Matter of Handshakes

Jackson did not rejoin the Court as a full-time member until the autumn of 1946, and on his return he found both a new chief and a new associate waiting for him. The new superior was Chief Justice Fred Vinson, the speaker at the Justice Black testimonial dinner that Jackson had declined to attend. Vinson had gone on to become director of the Office of War Mobilization and from there to the post of Secretary of the Treasury, where he became the strong man of the Truman cabinet. The stature and experience he had gained in the administrative posts as well as his long years in Congress and on the federal appellate bench had made him, in the opinion of many, the logical successor to Chief Justice Harlan Stone, who died in office on April 22, 1946.

The new Associate Justice was Harold H. Burton of Ohio, a Republican and long-time Senate friend of President Truman. Of course, Burton's friendship with the President was partly responsible for his appointment to the Supreme Court, but ironically, his Republican party affiliation was probably equally important, since it supported Mr. Truman's feeling that the institutional status of the Court demanded a bipartisan base. Burton's appointment to succeed Owen Roberts upon the latter's resignation in June of 1945 would have tended to balance the heavily Democratic Court.

Justice Burton kept a diary, and sometimes he kept it better than he knew, for on October 10 of the following year he chron-

icled an incident that touched on the very justification for his
own appointment—the extrapartisan selection of members of the
Court—and a rash of other factors.

> I noticed this morning when we came to conference—
> where each Justice greets the other—*Justice Jackson* was
> sitting beside me . . . when Justice Black came in. Jus-
> tice Black shook hands with him immediately—and
> Justice Jackson said, "Good morning, Hugo." Also during
> the conference today, Justices Jackson and Black joined
> in a brief discussion—all in the best of quiet manners. I
> mention this because of the popular idea . . . that they
> could not speak to each other.[27]

But the popular idea was not too far off the mark as Burton's
next sentence showed: "These were the first instances of their
speaking to each other that I have seen this fall."[28]

Had Burton been on the Court earlier, he would have noted
that the handshake he observed was the first such instance of civil
behavior between the antagonists since the stormy conference of
early June.

Jackson's departure for Nuremberg had stirred strong feelings
both on and off the Court. He had left behind an irate Black as
well as a number of other nettled people. Among them was Chief
Justice Stone. Stone detested extrajudicial assignments (he had
testily declined President Truman's recent invitation to head a
committee on traffic safety), and found Jackson's tenure at
Nuremberg, which he called a "high-grade lynching party," particularly unworthy of a member of the Supreme Court. Not only
were important cases carried over with four-to-four votes, but
the institutional arrangements of the Court suffered. "There has
been no group picture of the Court since I am on it," wrote the
newly appointed Justice Burton, "because Justice Jackson has
always been absent." Washington columnist Doris Fleeson noted
another element of discord. "Justice Black's temper has not been
sweetened this session by the fact that while Mr. Jackson is war-
criming, he has had to write twenty-six opinions which is five
more than runner-up Justice Douglas with twenty-one."[29]

Yet one man in Washington in early 1946—President Harry Truman—obviously did not regard Jackson's absence with disfavor. In office barely a week after Black's Jefferson Award testimonial dinner, the new President wasted no time in requesting Jackson's services as American prosecutor in the forthcoming trials at Nuremberg. It was not the first time Truman had come to Jackson with a request. When organizing the Senate investigating staff for the War Department contract investigation, which was to vault him from back-bench obscurity to national prominence, Senator Truman had sought the assistance of Jackson, who was then Attorney General, to find a committee counsel and later publicly recorded his appreciation for Jackson's help in doing so.

But on a larger scale, the President no doubt saw the prompt acceptance and execution of the nettlesome Nuremberg assignment as an example of Jackson at his best—intelligent, articulate, self-assured, decisive—and no doubt this impression underlay Truman's estimate of Jackson as presidential timber. Perhaps it was an unconscious preemption of Jackson for the presidential succession that accounted for Truman's seeming indifference to repeated recommendations that Jackson be appointed to fill the seat of Chief Justice left vacant by the sudden death of Harlan Stone. There were inconsistent accounts of the executive conferences concerning the selection of a new Chief Justice. Did former Chief Justice Hughes, for example, recommend Jackson or Vinson to President Truman for the job? Hughes's official biographer, Merlo Pusey, wrote that Hughes had recommended Jackson, an account that was approved by Hughes himself. The President, however, told Pusey in a letter that Hughes had recommended Vinson. Presidential Secretary Short did little to clear up the matter with another letter to Pusey in 1952: "If this conflicts with the understanding of other people like yourself, it still stands as the President's version of a two-man conversation on which apparently no notes were made by either one."[30]

The true story may never be known, but a great many people were confident that the succession would fall to Jackson, and

Justice Burton duly noted the following in his diary: "The probabilities of Chief Justice seem to be (1) Jackson, (2) Douglas, (3) Reed."[31]

The Elusive Office

Burton's assessment was reasonable, since Jackson had earlier missed appointment as Chief Justice because of a presidential desire for a bipartisan Court—the very reason Burton *was* appointed. This reason no longer obtained. "One can say," wrote Justice Frankfurter, "that F.D.R.'s choice for the succession to Hughes was Jackson. . . . He did not appoint him . . . in the summer of 1941 [because] the likelihood of war and the increasing partisan hostility to the President . . . complicated the choice of Chief justice. . . ." In fact, when Frankfurter advised the President to this effect, Jackson supposedly said, "he could well understand it," and the episode strengthened the ties of intimacy and affection between Jackson and Frankfurter.[32]

In his memorandum, Frankfurter went further and insisted that all thought about Jackson as Chief Justice was erased with Harlan Stone's appointment. In addition, Frankfurter said, "no evidence [would] be adduced and no thought be justified that he had any reason to believe that if such a vacancy did occur he would be named to it." Evidence subsequently came to light, however, indicating that Jackson believed just that. The record indicates that Jackson had indeed sought and obtained Roosevelt's assurances of consideration should the office of Chief Justice become available.[33]

These assurances, according to the author of a magazine article, were obtained through an intermediary, but by his own admission Jackson obtained them face to face. Nonetheless, the fragile hearsay nature of the available testimony drew a virtually impenetrable veil around the events that followed Stone's death in 1946. The narrative sequence, such as it was, began with a Washington columnist's news story of May 16, 1946. The story was essentially in two parts. One purported to be an "inside"

account of the stormy conference of June 9 of the preceding
year, in which Black reacted to Jackson's insistence on a dis-
clamatory statement on the denial of the *Jewell Ridge* rehearing
petition "with fiery scorn to what he regarded as an open and
gratuitous insult, a slur upon his personal and judicial honor."
As the Roberts retirement-letter incident suggested, it was not in
Black's nature to turn the other cheek. This lent a certain credence to the other part of Miss Fleeson's story, which purported
to quote the President directly. "Black says he will resign if I
make Jackson Chief Justice and tell the reasons why. Jackson
says the same about Black."[34]

Jackson subsequently insisted that the article was genuine in
the sense that one of the members of the Court had disclosed
what had transpired on June 9, 1945. "Nobody could have told
Doris Fleeson what she wrote unless it was somebody who was
present at the conference table," said Jackson in an interview.
Jackson felt an ongoing concern with a relatively new apparatus
in the media of politics, the Washington "inside" columnist. In
part, the rise of this new instrumentality was a function of new
experiments in communication; it was also a necessary for guid-
ing the behavior of the growing welfare state. Its judicial impact
was, however, less desirable.[35]

The concern of the Court with this new journalism began
early during the pendency of the *Southeastern Underwriters*
decision, when Drew Pearson (who a decade before had coined
the term "Nine Old Men") used his radio broadcast to undertake
a judicial forecast: "Prediction No. 1—*The Supreme Court*—
will hand down a split decision in favor of the Government and
against the insurance companies. . . ." Pearson was right and
Jackson believed that Pearson's information had come directly
from the Court. And again with the Hope Natural Gas case, the
division of the Court that had involved such irate accusations of
gratuitous law and biting counterdissents was exacerbated by
Pearson's accurate disclosure of Justice Roberts' indecision.
"Roberts was disturbed about the fact that he wasn't able to
make up his mind, but more disturbed about the fact that our
decisions were put on the radio Sunday instead of Monday."[36]

But the climax came with the succession controversy and with it the manifest conclusion that the Washington columnists—not unlike Black's transformation of the congressional hearing—were influencing events rather than just reporting them. The machinations of those columnists has been variously—and irreconcilably—described. Some described it as inflicting on Jackson that especial hatred that the *ultra* New Dealers bore toward the conservative ones. Others found an effort to win the presiding seat for Black, and the very vehemence of denials gave the suggestion a certain plausibility. Still others saw it as the opposite side of the same coin via a vengeful veto of Jackson's advancement. Here the mere hint of future judicial trouble was a powerful influence for the immediate disqualification of one of the antagonists.

Any attempt to associate Black with the effort, however seen, encountered the same impenetrable and commentless wall the Justice had displayed since the Klan controversy, and he flatly asserted, "I haven't made a statement of any kind to the press since coming up here. I don't expect to make any now." But in a roundabout way he did make a comment to a former law clerk after the publisher of the *Macon Telegraph* had sent him an issue of that paper containing an editorial entitled "Jackson is an Unmitigated Ass," accompanied by an article by John Temple Graves on the same subject. Here Black's terse comment was "I have nothing but sympathy for John Temple." This letter came after Jackson had publicly accused Black of possibly preventing his own appointment as Chief Justice. At second hand, irreconcilable assertions had been made on the question within the pages of the same publication—that on one hand Black had done nothing whatever to oppose Jackson and on the other hand that the Black position was expressed "through agents," supposedly Senator Lister Hill at the White House and Drew Pearson in the press.[37]

Four days after President Truman had nominated Secretary of the Treasury Vinson to the vacant Chief Justiceship and less than one day and one year after the stormy *Jewell Ridge* conference, Jackson fired off a fifteen-hundred-word cable from Nuremberg to the House and Senate Judiciary Committees, the latter of which was considering the appointment of Vinson. The addressee members of Congress must have been the most nonplussed persons in Washington, for the cable approved the Vinson appointment, and then undertook to explain the details of the *Jewell Ridge* conference. The cable detailed the bitter exchange of views, including Black's asserted declaration of war, and closed with, if not a counterdeclaration of his own, at least an ultimatum on former partners pleading before the Court: ". . . I wanted that practice stopped. If it is ever repeated while I am on the bench I will make my *Jewell Ridge* opinion look like a letter for recommendation by comparison."[38]

The End of the Affair

There were any number of consequences. On June 15, a somber President held a press conference and noted that Justice Jackson had wired him an advance copy of the charge, notwithstanding his own plea to defer further statement, and had shortly thereafter sent the cable to the congressional committees. He also answered a question as to whether Black had threatened to resign in the event of Jackson's appointment. "President Truman seemed to choose the words for his answer with care," one reporter noted. "He said firmly that he had never discussed the appointment . . . with any member of the Supreme Court. This answer did not seem to preclude the possibility that . . . a resignation threat . . . might have reached the White House in a roundabout way." More importantly, the President neither then nor at any time thereafter mentioned the possibility of Jackson's succession to the presidential office.[39]

What really prompted Jackson to write that damning cable? Years later a muckraking book, *The Truman Merry-Go-Round,* hinted that Frankfurter had served as Jackson's surrogate at home all the while keeping the absent Justice simmering abroad with tales of Black's maneuvers. The book infuriated Frankfurter who fumed, "I'm greatly tempted to sue both the publishers and the authors for libel." Jackson's behavior at Nuremberg was somewhat mystifying. His attempted cross-examination of Hermann Goering, for example, was seen by many as a disaster. In a widely publicized press conference, he passed out copies of his cables and, without any interchange with the nonplussed reporters, abruptly departed on a Denmark vacation. A few days later he wrote Frankfurter some sentiments that offer some revealing insights into his baleful view of Black.

> Black is now rid of the Chief whose reputation as a liberal made his opposition particularly effective and irritating. Black, as you and I know, has driven Roberts off the bench and pursued him even after his retirement. Now if he can have it understood that he has veto over the promotion of any Associate, he would have things about where he wants them.[40]

Other comments varied. On the Court, Justice Rutledge offered a sad but tolerant, "Too bad, but it's just like Bob. I'm not surprised." On the other hand, Frankfurter vigorously insisted that the Jackson explosion was not the result of disappointed ambition but rather "the boiling over of a disturbed state of mind regarding conduct over the years carried on under the protective privacy of the Supreme Court." Beyond the confines of government, Jackson caused a ten-day sensation with virtually every paper in the country taking one side or the other, and some condemning both. There were other and less condemnatory judgments of which the most tolerant was that of Arthur Schlesinger, Jr., who saw Jackson's outburst as

> the act of a weary and sorely beset man, committed to a harassing task in a remote land, tormented by the certainty that the chief justiceship had now passed forever out of his reach. Only someone who has lived the unreal life of an army of occupation can understand the violence of his response to the fragmentary reports of Washington intrigue; he reacted as a G.I. would to rumors of his wife's infidelity.[41]

Notwithstanding the sound and the fury, nothing came of the explosion, unless one counts the dismissal of Jackson by President Truman as a possible successor in office (although even had Jackson defeated Dwight Eisenhower in the 1952 election, he would have died before his term was half over). There were sequels, however; Jackson, according to Arthur Krock, went to his grave convinced that Black had maneuvered him out of the Chief Justiceship, and years later showed no disposition to forget or forgive the *Jewell Ridge* confrontation. He continued to insist that *Jewell Ridge* had been hustled through the high court "to help [John L.] Lewis win the strike, which meant nothing but money for [Crampton] Harris."[42]

Black came off the best of all, particularly when it is remembered that even had he disqualified himself in *Jewell Ridge,* the same result would have obtained as a result of an automatic affirmation of the lower court decision in view of the otherwise equal division of the Supreme Court. He soothed Frankfurter's expostulations of innocence over the *Truman Merry-Go-Round* assertions with a quotation from Omar Khayyam and the hope for "a good long talk" in the near future. He later published portions of their exchange in a posthumous tribute to Frankfurter in the *Harvard Law Review.* Even Jackson received a laurel from him—in his famous telecast of 1968, when asked to name the best lawyers he had ever seen, following John W. Davis, Black responded, "Bob Jackson. . . . He was always magnificent." He was even more generous as years later, a one-time law clerk explained that "as I recall, Mr. Justice Jackson (while at Nuremberg) had erroneously and publicly accused the Judge [Justice Black] of having opposed and possibly prevented Jackson's appointment as Chief Justice, the Judge once told me that another Justice, whom he did not name, had played that role and that Jackson was simply misinformed."[43]

History, however, demands not only a generous but a hanging judge, and Arthur Schlesinger, Jr., passed the sentence. Agreeing with Black as to Jackson's talent, Schlesinger added the mordant commentary that the great advocate "never presented a case so badly as he did his own against Black from Nuremberg."[44]

POSTSCRIPTUM

What made the Great Feud so bitter? There were many reasons, not the least of which was its character as the death throes of the New Deal.

There had been three New Deals, Black heavily involved in each. The first began with the Hundred Days Congress and ended with the aborting decisions of the Supreme Court's 1935 term. The second, rooted in the Seventy-fourth Congress, had as its landmarks the Public Utility Holding Company Act, Black's Fair Labor Standards Act, and other legislative acts aimed at a fundamental restructuring of American society rather than the essentially analgesic reform of the prototype predecessor.

Finally, there was the third New Deal, which has still to get its chronicler. Its matrix well may be the inner-circle Temporary National Economic Committee of 1938, whose concern with the essentially unregulated insurance industry sparked (under Thurman Arnold's antitrust leadership) the *Southeastern Underwriters* case. And just as the dogged Supreme Court dissents ultimately produced the reversing congressional statute, so did the counterpart dissents in the minimum-wage cases give rise to the aborting legislative action that ended once for all the use of the inflation-eviscerated Wage-Hour Act as a massive transfer of wealth to armor the American economy against the dreaded postwar depression.

As did the first, so did the third New Deal expire in the Supreme Court; but, in an ironic sequence, the stone that the builders rejected was about to become the cornerstone in the attempted construction of the egalitarian commonwealth at which all three New Deals had aimed.

CHAPTER TWELVE

The Great Seminar

Socratics, Statutes and Judges

Notwithstanding its distressingly personalized nature, the *Jewell Ridge* dispute had a larger context, wherein it was but a single pass at arms between Black and Frankfurter in what had already been an extended series. The series was to go on for a long time. The fact that in this case Jackson served as Frankfurter's surrogate was also typical, for the clash went forward, as often as not, through allies and associates. Yet, such were the complex differences of values, background and temperament that separated the antagonists that the alliances frequently changed, the issues shifted, and the nuclear center of controversy itself became blurred and indistinct. One line of cleavage, however, remained continuing and critical in the radical difference of perception that Black and Frankfurter separately brought to bear on the law and, more importantly, the process by which the law was applied. In this plane of encounter, *Jewell Ridge* fell into line as one more episode in the sequence that began with the Chicago dairy drivers injunction, the Harry Bridges and *Los*

Angeles Times contempt citations, and the unfolding flag-salute controversy. In this sequence Black and Frankfurter simply marched to different drummers, and there was no reconciling the difference of volume and measure.

And on top of this came a complicating interaction of personality. That Black and Frankfurter liked each other most of the time was evident enough, although both worked a little too hard and too obviously at the manifestation of friendship; however, the cross-chemistry of their relationship was a far more complex and subtle thing than any mere rapport of personal congeniality. Indeed, it would not become apparent until Frankfurter left the bench how professorial his influence on Black really had been. But this was not professorial in the sense of magistral, much less tutorial, but rather in the Socratic mode in which Frankfurter maintained that the question was more important than the answer. And Frankfurter did indeed ask the important questions, putting Black to the test and forcing him to positions. Their entire relationship could well be forecast by the presumptuous memorandum that Professor Frankfurter sent down from the Harvard Law School on the art of judging to the newly appointed Mr. Justice Black and the warm greetings that, a short time later, Black returned to the newly appointed Justice Frankfurter—"You know, of course, how happy I am that you are soon to sit by me on the bench."[1]

Or their exchanges might almost be so characterized, for, if Frankfurter remained the professor on the bench, Hugo Black continued to show from time to time the tactical skill that he had acquired in Alabama politics and in the United States Senate. Two diverse incidents in 1945 illustrated the technique. Writing in the experimental *PM* in early April, Irving Brant raised the question of Black's attack on the constitutionality of the corporate personality: "Well, he sometimes tells a story about a Senator who said that, when he wanted to accomplish something, he introduced two bills, the one he wanted passed, and the other that made the first one seem conservative." The other came in mid-October in a note recorded by Justice Frankfurter:

After going on the bench at 12 o'clock Frank Murphy
said to me that that talk of Black's was "the most revolutionary and destructive speech" that has probably ever
been made in the history of the Supreme Court. He
seemed terribly disturbed by it and said again and again
it was terrible. I then wrote him a note saying I quite
agreed . . . but wondered why he did not say at the
Conference what he had just told me and why he left it
for me always to take on Black when he takes such outrageous positions.

There was, of course, no question about the fact that Black was a
formidable adversary, although perhaps Justice Jackson, understandably enough, overstated the case when he observed that
"you can't just disagree with him . . . Reed is said to be easily
influenced and Black terrorizes Reed whenever he can." And
perhaps so was Frankfurter when he accused Murphy of being
"mesmerized" by Black.[2]

Frankfurter, however, was fully capable of giving every bit as
good as he got, and perhaps the only mistake he made in the
professorial role came in the self-conscious and self-defeating
efforts to abandon it. Here his clumsy and patronizing reference
to a "high-falutin" observation of Holmes, which he quoted in
his "art of judging" memorandum, was paralleled some six years
later in another communication to Black, which started off by
stating his own credentials with respect to the subject under consideration ("For nearly twenty years . . . I was at work on what
was to be as comprehensive and scholarly a book on the Fourteenth Amendment as I could make it") and closed by asking
"most humbly" for the materials that had led Black to a contrary
view.[3]

Yet the note also carried a passage that suggested the vast gulf
that lay between writer and recipient and the improbability that
Black could have responded with anything that might serve as a
bridge. In an anguished resurrection of *Swift v. Tyson* and without perhaps realizing the implication of his words or even of his
capitalization, Frankfurter asserted that "Hitler becomes the true
prophet if there is no such thing as Law different and apart from

the individuals who give it expression." Yet, to Black's hard-bitten view of reality, the vision of law as a thing apart—either as the brooding omnipresence in the sky, which was the object of Holmes's gibe, or the presence that Blackstone in a more serious mood said the judge carried within his breast—was an essentially profitless metaphysical speculation. Far more to the point, in his view of things, were those who give the law expression, and here he saw caveats of objectivity and self-restraint as delusive. His attitude on the point had been expressed years before, on the Senate floor, when he refused his consent to judicial and regulatory nominees, not on condemnation of character, but upon the insistence that background and experience inevitably shape attitudes and values. Indeed, he would soon assert a powerful counterproposition to the view of a mystic overlaw and its judicial exegetes as an excrescence licensing judges to "roam at large in the broad expanses of policy and morals and to trespass, all too freely, on the legislative domain of the States as well as the Federal Government."[4]

By singularly sharp irony these two divergent views of the judicial process converged in a reprise of *Jewell Ridge,* where the two Justices reached a common result from irreconcilable major premises. The occasion came in consequence of another round of demands by the redoubtable John L. Lewis, who reopened his contract demands while the government countered by seizing the mines and obtaining a federal court order against a work stoppage. On advice of counsel that the obvious letter of the Norris-LaGuardia Act had forbidden federal courts to issue injunctions in labor disputes, the miners walked out anyway, and the federal court in its turn fined the United Mine Workers three and a half million dollars and John L. Lewis ten thousand.

On appeal to the Supreme Court, the fines were modified and upheld. The new Chief Justice Vinson carried water on both shoulders as he agreed with the Black position that the Norris-LaGuardia Act did not apply to strikes against the government —a concededly tenuous description of the temporarily held mines—and then went on to agree with the Frankfurter doctrine that the restraining order was valid in its own right. For Frank-

furter found himself unable to agree that the Norris-LaGuardia
Act was inapplicable in the present case, and his reservations
carried great weight. Paralleling Black's intimate knowledge of
the Fair Labor Standards Act was his architectural encounter
with Norris-LaGuardia, an expertise he was not above pressing
in the cut and slash of conference. (Surprisingly, for all Black's
hostility to unrestrained judicial power and his protective concerns for labor unions, he participated in the Norris-LaGuardia
debates only to the extent of asking one procedural question.)
On this authority and with Justice Jackson's agreement, Black
insisted that while the federal court was without power to issue
the injunction at all, it nonetheless possessed the inherent prerogative of compelling obedience to its order while it determined
whether it had the power to do what it did.[5]

United Mine Workers presented, after its fashion, the issue
that had caused the two to part company in the *Harry Bridges*
and *Los Angeles Times* contempt proceedings, and with Reed
and Murphy in flat dissent, it produced the anomalous result of
punishing the miners for disobeying an order that a court had
not the legal authority to issue. In background and consequence,
the whole controversy produced a bilious state of affairs. One
unsettling note came from Drew Pearson's purportedly inside
story of the conference between counsel and the Chief Justice.
Another might be found in *Time*'s sour comment on the efforts
of Chief Justice Vinson to write an opinion accommodating his
unruly colleagues—"The Court might have confined itself to the
question of contempt . . . and let it go at that. But not this
Court. Boldly Chief Justice Vinson struck out into the jungle
country of the Norris-LaGuardia Act." It also provided a bristling preliminary to another Black-Frankfurter division on the
nature of judicial power growing out of another statute where
Black had a virtually proprietary interest, the Public Utility
Holding Company Act.[6]

The case was *SEC v. Chenery Corporation,* a controversy
growing out of the streamlining provisions of the statute, and one
that was triggered when the inside management group made
open-market purchases of securities with the avowed purpose of

maintaining their entrenched position in reconstituted organization. There was no statute, no regulation, no specific prohibition
against their doing what they did, but the Securities and Exchange Commission, acting on its interpretation of court decisions applying general principles of equity, set the transaction
aside as a violation of the fiduciary obligation that the insiders
owed the other stockholders and investing public generally.[7]

In a four-to-three decision in 1943, Frankfurter set the SEC
action aside on the ground that the Commission had misapplied
the judicial precedents under which it attempted to act. Running
through his opinion, however, was a note of reprimand to a mere
administrative commission that had taken upon itself the ancient
judicial prerogative of ascertaining and applying equitable principles. Speaking for himself, Murphy and Reed, Black entered a
vigorous dissent, which defended the administrative process
under which the Commission had acted and also reflected his old
view that saw the holding companies as rattlesnakes—". . .
they bought the preferred stock and then offered a reorganization plan which would give this stock a book value of four
times the price they paid for it."[8]

Duly admonished, the SEC "recast its rationale" and found its
divestiture order justified by the text of the statute and its own
administrative competence. With a straight face it once more
entered its order, which was again duly appealed to the Supreme
Court, where it met a doubly outraged Justice Frankfurter.
Frankfurter had been irked enough in the exchanges on the
original appeal, and the text of a note to Justice Reed suggested
the thin line that separated ideas and personalities: "Were I at
Cambridge I would be saddened to note that you underwrote an
opinion like Black's . . . I don't think I should be less saddened
because I am your colleague. I hate to see you bogged down in
such a quagmire of Populist rhetoric unrelated to fact." But now
the fact that the Commission seemed to have played him for a
fool was exacerbated by the realization that it had successfully
done so.[9]

The intervening years had converted Black's dissenting bloc to
ascendancy, and Justice Murphy accordingly upheld the Com-

mission on the basis of its revised reasoning. Moreover, in an effort to dispose of the case before term end, he had circulated his draft opinion only a week before adjournment date and thereby gave Frankfurter the option of inadequately stating his contrary views or of publishing them at a later date, when their psychological impact would be lost. It was, moreover, a problem that was increasingly plaguing the Court, but one that bore especially hard on Frankfurter's reflective temperament. ("I have to brood a lot even though I am clear about my view.") He threatened to embody his specific complaint in a passage of dissenting opinion, which in turn prompted Justice Murphy to remonstrate against the disclosures of matters proper only for "the private corridors of the Court," and Justice Rutledge noted that Frankfurter had once asked *him* to delete a similar reference. ("You will recall also . . . I did so in compliance with the suggestion.") Perhaps the words of his colleagues had their effect. Perhaps it was the memory of *Jewell Ridge.* In any event, when the dissenting views came down, the only expression from Justice Frankfurter was to note his concurrence in the opinion of Jackson, who protested the SEC making law after the fact and whose outraged tone could have come from any of the conservative bloc of the Nine Old Men.[10]

The Process of Law

  Chenery and *United Mine Workers,* for all their sharp note of confrontation, were essentially peripheral skirmishes in the long, running duel between Black and Frankfurter over the meaning of the four-word, twice-repeated phrase "due process of law" as it appeared in the Constitution of the United States. In the Fifth Amendment it qualified the power of Congress over life, liberty and property. In the Fourteenth it worked, textually at least, a counterpart restriction upon state power. Historically, it had served as a vast repository of judicial authority constraining actions of state and federal government alike in a double mode of operation. Procedurally, it insisted that what either government did be fairly done. Yet its exposition had gone on to a substantive dimension in an exegesis that asserted that there were some things government could not do at all.

In its Fifth Amendment context, the veto power of due process received its most famous application in the *Dred Scott* decision, which struck down the effort of the federal government to ban slavery in the territories. The Fourteenth Amendment consequences, with respect to legislation of the states, were particularly evident in the judicial proscriptions of the first third of the twentieth century with the protestations of Professor Felix Frankfurter and Senator Hugo Black being raised against what they saw as private opinion being enshrined as constitutional doctrine. From the pages of the *Harvard Law Review* Frankfurter insisted that "the veto power of the Supreme Court over the social-economic legislation of the States—presents undue centralization in its most destructive and least responsible form . . . The inclination of a single Justice, the buoyancy of his hopes or the intensity of his fears, may determine the opportunity of a much-needed social experiment to survive, or may frustrate for a long time intelligent attempts to deal with a social evil." And from the Senate floor, the gentleman from Alabama assailed the indefinability of the whole concept of due process: "No one has ever defined it. No one ever has marked its boundaries. It is as elastic as rubber."[11]

Understandably enough, the elimination of due process as a checkrein on economic legislation was one of the first triumphs of the New Deal's ultimate turnabout in judicial affairs. It was on this precise point that Justice Roberts' asserted switch of 1937 had come to pass in sustaining state minimum-wage legislation. On the federal side, Hugo Black's soaring view of the national commerce power swept all before it. Of that sweep, Justice Jackson wrote uneasily that "we seem to have no function but to stamp this act OK," and in a remarkably ironic development the Republican-controlled Eightieth Congress used the same rationale to scotch the entire array of Court-created overtime claims in the Portal-to-Portal Act of 1947.[12]

State criminal procedure was something else again, and here, notwithstanding the parity of the economic application of due process of law, its criminal implications continued to mean different things in state and federal proceedings. In the differentiation there was a certain element of continuity, for as early as 1833, in *Barron v. Baltimore,* the Supreme Court had held the specific provisions of the Bill of Rights—there the provision of the Fifth Amendment barring the uncompensated taking of private property for public use—bound only the federal government and not the state ones.[13]

Nor did the Civil War-engendered Fourteenth Amendment change anything. In 1884, in *Hurtado v. California,* the Court ruled that notwithstanding the guarantee of due process thereunder, a state might prosecute crimes on information of a public officer rather than the grand jury indictment demanded by the Fifth Amendment. Again, in 1908, it held that the Fifth Amendment's prohibition against self-incrimination bound only the federal government. The case was *Twining v. New Jersey*—Mr. Justice Black would have some things to say about it—validating indirect self-incrimination by upholding a comment of a state trial judge on a defendant's failure to testify. And in 1938, in Justice Black's first term and with the junior Justice concurring, it once more denied the application of specific provisions of the Bill of Rights to the states when it denied in *Palko v. Connecticut* any protection from the double-jeopardy clause of the Fifth Amendment to multiple state prosecutions for the same offense.[14]

Palko involved a double paradox. One was Black's joining a judicial denial of the "incorporation" doctrine, a thesis that was to be his jurisprudential hallmark, and the other was the resurrection in criminal proceedings required as the minimum due process of law in state proceedings of the natural-law intuitionism soon to be cast into outer darkness by *Erie Railroad.* Indeed, it would be hard to find a better statement of the whole natural-law concept than the "rationalizing principle that gives to discrete instances a proper order and coherence," to isolate these rights "implicit in a concept of ordered liberty and thus through the Fourteenth Amendment . . . valid against the states." And more importantly in terms of Black's future development, Cardozo went out of his way to indicate those provisions of the Bill of Rights that were not necessarily included in his comment—grand jury indictments and petit-jury trials, immunity from self-incrimination, freedom from double jeopardy. Notwithstanding the felicity of the Cardozo prose, the intense subjectivity of the test he proposed indicated that the uncertainty of "ordered liberty" due process would be as acute as that involved in economic regulation. Indeed, the very tests—"principle(s) of justice so rooted in the traditions of our people as to be ranked as fundamental" or outrages "so acute and shocking that our polity will not bear it"—recalled the very vagueness against which Black and Frankfurter had protested but a few years before.[15]

In a critical split, Black went on protesting, while Frankfurter did not, and by singularly appropriate development the opinion commonly accounted Black's greatest, *Chambers v. Florida,* marks not only the division between them but the beginning of Black's effort to fill the Fourteenth Amendment with the Bill of Rights itself rather than the elusive generalities of "ordered liberty" and its inevitably wide judicial discretion. He began cautiously enough, for the confessions he set aside on behalf of a unanimous Court could fairly fall within Justice Cardozo's insistence that due process in any form must necessarily give protection against torture, physical or mental. But some other aspect of the case also stirred him to the provisions of the Bill of Rights, perhaps the assistance of counsel, and the result was a seemingly offhand footnote to the effect that only a minority of the Supreme Court Justices who had considered the question ever agreed "that the Fourteenth Amendment was intended to be made secure against state invasion of the rights, privileges, and immunities protected against federal violation by the Bill of Rights."[16]

The footnote did not go unchallenged. In a "Dear Hugo" note of October 31, 1939, the very week in which the Court accepted *Chambers,* Frankfurter put the real questions to him:

Perhaps you will let me say quite simply . . . what I mean to say and *all* I mean to say, regarding your position on the "Fourteenth Amendment" as an entirety.

(1)I *can* understand that the Bill of Rights—to wit, Amendments 1–9 inclusive—applies to State action, and that *Barron v. Baltimore* was wrong. I think it was rightly decided.

(2) What I am unable to appreciate is what are the criteria of selection as to the nine Amendments—which applies and which does not apply.

This is not written to draw comment from you—not that I should not have pleasure in anything you may say. But I have written the above merely to state as clearly as I am capable of, what is on my mind.[17]

The note embodied Frankfurter's teaching technique at its best, with the man who spoke from a developed and systematic theory pressing the man who was in the process of developing his own. And in this process Frankfurter hit particularly hard at the weakest point, the applicability of the Bill of Rights to the states in the consequence of freezing as a constitutional imperative throughout the entire range of American jurisprudence the provision of the Seventh Amendment for jury trials in suits where the amount in controversy exceeded twenty dollars.

But there were procedural provisions and procedural provisions; and far different from the quaint anachronism of the Seventh Amendment was the command of the Sixth providing for the assistance of counsel. In the appeal of the initial Scottsboro proceedings, the Supreme Court had insisted that that concept of "ordered liberty" covered this in all capital cases, and ten years later the Justice from Birmingham cited that decision in a dissent in *Betts v. Brady,* which incorporated a double plea. One was that the right to counsel in noncapital criminal trials when tested by the traditionally vague tests of due process—"shocking to the universal sense of justice," "offensive to common and fundamental ideas of fairness," and so on—should be included within it. The other brought his views on the interplay of the Fourteenth Amendment and the Bill of Rights out of the footnotes and into his text: "I believe the Fourteenth Amendment made the Sixth applicable to states . . ."[18]

And again Frankfurter pressed him with the critical questions in a request for materials that would show that the Fourteenth Amendment was a compendium of the first nine:

> Are all nine so incorporated? Did the Fourteenth Amendment establish uniform systems of judicial procedure and freeze them . . . Is it conceivable that an amendment bringing about such a result would either have been submitted, would have been ratified . . . ? And if not all the nine Amendments, which of the prior nine Amendments are to be deemed incorporated and which left out?[19]

Despite Frankfurter's uncharacteristically humble requests for assistance, he was neither dissembling nor being difficult as he drew Black on. Rather, as his own pre-Court polemics suggested, he also had been struggling with the problem of judicial review in the democratic state. Unlike those of Black, his ideas remained where they had been in the early thirties. In fact, in his *Harvard Law Review* article, he noted the vagrant judicial vetoes interposed in the name of due process and concluded that "against these dangers the only safeguards are judges thoroughly awake to the problems of their day and open-minded to the facts that may justify legislation."[20]

Black's devotion to the adversary principle admitted no more play to the self-restraining judge than it did to the self-restraining trust. Yet, to cabin judicial discretion by his own judicial fiat would not only be the crowning perversion, as Frankfurter warned, but would in all probability be self-defeating as well—"what I am talking about is that if each temporary majority on this Court—and none is very long—in fact regards its presence . . . as an opportunity for translating its own private notions of policy into decisions, the sooner an educated public opinion becomes aware of the fact the better . . ."[21]

The professor had indeed asked the right questions, and he received his answers a few years later in *Adamson v. California,* an effort that Black regarded as his best on the Court. And not without reason for in his television exchange with Eric Sevareid

("What's the most important of those dissents that later became law in your mind now?"), he made it virtually his judicial creed: "That's the case where I asserted at full length for the first time my belief that the passage of the Fourteenth Amendment made the Bill of Rights applicable to the states." The rationale for that position, however, was not explained, and after a fashion it was almost as important as the result.[22]

Adamson was the *Twining* case of 1908 all over again. At issue was the dilemma posed by a state-granted right of freedom from self-incrimination and its virtual abrogation by another state-granted right of comment on silence plus the right of the prosecutor to inquire as to prior convictions of a defendant on the stand. Admiral Dewey Adamson insisted that the state of California had thrust a Hobson's choice upon him in this array of alternatives and had done so in violation of the Fifth Amendment of the Constitution, which guarantees freedom from compulsory self-incrimination. Justice Black agreed, and moreover, he carried three of his colleagues with him and thereby lost his proposition by the narrowest of margins. Nonetheless, showing that he had learned his lesson in a hard school, he set out the thesis that appealed from precedent to history itself:

> I am attaching to this dissent, an appendix containing a resume . . . of the Amendment's history. In my judgment that history conclusively demonstrates that the Fourteenth Amendment . . . was thought by those responsible for its submission . . . and by those opposed . . . sufficiently explicit to guarantee that thereafter no state could deprive its citizens of the . . . Bill of Rights. And I further contend that the "natural law formula" . . . should be abandoned as an incongruous excrescence . . . I believe that formula itself to be a violation of the Constitution in that it subtly conveys to courts, at the expense of legislatures, ultimate power over public policies in fields where no specific provision of the Constitution limits legislative power.[23]

Obviously the professor was not disposed to let this thesis pass unchallenged, and he counterattacked in a concurring opinion that agreed with Justice Reed's majority view but was in fact a special application of the counterdissent. Frankfurter denied that the Fourteenth Amendment was a covert way of imposing the whole Bill of Rights on the states, but illustrative of the widening gulf between himself and Black, he chose not to meet Black on the ground of historical exegesis. Instead he appealed to precedent, and precedent of a remarkable kind—"the judges who were themselves witnesses of the process in which the Fourteenth Amendment became part of the Constitution." There were, however, those who in due course chose to respond to Black on the grounds of history rather than law. Charles Fairman and Stanley Morrison framed a powerful rebuttal against Black's historical exegesis and accompanied it with the barbed comment, comparable only to the exchanges going on within the Court itself, that "the real significance of *Adamson* . . . is that four of the judges are willing to distort history, as well as the language of the framers, in order to read into the Constitution provisions that they think ought to be there," and they deplored the fact that the talents of Hugo Black should be so employed.[24]

There was one point and one paradox that went virtually unnoticed in the ensuing controversy, which saw the coinage of a new term of opprobrium—"law-office history"—and the charge of a Pulitzer Prize-winning historian that the Supreme Court flunked the course. In the inevitable demythologization of law of which the higher criticism was *Erie Railroad v. Tompkins*, the historical exegesis of the type pioneered by Black, for all its infirmities, could be put forward as being every bit as good a guide to decision as that provided by the interior and private revelation of untrammeled judicial discretion. There was, moreover, one remarkable element in the concepts of due process seen variously by Black and Frankfurter, an element that not only exemplified the difference between them, but suggested an area in which scholar had indeed learned from the master. For Frankfurter's quest for due process had always been to those ideas of "fairness" and "decency" that had been held fundamental by "English-speaking peoples," and it was the logical consequence of the special Frankfurter paradox whereby the Justice who had never spoken English before twelve accounted his visiting professorship at Cambridge as the happiest year of his life and confessed to an unbounding love of English legal institutions.[25]

And yet it was Hugo Black who, in *Adamson*, introduced the man who would be a recurring figure in the Supreme Court reports—John Lilburne, the Puritan dissenter of 1648—and who derived the Fifth Amendment's right of silence from Lilburne assertions, which Felix Frankfurter would find particularly congenial in spite of himself—"fair play," "fair trial," "the due process of law," and "the good old laws of England."[26]

The Winding Wall

If the most extensive Black-Frankfurter confrontation came on the salient of the Fourteenth Amendment, its most sensitive exercise came in the delicate church-and-state issue first posed by *Everson v. Board of Education*. The controversy was deceptively simple; indeed there were those who criticized the Court for even accepting the question of whether New Jersey might constitutionally reimburse parochial-school parents for the bus fares of their children. From the very first, Black thought the reimbursement permissible.[27]

Yet, others saw it differently. Thus, the issue split the Black bloc, as Wiley Rutledge not only passed over to join Frankfurter but served as his surrogate in an extended clash of opinions with his usual ally. And the sensitivity of the issue was further shown when Felix Frankfurter decided, after one draft of an opinion, that it was one on which he should not be heard; here he assumed a public silence comparable only to that that he had maintained in the Court-packing controversy and assertedly for much the same reason:

> I am the symbol of the Jew, the "red," the "alien." I would be heard and interpreted by what you call the average man—the reader of the Hearst papers, the *Chi-*

cago Tribune, the Legion, the D.A.R.'s, the Chambers of Commerce . . . Instead of bringing light and calm and reason . . . [I] would only fan the flames of ignorance, of misrepresentation, and of passion.[28]

But if the Frankfurter views went unstated on the record, they were insistently pushed in the conference room, and perhaps too much so. A friend had observed that his "push, push, push" of Franklin Roosevelt to put Learned Hand on the Supreme Court had probably guaranteed Hand's being passed over. Along the same line and notwithstanding Black's fondly posthumous recollection of Frankfurter's tactics in conference ("He fought long, hard, and loud . . . [He was] forceful, insistent, persuasive, eloquent, and at times explosive . . .")[29] it was just such a tactic that could propel Black into an obdurately inflexible position of his own.

There was another ironic twist in the mode in which the case presented the constitutional status of the parochial school to the two protagonists in the light of the ancestral proceeding of *Pierce v. Society of Sisters*—the 1925 decision in which the Court voided the Oregon Education Act compelling attendance at public schools by all children between eight and eighteen. The act was the only exclusively Klan-sponsored legislation adopted anywhere in the United States. Accordingly, the Court's action was widely hailed as a defense of freedom of religion—indeed it was even cited in the papal encyclical *Rappresentanti in Terra* —although it was in fact merely a defense of property entered under the due-process clause. And Frankfurter, in an unsigned editorial in *The New Republic,* noted that while the Oregon decision "gives just cause for rejoicing . . . a heavy price has to be paid for these occasional services to liberalism" and called the roll of all the state social legislation that had fallen under the judicial veto. And particularly interesting, given his future role in the flag-salute cases, was his criticism of phrases in the Oregon opinion concerning studies and good citizenship as "ample room for patrioteers to roll in their Trojan horses."[30]

Even before the bus case arrived, Frankfurter was already

showing his skittishness on the church-state issue and, as early as the beginning of 1944, was prophesying that the Supreme Court would come "to rue the implications of *Pierce v. Society of Sisters.*" His correctness in prophecy, at least by his own view, became manifest in the three months that followed argument in the bus case, and his vicarious confrontation with Black proceeded in a battle of draft opinions and a quest for allies. He assisted both Jackson and Rutledge in their dissents as Rutledge eventually turned out eight drafts of his opinion and Black responded with six. The Frankfurter insistence, however, pushed Black into a secularly absolutist major premise, for his ultimate majority opinion ("Neither a state nor the federal government . . . can pass laws which aid one religion, aid all religions, or prefer one religion over another") carried a sweep that the initial effort lacked. Yet there were others who found difficulties in following the premise into conclusion. "I flipped the leaves and missed the break," wrote Irving Brant, ". . . by gosh, on a point negatived by his own reason." Equally critical, but for a different reason, was Princeton's Edward Corwin, who insisted that historically the forbidden "establishment of religion" necessarily involved preference and who consequently attacked the "aid all religions" reference in Black's premise: "Undoubtedly the Court has the right to make history . . . it has no right to *remake* it."[31]

Yet it was to history that Justice Frankfurter appealed again and again in the secret debate within the Court. His arguments won over Jackson and Burton, who originally had been with Black, and he used a special historical appeal for the sorely perplexed Frank Murphy—now the Catholic swing man on an evenly divided Court—as "one who cares for your place in history, not tomorrow's headlines." Calling on an array of allies, from Cardinal Gibbons to Murphy's brother and sister, Frankfurter pleaded: "For the sake of history, for the sake of your inner peace, don't miss. No one knows better than you what *Everson* is all about. Tell the world—and shame the devil."[32]

Murphy's ultimate alignment with Black and Frankfurter's consequent loss of the battle in *Everson* did not dampen Frankfurter's zeal for the war. A year later church and state once more came up as *McCollum v. Board of Education* tested religious instruction on public-school property during school hours pursuant to a multidenominational program. Only Justice Reed thought the arrangement constitutional; the rationale of his eight colleagues who thought otherwise, however, divided the Court bitterly. For, after an initial Black opinion outlawing the arrangement on the basis of *Everson,* Frankfurter, in his own words on this topic a man driven by an "insistent" truth, called a caucus of the "anti-*Everson* lads" to restate the position for total separation.[33]

However, the division over means rather than ends raised the prospect that there would be neither majority nor plurality opinion, and a peace-making effort by Justice Burton initially produced merely a reiteration of stands. Frankfurter, calling Black's *Everson* opinion "mischief-breeding," asserted that only complete excision of any reference to it would permit his concurrence in Black's current effort. Black, never a man to recant, reiterated a conviction that *Everson* was decided right, dryly noted that contrary constitutional views were often regarded as mischievous, but offered to go along on any compromise that might reconcile points of difference.[34]

The consequence was a Black opinion that retained some *Everson* references but also incorporated some of the Rutledge dissent. Six Justices joined in the resulting effort, as Rutledge and Burton (but not Jackson) came over from the *Everson* dissenters, and Frankfurter, correspondingly, made concessions in his concurrence; nonetheless, it showed the depth of his feeling both in its doctrinaire literalism ("Separation means separation, not something less") and in its encomium to the public school (". . . perhaps the most powerful agency for promoting cohesion among a heterogeneous democratic people . . .").[35]

Frankfurter was, of course, right that any approach based on the line-drawing rather than categorical separation premised almost infinite judicial agony, and the difficulty of subsequent decision was underscored a few years later. Indeed each decision along the church-state wall predictably produced a public outcry and a prompt countermarch by the Court itself. Thus, the uproar over *Everson* helped produce the nearly unanimous result in *McCollum,* and in the consequent counteroutcry there resulted in its turn the next demarche in *Zorach v. Clausen.* In *Zorach,* the religious instruction was given off premises, but during school hours pursuant to a released-time program. A six-Justice majority of the Court found the differences critical and constitutional, and the majority opinion of Justice Douglas even asserted that "We are a religious people whose institutions presupposed a Supreme Being." It was a pronouncement that subsequently a legal thinker in the Frankfurter tradition would characterize as "famed, trouble-making, and essentially meaningless."[36]

Perhaps Black thought so too, for the *Zorach* case marked one of the few points of division between himself and Douglas in a constitutional context. Another difference from his usual way of doing things was the unusual sharpness, as in posing the question as one "whether New York can use its public-education laws to help religious sects get attendants presumably too unenthusiastic to go unless moved to do so by the pressure of the state machinery." And even more unusual than his acerbity was his company, for his fellow dissenters were Justices Frankfurter and Jackson.[37]

It would be too much to say that Frankfurter's doctrinely Enlightenment and *"Écrasez l'infâme"* view of the First Amendment drew Black in that direction. Nonetheless, Black's instincts drew in cognate intellectual roots going back to the Birmingham mills. ("The cheap-labor business infuriated . . . There was much anti-Roman Catholic feeling. They were making poor Italians . . . indentured servants . . .") Also involved was what he saw as "Roman Catholic hostility to Masons. Masons were always free thinkers. . . . This riled the Roman Catholics."[38]

Into this mental set, the anti-Catholic polemics of Paul Blanshard of the post-World War II period, and Black's marked and personally indexed copy of *American Freedom and Catholic Power* corroborated the observation of Hugo Black, Jr.:

The Ku Klux Klan and Daddy, so far as I could tell, had one thing in common. He suspected the Catholic Church. He used to read all of Paul Blanshard's books exposing the power abuse in the Catholic Church. He thought the Pope and bishops had too much power and property. He resented the fact that rental property owned by the Church was not taxed; he felt they got most of their revenue from the poor and did not return enough of it.[39]

The First and the Fourth

As the church-state cases suggested, Felix Frankfurter was a particularly formidable foe when the constitutional doctrine that, in a fashion, he shared with Black—that there is a difference in the binding character of the Constitution itself and what the Supreme Court from time to time said about it—was linked to some especially prized personal value. Obviously his doctrinal tenacity in the church-state cases derived from his membership in what, in the flag-salute dissent, he called "one of the most despised and persecuted minorities in history."[40]

This membership, curiously, was not without some anomalies of its own. He had long put off the religious side of his Jewishness, as his own admission and an oblique reference by Justice Frank Murphy ("Every member who signed that [McCollum] opinion save one was a believer") demonstrate. In fact, on this point Murphy scored a shrewd hit that outscored Frankfurter's imperial intelligence in the insight that the Massachusetts Justice did not really seem to like Jews unless someone started kicking them around.[41]

Derived from the same root was an almost obsessive concern to preserve what he saw as the fundamental underpinning of the First Amendment—the total constitutional inhibition and social tincturing of a resolutely secular state. Notwithstanding his disclaimer that he did not caucus to make his views prevail, here he did not caucus but led the caucus. In other matters he might brilliantly eviscerate the "seductive clichés" and "rhetorical flourishes" that had become engrafted upon the constitutional text. In church and state, however, he saw the Jeffersonian metaphor of the wall of separation as epitomizing the entire constitutional doctrine.[42]

There was another constitutional area of sensitivity, doubtless draining on the same roots, that Frankfurter was, by his uncharacteristically colloquial admission, "nuts about." Freedom from arbitrary searches and seizures was for him, as it was for Justice Brandeis before him, the embodiment of the most precious right of all—the right to be let alone. And in an arresting counterpoint of values he gave to the right to be free from an arbitrary search of person or property much the same absolution that was beginning to surface in Black's ideas of freedom of speech.[43]

Differences of experience, of course, had led to differences of perception. Black owed his whole political, and therefore his judicial, career to his ability to surmount a formidable opposition and a hostile press—whether on the Alabama courthouse square or on the dais of his investigating committee—to an ability to speak out and reach his audience. Searches and seizures were another thing. And it was quite another all the way from the Girard liquor cases of 1916, where his tactics offended his old teacher of the Alabama Supreme Court, down to the wrath of the Court of Appeals of the District of Columbia over the telegram seizures by his investigating committee some twenty years later.

Black had another difficulty. Giving direct effect to a constitutional guarantee was one thing, but dealing with its consequences and side effects quite another, for here surfaced once more that judicial discretion that he had set out to cabin and confine. Indeed in the compulsory incrimination cases he was not a bit sure that a judge's or prosecutor's comment on a defendant's silence in the face of accusation was the same thing as extorted testimony and only joined the assumption because the majority opinion insisted on doing so.

The Fourth Amendment carried an even greater difficulty. Here was no flat prohibition of searches and seizure, at least in the mode of the First Amendment's categorical assertion of freedom of religion, speech or the press. Rather, all that the Fourth Amendment proscribed were unreasonable searches and seizures, a critical adjective opening up by another door the same unlimited judicial discretion that the due-process clause afforded.

Not unexpectedly then, Black and Frankfurter parted company almost from the start. Once more the relativist and the absolutist came close to changing hats. For as Black's subsequent development made plain, he read the text of the Fourth in a narrow range of policy choices doubtless shaped by his activist experience as prosecutor and Senate investigator. Contrariwise, Frankfurter, activist philosopher but nonetheless philosopher, was as stated above "nuts about" search and seizure, with the Fourth Amendment being for him what the First was to Black. For, as Brandeis before him, Frankfurter saw it embodying the right most prized by civilized men—the right to be let alone.[44]

Moreover, his emerging status as the last Federalist—where Black was the undoubted catalyst—rejected the application of the Bill of Rights to the individual states. Rather, it permitted—indeed, almost compelled—a rigorous near-absolutism in those areas concededly under national control. And such was his leadership in that area that he himself headed up his own "Strange Alliance" of four, wherein he replaced Black in the libertarian quartet with respect to the war and postwar search-and-seizure cases.[45]

It was Black who concurred and Frankfurter who dissented, when warrantless federal searches of automobiles on grounds of asserted necessity came before the Court in *Davis v. U.S.* They differed on the warrantless seizures of illegally held ration stamps in *Zap v. U.S.*, and its plea that these were public, not private, papers. They were again divided on the basic application of the Fourth Amendment to the wiretaps and detectaphones challenged without success in *Goldstein v. U.S.* as to whether a nose might be used for a warrant in the detection and seizure of opium.[46]

Their sharpest point of difference, however, came on the virtually insoluble issue of seizures made without warrant but as an

incident of a lawful arrest. Here in *Harris v. U.S.*, Black supported Chief Justice Vinson's opinion that criminal evidence
might be so seized without warrant as long as it was in "plain
view" on the premises involved and notwithstanding the fact that
a search warrant would be required without the arrest. Then in
Tropiano v. U.S., shifts in both the composition of the Court
and individual opinions of the Justices saw Black standing fast
as the Frankfurter bloc wrote a triumphant turnabout requiring
search warrants for seizures in all cases of property as evidence
when time was available to apply for them.[47]

There was, moreover, a denouement to the latter sequence of
decisions and with a certain quiet drama it found Black and
Frankfurter as allies in dissent. The remarkable *entente* came
two years after *Tropiano,* as a turnabout of a turnabout in a case
virtually reinstating the old law on warrantless seizures incidental to lawful arrests. Understandably Frankfurter, sounding
exactly like Justice Roberts, sharply criticized the circumstances
of the turnabout as "reinforcing needlessly the instability of our
day by giving fair ground for the belief that law is the expression
of chance—for instance, of unexpected changes in the Court's
composition and contingencies in the choice of successors."[48]

The references once more disclosed how much of *Swift v.
Tyson* underlay so much of Frankfurter's juridical universe.
More remarkable, however, was the way in which much of its
sentiment was echoed by a parallel dissent of Justice Black. The
time was coming when Frankfurter's very words would be virtually adopted by Black. At the moment, however, his view was
cabined within the far smaller compass suggested a few months
earlier, when he concurred in *Wolf v. Colorado,* but for an entirely different reason than that set out in the majority opinion of
Justice Frankfurter. At that time Frankfurter, sustaining in a
state prosecution a procedure he would have struck down in a
federal one, upheld a conviction of an abortionist based on evidence taken without warrant on the grounds that the mystic "due
process" enjoined in the Fourteenth Amendment did not forbid
the seizure.[49]

In an illuminating index of his own emerging philosophy,

Black reached the same result by an entirely different route. Insisting once more that the Fourth Amendment's ban on unreasonable search was indeed binding on Colorado, he nonetheless took issue as to the consequences of violating the constitutional injunction. Here he insisted that the long-standing inadmissibility of such evidence in a federal court was mere procedural rule, which federal judges had made and Congress might very well unmake. He conceded that, subject to such congressional intervention, federal judges might also unmake what they had done. But then, possibly suggestive of Frankfurter's influence, he went on to suggest in *Rabinowitz* that the exclusionary rule was hardly a measure of "what is wise judicial policy." And the uncharacteristic juncture was significant for another dimension, for it measured a change in the Court as well as in the man.[50]

CHAPTER THIRTEEN

Fair Deal and Cold War

Changing of the Guard II

The hard-lining turnabout from *Tropiano* to *Rabinowitz* came to pass not so much as the reconsideration of prior views but in new opinions of new men. In fact, in *Rabinowitz* only one Roosevelt appointee, Justice Stanley Reed, was numbered in the five-to-four majority. Joining him, however, were all four Truman Justices—Vinson, Clark, Burton and Minton—and the new bloc stood steadfast on the need for toughened procedural requirements in criminal matters. It was a symbol, as good as any, of both a changing face of the nation and the changing direction of a reconstituted Court.

The reconstitution was not without its own ironic dimension, particularly in the succession to the libertarian Justices Murphy and Rutledge. The replacement of Murphy by Attorney General Tom Clark was commonly accounted a signal gain for both Court and country; popular and legal opinion was accurately reflected by *Time* Magazine, which noted how the style of Murphy's opinions changed with every change of law clerks and that their substance reflected "an eager beaver who is all heart and sniffles whenever the legal hunt picks up the scent of something human."[1]

There was the judgment of another kind of time, however, which was to vindicate another side of Murphy's visceral jurisprudence, and do so in a sequence not unlike the changing historical fortunes of the first dissenter from constitutionalized segregation, Justice John Harlan. For, while Harlan had written of the "inoculation of race," he had not labeled the phenomenon. Well in advance of the popular coinage, however, Murphy became the first Justice to use the word "racism" in a Supreme Court opinion, bringing the word into the reports via a bitter dissenting opinion in *Korematsu*. (By one of those historical paradoxes he was succeeded by the man who had a relatively minor role in the Nisei transportations and who would later— perhaps in partial consequence of the Murphy dissent—refer to that episode as one of the few regrettable items of his own long public life.)

There were other aspects of Murphy's character and personality that softened in the backward view of the whole man. Certainly the self-righteous humanitarianism, itself the obvious overcompensation of an immigrant-arriviste self-doubt and insecurity, was more than offset by the affectionate humor that showed itself in the shadow of death. "One of the nurses," he wrote from the sequence of his terminal hospital stints, "said, 'Oh, I would like to meet that Justice Douglas. Don't you think he would be an interesting man to know?' I replied, 'Miss, he might have been acceptable and interesting fifteen years ago.' Best wishes to you, dear Bill. . . ."[2]

The succession of Clark to Murphy also involved, after its fashion, an index of change in the institutional Court. In a departure of sorts from customary ways of doing things, Harry Truman refused to replace Murphy with a coreligionist in what was increasingly called the Court's Catholic seat. Yet, even this action underscored in its negative way the mode in which a new norm of American pluralism was slowly taking its place alongside the traditional sectional calculus. Indeed the downgrading of sectionalism was apparent in the succession to the other decedent of the New Deal Court, Wiley Rutledge. For, in perhaps the last expression on the subject, Franklin Roosevelt himself told Rutledge, the other possible nominees for the Court at the time had all qualifications save one—"Wiley, . . . they didn't have geography—you have that."[3]

But geography seemed considerably less important in the selection of Rutledge's successor, which turned out to be Sherman Minton, onetime Indiana Senator. But Minton's Indiana roots had been considerably attenuated in his years on the Circuit Court of Appeals for the District of Columbia. Nor was any special mention made of them when, a full decade after his consideration by Franklin Roosevelt for the vacancy that ultimately fell to Black, Minton finally moved up to that position from a lower court. *Time* tartly noted that Minton had been mentioned for just about every vacancy that had turned up in the interim, but went on to suggest that the new Justice would be "a competent and liberal judge, if no earth shaker." Irving Dilliard voiced the widespread assumption that Minton would be a coadjutor, if not a disciple, of Black. "They served together in the Roosevelt ranks . . ." Dilliard recalled; "the prospect is that the newest Justice will be looking to the senior member for at least some guidance in his first term. Beyond that it is foolish to forecast."[4]

As things turned out, forecast in the short run proved hazardous. Back in 1938 Minton had introduced a bill in the Senate that would make it a felony to publish a "known untruth." Punishment could include up to two years' imprisonment and a $10,000 fine, with the offending journal losing its mailing privileges for six months. And this was a better indication than past rapport with Black. And before Minton's first term was out, he had shown a disposition to "gag the newspapers" (as W. J. Cash called it), and it was not Black's counsel that was predominant. In fact, the *Rabinowitz* weather vane of the new direction the Court was taking had been written by Minton himself, and his influence also showed itself in another and more subtle mode. This was in the equally decisive but less apparent results that came to pass in the Court's refusal to act at all. In cases actually before the Court, the quartet of Black, Douglas, Rutledge, and

Murphy needed only one vote to work their will in any particular controversy. And even if they could not win, they could at least bring the case to the Court and get their views on record and appeal to the intelligence of a future day. For under the "rule of four" the votes of that number of Justices determined whether (in the great majority of instances) a case would come before the Court at all. Thus the Black quartet had virtual control of the calendar and the docket.[5]

But it was this authority that evaporated when the quartet was reduced back to the original duo of Black and Douglas. The consequences were duly noted in a bristling *New Republic* article by Yale's Fred Rodell in the year-ending issue for 1949. A defender of the Court might rise to its defense with respect to some of the items, for Rodell charged a deplorable judicial inaction— or perhaps reaction—in the areas of union security, civil liberties and economic regulation. More acute, however, was the accusation that went not so much to a change of tactic as to a shift of philosophy, and it was summed up in the title "The Supreme Court Is Standing Pat."[6]

Alienation and Sedition

The hardening attitude of the Court in cases involving domestic crimes was obviously related to the outbreak of that war that was called cold and involved the first full-scale American encounter with subversion as an avowed and massive instrumentality of belligerency. There was, of course, more to the national mood than the confrontation with Soviet imperialism. The inevitable postwar disillusion, which a generation before had manifested itself in the red hunts and the Ku Klux Klan, emerged once more. And perhaps the comparatively libertarian policy of World War II only intensified the character of the postwar reaction. Again there surfaced the strain of endemic anti-intellectualism, this time intensified by the disproportionate involvement of American intellectuals in what seemed at the time as radical chic, but which in hindsight bore the sinister overtone of treason.

The new mood of insecurity, however, also had a long-lived strain to draw upon with earlier manifestations running back to the 1798 Alien and Sedition Acts of John Adams' administration. Here it fell to Black's historical sense to note that the contemporary mood of the country was such that the Court was giving the 1798 statute a far broader meaning than it was given by one of the most vociferous champions of antialien and antisedition legislation. And, coincidentally enough, the initial statutory manifestations of the new insecurity, emerging even before American belligerency, bore the official title of the Alien Registration of 1940; unofficially it was known as the Smith Act, and only a minor portion of its provisions involved aliens at all. Nonetheless that particular portion—a prohibition against teaching or advocating violent overthrow of the government or conspiring to undertake such teaching or advocacy—had complete prewar roots, which were manifested in the growing popularity of the Dies Committee in the late thirties and the subsequent institutionalization of the body under the name of the House Committee on Un-American Activities.

The parliamentary fortunes of the committee were also an excellent weather vane. In 1945, 186 votes were cast in the House against its continuance; by 1950 only 12 could be mustered. The committee reaped where its predecessors had sown; "merciless exposure" for itself alone was carried to new dimensions and from thence into substantive law. In 1943 the committee's efforts had attached a "red rider" to an appropriation bill and forbade payment from any funds thereunder to a group of fellow-traveling government employees who had drawn Chairman Dies's wrath. Pressed by the financial exigencies of the war, Franklin Roosevelt signed the bill under protest, and his reservations were amply vindicated when the Supreme Court in *United States v. Lovett* unanimously voided the rider as a constitutionally prohibited bill of attainder. Black wrote the declaration in which there were uneasily balanced a declaration of his own constitutional faith and a manifest dislike of voiding a congressional statute—"Much as we regret . . . we have no alternative here."[7]

Both his tone and the Court's stance were to change as an essential judicial retreat was concealed under a Fabian tactic deriving substantive results from procedural formulas. Thus the growing tension between Court and Congress on the right of legislative committees to compel testimony was, in *Christoffel v. U.S.,* deflected on the grounds that the absence of a quorum excused perjury. Yet there was only a limited amount of retreat afforded by such a rationale; and in the opinion of one observer, it was only the flight of a Soviet espionage agent duly haled before a committee, that prevented a full-blown confrontation at a time when the forces of liberalism were comparatively strong.[8]

For it was in the latter controversy, *Eisler v. United States,* that Justice Frank Murphy wrote what was to be his judicial epitaph—"Law is at its loftiest when it examines claimed injustice even at the instance of one to whom the public is bitterly hostile." But a few weeks later Murphy was dead, and within a comparatively short time the composition of the Court had undergone a change in values and attitude. Thanks to the four Truman appointees, or what Black bitterly called the "new majority," the Court moved closer to that aspect of public temper that John Lord O'Brian labeled "preventive law."[9]

For subversion as a technique relying on stealth, dissembling and betrayal had produced its own counterpathology in efforts to diagnose and anticipate treasonous action by the early discovery of subversive ideas. The corpus of the new jurisprudence accordingly comprehended statutes, executive orders, loyalty oaths, blacklists and private agreements. And here the executive and legislative branches vied with each other in a contest of repression. Shifting the fundamental balance from reasonable doubt concerning loyalty to reasonable grounds to suspect it, Harry Truman issued Executive Order 9835, authorizing the dismissal of any government employee if there are "reasonable grounds" to question his loyalty. And the Eightieth Congress responded with its Taft-Hartley Act provision requiring an anti-Communist affidavit of officers of all unions resorting to the National Labor Relations Act.

The requirement was grudgingly validated by the Court in

American Communications Association v. Douds, although the rationale was hardly satisfactory. *Time* called the judgment a "four-way stretch" as three Justices disqualified themselves, and the remainder split badly. Five believed that a disclaimer of Communist affiliation might be exacted; three affirmed that a statement of nonbelief as well might be taken, with Justices Frankfurter and Jackson waffling on the point. Black was the only out-and-out dissenter, as he quoted a passage from Charles Evans Hughes that he would use again as the last words of his career:

> The greater the importance of safeguarding the community from the incitements to the overthrow of our free institutions . . . the more imperative the need to preserve inviolate the constitutional rights . . . therein lies the security of the Republic, the very foundations of constitutional government.[10]

His appeal went unheard, and his concerns mounted. A new figure entered the milieu of concern and insecurity, even giving it his name, as on February 9, 1950, Senator Joseph R. McCarthy of Wisconsin spoke in Wheeling, West Virginia, holding in his hand, so he said, a list of fifty-four Communists in the employ of the State Department. The supposedly incriminatory document, conspicuously exhibited but never put in evidence, was the old trial lawyer's ploy that Chairman Black had used to great effect in his own day. And there were other elements of resemblance. One was the defamatory leading question; another was the instinct for media; a third emerged in the implacable hatred of a section of the public where virtually all shades of liberal and intellectual opinion united in a loathing that had no earlier counterpart, save perhaps that which the business community had reserved for Hugo Black two decades earlier.

Indeed, in a remarkable bit of symbolism, the legislative investigating committee was producing other fruit, including the conviction of a former law clerk for Justice Holmes, formally for perjury and informally for espionage. Character testimony from two members of the Court and an *ex parte* averment of confidence from the Secretary of State availed the defendant nothing. Rather, the only consequences seemed to be a demand by the Illinois Department of the American Legion for loyalty oaths for the Supreme Court Justices and a bill in the House of Representatives to forbid their future expression of character testimony.

The stage was accordingly set for the judicial denouement of the cold war. On June 4, 1951, the Court pronounced two judgments on the current antisubversive campaign. One came 6 to 2 in *Dennis v. U.S.*, sustaining the conviction of the top eleven Communists for violating the Smith Act's prohibition of conspiracy to teach or advocate violent overthrow of the government. Closer was the 5 to 4 decision in *Garner v. Board of Public Works,* which upheld a Los Angeles requirement that municipal employees evidence by oath and affidavit their non-membership in any group pledged to similar ends. In probably unintended *double entendre, Time* headlined its story "Black Day for Reds," but other views were more somber in fact if not in coloration.[11]

The New Republic deplored "what the Court has destroyed," and this was the essential tenor of Black's surprisingly brief dissents. In *Garner,* he regretted the doubt that had been thrown on the earlier *Lovett* holding. In *Dennis,* he was more forceful, emphasizing that the defendants were not charged with doing anything, and denouncing the result as a "virulent form of censorship of speech and press" in abandonment of the clear-and-present-danger rule that Justice Holmes had enunciated thirty years before. And the tone of regret that had accompanied his views in *Lovett* had also been abandoned. In a brief compass and in a curiously conditional syntax he managed to reprimand both his present colleagues on the Court and his former ones on Capitol Hill. ("So long as this Court exercises the power of judicial review, I cannot agree that the First Amendment permits us to sustain laws suppressing freedom of speech and press on the basis of Congress' or our own notions of mere 'reasonableness.'") He also had a few words for his fellow Americans:

Public opinion being what it now is, few will protest the conviction of these Communist petitioners. There is hope, however, that in calmer times, when present pressures, passions and fears subside, this or some later court will restore the First Amendment liberties . . . where they belong in a free society.[12]

Unquestionably Black's sympathetic stance rested on his recollection of the storm that had attended the disclosure of his Klan membership and his knowledge of and insight into the ordeal of *ex post facto* judgment upon an action that seemed harmless enough at the time. There were those who disagreed, suggesting that the Communist Party U.S.A. did not quite stand *pari passu* with the vegetarians or Prohibitionists. Nor was all suppression. In *Joint Anti-Facist Refugee Committee v. McGrath*, a majority of the Court granted the request of three organizations to be removed from the Attorney General's list, where they had been placed without notice or hearing in the interests of merciless exposure; here Black wrote a concurring opinion denying any executive power to issue "these pseudo bills of attainder" and to it he appended Macauley's account of a parliamentary proscription "which took place when popular prejudice was high." Again, in *Blau v. U.S.*, he spoke for a unanimous Court upholding the rigorous tradition begun by John Marshall ("from Mr. Burr to Mrs. Blau," punned *Time*), safeguarding a recalcitrant witness against self-incrimination and where he quoted Blackstone and threw in the tyrant Dionysius for good measure.[13]

A Family Affair

Yet, the reverses were many and the victories few, and as the Court convened for the October 1951 term, an observer noted how Black and Douglas seemed to stand "alone, discouraged, and embittered." Then, at what must have been the worst of all times for it, Black's wife died in the closing days of the year. "She is altogether a grand person," Felix Frankfurter had written years before, ". . . with unusual talents for mitigating difficulties and softening hard feelings." She had wept when Senator Black had flayed a utility magnate. And she had captivated Franklin Roosevelt—"Josephine, you are beautiful. . . . Don't think I'm harmless just because I'm crippled." It was a double tragedy, for she was barely on the threshold of middle age.[14] "She ought to be the last of her generation to die," mourned her stricken husband, "not one of the first. Life is wrong—it's just wrong."

In her own quiet way she had been a part of the Washington scene for so long that it was hard to believe she was only fifty years old. At twenty-eight, she had been the youngest of the Senate wives when Black first took his seat, and the youngest of their three children was born after that time. Utterly without pretense or pretensions, she probably found the Birmingham years the best, and perhaps her favorite of their residences was the house in the hills overlooking Birmingham. Her participation in Washington social life was low-keyed, for the Black parties ran to small groups and good talk, with the Justice himself frequently serving as cook.

And throughout the years the domestic Black chronicle did seem to prove Tolstoy's law that all happy families are alike. Not that the home life had been without concern. Josephine's gentle, artistic nature was underlain with a touch of melancholy, as the Southern euphemism had it; indeed, liquor allegedly first came into their house in response to a physician's suggestion for a touch of sherry. And the hearing of one of the children had been a source of continuous worry, its possible consequences had partially underlain Black's consideration of a return to the practice of law as his second term approached its close. Ironically enough, the tumultuous days following his nomination to the Court had been spent, not on the Senate floor or in its lobbies, but over at Johns Hopkins Hospital in Baltimore on this very matter.

But over-all the years had passed placidly enough. The boys followed their father in the law, the older, Hugo junior, after graduating from Alabama went on to the Yale Law School, where he served on the prestigious *Yale Law Journal* and was president of the law-student association as well. Sterling Foster, named for his maternal grandfather, went to Arizona and thence to Columbia. And the baby of the family, Martha Josephine ("JoJo"), after a Washington girlhood that included a President of the United States playing piano at a slumber party, opted for Bryn Mawr. The progress of domestic events—a graduation at an Army Officer's Candidate school or a Bryn Mawr commencement—provided the occasions for the Justice's rare public speeches. And through it Josephine Foster Black went her way taking an occasional course in constitutional law ("No, my husband doesn't help me with my homework") and trying her hand at her painting, which took the grand prize in one of Washington's Famous Amateur contests. ("To learn a new craft after forty is a laborious process. What I paint never satisfies me, but there is always a new white canvas, some nice 'squashy' paints and another day—so it doesn't bother me.")[15]

For all Black's steel, the loss came close to being devastating. "I cannot think of her without tears," he wrote a favorite niece. "This I know should not be, since I keep telling myself how fortunate I was to have had her for thirty years." Chief Justice Vinson summed it all up in his eulogy, which commented upon that combination of "friendliness of the South and the stern discipline of the Scottish Presbyterian faith," as she was buried on a cold, rainy day in Arlington cemetery. Indeed, the remarkable combination of talents noted by the Chief Justice was apparent in the grave site itself, for she held her claim both as a veteran's wife and a veteran in her own right.[16]

But, then, both Foster girls were remarkably talented, and Virginia Foster not only shared her sister's gifts, but had also married an unusual lawyer in Clifford Durr, of Montgomery. Like Black, Durr was energetic, free-thinking and scholarly (he had gone to Oxford on the World War I equivalent of the G.I. Bill). He and his wife had been moving spirits in that heterogeneous collection of Southern liberals, the Southern Conference for Human Welfare, and he made a welcome addition to the Federal Communications Commission, to which he was appointed in 1939, thanks to the influence of his Senator brother-in-law once removed.

There was a negative aspect to his service here, for Justice Black regularly and scrupulously disqualified himself whenever an FCC matter came before the Court. A disqualification of another sort had been suggested when Durr left the Commission in early summer of 1948, and the news reports of a testimonial affair in New York detailed a remarkable display of tributes from a variety of sources. Assured of presidential reappointment, he nonetheless preferred to go out with his term rather than participate in its loyalty-security programs. And another indication of the crisis of the times came with the subsequent filing of Virginia Foster Durr for the Senate seat from Virginia on the newly formed Progressive (Henry Wallace) ticket.

The formal political breakaway of the leftists rang the death knell of the Southern Conference, whose laureate Black had been twice before, and perhaps its most able achievement was that it lasted as long as it did. Certainly Black understood the web of tensions and frustrations that underlay his sister-in-law's move just as he understood those prompting the contemporaneous walkout—under the goad of a civil-rights plank—of half of the Alabama delegation at the Democratic Convention. Indeed, events at the convention prompted what might be called one of his few political actions and perhaps the first for Harry Truman's Fair Deal.

Certainly Black had never felt any sense of true rapport with the Truman entourage in the same way in which he had been so thoroughly and congenially at home with Ickes, Norris and other nuclear New Dealers, and his low-keyed and selective social life guaranteed an even further insulation from public affairs after the New Deal exodus from Washington. Not that he had anything but the warmest feelings for Roosevelt's successor himself. ("Oh, I was very fond of Harry. I campaigned for him in the State of Missouri.") And it was doubtless the defections of both left and right, both so close to home, that prompted his telephone call to the President the morning after Truman had gone to Philadelphia and roused a tired and demoralized convention with a fighting speech.[17]

Black recalled that he had called the President early the next

morning, since they were both early risers. "I want to congratu-
late you on your speech last night. Now a lot of people don't
think you could be elected now, and I'm one of them. But I think
you can be elected if you'll make exactly that same kind of appeal to the people all over the United States." And Black also
recalled the President's reply: "I agree to everything you've said.
Of course, I couldn't get elected now. But I'm going to make that
same kind of speech and I'm going to get elected."[18]

And Truman made the speech and he was elected. Running
with him for Vice-President was Senator Alben W. Barkley, of
Kentucky, who had entered the Senate the same day as Black
and who had also roused the convention as the Democratic key-
noter. (How far away the proposed presidential apprenticeship
of Robert Jackson seemed to be.) The subsequent whistle-stop
campaign and surprise election of Harry Truman were accounted among the upsets of American political history. And
least remembered campaign data were the speeches of Earl
Warren, Barkley's opposite number on the Republican ticket;
they included a proposal for a crusade to show what's right with
America and a diagnosis that what was wrong with America was
the coddling of Communists.

Yet, there were some other memorable aspects, and they
loomed ever larger in retrospect. While the Southern Conference
for Human Welfare had been dissolved, an ever more mortally
wounded symbol of the past was the long-time conference foe
Eugene "Bull" Connor, who now led the Alabama convention
walkout (after failing to get the organist to play "Dixie") into
the driving rain. Connor again surfaced into national prominence when he arrested the Progressive vice-presidential candidate, Glen Taylor, for using the "Negro" door to enter a black
Birmingham church. ("There's not enough room in town for
Bull and the Commies.") Taylor appealed his subsequent conviction all the way to the Supreme Court, which, over Black's
objection, declined to hear it.[19]

Yet on the very day *The New York Times* was reporting Mr.
Connor's political views, a unanimous Supreme Court was decid-

ing *Shelley v. Kraemer,* which outlawed judicial enforcement of racially restrictive covenants. Contemporaneously, parallel thrusts at resolving the American dilemma occurred in a mode even closer to home. A week or so before *Shelley,* W. T. Coleman had been named law clerk to Justice Frankfurter and thereby became the first black to hold such a position. And before the year was out, William Hastie, sometime Dean of the Howard Law School, assumed office as a judge of the United States Court of Appeals for the Third Circuit and thereby worked something of a counterpart development in the realm of the judiciary itself. And given the rising role which the clerks to the Supreme Justices were supposed to have, there would be those who said young Coleman had scored the bigger breakthrough.[20]

The Duel Rejoined

The shortened docket of the Truman Court compacted the area of encounter between Black and Frankfurter, but diminution in range seemed more than offset by increase in intensity, which in turn seemed to have its own annealing effect on the contour of Black's emerging philosophy. And not only new times, but the response to new ways of doing old things served to bring out both affinities and differences.

For not all was difference. The single issue of whether prurient phonograph records came within a statute forbidding interstate shipment of "any filthy book, pamphlet, picture, motion-picture film, paper, letterwriting, print or other matter of indecent character" could find the two standing together in an unavailing negative dissent. Again, a luminous insight on personal perceptions was provided by the bombardment of the captive riders of Capital Transit Company with selected radio programs. Calling himself "a victim of the practice," Frankfurter refused to trust himself to sit on the case. Black, on the other hand, did sit and differentiated his objections—that musical programs would not violate the riders' First Amendment rights, but that any "broadcasting of news, public speeches, views, or propaganda of any kind" most certainly would.[21]

But the collision between the right to speak and the right to be let alone—in an oblique way the heart of the Black-Frankfurter differences—received its fullest treatment when it split them asunder in the sound-track case of *Kovacs v. Cooper.* Formally, the case overcalled one of its outstanding Jehovah Witnesses decisions, as it upheld a Trenton ordinance prohibiting amplifying equipment from that city's streets. Black not only protested the turnabout, but went on in a passage that recalled the face-to-face effort that won him senatorial office in the face of the opposition of the Alabama establishment in noting that "there are people who have ideas they wish to disseminate but who do not have enough money to own . . . publishing plants, newspapers, radios, moving-picture studios, or chains of show places." Contrariwise, Frankfurter showed both his own predilection for privacy in denouncing "aural aggression" and his rising apprehension over the expansion of the *Carolene Products* footnote into what was rapidly becoming the Black doctrine, the superpreferred position of the First Amendment. Here he was at his waspish best in the cutting description of the typographical origins of the dispensation ("A footnote hardly seems to be the way of announcing a new constitutional doctrine") and more delicately indicated that the footnote had gone down in the face of Black's opposition. And on the whole, he bestowed the ultimate pejorative in his lexicon of reproach, "mischief-breeding."[22]

Two cases decided at the beginning of 1950 gave the occasion for Black's answers. One, *Rochin v. California,* concerned the seizure of critical evidence via the action of three Los Angeles deputies in pumping out the defendant's stomach, and here Frankfurter wrote for the Court in reversing the conviction on the traditional, if nebulous, due-process grounds, that the police action departed from the fundamental standards of decency and fairness of English-speaking peoples and shocked the judicial conscience.[23]

Black concurred in overturning the conviction, but his nomi-

The candidate for the Senate, 1926.

American Gothic: Hugo Black at 6 years of age (1892), fourth from left. Left to right: O. E. Black, Robert L. Black, William L. Black, Hugo, Mrs. Martha Black, the future Mrs. Daisy Rozelle, Mrs. Ora Garrett, Vernon Black, and Pelham Black.

Hugo Black as a young man.

The strikingly beautiful Josephine Foster, whom Black married in 1923.

Three powers of Alabama: left to right, Senator-elect Hugo Black, Governor Bibb Graves (both Ku Klux Klan members) and returning Senator Oscar Underwood (Klan victim), 1927.

Associate Justice Hugo Black (center) with Alabama congressional powers—Speaker of the House William B. Bankhead (left) and Junior Senator John Bankhead—at the Capitol as Congress struggled toward adjournment, 1938.

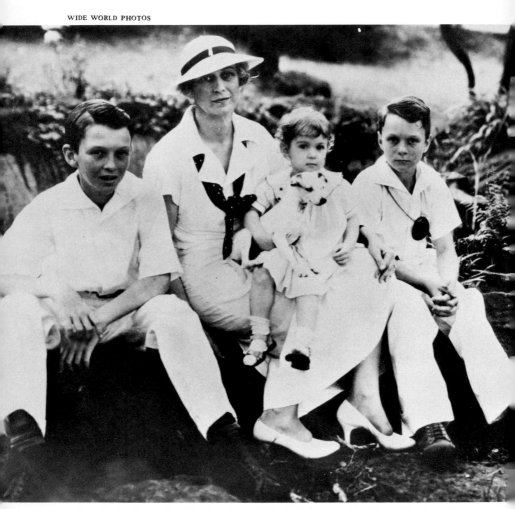

Court-nominee Black's family, 1937. Children with Mrs. Black, left to right: Hugo L., Jr., Josephine, and Sterling Foster.

Franklin D. Roosevelt. "He was magnificent."—Hugo Black

Warm friend and intellectual ally Senator William E. Borah, the Lion of Idaho.

The Gentle Crusader, Senator George W. Norris, Nebraska independent, fellow maverick and close personal friend of Black.

Black with Eleanor Roosevelt, May 14, 1949, at a Women's National Press Club dinner.

Black strolling with his wife Josephine.

Hugo Black's letter of resignation from the Ku Klux Klan, July 9, 1925.

Black on national radio as he denies any present affiliation with the Klan, October 1, 1937.

Home in Alexandria the day after the wedding, September 12, 1957: Justice Black and his second wife, Elizabeth S. DeMeritte.

The grandfather.

Eight Old Men and the Junior Justice. Junior Justice Black is at upper right, and Chief Justice Charles E. Hughes is center, front row.

The New Deal Court. Black is seated on the left of Chief Justice Harlan F. Stone.

The Truman Court. The air of levity is quite misleading. Black, now Senior Associate Justice of the Supreme Court, is seated in the place of honor on Chief Justice Fred M. Vinson's right.

The Warren Court—or, as many observers termed it, the Black Court. Black, still Senior Associate Justice, is seated on Chief Justice Earl Warren's right.

The Burger Court. Black is seated between his distant cousin John Harlan and Chief Justice Burger, with whom he had an unusually cordial rapport.

Reading in his chambers. A late photograph of Justice Black.

nal agreement was in fact dissent. In his view, the Fifth Amendment ban on self-incrimination applied to California as well as the United States—he had said that before—and he now held that that ban covered not only admissions extorted from the mind but also objects extracted from the body. And in something of a waspish professorial streak of his own, he made a point with two Socratic questions of his own: why should the Court consider "only the notions of English-speaking peoples to determine what are immutable and fundamental principles of justice"; and "what avenues of investigation are open to discover 'canons' of conduct so universally favored that this Court should write them into the Constitution." He then gave a hint of what the answer should be in referring to contemporary abridgment of expression and its inevitability under an "accordion-like" judicial formula, before suggesting its substance—"the absolute and unqualified words of the Fifth Amendment."[24]

And he hammered home this canon a few months later in *Beauharnais v. Illinois,* where the Court sustained an Illinois group libel law and with it the conviction of a racist pamphleteer ("Awake, Chicagoland, awake!") who sought "one million self-respecting white people in Chicago to unite (and prevent) the white race from being mongrelized by the Negro." Frankfurter wrote the Court's opinion sustaining the statute as the legitimate response to a state history of racial turbulence linking the lynching of abolitionist Elijah Parish Lovejoy in 1837 to Cicero riots in 1951. He got a responsive comment from the unsuccessful petitioner, one that might have served as the basis of another prosecution—"this is the will of his masters: the American Jewish Congress, the Anti-Defamation League, and certain notorious interracialists." He got an equally outraged, albeit more scholarly one from his senior colleague. For Black recorded his dissent in historical allusions which ran from Fox's Libel Act to the Star Chamber and the use of standards of decency, whatever those might be, as guides for judicial decision. And he, in addition, tartly regretted that the First Amendment's guarantee of free speech and press were not "given the respect of a passing mention." He also restated his response to the problem of "case-by-case, day-by-day majorities of this Court," in a terse phrase that, insistently reiterated, proposed that in the constitutional text absolute and unqualified meant absolute and unqualified. Hence the unconditional ban on laws abridging freedom of speech or the press meant that, with respect to the Illinois statute, "the First Amendment, with the Fourteenth, forbids such laws without any 'ifs,' 'buts,' or 'whereases.' "[25]

The Causes Célèbres

The kaleidoscopic Black-Frankfurter interplay ran on through a variety of encounters. The two divided in *Feiner v. New York* on the right of the police to maintain public order by arresting a speaker who had been stirring the anger of an unfriendly crowd. They divided again in *Breard v. Alexandria* on the constitutional power of a municipality to bar uninvited solicitors from calling on private homes. They united in *Adler v. Board of Education* to unavailingly protest the exclusion of Communist teachers from the New York public-school system. They united again in *Sacher v. United States* to record a futile protest against the summary sentences for contempt that Judge Harold Medina had inflicted on the unruly counsel at the close of the first great Communist trial.[26]

They also stood together in the two leading cases of the Truman Court, once in a common conclusion reached from a common premise and again in a joint judgment, where agreement joined diverse starting points. For the diversity in temperament and point of view was most obvious in *Youngstown Sheet and Tube v. Sawyer*. Coming up from the lower courts in 1952, it placed in issue President Truman's plea of the exigency of national defense and the inherent power of his office. Both were involved in his seizure of the strike-bound steel industry. And it also tested how both Black and Frankfurter saw the Presidency and the courts.[27]

On its face the claim of inherent presidential power was as plausible as claims of inherent judicial authority, and after argument of the point, three Justices of the Supreme Court came to agree that such inherent authority to act did exist. The view, however, was that of a dissenting minority, which numbered neither Black nor Frankfurter. Rather, it was Black who wrote the opinion of the Court, which held that the President had no legal capacity to do what he had attempted.

Black's opening proposition not only showed the parliamentarian par excellence, but denied the presidential assertion at the threshold: "The President's power, if any, . . . must stem either from an Act of Congress or from the Constitution itself." Manifestly, such a question yielded its own answer: "The Founders of this Nation entrusted the law-making power to Congress alone in good times and bad . . . This seizure order cannot stand." It was one of his better pinewood efforts; at once plain, tough and springy. Unhappily, diversity among his colleagues took away some of its force, for of the five who agreed with him, four felt impelled to write separate opinions. They included Felix Frankfurter, whose effort was a remarkable combination of polar opposites. One was a flick of intellectual hauteur—"The considerations . . . seem to me more complicated and subtle than may appear from what MR. JUSTICE BLACK has written." But the other element was an exercise in humility; his analysis began, not on the power of Harry Truman to seize, but on the capacity of a federal judge to sit—"our first inquiry must be not into the powers of the President but into the powers of a District Judge. . . ."[28]

In dissent an angered Chief Justice Vinson wrote for himself and two colleagues in unavailing support of the attempted presidential takeover and in denunciation of the "diversity of views expressed in the six opinions of the majority" by which that takeover was undone. He failed to impress *Time*, which first noted how Black delivered his opinion in but fifteen minutes, with an Alabama half-drawl and an "austere logic [which] fitted the gravity of the case." Contrariwise, the magazine unsympathetically reported how the Chief Justice's one-hour dissent "lumbered into an extraordinary proposition" of inherent presidential powers drawn from sources as noteworthy as the Korean War and the United Nations charter. And *Time* reflected the appreciative reception of the decision in the halls of Congress, where members hailed the Court as well as their former colleague, and a Senator who one day would be a leader of the movement to shear the Court's jurisdiction now proposed that jurisdiction be made permanent by constitutional amendment.[29]

Understandably, presidential reaction was considerably different from the congressional. Harry Truman had announced that he would abide by the Court's decision, and he had also indicated an intention "to put the cat on Congress' back." The cat seemed to get placed quite the other way, however, for Congress voted down two seizure bills and instead passed a resolution "requesting" the President to apply the hated Taft-Hartley Act. It was hardly a time of triumph for Truman. "He was so upset," Justice Douglas recalled, "that Hugo Black gave him a party." And the party was a remarkable effort as the Court undertook to soften the blow they had inflicted. "We all went and poured a lot of bourbon down Harry Truman . . . He didn't change his mind, but he felt better, at least for a few hours."[30]

The other hallmark case of the Truman Court wound up on a very different note, for its end was the execution of a sentence of capital punishment. In further contrast, its tortured sequence was remarkably unlike the swift progress of the steel-seizure controversy both up and down the judicial ladder. For the case of *United States v. Rosenberg* had been in the courts a long time. It had been heard repeatedly at the trial level, appealed to the circuit court several times, and produced no less than seven arguments before the Supreme Court itself. At the close, however, it moved with remarkable speed including a special term of the Supreme Court—the first since the trial of the Nazi saboteurs a decade earlier—providing the final element of dispatch.[31]

The special summer term involved what was in every sense the last appeal of Julius and Ethel Rosenberg from a sentence of death, technically for conspiracy to violate the Espionage Act of 1917 and in fact for transmitting atomic secrets to the Soviet Union. The sentence had been taken through a battery of appeals throwing up almost every conceivable defense including the assertion that the First Amendment freedom of speech included communications of American spies with foreign governments and that the Espionage Act was unconstitutional. Passed over, however, was the possible impact of the Atomic Energy Act of 1946, which permitted the death penalty for disclosing atomic secrets only upon jury recommendation and, moreover, requiring a specific finding of intent to injure the United States. Neither condition had been met in the Rosenberg case.

The critical legal point, unexamined in repeated proceedings on the three federal levels, was in fact presented only after the Supreme Court had adjourned on June 15, 1953, with the final action of the term denying a Rosenberg plea for a stay of execution for the sentence scheduled to be carried out three days later. The disposition was not unanimous, for Black, Douglas, Frankfurter and Jackson found themselves in a rare dissenting partnership. And literally at the eleventh hour, two attorneys who were strangers to the entire proceeding presented the critical point as to the Atomic Energy Act to Justice Douglas as he was packing for vacation.

Pressed by Douglas as to why they had not contacted another judge, the volunteers responded that Black had gone to the hospital for minor surgery (leaving word that he would entertain no petitions) and that no other Justice was available. After a night's research, the issue appeared substantial enough to warrant issuing a stay of execution, which he did before leaving on his delayed vacation ("rushed off" in *Time*'s unsympathetic phrase). But he had not counted on the sensibilities of his chief. He got no further than Erie, Pennsylvania, when he found himself summoned back to Washington for a special term convened on the very day of the scheduled execution. Other members of the Douglas family also became involved. On a Scarsdale-Manhattan train, an impetuous passenger asked the president of the Statler Corporation: "Are you the brother of the son of a bitch who issued the stay of execution in the Rosenberg case?" which was no way to refer to Julia Fiske Douglas or her son. The affirmative rejoinder came as a right to the mouth, which knocked out five of the questioner's teeth. The victim later sued for $50,000, a demand (subsequently compromised) for $10,000 per tooth as Arthur Douglas noted mathematically.[32]

The term was duly held—Black postponed his surgery and returned from the hospital—and after a few hours of argument and a few more of conference the Court next morning dissolved the Douglas stay. Like the Nazi saboteurs before them, the Rosenbergs were electrocuted virtually on schedule. Black held out against it to a solitary finale. On the specific issue of dissolving the Douglas stay, he was numbered with its author and Justice Frankfurter in a dissenting trio. On the final act of the Rosenberg drama in the Supreme Court—a last plea for a stay, not to review a question of law, but to seek presidential clemency in view of the divisions of the court—the record noted a terse denial with the additional notation, "Mr. Justice Black dissents." Years later he contrasted the case with that of Sacco and Vanzetti: "I don't know that they [Sacco and Vanzetti] were guilty, but I know that they didn't get a fair trial. Re the Rosenbergs: I believe them to have been guilty, but the prosecution wasn't conducted under the right law."[33]

Not years later, but before the summer was out, there was something of an ironic sequel to the Rosenberg case. The Chief Justice, who had insisted that Rosenberg execution go forward as scheduled, did not survive them by one hundred days. And Black, increasingly pressed into a dissenting minority, doubtless saw no cause for optimism in any possible successor the President, whose clemency the Rosenbergs had vainly sought, might appoint.

Part Five

The Great Divide

CHAPTER FOURTEEN

The Brown Decision: The Black and White of It

"Yes, the unanimity of the Court in the Segregation *decisions rightly gave the widest comfort. . . . Maybe one of these days the story will be known how it came to pass."*—FELIX FRANKFURTER, to C. C. Burlingham

I. THE AMERICAN DILEMMA

The New Chief Justice

"I made straightway for the chambers of Mr. Justice Black . . ." recalled Earl Warren concerning journey's end to the abrupt five-day transition from the governorship of California to the Chief Justiceship of the United States. "He welcomed me to the Court and offered his assistance in every possible way. He then took me to the chambers of the other members of the Court who were also most cordial in their welcome." By the time the round of introductions was over, it was almost noon and time for senior Associate Justice Black to administer the constitutional oath to his new chief in the customary private ceremony in the

297

conference room. The members of the Court then filed into the courtroom itself, where Warren again was sworn, this time to the judicial oath and once more at Black's hands.[1]

The day was October 5, 1953, as good as any to mark the onset of the great judicial revolution, although then little radicalism seemed suggested in the man whose name the revolutionary tribunal was to bear. Yet Warren's very entry onto the judicial scene was portentous: the new Chief Justice took his seat under recess appointment and without Senate confirmation, as Dwight Eisenhower did what Franklin Roosevelt had dared only to threaten—forgo advanced advice and consent and confront the returning Senate with the *fait accompli* of a sitting Justice engrossed in the work of the Court. As things were to turn out, Warren's exit would be on an equally unprecedented and provisional note—retirement subject to the appointment and qualification of a successor.

Beneath the seemingly uncomplicated and almost glacial calm exuded by the new Chief Justice lay an extraordinary combination of complexity and will galvanized by an abounding energy. And to this was to be coupled an intense sensitivity to the prestige of his Court and a profound sense of identification with it. Indeed, his initial astonishment at the small staff of the high judicial office—a secretary, a messenger, a brace of law clerks—compared with the two hundred aides who had done his bidding as governor of California presaged something of that sensitivity and identification.

On October 5, 1953, however, the new Chief Justice's judicial attitudes and philosophy were just another of the unknowns in the towering issue facing the Court he had been called to head—the constitutionality of the "separate-but-equal" doctrine in public education. The preceding December there had been one inconclusive pass at arms before the Court in the first fundamental re-examination of the question in over half a century. A decade before, however, the issue had been both appropriately titled and massively analyzed in *An American Dilemma,* by Gunnar Myrdal, a member of the Swedish Academy and perhaps the world's foremost social scientist. A decade later a distinguished

literary magazine would list the book as the second most important work to appear during its own institutional existence.
(First was Lord Keynes's *The General Theory of Employment,
Interest and Money,* and third was Hitler's *Mein Kampf.*)
And in an arresting example of the interplay of the world of ideas and
the world of reality, it was unquestionably Warren's citation of
the work in *Brown,* the landmark opinion of his revolutionary
Court, that brought about the commemorative acknowledgment
in the journal of literary criticism.[2]

The book's title summed up the contradiction between the
American ideal and American practice; its theme focused on a
critical pressure point of that contradiction—the legal infrastructure in the Southern and border states "separating the two groups
in schools, on railroad cars and on street cars, in hotels and
restaurants, in parks and playgrounds, in theaters and public
meeting places . . . with the explicit purpose of diminishing, as
far as was practicable and possible, the social contacts between
whites and Negroes. . . ."[3]

Remarkably enough, Myrdal had had a personal encounter
with the operation of such separate-but-equal legislation; perhaps
it underlay in part his observation that "by traveling around the
country, in particular in the South, to see things with my own
eyes, I was shocked and scared to the bones by all the evils I
saw." He was present in Birmingham at the first meeting of the
Southern Conference for Human Welfare, when Police Commissioner Theophilus Eugene "Bull" Connor—later world famous
for his pronouncement, "We're not going to have white folks and
nigras segregating together in this man's town"—imposed the
local segregation ordinance upon the gathering. Myrdal made no
reference to the incident in the book, nor did he mention the
newly appointed Justice Black's speech before the conference
accepting its first Thomas Jefferson Award. He did, however,
single out Black as one of the most prominent Southern liberals
and noted that it seemed "easier for a Southern liberal to win a
seat in Congress than to be really influential at home."[4]

Black's political career strikingly epitomized Myrdal's epi-
gram. Paradoxically, Black could filibuster against an antilynch-

ing bill as an unconstitutional extension of federal police power and in the very act extol the plenary reach of the commerce clause. ("Economically, in trade and commerce, this Nation is one, indivisible and inseparable. . . .") Alone of all the Senators, he could denounce Herbert Hoover's use of force to oust from Washington the protesting veterans of the Bonus Army, and, at the same time, tell some Vassar-Wellesley protesters against the Scottsboro case to give their sympathies to crime in the Northern cities. As chairman of the Senate Committee on Education and Labor he could extol the great transforming power of education, while declining to give the minority school systems any legal assurance of a pro rata share of federal assistance.[5]

And yet a fellow American, in an infinitely better position to perceive and, indeed, to regret the paradox than Gunnar Myrdal ever was, struck the balance on Black and found it good. "He seemed to me," earlier, Walter White, then Executive Secretary of the National Association for the Advancement of Colored People, recalled, "to be the advance guard of the new South we dreamed of and hoped for. . . ." The evening of Black's nomination to the Supreme Court saw a remarkable and earnest colloquy, as the head of the nation's then most militant civil rights organization warned the senior Senator from Alabama of "being on the spot" when any issue involving a minority came before the Supreme Court. "He told me frankly and soberly," White wrote a friend, "that he realized this and that he hoped that he would be able to measure up to what I and others of his friends expected of him."[6]

Black did measure up, although the start was faltering. He disqualified himself in the third Scottsboro case at about the time his Senate successor involved him in another filibuster against antilynching by reading his earlier speech into the *Congressional Record*. In fact, during that debate, Senator Tom Connally of Texas brandished a copy of the bill and warned his colleagues that there was a man on the Supreme Court who was prepared to hold it unconstitutional. But on Lincoln's Birthday of 1940, Black cleared up all doubts as he spoke for a unanimous Court in

Chambers v. Florida, striking down a Florida death sentence imposed on four black tenant farmers accused of murder: "Under our constitutional system, courts stand against winds that blow as havens of refuge for those who might otherwise suffer because they are helpless, weak, outnumbered, or because they are nonconforming victims of prejudice and public excitement."[7]

Chambers was a difficult opinion for Black. The case involved going against two principles he held particularly dear. One was overturning a jury verdict; in *Chambers* the jury had found that confessions produced by night-long interrogation incommunicado were nonetheless voluntary. Another, strongly underscored in his antilynching filibuster, was an antipathy for using the Fourteenth Amendment as a vehicle for federal interference with state judicial process. Indeed, Black had voted against taking *Chambers* in the first place, and the assignment to write the opinion placed him in the sharpest of dilemmas. "But the evidence of oppression and injustice would not down. The opinion Black wrote, after great internal struggles, was a turning point . . . [foreshadowing] much of what was to become his mature [judicial] philosophy."[8]

That maturing judicial philosophy placed Black in the forefront of the slow, case-by-case judicial resuscitation of the constitutional rights of the black minority—fair trials, education, suffrage—a process duly noted and commended in *An American Dilemma*. Myrdal, however, also indicated that these efforts would be peripheral until the Court laid the ax to the root by reversing the judicial veto which its *Civil Rights* decision of 1883 had laid on congressional legislation in the area of public accommodation. Curiously, however, for all the attention the book gave segregation legislation, it omitted any mention whatsoever of that legislation's constitutional underpinning—the 1896 decision of the Supreme Court in *Plessy v. Ferguson*. It was there, over the spirited, sole dissent of the first Justice Harlan ("Our Constitution is color blind. . . ."), that the Court upheld a Louisiana statute requiring all railroads carrying passengers in that state to provide equal but separate cars for the white and colored races.[9]

The issue of separate-but-equal went back at least to 1849, when *Roberts v. City of Boston* held that a legal command for equality could be squared with a legal command of enforced separation. Although *Roberts* had no constitutional force in suggesting the content and meaning of the Fourteenth Amendment, its spirit was evident in the amendment's very origin. For the Thirty-ninth Congress, which had framed the amendment, also had segregated galleries. ("Why is [it] that [you have] separate places for the races even in your own Chambers?" Maryland's Senator Reverdy Johnson asked his colleagues. "Why are they not put together?") But Congress did not put the races together, either in its galleries or in the educational institutions under its direct jurisdiction. Particularly its action in continuing a segregated school system in the District of Columbia seemed decisive to the Court that decided *Plessy v. Ferguson;* the Court did not so much approve the Louisiana segregation statute as confess an inability to say that enforced segregation on a railroad train was "unreasonable or more obnoxious to the Fourteenth Amendment than the acts of Congress requiring separate schools for colored children in the District of Columbia. . . ."[10]

Yet, the true constitutional infirmity of separate-but-equal may have been that the Thirty-ninth Congress had ordained the impossible. Myrdal insisted that segregation could work economically only by systematic deprivation of the weaker group because the duplication required for true equality would be economically ruinous. Certainly the cumulative evidence of the end product bore out his words. "The great difference in the equality of service for the two groups in the segregated setups of transportation and education is merely the most obvious example of how segregation is an excuse for discrimination." But this truth had a double edge. The accomplishment of the long-run strategy of bringing down the spirit of *Plessy v. Ferguson* depended tactically on a Draconian insistence on its letter. In the tactic, as Myrdal noted, lay the reforming group's broadest common ground, most obvious legal appeal, and mode of exposing the inherent contradiction of the formula.

At the beginning of the 1950s a trio of cases involving "the segregated setups of transportation and education" afforded a spectacularly triumphant application of both the tactic and the strategy. Tactically, the demand for absolute equality was repeated; strategically, that demand was expanded beyond quantitative to qualitative parity. In *McLaurin v. Regents*, a black graduate student at the University of Oklahoma was accorded the use of the same classrooms, library, and cafeteria used by white students, but was confined to placarded ("Reserved for Colored") desks and tables. The Supreme Court, holding the separation unconstitutional, found that this was not an equal educational opportunity, because it denied some of the intangible benefits of education that derive from association with fellow students. Matching this insistence on the "intangibles" of full parity—an essentially twentieth-century insight—the Court in *Henderson v. United States* struck down as an impermissible burden on national commerce (under the Interstate Commerce Act) the designation by the Southern Railroad of a separate, curtained table for Negroes in its dining cars, the unavailability of which had caused the petitioner to go hungry on a trip from Washington to Birmingham. In *Sweatt v. Painter* disparity was exposed by the mere comparison of a concededly separate and hastily established law school at the black Texas State University with the prestigious white counterpart of the University of Texas. More importantly, in *Sweatt* the Court's *Plessy v. Ferguson* measure became calibrated, not only to the measures of faculty, degrees, library, and law review, but also by "qualities which are incapable of objective measurement but which make for greatness in a law school . . . reputation of the faculty, experience of the administration, position and influence of the alumni. . . ."[11]

Under the field-marshalship of Thurgood Marshall and the Howard Law faculty, the petitioners in *Sweatt* had indicated the ultimate overthrow of the quantitative by the qualitative in suggesting *Plessy* be reexamined on the basis of the perceptions of contemporary culture. The eventual result of this probe was, of course, obvious—that the psychological effect of segregation on the segregated necessarily flawed the accommodation or service involved and hence prevented equality of use and enjoyment.

Judicial response to these unanswered nuances of the trilogy—particularly, the constitutional consequences of the psychological reaction of the segregated minority and how that reaction might be ascertained—was not so much denied as deferred. The question was unavoidably posed in a quintet of new controversies—from Kansas, South Carolina, Virginia, Delaware, and the District of Columbia—moving inexorably up the judicial ladder. Moreover, the challenge was asserted, not to graduate or professional training, but to elementary education itself. It thereby presented the greatest potential in both hazard and hope. On one hand, the public temper, which saw no harm in veiling the face of a fellow passenger in a diner (whatever his reaction might be), could hardly be expected to endorse the prolonged, compulsory and intimate association of small children. Yet balanced against this attitude was the American vision that saw education as the most fundamental transformation of all and that, appropriately applied, could sweep away all other discriminations before it.[12]

The Supreme Court had not been immune from the burning national issue. It had been cropping up in the Court's own institutional life in one way or another over the past decade and a half. In 1939, because of segregated seating arrangements, what was to have been a private recital of Marian Anderson in Constitution Hall became a public concert at Lincoln Memorial wherein invitations to the Supreme Court produced one acceptance. In 1947, a household controversy—whether the black Supreme Court messengers should attend the law clerks' and secretaries' Christmas party—took almost an hour's debate at the weekly judicial conference before being settled by an affirmative 6-2 vote. In 1950, the stark constitutional issue was presented without any pretense of *Plessy v. Ferguson* trappings when Glen Taylor, the Progressive vice-presidential candidate, unsuccessfully sought review of his Birmingham conviction for using the colored instead of the white door to enter a church. ("There's not enough room in town for Bull and the Commies.") The Supreme Court denied certiorari.[13]

The Anderson concert, the Christmas party controversy, and the Taylor case had all occurred prior to Warren's accession to the Court, and accordingly shed no light on where he might stand on the basic issue. Indeed, the very speculation as to where he might stand underscored the haphazardness of the constitutional process. A number of other men had been mentioned for appointment as Chief Justice following the death of Fred Vinson—John Foster Dulles, John J. McCloy, Robert A. Taft—and the views of any one of these men might have entailed a different sequence of events. And certainly that sequence of events might have been decidedly different, for example, had James F. Byrnes not broken with Harry Truman, but instead sought and obtained the Chief Justiceship on the death of Harlan Stone in 1946.[14]

Earl Warren's record as governor of California—innovative, activist, progressive—had already been written. Yet, there was also a thread running through that record that afforded food for thought. Foremost was his vigorous advocacy of the Nisei relocations before the fact and his vigorous defense of that action afterward. More recently, there had been his firm stand for loyalty oaths for the University of California faculty, a matter that reportedly had been decisive in President Eisenhower's choice. In fact, just some months before appointment, and while Warren was still being mentioned as a possible Republican nominee for the Presidency, an article in the *The New Republic* looked at the record with considerable apprehension. In addition to the Nisei relocations and the loyalty oaths, the author found other disquieting items—opposition to both a parole for Tom Mooney* and a California court appointment for Max Radin,† an asserted advocacy of migrant-farm-worker disfranchisement but of agricultural superrepresentation otherwise, and less-than-successful

---

* Mooney had been sentenced to death for the murder of ten persons killed by a bomb in a parade in San Francisco in 1916. His sentence subsequently was commuted to life imprisonment.

† Radin, a professor at the University of California Law School, a distinguished liberal and a man with a passion for justice, was appointed to the California Supreme Court in 1940. His confirmation was opposed by Warren, and his name subsequently was withdrawn.

efforts to secure fair-employment legislation. The interrogative caption of the article summed it all up: "How Liberal Is Warren?"[15]

The Limits of Politics

Relevant as that question was in a political context, it took on a special significance in a judicial one. In grappling with its foremost dilemma the American political process seemed to have reached the limit of its effectiveness. Notwithstanding the triumphalist prose of *The New Republic* hailing the 1950 trilogy of *Sweatt-McLaurin-Henderson* as "Jim Crow in Handcuffs," the more obvious fact seemed to be that the swart bird had but lost some tailfeathers. To be sure an occasional black passenger might dine in dignity; nonetheless, the appropriate counterpart of *Henderson* might be glimpsed in the Freedom Train episodes of just a short time before. Here the issue was not dining but something more fundamental, and the recurrent controversies over whether segregation would be imposed on lines of citizens waiting to view the organic documents of American liberty provoked a bitter poem:

> Can a coal-black man drive the Freedom Train?
> Or am I just a porter on the Freedom Train?

The political process had not failed for want of effort. As early as 1946 Truman had taken a firm stand for equal employment opportunity. But despite an upset electoral victory two years later on a platform that included a strong civil-rights plank, despite an eloquent and landmark remonstrance against "imposing a caste system on a minority group" by a prestigious presidential commission, despite majorities in both houses of Congress, Harry Truman's Fair Deal proposals all came to naught. Superficially, of course, there were any number of things to be blamed, and those ranged from congressional structure—seniority, the committee system, the Senate filibuster—to the Truman administration's effort to restore party harmony after the bitter 1948 campaign. Deep down, perhaps, there was another reason.[16]

This reason, the most subtly corrosive of all, said Myrdal, was the vague and optimistic assumption that in time things would somehow work themselves out. But all the evidence suggested that things were not working themselves out, particularly in the area of congressional action, which Myrdal saw as the indispensable element of change. The very abortiveness of legislative proceedings only underscored how legislative developments increasingly lagged behind judicial ones. The mere reporting from a House committee to the floor of a doomed antilynching bill— the very type Calvin Coolidge had recommended at the beginning of Hugo Black's first Senate term—was accounted a signal victory. Mere House passage of an antipoll-tax and fair-employment measure, both defeated by Senate filibuster, was accounted an even greater triumph. By the time Harry Truman's second term was over, Professor Edmund Cahn summed up reformist sentiment with the bleak observation that the "legislative process that had appeared so promising in the middle forties seemed to have come to a definite and protracted halt."[17]

If anything, this observation understated the case. By the time of Dwight Eisenhower's inauguration the process would have been better described in terms of total cessation. Nor could much hope be seen in the modest promises of the new President to do what he could to end segregation in the District of Columbia and throughout the federal government. These promises contrasted strikingly with the soaring but unaccomplished proposals of his predecessor, not only in their distrust of centralized power but in their unambitious estimate of what might be done.

Within a few months of his inauguration the new President received assistance in redeeming his pledge from a quarter that no one, not even Gunnar Myrdal, had suggested as an apparatus of political and social change. On the very day the Supreme Court decided to set Linda Brown's case down for reargument it also ended forthwith theater and restaurant segregation in the nation's capital. The mode was resuscitation of an 1873 District of Columbia statute that most parties in interest thought had been repealed long before. The swift and summary nature of the change—in the sharpest contrast to congressional do-nothingism —and the prompt public approval suggested that Congress, not the Court, was out of touch with the dominant public mood.[18]

A further indication of the merits of decisive action and the supportive popular response was suggested by the progress of military desegregation, initiated under a Truman executive order. Hence, even though the first session of the new Eighty-third Congress came and went without substantial legislative action on America's foremost problem, and even though the Republicans in power seemed doubly disposed to emulate the inaction of the Democrats, as the Supreme Court approached the 1953–54 term and its new Chief Justice other signs of the times could be seen as justifying an editorial headline in *The New Republic:* "Exit Softly, Jim Crow."[19]

Brown v. Board: The Record and Beyond

Present and set down for argument at that term was Linda Brown's case out of Topeka, Kansas. It had been there since June 7, 1952, when the Court agreed to hear it in a deceptively colorless *per curiam.* Some of that deception fell away the following October, when the first advance sheets for the new term suggested the national dimensions of the issue, and consolidation with counterpart South Carolina, Delaware, Virginia, and District of Columbia litigation was ordered. First argument was accordingly scheduled for December, and the Court's temper with respect to it was suggested by another entry in the reports shortly before Thanksgiving—a tart judicial inquiry of November 24, 1952, which observed that the Kansas Attorney General had neither appealed nor filed a brief and asked if such inaction was meant as a concession of the unconstitutionality of the state segregation statute. Another element was added shortly after the election, in the belated appearance of the Department of Justice on behalf of the petitioners.

At last came the display of advocacy on December 9, 10 and 11, 1952, wherein the high spot was the confrontation pitting the great John W. Davis, still at the mastery of his powers at seventy-nine, and forty-four-year-old Thurgood Marshall of the N.A.A.C.P. But, although the encounter provided great advocacy, it afforded little argument, for the antagonists never seemed to be at issue. The two lines of address resembled nothing quite so much as the nineteenth and twentieth centuries passing each other on parallel but never-meeting planes. Davis pleaded eloquently against moving the landmark that the Fathers had set. ("Somewhere, sometime to every principle comes a moment of repose where it has been so long often announced, so confidently relied upon, so long continued, that it passes the limits of judicial discretion and disturbance.") Marshall, however, was not to be outdone in either eloquence or pragmatism. ("Even if [segregation] was necessary in 1895, it is not necessary now, because people have grown up and understand each other.")[20]

Much the same void was exhibited in briefs. Here, as in oral argument, a second thrust of the petitioners' case lay in an exhibit evaluating, in the light of modern knowledge, the consequences of racial segregation, signed by thirty-two sociologists, anthropologists, psychologists and psychiatrists.

The 1952–53 term closed without an answer to either thesis. Instead, the cases were set down for reargument on a remarkable sequence of four interlacing questions largely turning on cause rather than consequence: (1) whether the Fourteenth Amendment had actually abolished segregation of its own force, (2) whether the "intentions of the framers" contemplated some future Court or Congress doing so, (3) whether such abolition was within the ambit of the federal judicial power, and (4) if the latter development were to be the case, whether such power might be best exercised (a) by admitting petitioners forthwith to schools of their choices, (b) by reorganization of school districts, (c) by the appointment of special masters to oversee the cases, or (d) by returning the cases to "courts of first instance."[21]

The convoluted questions suggested a few answers. One was that the issue might be around for a long time, and that the current opinion of the Court was merely *Brown I*. More substantive was the implication that the Court was willing to strip away almost a century of encrusted overlay and reexamine the original understanding of the Fourteenth Amendment. Beyond this was the real thrust. Justice Frankfurter, in a somewhat malaprop metaphorical reference to the array of questions, cautioned the Court not to "tip the mitt," by looking in the opposite directions. The mitt had indeed been tipped, however, as Thurgood Marshall's comment indicated: "A nothin'-to-nothin' score . . . means we win the ball game."[22]

Obviously, things were not quite that simple, for the historical quest for the meaning of the Fourteenth Amendment might not produce a standoff score, or as Marshall later put the hazard, the "golden gate" might well turn out to be a "booby trap with a bomb in it." The difficulty was the questionable capability of the Supreme Court of the 1950s, far more remote from the Thirty-ninth Congress than the *Plessy* Court, to nonetheless more clearly perceive that body's intention. Nevertheless, Marshall plunged into the terra incognita, and where a year earlier he had brigaded the views of social scientists, he now called upon historians. In fact, he held a veritable seminar on the subject in New York in September 1953 ("the smartest move I ever made in my life"), wherein the muse of history became the queen of law. His new "historical" brief ran to 235 pages. The South Carolina reply covered 90, with 145 more of appendix. The Department of Justice brief covered 188, with twice that amount in its appendix.[23]

As had happened a year earlier, the *Brown* arguments were once more postponed, from October to December. The reason was not procedural consolidation, however, but the need for the new Chief Justice to acquaint himself with the massive and formidable briefs. Hence, it was almost a year to the day when the encounter was resumed, and from 1:05 P.M. on December 7 to 2:42 P.M. on December 9 a magistral burst of advocacy—again featuring a Davis-Marshall exchange—reviewed the intentions of the Thirty-ninth Congress. This time another element constantly intruded: apprehension and concern with public response, acquiescence, and obedience.

The dominance of the latter issue and the subordination of the former were apparent when the new Chief Justice read the opinion of a unanimous Court at 12:52 P.M. on May 17, 1954. If the intricately filigreed questions of *Brown I* suggested Justice Frankfurter, *Brown II*—lumbering, bearlike, and overpowering—bore the stamp of Earl Warren. All the subtle argument and scholarly research as to what the Thirty-ninth Congress had on its mind was dismissed with one word—"inconclusive," and Thurgood Marshall had his zero-to-zero ball game with a scorer's note in the observation that the Court could not "turn the clock back to 1868, when the Fourteenth Amendment was adopted, or even to 1896, when *Plessy v. Ferguson* was written."[24]

The discard of the past provided the key to the present. After a discussion of the growing place of education in American life and government as well as its impact on the democratic process, and, perhaps most critical, of the traumatic psychological impact of segregation on the segregated minority, the Chief Justice came to the key sentence in which he distinguished (but did not overrule) *Plessy* from the current controversy: "We conclude that in the field of public education the doctrine of 'separate but equal' has no place."[25]

Given the categorically absolute tone of the decision ("We have now announced that such segregation is a violation of equal protection of the laws"), the real surprise was that it did not admit a single child to a single school. *Brown II* called for a *Brown III* argument on the fourth of the arabesqued questions, that concerning remedy, where enlightenment had been requested the preceding year.[26]

A separate companion opinion was necessary to dispose of the District of Columbia issue involving as it did national rather than state power. It also involved the difficulty that the Fifth Amendment, on which the Washington petitioner's appeal was pitched, unlike the Fourteenth, contains no reference to "equal protection of the laws." This meant that if relief was to be forthcoming at all it was to be secured under the nebulous bonds of "due process."[27]

The difficulty did not detain the Chief Justice for a minute. Citing among other authorities *United States v. Korematsu,* which had validated the relocation-camp incarceration of almost one hundred thousand American citizens and their relatives solely on the basis of race, the companion opinion reached its conclusion on a manifest and common-sense proposition: that if the Constitution outlawed segregation in education by the states, it was "unthinkable" that it imposed a lesser duty on the federal government. The logic had an irony transcending *Korematsu.* A century earlier in *Dred Scott v. Sandford* another Chief Justice had used the same judicial reasoning—the logic of unthinkability ("No one . . . would think a moment . . .")—to use the self-same words of the Fifth Amendment as a mode of extending slavery throughout the American territories.[28]

The issue of remedy came on almost a year later, and almost as an anticlimax. Once more scheduled argument had to be deferred, this time in consequence of the death of Justice Jackson in early October, 1954, and the subsequent Senate delay—in a sense, the first fruits of resistance to *Brown*—until the following March in confirming the second Justice Harlan as his successor. But on May 31, 1955, Chief Justice Warren once more spoke for a unanimous bench in *Brown III* and sent the cases back to the lower courts with a phrase that would be long remembered: that racial segregation in the public schools must be ended, not necessarily overnight, but "with all deliberate speed."[29]

The phrase itself became almost as much the subject for debate and reflection as the key decision, for, notwithstanding the Chief Justice's brave rhetoric that "constitutional principles cannot be allowed to yield simply because of disagreement," the plain fact was that constitutional principles were being allowed to yield precisely for that reason. At the time, however, the abstract outlawry of educational segregation provoked the larger commentary, or perhaps noncommentary, of which President Eisenhower's was the most conspicuous.[30]

Other response was neither covert nor restrained and Warren's efforts and particularly footnote 11 of *Brown II* drew a variety of fire. Professor Edmond Cahn wrathfully denounced the citation of sociological data. ("I would not have the Constitutional rights of the Negroes—or of other Americans—rest on any such flimsy foundations as some of the scientific demonstrations in these records.") The Chief Justice of Florida was likewise scandalized, albeit from an opposite point of view, by the citation of "the Scandinavian sociologist," Gunnar Myrdal. ("What he knew about Constitutional law we are not told nor have we been able to learn.")[31]

Nevertheless, the spring of 1954, the spring of *Brown II,* was a springtime of hope, with a euphoria almost impossible to remember in the light of subsequent events. Down in Atlanta at the N.A.A.C.P. convention, Channing Tobias greeted the decision, not in the accents of victory, but of moderation, and promised his organization would work for its mandate in a spirit of "give and take." In Washington, Senator Allen Ellender of Louisiana asserted that white Southerners were "law-abiding citizens and the Supreme Court's decision is the law of our land." Felix Frankfurter captured something of the spirit of the spring of 1954 when he was able to write an old friend:

> Yes, the unanimity of the Court in the *Segregation* decisions rightly gave the widest comfort. Particularly heartening is the predominantly moderate tone of the southern press and with a few conspicuous exceptions, even the southern public men are more sober than I should have expected them to be. Maybe one of these days the story will be known how it came to pass.[32]

Brown v. Board: The Vinson Story

Frankfurter made another observation in his letter, and it touched the very heart of what had transpired in *Brown:* "One does not have to be a soothsayer to know that the new Chief Justice is one person and his predecessor another." The passage cryptically summarized the sequence of events that brought a divided Court to the unanimous opinion of May 17, 1954.[33]

Just two short years earlier, on June 9, 1952, the Justices by a seven-to-one margin voted to hear the case. Justice Jackson cast the negative vote; Chief Justice Vinson's vote was not recorded. The real divisions, however, appeared at the conference of December 13, 1952, following the first round of argument. Here a remarkably diverse quartet favoring reversal of *Plessy*—Black, Douglas, Minton, and Burton—confronted a doubtful Chief Justice Vinson and the varyingly doubtful Reed, Frankfurter, Jackson and Clark. As significant as the fact of division was its character.[34]

This doubt was epitomized by the Chief Justice's perplexity as to the action of the Thirty-ninth Congress in dealing with the public schools under its jurisdiction. But Vinson also indicated that the Court might have to act if Congress did not, and the just concluded election of the Eighty-third Congress in the first Eisenhower landslide obviously heightened the chances of the latter contingency coming to pass. At the moment he seemed to favor continuing the euthanasia approach of the past, wherein the Court hastened the demise of *Plessy* by affirming its letter and denying its spirit.

But there seemed another element present: an obviously increasing concern over judicial legislation in the area of civil rights. The Chief Justice's questioning of petitioner's counsel during oral argument had been seen as less than sympathetic. More suggestive was his forthcoming dissent from *Barrows v. Jackson,* the last official word on civil rights. There he was to break what had been the Court's long unanimity and disagree with the veto which *Barrows* placed on state-court enforcement of suits by whites against whites for sales of real estate to blacks in violation of racially restrictive covenants.[35]

Something of the same apprehension beset Felix Frankfurter. The historical intentions and the original understandings of the Thirty-ninth Congress as expressed in the Fourteenth Amendment had been on his mind a long, long time. "For nearly 20 years," as he told Black back in 1947, "I was at work on what was to be as complete and as scholarly a book on the Fourteenth Amendment as I could make it." From that study he had concluded that the states were under no constitutional ban insofar as legally imposed segregation was concerned. The federal government and the District of Columbia, however, were another thing again. Here he saw the far more obscure and latitudinous due-process clause of the Fifth Amendment as a readily available source of judicial power.[36]

Almost predictably, Hugo Black disagreed. Black's antipathy toward judicial resort to due process as a superlegislative veto authority had been established as far back as his first Senate term. But that was not at issue; what was in dispute was the meaning and content of the Fourteenth Amendment vis-à-vis state power. Here Black had made his own independent study, best exemplified in the lengthy appendix attached to his dissent in *Adamson v. California,* but manifested also in one of the dissents at the beginning of his judicial service. That study had been undertaken in the context of Black's long-standing duel with Felix Frankfurter over whether the Fourteenth Amendment incorporated the Bill of Rights. It posed special complications for the issue in *Brown.* The very Congressman John A. Bingham whom Black had hailed in his *Adamson* appendix as "the James Madison of the Fourteenth Amendment" had insisted that the Civil Rights Act of 1866 be amended to eliminate prohibition of state segregation laws. To be sure, the inference was as long as it was broad, for the evidence also suggested that Bingham felt this result should be effected by amendment rather than by statute.[37]

Black preferred to take his stand with the first Justice Harlan that segregation as a constitutional issue was ruled essentially by the Thirteenth, Fourteenth and Fifteenth Amendments *ensemble,* rather than by the legislative history of any one. The consequence was simple: that slavery with all its incidents, consequences, and secondary pathology—including separation by reason of color—lay under the continuing ban of the organic law.

The specific letter of the Fourteenth Amendment also was available to support his view and what was perhaps his line of argument at the December conference, reconstructed from subsequent expression. Thirteen years after *Brown II,* Justice

Douglas gave one view of what that case decided—that "notions of what constitutes equal treatment for the purposes of the equal-protection clause *do* change." It drew a bristling dissent from his long-time coadjutor: "I do not vote to hold segregation in the public schools unconstitutional on any such theory. I thought when *Brown* was written, and I think now, that Mr. Justice Harlan was correct in 1896 when he dissented from *Plessy v. Ferguson.*" And still two years later in a television program Black elaborated his defense of an unchanging equal-protection clause:

> My view was, we had a simple question: does that give the colored people of the nation equal protection of the law? . . . Well, I lived in the South, practically until I came up here. . . . I didn't need any philosophy about changing times to convince me that there was a denial of equal protection of the laws.[38]

Frankfurter, however, had no desire to take a stand with the first Justice Harlan, and what Frankfurter had to say earlier in *Adamson v. California,* on the incorporation of the Bill of Rights in the Fourteenth Amendment, was not without relevance to the decision he faced in *Brown:*

> Between the incorporation of the Fourteenth Amendment and the beginning of the present membership of the Court —a period of 70 years—the scope of that Amendment was passed upon by forty-three judges. Of all those judges, only one, who may respectfully be called an eccentric exception, ever indicated the Fourteenth Amendment was a shorthand summary of the first eight Amendments theretofore limiting only the Federal Government, and that due process incorporated those eight Amendments as restrictions on the powers of the States. Among those judges were not only those who would have to be included among the greatest in the history of the Court, but—it is especially relevant to note—they included those whose services in the cause of human rights and the spirit of freedom are the most conspicuous in our

history . . . Miller, Davis, Bradley, Waite, Matthews, Gray, Fuller, Holmes, Brandeis, Stone, and Cardozo. . . .[39]

He might have added, vis-à-vis the current issue, Hughes, Murphy and Rutledge. Still, by early 1953 Frankfurter had made the break with the past, although the agony of his choice was suggested by a work of supererogation—having "one of the most dependable law clerks he ever had" read "every word" in the old *Congressional Globe* relating to the formulation of the Fourteenth Amendment.[40]

In any event, with the advent of 1953 his thoughts turned from right to remedy, and his writing skills appeared in the ceaseless drafting and redrafting of a memorandum to his fellow Justices concerning what form the Court's forthcoming decree should take. This overt change of position, together with that of Justice Tom Clark—who insisted that whatever be done be done with a gentling hand but whose ultimate judicial position had been forecast by his stand against residential segregation as Attorney General—reduced the previous five-man majority reluctant to overrule *Plessy* to an unconvinced trio of Vinson, Reed, and Jackson.

Along this line, the arabesqued questions that came out of *Brown I* were drawn largely from Frankfurter's views on the direction in which the Court should proceed and his recommendation that the Court should conceal that direction by looking in opposite directions. Concealment went only so far, however, for Frankfurter had a characteristically tart response to suggestions that the Court indicate that the questions had been framed at the request of the Department of Justice:

1. We ought to assume full responsibility for the questions we put to counsel, and what is perhaps more important
2. The objections which both parties will naturally have . . . John Davis, *et al.,* because they do not want any intimation.that the merits will go against them, and Thurgood Marshall because he wants a decree on the

merits unqualified—ought not to be allowed to be resolved into resentment against the Government for
bringing up this matter in the first place. . . .[41]

The Changing Cast

The second *Brown* conference was held December 12, a year
to the day less one since the first meeting of the Court on the
merits of the case. The meeting mixed the old and the new. One
new element was the position of Justice Frankfurter, who four
days earlier had circulated among the Justices a memorandum
that compressed the *tour de force* of his historical research on the
origins of the Fourteenth Amendment into a brief phrase—"in a
word, inconclusive." It was to give the Chief Justice a key term
for his *Brown II* effort.[42]

Also completely new were the words and attitudes of the Chief
Justice of the United States, and these differed strikingly from
those of his predecessor. The historical difficulties that had beset
Vinson moved Warren not at all. Instead, almost at the opening,
he tersely restated the Harlan-Black concept that it did not take
research but only a knowledge of the plain meaning of plain
words to know that segregation violated the Fourteenth Amendment and the Thirteenth and Fifteenth as well. Insisting that the
practice was based on a presumption of racial inferiority and had
no place today, whatever its past may have been, Warren proposed that the only duty of the Supreme Court was "to abolish
[it] in a tolerant way." The statement also indicated that the
Warren style, which had been developed in eleven years in state
government, was to continue in the Chief Justiceship—innovative, policy-making, advocative, persuasive.[43]

Only two of the Justices present seemed disposed to dispute
their new Chief. Stanley Reed, conceding that the Constitution
of *Plessy* and 1896 might not be the Constitution of today, denied Warren's assumption that segregation necessarily rested on
an assumption of racial inferiority and suggested the arrangement might be justified as an application of the police power of

the state. A far harder opposition seemed to lie with Robert Jackson, whose files contained a bristling memorandum ("A Random Thought on the Segregation Cases") and whose disclosure some years later would itself trigger a separate and independent controversy. At the time, however, its thrust illuminated some of the argument among members of the Court:

> I realize that it is an unpopular and unhumanitarian position for which I have been excoriated by my "liberal" colleagues, but I think *Plessy v. Ferguson* was right and should be affirmed. If the 14th Amendment did not enact Spencer's *Social Statics* it just as surely did not enact Myrdal's *American Dilemma*.[44]

Yet, Jackson did not take this line of address at the conference. He did much the same thing, however, in softer words, suggesting that he knew no judicial way to reverse *Plessy* but that he was prepared to join—if so labeled—a frankly political decision reaching this end. All through argument before the Court his comments had indicated the issue was essentially one for political resolution. ("I suppose that realistically the reason this case is here is that action couldn't be obtained from Congress.") His complete response to that impasse was such that a quarter century later a former law clerk would say that "to this day . . . I am not exactly sure what Justice Jackson's views were."[45]

The winning over of the minority became the Chief Justice's key strategy, and he approached it with the same bland but hydraulic and pervasive manner that had worked his will time and time again with a recalcitrant legislature. Five days after the conference Justice Burton was recording the Chief's tactic—"to try [to] direct discussion of segregation cases toward the decree—as probably was the best chance of unanimity in that phase." Here Burton put his finger on the critical element of any reversal of *Plessy:* the indispensability of organic unity and the necessity that the Court speak with a single voice.[46]

In a later commentary—written in the subsequent fallout of *Brown* and therefore applicable a fortiori to the germinal litigation—Frankfurter suggested the double necessity for judicial unanimity. One was negative—to foreclose "any possible mis-understanding, especially by those fired with a zeal to pervert, that there was any qualification to the responsibility for every member of the Court for the Court's decision." The other was positive—to make "the transcending issue" not segregation but "respect for law as determined so impressively by a unanimous Court in construing the Constitution of the United States."[47]

The means of securing the impressive and unanimous determination took the form of a double envelopment. The first fold was to align the plurality who already agreed to *Plessy*'s reversal on the mechanics of reversal and hold them together. Concessions obviously had to come from this revisionist quartet whose initial disposition was to effect the overthrow out of hand. The second was to coax the others into the group. Here also Frankfurter came to the fore. Well before the second conference of December 12, 1953, he was helping to shape the tactic of remedy via the phrase "with all deliberate speed." It was an ancient chancery line, one that Holmes had used half a century before, one that Frankfurter himself had used repeatedly and without attribution and that he incorporated in a secret memorandum to the Court—"The typing was done under conditions of strict security." This was the phrase that was much criticized and long regretted; at the time, however, it yielded two enormous advantages, distinct but related. Primarily, it fitted the vague mood of hope that the problems of race in America would somehow and in some way work themselves out. Tactically, it later gave the Chief Justice the resource of flexibility. It was a remedy of compromise, and in the short run, massed the Court on a common front regarding the fundamental constitutional issue.[48]

In many ways, massing the Court involved the same delicate game of feint, charm and persuasion that Warrren had played a thousand times in Sacramento. On the Court, as in the legislature, each side held some trump cards; in *Brown,* however, the potential dissenters had a bargaining position out of all proportion to their numbers. Yet the Chief Justice was not without some bargaining leverage of his own on this proposition, where the key issue (as Frankfurter suggested) was the institutional character of the Court itself and where the consequences of a divided decision could be equally chilling when turned either way.

In any event, a unanimous opinion is the product of all participants, and the role of the Chief Justice was essentially that of orchestral intermediary. Perhaps some members of the Court were more open to his advocacy than others, as for example, Justice Reed, whose concession on a changing Constitution had stipulated away half the intellectual opposition and whose heart had already demonstrated it was in the right place. Notwithstanding a rural Kentucky background, Reed was the one who wrote the landmark opinions ending the color bar in party primaries and integrating common passenger carriers in interstate commerce.

Throughout the spring of 1954 the Chief Justice backed and filled with the issue of remedy as his major ploy, and by May 8, 1954, Associate Justice Burton's praise of the draft effort to date ("a magnificent job that may win a unanimous court") suggested the end of the trial was in sight. On May 12 the close was even nearer at hand (It looks like a unanimous opinion"). The entry at the conference of May 15 recorded the draft being "finally approved" and therewith Warren's triumph.[49]

But he had help.

"When the inner history of [the *Brown*] case is known," the late Professor Bickel noted, "we may find that [Justice Frankfurter] was a moving force in its decision." Frankfurter's contributions lay at several levels. One may have been a role as devil's advocate, masking the strong feelings he obviously had ("as one who, for years before coming on the Court, was a member of the legal committee of the N.A.A.C.P.") and testing the arguments put forward. But most conspicuous and, in retrospect, most ironic, was the suggestion of "with all deliberate speed." At the time it seemed the tactic of consensus when consensus was indispensable. Years later, Justice Black looked back with regret:

> It seems to me that it probably delayed the process of outlawing segration. It seems to me, probably, with all def-

erence to the opinion of my brethren, all of them, that it would have been better—maybe—I don't say positively —not to have had that sentence.[50]

Ironically enough, Felix Frankfurter also agreed, ambiguously asserting some years later that the sentence "was used without credit [against my protest] in the segregation opinion."[51]

In truth, Frankfurter's contribution in the area of phrasemaking did not lie in the increasingly controverted sentence concerning speed but in the single word "inconclusive" with which he summed up the legislative history of the Fourteenth Amendment and which was incorporated in a key sentence in the *Brown II* opinion. His private opinion of that history was even less complimentary—"How anyone could have gone through the debates in Congress on the subject of the Fourteenth Amendment and have respect for the intellectual clarity of hardly anyone in that debate beats me." But the important thing was that he had laid his towering reputation for integrity ("I feel about accuracy the way Queen Victoria felt about chastity") on the line in attesting that the legislative history was indeed inconclusive.[52]

Even after Frankfurter had settled the question of legislative intent, the conclusion did not come easily to him. He was indeed the last Federalist, scrupulously concerned with keeping the ancient balance the Fathers had set between central power and local authority, and beyond that, with keeping the judicial power within its appointed limits.

> My starting point is . . . the democratic faith . . . the right of a democracy to make mistakes and correct its errors by the organs that reflect the popular will—which regards the Court as a qualification of the democratic principle and desires to restrict the play of this undemocratic feature to its narrowest limits.[53]

Yet, despite this starting point he did come over. Why? Perhaps it was the passage from Holmes he was so fond of quoting:

The life of the law has not been logic: it has been experience. The felt necessities of the time, the prevalent moral
and political theories, institutions of public policy, avowed
or unconscious, even the prejudices which judges share
with their fellow-men, have had a good deal more to do
than the syllogism in determining the rules by which men
should be governed.[54]

Frankfurter may have made one other contribution to the
unanimity of *Brown* in the evolving position of Justice Jackson.
On March 30, 1954, Justice Robert Jackson suffered a heart
attack and, from that day until the reading of the *Brown II*
opinion on May 17, was confined to the hospital. For that reading he came directly to the bench from his hospital bed to add his
physical presence to the display of institutional solidarity. Five
months later he was dead. The following year his Godkin Lectures were published posthumously by the Harvard University
Press. If the controverted memorandum were in fact an index of
Jackson's views during the pendency of *Brown,* then a remarkable passage in the lecture could have been framed, *in vitro* at
least, as a dissenting opinion in *Brown II:*

A cult of libertarian judicial activists . . . appears to
believe that the Court can find in a 4,000-word eighteenth-
century document or its nineteenth-century Amendments,
or can plausibly supply, some clear bulwark against all
dangers and evils that today beset us internally. This as-
sumes that the Court will be the dominant factor in shaping the constitutional practice of the future and can and
will maintain, not only equality with the elective branches,
but a large measure of supremacy and control over them.
. . . But it seems to me a doctrine wholly incompatible
with faith in democracy, and in so far as it encourages a
belief that the judges may be left to correct the result of
public indifference to issues of liberty in choosing Presidents, Senators, and Representatives, it is a vicious teaching.[55]

What aborted the dissent, if dissent it was, and won Jackson over? Surely not the friendly persuasion of the Chief Justice, who occupied the office for which Jackson had been twice passed over. Jackson did have one close friend on the bench in Frankfurter—the only one, if a book so scurrilous that Frankfurter wanted to sue for libel is to be believed. But Jackson was always his own man, whatever the counsel of friends, and his final decision was very much of his own making. Perhaps in those months in the hospital, overshadowed with the intimations of mortality, another and wholly different consideration was both critical and decisive—the memories of Nuremberg, where he had served as a prosecutor of the Nazi war criminals and had seen, as few men have, the ultimate pathology of race and the Caliban state.

Brown v. Board: The Black Footnote

Despite—or perhaps because of—the fact he was the only member of the Court from the deep South, Black was in the forefront of the revisionist bloc. He had acquired some credentials much earlier when he was the only member of the Supreme Court to accept Secretary Ickes' invitation and attend the Marian Anderson concert at Lincoln Memorial. ("Only ten Senators attended," Ickes wrote, "and only one Justice of the Supreme Court—Black—who was a former member of the Ku Klux Klan.") More recently, he and Douglas had been the only members of the Court willing to hear the head-on and unadorned confrontation to segregation presented by the Taylor case of 1950.[56]

A reference to the latter episode and a measure of the progress of ideas came when the Southern Conference for Human Welfare honored Black a second time. The second event, some six years after the first, occurred a week before the death of Franklin Roosevelt in 1945. This time there was no imposition of segregation laws but instead a glittering and fully integrated gathering at Washington's new Statler Hotel. At the meeting, Charles Houston, general counsel of the N.A.A.C.P., recalled the Anderson event: "After the concert, Negroes sought Mr. Justice

Black's autograph more than [that of] any other person except Miss Anderson herself. People have an uncanny instinct for recognizing their friends."[57]

Black was hailed that night by the future Chief Justice Vinson as "an unmistakably Southern but genuinely national statesman," and a passage in Black's reply forecast both his *Brown* concurrence and the consequent tension between the two loyalties. ("The conditions which created fascism abroad must not be allowed to exist here—the placing of some groups in a preferred class of citizenship at the expense of other groups.") Perhaps the oblique phrase was especially applicable to Houston, whose Supreme Court appearances involved a lunch at Union Station—the only nearby place he could eat—and to whom the dining facilities in Washington, from the drugstore lunch counters to the Statler itself, remained as closed after the festive evening as they were before.[58]

In any event, it was precisely Black's Alabama origins that give his concurrence in *Brown,* and through it the decision itself, an ultimate credibility. "How wonderful the unanimity of the Court," wrote the venerable C. C. Burlingham, dean of the American bar. "Black's concurrence is marvelous. He is as good a Southern Democrat as any of the Governors and Senators."[59]

But goodness as a Southern Democrat did not carry with it freedom from the price exacted, and some years later Chief Justice Warren suggested what that price was when he declined praise for the decision and insisted, instead, that it go to the Southern Justices—Reed of Kentucky, Clark of Texas, and Black, who had to go home thereafter. In Black's case there was a degree of rhetorical license, for Black did not go home, at least for a long time to come. Ironically, his southward trip, which caused him to miss the historic December 1953 conference on *Brown II,* was the last public journey he was to take to his native state for over a decade. He did not need critical senatorial oratory to know that there would be "a more or less hostile attitude on the part of many people, partially because of a feeling that I have participated in opinions which many people thought were bad for Alabama and the South." He was right, as the expostulation of an unidentified Congressman showed—"Why didn't I kill that son of a bitch, Black [when] we were in the Army together?" And in the same spirit, his law-school class declined to send him an invitation to their fiftieth anniversary.[60]

The real price was exacted vicariously, however, and it was that much harder to suffer. "Hugo, Jr., and Graham are at Birmingham, no children yet," the Justice had written a few years before *Brown II*. "Hugo is doing well in the practice and loves it." The son and namesake, educated in Alabama and practicing law in his parents' home town, obviously had the most promising of political futures in a state where the Bankhead dynasty was proof that family names would be taken seriously. All that passed with the *Brown* decision. Indeed, he had to pronounce the sentence when his son's sure-fire candidacy for the Birmingham seat in Congress was about to be launched—"This is your chance, son, but I've got to tell you something. . . . We've got some cases . . . challenging segregation . . . I don't believe segregation is constitutional."[61]

It all had been forecast some two decades before when Walter White, Executive Director of the National Association for the Advancement of Colored People, appraised the assurances (". . . he hoped that he would be able to measure up to what I and others of his friends expected of him") just tendered by the senior Senator from Alabama, who was about to become the junior Associate Justice of the Supreme Court: "Somehow or other, I feel quite confident that he is going to do so. I do hope we won't be fooled by him."[62]

Nor were they.

Part Six

Mr. Justice:
Part Two

CHAPTER FIFTEEN

Dr. Myrdal's Postscript

Of Men and Institutions

In the closing lines of *An American Dilemma,* Gunnar Myrdal made his famous point that, notwithstanding widespread popular belief that race relationships would gradually work themselves out, the odds were that they would do no such thing. On the contrary, he insisted, the seeming equilibrium of the times was illusory, becoming increasingly negative, and indicated an urgent need for social engineering to deal with the profound difficulties that lay ahead. He suggested no specific control framework to provide such engineering but indicated—particularly by his stress on the necessity of reversing the civil rights cases—that somehow it was to be provided within the national political process.

Myrdal may have lacked clairvoyant perception in failing to forecast both the failure of that process and the reluctant judicial *Putsch* that made good the default, but he provided a prophetic flash of insight into what was to come when he restated his basic proposition in a ponderously captioned appendix, "A Methodological Note on the Principle of Cumulation," and proposed that principle as a basic law of society—that change, once started, attained a momentum out of all proportion to the force of the original push. There was nothing essentially new here. Edmund Burke had said the same thing in a different and remarkably apposite idiom in that passage in his *Reflections on the Revolution in France* wherein he insisted that there is a process of upheaval change that is progressive as well as irreversible, and in it the medicine of a constitution becomes its daily bread.[1]

Hence, appetite came with eating in the very necessities of the case, and notwithstanding the conscious intent and even deliberate will of its authors, *Brown* could not be an isolated, nonrecurring act of political intervention by the judiciary. Rather, once taken, it became the critical point of departure of ongoing change. Yet, the course of that change, as the mutational development of both Court and Chief Justice was to show, was something considerably more complex than a simple, lineal sequence.

The several faces of the process as well as their essential, if lagging, interconnection might be glimpsed in several sequences. One was the contrast between the agonizingly slow implementation of *Brown III* on one hand, and the forthright opening of public recreational facilities, which was ordered in terse, imperious and faceless *per curiam* opinions. Nor did the contrast go unnoticed; for, ironically, the summary orders cited for their authority the theses on necessity and damage ("neither of these points can be made about golf-playing or swimming," gibed *The New Republic*) undergirding the decision where the Court was slow to act. And the Court was slow to extend its judicial protection to other discrete and insular minorities. Yet it moved crabwise in that direction, and someone later marked the index of the pilgrim's progress in the diminishing differences of Warren and Black. For the twenty-two cases wherein the Chief and senior associates ranged on opposite sides in Warren's first term shrank to twelve in the second, and numbered only three in the third.[2]

The point of this beginning, a few months before *Brown II,* saw Warren and Black part company on the constitutional claims of both the criminally and the politically accused. Indeed on the appeal of Patrick Irvine, Long Beach bookmaker, they parted company twice over. Irvine had publicly disclosed his occupation by the purchase of the gambling stamp that federal law required, and the process of his incrimination was completed when the local police overheard conversations picked up by a microphone that they had installed without warrant or authority in his bedroom. Robert Jackson commented on the procedure in incandescent wrath ("almost incredible if it were not admitted"), but he nonetheless upheld Irvine's conviction on the basis of the Wolf case—that the restraints of the Fourth Amendment against unreasonable searches and seizures did not bind the states. Nonetheless, he proposed, Warren alone of the concurring Justices agreeing, that a copy of the record of the case be sent to the Attorney General of the United States for possible prosecution under an appropriate federal statute.[3]

While there was something that ran against the grain in the idea of a constitutional right whose protection was unavailing, Jackson's opinion was nonetheless in the common-law tradition which denied that a proven criminal should go free simply because the constable had blundered. Black, however, was prepared to say that the criminal should, and not on the ground of the concealed microphone. Instead, his emerging constitutional fundamentalism pleaded for a rigorous interpretation of the Fifth Amendment as the stamp Irvine had so unwillingly bought and binding California to it: ("It is enough for me that Irvine was convicted in a state court on a confession coerced by the Federal Government. I believe this frustrates a basic purpose of the 5th Amendment.") And onetime prosecutor and former legislator, he also regarded the suggested reference to the Attorney General as gratuitous—"Prosecution, or anything approaching it, should be left to government officers whose duty that is."[4]

Warren also stood apart from the dissenting Black in a spate of security cases that followed hard on the heels of Irvine. He joined five of his colleagues, over the dissent of Black, Frankfurter and Douglas, to uphold New York's suspension of the medical license of Dr. Joseph Barsky, a Brooklyn physician who had been convicted of contempt of Congress in refusing to turn over the records of the Joint Anti-Facist Refugee Committee to the House Committee on Un-American Activities. Again the Chief Justice was numbered with the Court, Black and Douglas dissenting, in upholding the deportation of Robert Galvan, long-time alien resident, pursuant to the proscription which the Internal Security Act of 1950 had placed upon Galvan's prior and perfectly legal membership in the Communist Party.[5]

Next term, however, there came a subtle and significant shift and, appropriately enough, race was the catalyst. A year to the day after *Galvan,* the Court upheld an all-white cemetery's refusal to accept the body of an Indian war veteran. More noteworthy, however, was that Warren was numbered in the dissenting partnership of Black and Douglas. It was the prelude to a more conspicuous change of position in a security case that followed shortly thereafter, wherein the Chief Justice carried his Court with him, in voiding a "post audit" procedure that had forfeited the security clearance of Dr. Frank Peters of the Yale Medical School. He did more than this, however, for he unveiled the Fabian tactic that was to be the standard ploy in the judicial protectorate of the politically accused—a deft thrust that gained its result by seizing on some peripheral procedural issue and avoiding more substantive issues. Thus Warren passed over the entire legitimacy of the executive loyalty program itself to find that no "post audit" procedure had been authorized by it. And while he and Black were now on the same side, Black's obdurate concurrence indicated that the rapport had still some distance to go—"I wish it distinctly understood that I have a grave doubt as to whether the Presidential Order has been authorized by any Act of Congress. That order . . . [embodies] a broad, far-reaching, espionage-system program over government employees."[6]

That rapport was finally achieved two years after *Brown II,* when the profile of Warren and the Warren Court emerged in unmistakable clarity with the reversal of Communist Steve Nelson's conviction for sedition under the Pennsylvania statute. Ironically, the ground was that federal action—the much criticized Smith Act—had covered the entire field. ("Only Feds for

Reds," *Time* headlined.) And a week later the constriction of state antisubversive powers continued as the Court forbade New York to fire a prickly Brooklyn College professor named Harry Slowchower for his behavior before the House Un-American Activities Committee. To *Time,* and doubtless the public at large, Slowchower was "an evasive smartaleck" who named Josef Stalin as the one person he suspected of Communist Party membership, but declined to answer at all when his own affiliation came up. Yet, the constraining of state power did not mean the expansion of the federal counterpart, for with Warren numbered among the majority, the Court wound up the 1956 term with a reprise of its Fabian ploy lifting the legal framework of the overall loyalty program from nonsensitive government agencies. Even more illuminating of the change was Warren's association with Black and Douglas to dissent from the Court's dismissal of the appeal of a security-suspect employee protesting his discharge by a private employer.[7]

Time, somewhat prematurely but prophetically, took note of the Court's "deliberate course to the left," and *Business Week* suggested the underlying cause: "Note the Supreme Court split with Chief Justice Warren, Eisenhower's appointee, lining up time after time with Justices Douglas and Black, the old New Deal liberals. It causes a lot of comment in Washington." And then in mid-June as the 1956 term approached its close, James "Scotty" Reston pronounced the appraisal of the establishment press as he entered in *The New York Times* the view that Chief Justice Warren was now a member of the liberal wing of the Court, "since he joins Justices Black and Douglas' dissents in many cases." But Black had another view of the matter:

> It's too bad the papers are pretending that Warren has been changed under the influence of me and Douglas. He came into the Court with the same ideas I had. He got them in California, I in Alabama. No wonder the Democrats backed him; Republicans backed me when the Democratic big businessmen opposed me. I like Warren very much.[8]

Of Counter Causation

The principle of cumulative causation was capable of application in any number of directions, and one counter to the line of departure chosen by the Court began to show itself after *Brown III* and indicated that Senator James O. Eastland's bitter condemnation was far more prophetic of things to come than the N.A.A.C.P.'s magnanimity in victory or Senator Allen Ellender's irenic declaration that the decision represented, after all, the law of the land. For, showing itself at about the same time, the emergence of Warren's ultimate position was a developing counterposition asserted in the calm, yet implacable tone of the Declaration of Constitutional Principles. Better known as the Southern Manifesto, and signed by ninety-six Southern members of Congress (Senator Lyndon B. Johnson of Texas was a notable exception), the Declaration was released March 12, 1956; it charged that the Justices had substituted "personal political and social ideas" for established law in *Brown II,* and it pledged an unremitting effort to overthrow that judgment by all legal means.

The Manifesto had any number of other characteristics. One was its character as pressure at the periphery rather than conspiracy at the center. Indeed any number of Southern Senators and Representatives, predisposed to moderate positions as a consequence of their enlarging Washington experience and perspectives, went over to extremist hostility as a consequence of local pressures and grass-roots challenges.

And yet another facet was its symbolization of a permanent base upon which might be piled other elements of hostility to the Court in a sequence of cumulative countercausation to the one that was transpiring on the Court. For the outlawry of state sedition statutes on the ground of federal preemption provoked a wave of genuine apprehension over misplaced judicial intervention in the cold war but permitted ideological outrage to unite with sectional resentment and do so in an idiom of criticism that said not one word of race. The legislative focus, moreover, took the classic legislative responses. "Most of the attacks on the

Court," *Time* noted, "are emotional instead of cerebral. Most of
the 70-odd congressional bills are bad ones with little likelihood
of passage in the foreseeable future. But the widespread reaction
against the Court's use as a social institution is a clear and
present danger."[9]

The clearest and most present danger threatened the venerable
doctrine of preemption—that laws within the scope of the
national authority swept away inconsistent state ones. Some proposed congressional countermeasures went only to reversal of
Nelson and the reinstatement of state antisedition laws. Others,
however, proposed to uproot the historic doctrine, root as well as
branch, and permit all state laws to stand unless Congress specifically enjoined their invalidity. Yet, illustrative of the rising mettle
of the Warren Court and its growing sense of security in the
face of the hostile, if variegated, coalition in Congress was its
action of May 1956, when it struck out on still another front and
reiterated the doctrine by vetoing the application of the Nebraska
right-to-work law to railroad unions to the extent of inconsistency with the Federal Railway Labor Relations Act.[10]

The action added yet a third layer of hostile criticism to go
with that attending the desegregation and security decisions, and
perhaps the very base and depth of the resentment provoked a
bitter personal tone, which increasingly focused around Warren
himself. Yet the increasing fusillade of criticism was self-defeating and tended to harden, not shake, Warren's views. Part of the
Chief Justice's reaction was rooted in his character and personality—beware the genial Swede, ran an ancient blue-collar-Irish
counsel of caution. And there was another factor.

This was the Chief Justice's round-the-world trip during the
vacation months of the summer of 1956 whose decisive influence
in terms of attitude and determination could be compared only
with Woodrow Wilson's tumultuous European reception of
1919. Indeed, far surpassing the character of the welcome given
Wilson was that triumphal Indian experience in which the Chief
Justice was hailed from Bombay to Calcutta as the liberator of
America from the tyranny of color and caste and that reached its
climax in the stormy and sustained applause that broke out at the

University of Delhi, when the reading of his LL.D. citation reached the part of the honoree in breaking the color bar.

The Indians were not alone; in the United States, university after university vied to claim the Chief Justice as its own, *honoris causa*. And surpassing anything the academic world had to offer anywhere was the controversy that surfaced in the campaign of 1956 as to whether Vice-President Nixon had inserted a comma between "great Republican" and "Chief Justice Earl Warren" in framing his own particular tribute to the author of the *Brown* decision.

Changing of the Guard III

The transformation of the Warren Court involved changes in membership as well as changes in attitude, and both processes opened from much the same deceptive starting point. Certainly the replacement of Robert Jackson by John Marshall Harlan in late 1954 indicated no radical shift of direction. Yet, even here the spirit of changing times tinctured the process of succession. It was widely noted the new Justice was the grandson of his dissenting namesake in *Plessy v. Ferguson,* and doubtless that fact alone underlay much of the delay in Harlan's accession to his new office.

The President began the delay by withholding the nomination until the congressional elections were out of the way, and the Court correspondingly deferred argument on what was to be *Brown III.* Delaying submission, however, seemed to produce still more inaction, and here Senator William Langer's opposition—a protest over the lack of Supreme Court appointments from North Dakota—and a vocal concern for "experience" were but the top of the iceberg. For it was not until spring of 1955 that Harlan finally took his seat, and his hearings revealed all the standing suspicions of the Court plus a new one, which took the form of an apprehension of a judicially enlarged treaty power eroding national sovereignty.

Philosophically, the continuity from Jackson to Harlan had a variant note in the changed relationship of the holder of that chair with the senior Associate Justice. Not that Black and Jackson had not made an effort to put the confrontation of 1946 behind them, but the very vigor of a statement by Jackson in 1952 indicated just a little too much: "From that day to this, Justice Black has treated me with respect as one gentleman to another. We've never exchanged a harsh word. Relations were never as harmonious between us as they have been since [my return]."[11]

John Marshall Harlan never had to make such a statement for his long-term rapport with Hugo Black—a distant cousin as things turned out—was one of those relationships in which two men agreed in all things except opinion. And even in opinion they could occasionally be in accord. In fact, Harlan was to write the opinion differentiating abstract advocacy of insurrection from specific exhortation, thereby weakening the thrust of the Smith Act. Indeed, on occasion he could press beyond Black's libertarian ideas, as when he not only wrote into the United States Reports the word that Mae West said she could not be paid to speak but also established the constitutional right to exhibit its written form to women and children.

And this seeming paradox, which symbolized so much of the character of the Warren Court, had its counterpart in the next Eisenhower appointment, the Roman Catholic who was to write into ruling the constitutional right of contraception for all, including minors. Unlike John Harlan, however, William Brennan came to the Court with something of a reputation for outspokenness, and Dean Griswold of Harvard subsequently compared him to Holmes in the complexity of his attitudes and philosophy. Indeed, the complexity was underscored at the very threshold of the Court in his response to Senator Joseph McCarthy on the import his own libertarian speeches held for legislative antisubversive efforts: "Senator, I can think of no more vital or important object than rooting out subversives." (His response apparently did not convince the interrogator, for McCarthy cast the only negative vote on confirmation.)[12]

Brennan succeeded Black's old Senate confidant, Sherman

Minton, in a sequence of successions that had its own special element of irony and surprise. For, notwithstanding the presumption that Minton would be almost a natural ally of Black on the bench, perhaps no member of the Court ever fitted the role less. Contrariwise, the role of Brennan was subject to no such advance appraisal; but, as things turned out, the New Jersey Justice teamed up with Black, Douglas and the transformed Chief Justice, a libertarian quartet reminiscent of the one that the old New Dealers had once made with Rutledge and Murphy and that the jargon of the day, paraphrasing the initials of a well-known ad agency, christened as "B. B. D. & W."[13]

The development was largely unforeseen, particularly to the appointing President who sought not another Rutledge or Murphy, but (as he later told Arthur Krock of *The New York Times*) a candidate in the mold of Chief Judge Arthur Vanderbilt of New Jersey. And, *prima facie,* Brennan seemed to fit the mold, for he reputedly had been the protégé of Vanderbilt on the state bench. The President had not, however, confirmed that desirability of appointment with the Chief Judge, and Vanderbilt's comment on learning of the Brennan appointment not only expressed a difference with the presidential estimate of the appointee but also summed up that unpredictability of the appointive process in an obvious reference to the mutational development of the Chief Justice of the United States: "He's done it again. He's pulled another one."[14]

Dwight Eisenhower is later reputed to have said that he had made four appointments to the Supreme Court and regretted two and a half of them. And for his part the first appointee responded by compressing in a single sentence the phenomenon of cumulative causation that had taken Gunnar Myrdal a whole appendix to describe: "I doubt if the President expected us to take the stands we have taken."[15]

CHAPTER SIXTEEN

The Darkling Plain

Red Monday

The extent to which President Eisenhower had done it again was underscored as the decisions for the 1957 term began to come in. Something of a foreshadowing prelude appeared in *Schware* and *Konigsberg*, both decided May 6, 1957, and both holding that past membership in the Communist Party, admitted or suspected, could not be used to deny admission to the bar. The decisions were undertaken without the participation of Stanley Reed, who had resigned the preceding February. Neither was the fifth Eisenhower appointee, Charles Whittaker, of Missouri, involved in them, nor did he have to be. The Court divided 8 to 0 in one case and 5 to 3 in the other, with Black writing the opinion in both.[1]

The bar admission stirred up much hostile comment, but this was dwarfed by the outpouring that soon followed after *Jencks v. U.S.* reversed the conviction of a labor leader who had filed a false non-Communist affidavit, and ruled that the government must produce all FBI reports forming the basis of testimony in criminal trials. President Eisenhower ("never been so mad in my

339

life") found it doubly enraging, for not only did the opinion give the defendant far more than he asked for—that the trial judge, not the jury, inspect the relevant documents—but it was written by his recent appointee Mr. Justice Brennan. Far more memorable and certainly more widely quoted was Justice Clark's bitter dissent that his new colleague had just opened the FBI files to the criminal "and thus afforded him a Roman holiday for rummaging through confidential information as well as vital national secrets."[2]

The stage was thus appropriately set for that quartet of opinions that came down on June 17, 1957, and made that day thereafter known as "Red Monday." In an opening rebuff to the administration, the discharge of a State Department careerist was set aside on the grounds that the Secretary had not followed his own regulations, even though an act of Congress had granted him absolute discretion in such matters. In a second thorn in the presidential side, the second Eisenhower appointee, John Marshall Harlan, reversed the Smith Act convictions of the second-string Communist leaders in a thesis that differentiated between conspiring to advocate overthrow of the government as an abstract philosophy and conspiring to do so as a workaday act. He failed to persuade Justice Clark, who scored "the artillery of words," and he also failed to persuade Black and Douglas, who would have none of his distinction and who repeated the insistent thesis they had raised at the trial of the first-string Communists to the effect that the advocacy provision of the Smith Act was unconstitutional on its face, with the defendants being entitled to directed verdicts.[3]

The remaining parts of the quartet came in constraints laid on legislative committees at both state and federal levels. In one action the Court freed a recalcitrant witness from a conviction for contempt of the House of Representatives and its Committee on Un-American Activities. In the other it did likewise for a leading Marxist theoretician who had fallen afoul of the New Hampshire Attorney General serving as a one-man body of legislative inquiry. There were some arresting individual aspects to the cases. The Chief Justice made a heroic effort to suggest that the new investigations were qualitatively different from those his senior colleague had undertaken in the 1930s. ("The new phase of legislative inquiry involved a broad-scale intrusion into the lives and the affairs of private citizens.")[4]

The past was also present in two references in the government's brief, duly incorporated into Justice Clark's dissenting opinion. One quoted from Senator Black's article in the February 1936 issue of *Harper's,* "Inside a Senate Investigation," which upheld the widest scope of inquiry and defended pitiless exposure for its own sake. The other was a *New Republic* contribution by Professor Felix Frankfurter, of the Harvard Law School, whose thesis was bluntly put in its title, "Hands Off Investigations." Black serenely ignored the thrust, but with Frankfurter the tormentors drew blood and indeed had done so for some time—"How 'they' wallow in that piece of mine . . . published more than thirty years ago."[5]

Crimes and Cellophane

As the 1957 term came to its close, the Warren Court left its mark on several areas other than security and subversion. A triply sensitive combination of race, sex and crime came in *Mallory,* where the Court enlarged the list of its enemies by reversing the conviction of a black rapist, not on the grounds of innocence, but rather because the District of Columbia police had not complied literally with Section 5(a) of the Federal Rules of Criminal Procedure requiring arraignment before a magistrate without unnecessary delay.[6]

Apart from its sensitive combination of essentially extrinsic elements, there was no revolutionary dimension to *Mallory.* Rather, the ruling faithfully conformed with the 1943 precedent of *McNabb v. U.S.* Yet the extrinsic elements could not be ignored completely. The changing ethnic curve of the rising crime cycle was a brutal fact. So was the subsequent career of the defendant who gave his name to the *Mallory* case and who thereafter went from rape to rape and was fated to die, almost in that act, by a policeman's gun. And while Justice Frankfurter, who wrote the opinion, was undeniably right in his contention that constitutional precedents were frequently obtained by people who were not very nice, it was also true that Mallory's subsequent victims might take another view of the matter.[7]

For, as New York's Chief of Detectives Frederick M. Jussen would later assert, "I wouldn't say that the Supreme Court decisions have directly led to more crime on the streets, but remember this: A criminal freed on a technicality is almost always going to be a recidivist." And perhaps in ultimate irony, the man ultimately punished for Mallory's first crime had nothing to do with it. "Mallory, Mallory," a senatorial inquisitor was to intone for Chief Justice-designate Abe Fortas, "let that name ring in your ears."[8]

And, as if *Mallory* coming atop the security and subversion decisions were not enough, the Warren Court had one more element to add for its roster of critics. For on Red Monday the Court also handed down its decision in the famous du Pont case, or more precisely *du Pont II*. For, like *Brown* before it, *du Pont* was entitled to an ordinal number; it was an integral part of an organic sequence of decisions involving the same parties and the same essential point of law. There was a difference. While the *Brown* cases embodied a continuity of set and direction, *du Pont* involved both the sharpest of turnabouts and the briefest of time frames.[9]

Decided in 1956, *du Pont I* held that control of virtually all the cellophane production in the country did not amount to a monopolization denounced by the Sherman Act. Rather, the critical question was held to be the defendant's control of the over-all market for flexible packaging materials, and tested by this standard, the government's suit failed to state a case. The sophisticated economic rationale, particularly the use of cross-elasticity of demand to test the relationship of seemingly unrelated products, was hailed as a new beginning in antitrust and the embodiment of the Eisenhower administration's promise to bring order out of the chaos that had beset this branch of the law.

Yet, the applause for *du Pont I* was far from universal. There were those who saw it as judicial legislation rampant and an affront to common sense as well. Moreover, the new dispensation went against the grain of both the jurisprudence of certainty and that ongoing American apprehension that the "heejus monsters" (as Theodore Roosevelt, per Mr. Dooley, called the major corporations) should be bridled with the strictest of controls. And within this group had to be accounted a trio of Supreme Court dissenters—Black, Douglas and Warren—who denounced *du Pont I* as a sophistry compatible with a completely monopoloid economy.

With the accession of William Brennan, however, and three disqualifications (as Justice Whitaker joined the initial Clark–Harlan recusations), the minority of three in *du Pont I* became a plurality of four in *du Pont II*. The new decision did not purport to disturb the old in the slightest, and formally this was indeed the case. But in fact the reversal was utter and complete as *du Pont II* breathed a new Draconian spirit into antitrust as it held du Pont's 25 percent stockholding in General Motors illegal, not only when the government brought its recent suit but when the stock was bought almost half a century before.

It was the elastic time dimension that perhaps accounted for the almost seismic shock wave that followed. *Time* reported that *du Pont II* "stunned both sides" in stretching the antitrust laws so far that even the trustbusters "gasped." The *Wall Street Journal* called the decision "incredible" and the *New York Herald Tribune* asserted that "the whole American corporate structure is shaken." And given Justice Black's Darwinian view of the competitive business process, that was exactly what was intended.[10]

The Gathering Storm

Perhaps the occasionally abrasive tone in Black's opinions in the first half of the 1950s reflected the six long and lonely years he lived as a widower; for a while those years had been shared by his daughter, but she left on her own career, and the senior Justice resided by himself in the pleasant house in Alexandria.

344 Hugo Black and the Judicial Revolution

Most of those years involved disappointment and defeat on the bench, but a triumphal change seemed to come with the 1957 term, and in a happy coincidence, its conclusion was duly noted by an adoring niece. For that September Black "handed down a decision . . . where there was no dissent at all; in fact, many people wrote concurring opinions. It was truly a good thing that Elizabeth De Meritte agreed to change her name to Mrs. Hugo Black." Mrs. De Meritte, a still-youthful Birmingham grandmother and the sister of an admiral, was at the time his secretary, and as a former law clerk put it, she had been so installed by the Justice's matchmaking children with malice aforethought.[11]

Friends and associates noted how the marriage seemed to give Black a new lease on life, and it could not have come at a better time. Counterbalancing the rise in his judicial fortunes was the revitalization of the antijudicial coalition in Congress. Red Monday had done its part; so had *du Pont II*. *Jencks* and *Mallory* in tandem were particularly formidable, for together they stirred up the friends and admirers of the FBI both to reverse judicial action and to avenge a prior defeat. ("After that [*McNabb*] decision in 1943," wrote Justice Frankfurter, "the Department of Justice and, I was advised at the time, particularly the FBI made a fierce drive to have Congress change the *McNabb* ruling by legislation.")[12]

The seventy-odd bills that had been introduced into the Eighty-fourth Congress were but prelude to the flood tide of proposed anti-Court legislation that came in with the Eighty-fifth. News magazines observed that not since the Nine Old Men shot down F.D.R.'s Blue Eagle had the Supreme Court been such a subject of general comment. Indeed before the summer of 1957 was over, an anti-*Jencks* statute protecting the FBI files was on the President's desk. It emerged as a prophetic compromise of covert cooperation between the Court's critics and the Court's defenders. But it also stood as a symbol of formidable attack to come in a legislative counteroffensive forming along several lines.

One proposal, carried over from past sessions of Congress, was for a second Smith Act, wherein the author of the original statute to bear that name now recommended the virtual abolition of federal preemption, and the corresponding enlargement of state jurisdiction, in the areas of subversion. A second was an omnibus measure, sponsored by Senator William E. Jenner of Indiana, seeking to abolish Supreme Court jurisdiction in the controverted areas of bar admissions, subversion and security. Yet a third would have ended the power of federal courts to issue the great writ of habeas corpus in connection with state criminal trials and thereby end collateral federal inquiry into those proceedings. And a fourth, undoubtedly the most formidable, proposed reversing *Mallory* by providing that no confession should be inadmissable in the federal courts solely by reason of delay in the defendant's arraignment.

There were other proposals. Congressman Robert L. F. Sikes of Florida called for a constitutional amendment setting up the Senate as a super-court of appeals on any decision involving states' rights. Senator Herman E. Talmadge of Georgia would require the Supreme Court to give all parties in interest an opportunity for full hearing before acting on a lower-court decision. Senator Talmadge's state legislature called for the impeachment of Black, Clark, Douglas, Frankfurter, Reed and Warren for high crimes and misdemeanors. Representative Carl Vinson, dean of the state's delegation, said that he would neither introduce nor vote for such a measure, but offered his own remedy— a constitutional amendment that would bar the Court from overturning a precedent over fifty years old.

The spate of the proposed constraints was not without its ironic side. Senator Thomas C. Hennings of Missouri, who had emerged as the Court's strongest defender, duly noted that the two principal elements seeking to harness the judiciary—the Southern Democrats and the conservative Republicans—had been the very groups whose earlier judicial protection had produced the bitter anti-Court criticism—indeed, the constitutional crises—of 1868 and 1937. But an even more consummate irony came in Britain in mid-1957 during a joint meeting of the American Bar Association and the British Law Society. At the very moment when Winston Churchill was paying his own tribute to the Supreme Court at an A.B.A. dinner, a committee of the association was presenting a report suggesting that judicial zeal to protect individual rights could endanger national security. More than this, the Association itself was tabling a resolution urging lawyers to refrain from "contemptuous criticism" of their highest American tribunal. Perhaps the proposal should have been framed in extraterritorial terms, for the British hosts were reportedly shocked at what they heard from their American guests.[13]

They would have been more shocked had they been present at some congressional hearings on the other side of the Atlantic, when the forthcoming showdown in the last session of the Eighty-fifth Congress began. It was not a prospect that defenders of the Court found particularly promising. The swift passage of the anti-*Jencks* statute in the previous session was ominous enough; the prospects for the remaining items were enhanced when the critics of the Court seemed to receive two powerful intellectual assists and some others not so intellectual.

In February the venerable and enormously respected Learned Hand delivered the Holmes Lecture at Harvard. It was widely regarded as a criticism of the Supreme Court in general, and its anti-Black implications were also manifest. Hand was urbanely skeptical of the possibility of extracting categorical certainties on judicial power from the constitutional text; and he was even more corrosive on the effort to exalt personal rights over property rights. And even more mordant was his closing line of tribute to deceased friends. "In the universe of truth, they lived by the sword; they asked no quarter of absolutes, and they gave none." Most memorable, however, was his obvious thrust at the Chief Justice of the United States: "For myself, it would be most irksome to be ruled by a bevy of Platonic Guardians, even if I knew how to choose them, which I assuredly do not."[14]

And then in the following month, Arthur Corwin, of Princeton (emeritus), virtual dean of American constitutional scholars and vigorous critic of the pretensions of an earlier Court, reflected on Red Monday and then wrote *The New York Times* that "on June 17 last the Court went on a virtual binge and thrust its nose into matters far beyond its competence with the result (in my judgment, at least) it should have its aforesaid nose well tweaked. . . . The country needs protection against the aggressive tendency of the Court."[15]

Somewhat less lofty but substantially the same were the verdicts coming from the National Association of New England Women, the National Association of Manufacturers, the American Legion, and the National Association of Former Agents of the Federal Bureau of Investigation. On the other side of the line were ranged, sooner or later, *The New York Times,* the AFL–CIO, the American Bar Association, and the Eisenhower administration. There were some points where a position on the line of battle was difficult to discern. Thus, Justice Douglas in his current book, *The Right of the People,* held his own Court partly to blame for an asserted erosion of American ideals; contrariwise, a determined ban of dissidents at the D.A.R.'s annual convention forced an anti-Court resolution to be reworded from "must" to "should" with respect to prior judicial experience of future Justices. And Learned Hand disclaimed the implications of his Holmes Lecture in asserting that current proposals for statutory overcall of Supreme Court decisions "would be detrimental to the best interests of the United States."[16]

Long Hot Summer I

In a surge reflecting the popular mood, a sequence of anti-Court bills swept through the House of Representatives by enormous majorities—to narrow federal preemption; to constrain the great writ of habeas corpus; to repeal *Mallory;* to withdraw jurisdiction over bar-admission controversies. The Senate seemed particularly receptive. Already its temper had been indicated by the hostile questioning of Potter Stewart, nominated to replace the ailing Harold Burton (had he been a "creative" judge in prior circuit-court service, did the Constitution mean today what it meant in 1787, did he agree with the reasoning in *Brown II?*), as well as by the seventeen votes cast against his confirmation.

And in the Senate the initial blunderbuss withdrawal of jurisdiction had been recast into specific proposals that took the Warren Court at its Fabian word and undertook to rewrite the statutes involved.

Yet it was in the Senate that the revisionist movement encountered three formidable and ultimately aborting barriers. Extremely important was the necessity of an early adjournment in an election year. Equally significant were the political instincts of the majority leader, Lyndon Johnson, who had no intention whatever of rending the gossamer unity of the Democratic party by either passing or defeating the anti-Court measures. And significantly critical was the attitude of a band of Northern and Western liberals, led by Senator Hennings, who put forward their view of what the issue was about:

> A view of overriding a decision of the Supreme Court cannot be considered in isolation. Just as our opponents desire to overrule the Supreme Court for its symbolic effect, so we desire to present fully the symbolism involved in supporting the Court and particularly in having the free world know that America is proud of the humanitarian decisions of its highest court.[17]

The thesis was coupled with a demand to put the whole revisionist congeries over to the next session of the next Congress. More to the point was the threat, coupled with the request, to hold Congress in session by a variety of devices including the filibuster itself.

The combination proved decisive. Some proposed legislation went to a conference committee, from which it never emerged; some was laid on the table; and the anti-*Mallory* bill, really regarded as the test case, went down in a parliamentary snarl. Seemingly the consequence of an inadvertent violation of Senate rules, the disposition had in fact been approved by the Democratic policy committee, and "the attack on the Warren Court, which had come in with a thunderclap, went out with a sham battle over a point of order."[18]

Long Hot Summer II

"I think we must choose on whose side we stand," asserted
Senator Paul Douglas in his own expression of the symbolism
involved in the Senate debate. "Do we stand on the side of Governor Faubus or do we stand on the side of the Supreme Court?"
For the governor had surfaced as a symbol of another variety. A
full year before the Senate standoff he had provided a full-blown
crisis in Little Rock when he blocked a cautious, judicially approved program of school desegregation by calling out the
National Guard and blocking the entry of a handful of black
students to Central High School. The effort was balked by the
imposition of a special restraining order and the arrival of the
paratroops of the 101st Airborne. But the fundamental instability of the situation persisted throughout the school year.[19]

At the close of that year, the inevitable turbulence produced a
request for a thirty-month moratorium on further desegregation
efforts, which the local federal district court promptly granted.
This was in turn overruled by the regional court of appeals, and
the issue eventually came on for decision to the Supreme Court,
which, appropriately enough, held a special summer session on
the issue. For the issue was not the local problems of an individual school board. Rather, as Justice Burton noted in his diary,
what was at issue was "the first real test of the power of the
federal courts to implement the *Brown* decision."[20]

The opinion that came out of the special summer session more
than bore out Burton's estimate of the gravity of the cases and its
content had been forecast by Black's interrogation of the counsel
of the respondent school board:

> JUSTICE BLACK: Is your argument based on the premise
> . . . that it requires a 2½-year period in which state
> laws purporting to override the *Brown* decision could
> have been tested in the courts?
> MR. BUTLER: Yes sir, I think that is our position.[21]

Mr. Butler got his answer in two parts. On September 12, 1958, the Court tersely ordered the immediate integration of Central High School. Seventeen days later an extraordinary opinion signed by all the Justices not only slammed the door but threw away the key in a total condemnation of all efforts to evade the decree. More than this, the Court insisted that *Brown II* "is the supreme law of the land" and no state official "can war against the Constitution without violating his undertaking"—in sum, that Governor Faubus was, like every other public official in the United States, fully bound by the decrees in *Brown II* and *Brown III* as if they had been in the Court as litigants.[22]

His second answer came in Frankfurter's concurring opinion, which was handed down in October, and as a Southern lawyer he was a particular addressee. There was some surprise that Frankfurter had taken some of the edge off the initial unanimity of the Justices, and he defended his action in a letter to an old friend:

> Do any of your lawyer friends really think that I wrote my concurring opinion . . . because I thought I could do better than the Court did? Nothing could be further from the truth. . . . My opinion . . . was directed to a particular audience, to wit: the lawyers and the law professors of the South . . . I myself am of the strong conviction that it is to the legal profession of the South on which our greatest reliance must be placed for a gradual thawing of the ice, not because they may not like the termination of segregation but because the lawyers of the South will gradually realize the transcending issue, namely, respect for law.[23]

Black apparently was dubious about the wisdom of Frankfurter's venture into concurrence. Black was, of course, the Court's only expert on Southern lawyers. But, apparently too, he changed his mind and was one of the Justices who, according to Frankfurter, "very generously said that in view of the returns that have come in, they were wrong and I was right in the expectation which led me to write as I did . . ."[24]

Broken Reprise

If Black was among the Justices who congratulated Frankfurter for the special effort in Little Rock, he was ranged conspicuously on the other side in the development that blunted the second thrust of the congressional revisionist effort. For the new Eighty-sixth Congress started off on much the same note as its predecessor, with an array of anti-Court bills sweeping through the House by wide margins. There were, to be sure, some new elements. One was a young Republican Congressman named John V. Lindsay, who broke tradition and his freshman silence to denounce the proposed legislation as unnecessary, irresponsible, uncertain and chaotic. On the other hand, endorsement of the change came from the American Bar Association, now minus the membership of the Chief Justice. (It continued to hold that of Associate Justice Black, who once said, perhaps half in jest, that it was the only organization that he ever regretted joining.)

Even though passage of Court curbs had been forecast by prophets as acute as Speaker Sam Rayburn, the revisionist drive in the Eighty-sixth Congress turned out to be as abortive as in the preceding one. Again a number of elements, not necessarily repetitive ones, combined to undo the effort. The insecurities of the cold war were obviously ebbing. The judicial revolution was gaining some legitimacy. Some of the principal revisionists had left the legislative field. And the Court itself contributed to the lessening of tensions.

Not that it gave ground cravenly. Indeed it stood fast on certain salients, setting aside a ten-thousand-dollar fine on the N.A.A.C.P. for failing to turn over its records to the authorities in Black's native state and reasserting the right of suspect defense-plant workers to confront and cross-examine their accusers. But the edge of all this was blunted by a set of decisions that ran quite the other way. One group permitted state and federal authorities to successively try a defendant for the same single act.

Another group, more importantly, reexpanded the scope of federal and state legislative investigations.[25]

The judicial compromise—*turnabout* is too strong a word— was essentially the work of Felix Frankfurter, who crossed over from earlier libertarian positions and distinguished his new opinions with great care from his older ones. Some acid observers, however, saw no distinction whatever. Indeed, at least one suggested that the only analogy in the past was the famous switch in time which Justice Owen Roberts had undertaken two decades earlier. Irrespective of the validity of the comparison, the two incidents had one point in common, and this was the effective disarming of the critics of the Court.

Black refrained from including that particular analogy in the extended historical review that he included in his dissent. He also refrained from extrajudicial comment and thereby differed from his long-time colleague, Justice Douglas, who made a speech insisting that the Supreme Court was not about to take "a back seat" in the American system of government. But there could be no doubt Douglas spoke for both.[26]

But the only time Black's name appeared in the press during the détente was on a matter unconnected with the immediate work of the Court, on April 5, 1959, when the wire services reported the marriage of his daughter, Martha Josephine ("Jo Jo") to Mario Pesaresi, a New Jersey psychiatrist. A few days later, however, *The New Republic* stitched together his latest opinions under the caption "Black Dissenting" and noted that "an indictment of this character cannot fail to be disquieting."[27]

Yet if the view was disquieting, the viewer was not, and a significant tribute to the senior Justice's intellectual and moral stature came when Charles Curtis, of the Boston bar, delivered the prestigious Gaspar Bacon Lecture:

> Twenty years ago, after Black's first term of Court, I wrote an article about him in the *Atlantic Monthly* . . . I spoke of his "disrespect and distaste for judicial statesmanship." What shall I say now, after his twenty judicial

years? . . . I say that Justice Black is a child of the 18th century enlightenment and the spiritual heir of Thomas Jefferson. Are we not all his heirs? Are we not all children of the enlightenment?[28]

CHAPTER SEVENTEEN

Arrivals and Departures

The Lady in Court

A *New Republic* editorial, "Black Dissenting," echoed the senior Justice's strong remonstrance against the Court's current Thermidorian retreat. But it also noted that Black's strongest dissents had been handed down two weeks before the adjournment of the 1959 term and thereby failed to reflect several important decisions wherein the Court may not have been so insensitive to its "highest duty" as the dissenter had feared. And singled out for especial reference in this area of judicial second thought was *Kingsley v. Board of Regents,* which overruled New York's ban on the film version of *Lady Chatterley's Lover.* The *New Republic* rejoiced particularly that the lady was not for burning, but it tempered its joy with the regret that six different opinions were deemed necessary to explain why New York could not suppress her advocacy of adultery.[1]

The judicial label was itself a luminous index of both cultural and moral transition and the complex reciprocating sequence linking law and life. For obscenity, perhaps by its very nature, was one of those things whose outlawry was taken for granted as resting on custom and consensus rather than law. It was thus absent from that long list of judge-made, common-law crimes that otherwise ran to matters as diverse as eavesdropping or being a common scold, and statutory constraints did not emerge in either America or Britain until the middle of the nineteenth century. Understandably enough, the American constitutional aspects of obscenity came quite late in a milieu where the First Amendment protection of speech and press were perceived almost entirely in terms of political communications, and media otherwise was by almost universal account placed outside its ambit. Doubtless scholarly readers of *Playboy* in the early seventies would look back in astonishment at that for which *Esquire* almost lost its mailing permit three decades earlier. Yet as late as 1938 it was possible for the *Harvard Law Review* to carry a definitive article on censorship and say not a single word about any constitutional dimension of the subject.[2]

The initial decision came slowly and, in view of what was to follow, was surprisingly easy at the outset. In *Butler v. Michigan*, for example, there was really no difficulty in overruling the literally Victorian doctrine of *Regina v. Hinklin* and with it a Michigan statute that banned all material with a tendency to corrupt youth. ("Surely this is to burn the barn to roast the pig.") The size of the blaze, however, was another matter, and over it the uneasy libertarian partnership of Black and Frankfurter came asunder.[3]

The first occasion of parting was the companion cases of George Alberts and Sam Roth, charged with violations of the obscenity statutes of California and the United States, respectively. Justice Brennan upheld the convictions in a majority opinion that placed obscenity beyond the bounds of constitutional protection in a calculus that almost matched the Internal Revenue Code for turgid obscurity. The critical definition isolated material that dealt with sex—"a great and mysterious force in human life . . . a subject of absorbing interest to mankind through the ages"—in a manner appealing to the prurient interest and without—utterly without—redeeming social importance. But there was more than this, for the calculus was to be applied to the dominant theme of the work taken as a whole, in the eyes of the average person using contemporary standards. He failed completely, however, to win two of his colleagues to the formula as Douglas, with Black's concurrence, probed behind the components and inquired how the community conscience might be ascertained for a work dealing with sex and not for one concerned with politics or philosophy.[4]

It was a good question, for the community conscience with respect to sex was in a profound state of uncertainty. Massachusetts found Lillian Smith's *Strange Fruit* to be obscene in 1946, but cleared Kathleen Windsor's *Forever Amber* in 1949. New York, California, Wisconsin, Illinois and Massachusetts turned up at loggerheads on the character of *Tropic of Cancer*. And perhaps the most extraordinary event of all, and a true sign of the times, came in the 4-to-4 vote of the Supreme Court that left standing the New York ban on Edmund Wilson's *Memoirs of Hecate County*—a tie vote that came to pass as a consequence of the erudite and fastidious Justice Frankfurter's self-disqualification on the grounds of friendship with the accused pornographer.[5]

Part of the difficulty, of course, was rooted in the verbally incommunicable and intensely subjective nature of the response to the subject-matter. ("I know it when I see it," was to become a classic Supreme Court dictum.) And for Black this circumstance both symbolized and encompassed judicial incompetence, administrative unworkability, and violation of the plain constitutional command. Moreover, it enabled him to play the role of both the Alabama Baptist and the ultralibertarian in forgoing what was surely the most extraordinary evidentiary proceeding in Supreme Court history up to that time—a special viewing of *Lady Chatterley's Lover* in the Supreme Court conference room.[6]

For, unlike his eight colleagues, Black did not attend the showing. He did associate himself in Justice Douglas' concurring opinion, which followed the tradition of Blackstone and Story in declaring that if free speech meant anything at all it at least covered freedom from prior restraint. Reminiscent of Malcolm Muggeridge's dictum on pornography—unnecessary for the young, useless for the old, unseemly for the middle-aged—he added a concurrence of his own, gently teasing the other members of the court on their singular inability to apply the psychophysical litmus of prurience, "This Court is about the most inappropriate Supreme Board of Censors that could be found."[7]

There was more here than the inability of elderly men to respond to the media of excitation. There was also the inevitable book-by-book ("look-by-look") appraisal, which not only would take an incredible toll in time, but also carried the personalized and unpredictable judicial supremacy that he had already found anathema in the areas of economic regulation and criminal justice. And by the next term of court he was ready with a counter-calculus of his own. The occasion came with a state statute that punished the possession, knowing or unknowing, of obscene material held for sale. The unanimous judgment of the Court voiding the statute was achieved by different premises, and the varying logic of Black and Frankfurter divided them once more on the same line of cleavage that emerged in final procedure. Frankfurter concluded that the trial court had improperly excluded evidence about the literary standards of Los Angeles. Black, on the other hand, would have nothing of the community conscience there or any place else—"[The First] Amendment provides, in simple words, that 'Congress shall make no law . . . abridging freedom of speech or of the press.' I read 'no law abridging' to mean no law abridging."[8]

The Jurisprudence of Italics

The concurrence in *Smith v. California* was not the first time that Black had made something of a profession of faith in constitutional absolutes. In one form or another it had been the thread running through his quest for the grail of constitutional law. It underlay his selective parliamentarianism, his exegesis of texts, his appeals to history, and even his seemingly vain but nonetheless untiring effort to bind the states to the Bill of Rights. But the stark literalism was something else again.

And any doubt that he meant what he said in *Smith v. California* was dispelled when he gave the inaugural Madison Lecture at New York University in mid-February of 1960. His text, not without irony, was the one that Hand had chosen for the Holmes Lecture at Harvard some years earlier; and predictably enough, Black extrapolated the Bill of Rights to some remarkably different conclusions. For, where Hand paid tribute to old companions who had asked no quarter of absolutes and had given none, Black reiterated his profession of faith in a passage wherein punctuational stress was necessary to capture the total emphasis of the speaker: "It is my belief that there *are* 'absolutes' in our Bill of Rights, and that they were put there on purpose by men who knew what words meant, and meant their prohibitions to be 'absolutes.' "[9]

There was far more to the lecture than this. It included an appeal to history in the story of the Puritan dissenter who had claimed his own freedom from self-incrimination and was emerging as one of Black's more illustrious heroes. There was a reprise of the American experience in repressive legislation and an article-by-article commentary on the Bill of Rights itself. And there was also the fictitious account of a nameless Judge X—no other, of course, than Felix Frankfurter—who "balanced" the legislative findings of national necessity against uncompensated expropriation of private property notwithstanding the express command of the Fifth Amendment.[10]

Frankfurter published no reply, but that did not mean disputation was at an end. Alexander Bickel, Kent Professor of Law at the Yale Law School and sometime Frankfurter law clerk, led off in *The New Republic* with some reflections whose title, "Mr. Justice Black: The Unobvious Meaning of Plain Words," so epitomized his point as to make further commentary superfluous. It was a remarkable personal tribute ("The observer not only can bring himself to admire the capacity of so powerful a figure as Justice Black, he cannot bring himself not to. And it isn't really candor or capacity that is in question") with a formidable intellectual attack. First under fire was the Black logomachy on due process—that whatever the content of the phrase meant it must be granted. And from here Bickel passed to the principal thrust of his attack: the utility of illusion, the justification for creating it, and the possibility that illusion, engulfing the judiciary, could run to an ultimately devasting reaction.[11]

Hard on the heels of the Bickel article and in the same journal of opinion came another passage from the Yale Law School. This one was written by Professor Louis Pollak, former Rutledge law clerk and future dean, who reviewed a book of yet a third Yale professor, Charles L. Black's *The People and the Court.* Generally, the review was favorable, for it agreed with Professor Black's thesis that judicial review and the democratic process were compatible. But it then went on to approve Justice Black's conclusions while demurring to the absolutist logic. It also took note of the Bickel article and the Black-Frankfurter confrontation, and disclaimed any power of attorney "to accept in Professor Black's name a call to active duty in a crusade against Justice Frankfurter or anybody else."[12]

Seven months later Professor Black spoke for himself in a *Harper's* article, "Mr. Justice Black, the Supreme Court, and the Bill of Rights." Noting that the Madison Lecture had touched on the national interest itself, the Yale scholar went on to examine the beliefs that often set his judicial namesake apart from the other Justices and raised the question as to a country going through an erosion of constitutional guarantees, whether Justice Black's position represented a lost cause, and whether the American people would favor that position once they realized the gravity of the issue.[13]

After a characteristically vivid and eloquent analysis, Professor Black reduced the issues to two. Primary was the conclusion that even an absolutist logic necessarily began with definitions, and these—by definition, so to speak—had an inherently exclusivist character. Second in rank but virtually equal in sanction was the pragmatic counsel that even a nominal absolute had to yield to an extreme case—that notwithstanding the universal constraint against interrogation by torture, no prisoner who had secreted an armed atom bomb would be permitted to smile blandly at his interrogators in the police station. And he then phrased a doubting rejoinder to the categorical jurisprudence of italics:

> May not one infer that enforcement of the Bill of Rights guarantees is *necessarily* a process of not giving effect to "absolutes" but of balancing asserted claims of public interest that motivate the curtailment of freedom?[14]

From this point, Professor Black concluded, the real issue at stake was a question of argument and priorities. And here formal logic necessarily yielded to vital reality, as he propounded two answers to his own questions. The first was that the very "balancing" that Justice Black decried was an inescapable part of the process of definition itself. The second was that infringement of liberty committed in the name of definition must at least be phrased in terms "that can be swallowed by people who speak standard English." More importantly, it must give rise to a special order of magnitude.[15]

In the process of expounding his reflections, Professor Black indulged in a number of *obiter dicta* of his own. One was the aside that "Mr. Justice Black himself recognizes, as of course he must, that even 'absolute' rights have the limits that inhere in their own definition. . . . No one would argue, for example, that the 'free speech' protected by the First Amendment includes mere personal slander. . . ." And more *entre nous* was the suggestion that "Mr. Justice Black is an experienced judge with a long head" and should not be taken at the obvious meaning of his plain words.[16]

Professor Black was badly mistaken. A few months later the Justice was the subject of a public interview at the annual convention of the American Jewish Congress and vigorously repudiated the interpretations that had been placed on his Madison Lecture. He did more than this; he foreshadowed what would be regarded as the second major *volte-face* of his life. A consequence in part of discontinuities that lay ahead, but in part also of the jurisprudence of italics that was rapidly coming to form the core of his constitutional thought:

I learned a long time ago that there are affirmative and negative words. The beginning of the First Amendment is that "Congress shall make no law." I understand that it is rather old-fashioned . . . to say that "no law" means no law. It is one of the most amazing things about the ingeniousness of the times that strong arguments are made, which *almost* convince me, that it is very foolish to think "no law" means no law. But what it *says* is "Congress shall make no law respecting an establishment of religion" and so on. . . . Then I move on to the words "abridging freedom of speech or of the press." It *says* Congress shall make no law doing that. What it *means*—according to a current philosophy that I do not share—is the Congress shall be able to make just such a law unless we judges object too strongly.[17]

Most of the interview was restatement, including the reiterated emphasis on the sweep of the First Amendment ("without any ifs, ands, buts or whereases"). There were elements of novelty, however. One was a reply to Professor Black on the issue of defamation. "I do not hesitate as far as my own view is concerned as to what should be and what I hope will be the constitutional doctrine that just as it was not intended to authorize damage suits for mere words as far as the Federal Government is concerned, the same rule should apply to the states." But even more pregnant was the thesis, also the fruit of the long constitutional quest, that reached the same result that Learned Hand asserted in his Holmes Lecture and denied any essential difference between those rights called personal and those called proprietary:

We have a system of property in this country which is also protected by the Constitution. We have a system of property, which means that a man does not have a right to do anything he wants anywhere he wants to do it. For instance, I would feel a little badly if somebody were to try to come into my house and tell me that he had a constitutional right to come in there because he wanted to make a

speech against the Supreme Court. I realize the freedom
of people to make a speech against the Supreme Court,
but I do not want him to make it in my house.[18]

Causation Continued

The great debate between Black and Frankfurter really
masked far more than it revealed. At issue was not the judicial
revolution, but rather the extent of its momentum and sweep.
And here the proposition that had set the Court in motion—that
judicial power not only grows out of political impasse, but has
the duty and the sanction to impose the results that the democratic process should have reached—could not in the very nature
of the case be confined to the impasse litigated in *Brown I, II* and
III. For there were any number of minorities within the sweep of
the *Carolene Products* footnote, discrete, insular, and highly visible as well.

Frankfurter, however, did struggle valiantly to keep the genie
from getting wholly out of the bottle, and perhaps struggled all
the harder as a consequence of having yielded to the Promethean
temptation of the Brown case. Perhaps with a passing acknowledgment of the sardonic comment—that desegregation was not
a constitutional right till May 17, 1954—he stood uneasily upon
the dictum of Charles Evans Hughes that the Constitution was
exactly what the judges said it was, nothing more and nothing
less. And his preference was for the less of it, in as much as he
also stood in the Holmes tradition that judicial exegesis should be
minimal and should take the great provisions of the constitutional text as vital rather than formal—"not simply by taking the
words and a dictionary, but by considering their origins and line
of growth."[19]

But for Black the course of his own development had brought
the conclusion that constitutional adjudication lay exactly in
taking the words and a dictionary (1787 edition). But it also
involved a judicial response whenever the meaning of those
words demanded judicial action. The consequence was a judicial

world view that did not really collide with that of Felix Frankfurter. But there was a difference in character, for the judicial
sanction, as envisaged by Black, gained in intensity as it narrowed in focus, becoming precise, predictable and automatic.

Ironically enough, the character of the Black-Frankfurter duel
and the dynamics of combat were badly clouded over by the
ongoing revisionism in the loyalty-security cases, which suggested quite the opposite of what was coming to pass. The reports showed Frankfurter ascendant and Black in unavailing
protest. And this was not the case, even though some indications
were otherwise. One was that of the luckless defendant in
Uphaus v. Wyman, who remained under indefinite sentence for
obstructing New Hampshire's legislative inquiries. Here *The
New Republic*'s T.R.B. noted, in "Poetry, Thoreau, and a
Bible," that, because the seventy-year-old Dr. Uphaus was in jail
for consorting with "oddballs and idealists," whom he refused to
name, everyone else was in jail too. And Black sounded a parallel note in dissent when he suggested the analogy of John Bunyan. "He was arrested for preaching, and efforts were made to
make him agree not to preach anymore. . . . It is perhaps one
of the ironies of history that the name of John Bunyan, a poor
tinker and preacher, is at least as well known and respected
today as [that of] the great Chief Justice of England who permitted him to languish in jail."[20]

And while Frankfurter was the author of neither the first nor
the second *Uphaus* opinion, Black might as well have named him
in the second dissent, for the protestation was framed against
Frankfurter's views and Frankfurter's vocabulary:

> I think the summary dismissal of this appeal . . . is a
> sad indication of just how far this Court has already de-
> parted from the protection of the Bill of Rights. . . .
> Such retrogression follows naturally from the Court's re-
> cent trend toward substituting for the plain language of
> the Bill of Rights elastic concepts which permit the Court
> to uphold direct abridgments of liberty unless the Court
> views those abridgments as "arbitrary," "unreasonable,"
> "offensive to decency" or "unjustified on balance," for

these concepts reduce the absolute commands of the Constitution to mere admonitions.[21]

And in another reprise of a case that had been before the Supreme Court once before, the thrust against his long-time colleague was even sharper. In objecting to *Koenigsberg v. State Bar*'s conclusion, which barred the petitioner from becoming a California lawyer—now for obstructing the bar association's investigation—Black struck straightway at the heart of Frankfurter's constitutional *ethics*. ("It . . . seems to me that the Court's 'absolute' statement that there are no absolutes under the First Amendment . . .")[22]

Much the same strain ran through Black's protest against the legitimation of the anti-Communist statutes. In *Communist Party v. Subversive Activities Control Board,* involving registration of the party under the Subversive Activities Control Act of 1950, and again in *Scales v. United States,* involving the fundamental ban in the Smith Act on advocacy of overthrow of the government, Black bitterly protested the Frankfurter concept of balance. In the first case his views focused on a historical framework. ("Mr. Pitt proved, in 1799, that he was master of the concept and language of 'balancing' in his speech urging . . . laws to muzzle the press of England . . . And there certainly was no shortage of 'balancers' in our own Congress when the Alien and Sedition Acts of 1798 were passed.") In relation to *Scales,* however, he spoke to the present. ("This case reemphasizes the freedom-destroying nature of the 'balancing test' presently in use by the Court. . . . This doctrine, to say the very least, is capable of being used to justify almost any action Government may wish to take to suppress First Amendment freedoms.")[23]

Yet, for all the dissenting rhetoric, Black scored spectacularly in another and more permanent area of constitutional law in *Mapp v. Ohio.* In personal terms, the triumph came in the change of views of Justice Tom Clark with respect to state searches and seizures and thereby turned the initial dissent of Black, Douglas, Brennan and Warren into ruling case law. Indeed, Black had to make an adjustment himself, for he had never viewed the latitudinarian ban of the Fourth Amendment on merely unreasonable searches and seizure the way he did the unqualified commands of the First and the Fifth. Earlier he viewed the inadmissibility of illegally seized evidence into federal trials merely as a judicial rule of evidence and not a constitutional command. But now he read the Fourth Amendment into the Fifth, for self-incrimination, and saw a "precise, intelligible, and more predictable constitutional standard . . . dissipating doubt and uncertainty." And he accordingly departed from his prior view and joined in the judgment that illegally obtained evidence was barred from all American courts by the text of the Constitution itself.[24]

There was another context in which *Mapp* might be seen, and it was not unlike the one that brought *Brown* to pass. For the basic constitutional posture of the criminally accused throughout the United States was not unlike that of blacks prior to *Brown II*. In both there was a continuing impasse in which the political process was unavailing. Indeed, on the criminal-procedure front the Supreme Court's indignant wrath at the emetic searches in *Rochin* and the bedroom bugging of *Irvine* could be matched only by the indifference in the states in doing anything about it. The result was already preordained when the Supreme Court did act in a decision that was spiced with a Black thrust at the long-held views of Justice Frankfurter. ("We again reject the confusing 'shock-the-conscience' standard.")[25]

And the interconnection of the judicial protectorates over the discrete and insular minorities was underscored when the Court acted in *Gomillion v. Lightfoot*. For here it intervened, not in the function but in the very structure of state government. The dispute was occasioned by the petitions of the blacks of Tuskegee, Alabama, that they had been gerrymandered out of the political process, and the Court responded with an order that provided for a redistricting in which all political rights were brought into line.[26]

After its fashion, the Tuskegee decision could be justified as a mere by-product of the Brown case or at least as its logical consequence. But another line of analysis as well as the essential interconnection of the discrete and insular minorities forming the Court's protectorates was suggested within the week. It came at the behest, not of black Alabamians but of white Tennesseans, but the gist of the petition was essentially the same—a functional exclusion from the electoral process that was politically unreformable.

The Last Federalist

A fourth group was added to those already enjoying the juridical protection of the Supreme Court when the Court decided to hear *Baker v. Carr.* Unlike the others—racial minorities, moral and religious dissidents, and defendants in criminal prosecution —the new, discrete and insular minority was actually a majority in all things except political power. It comprised the inhabitants of the great metropolitan communities that almost everywhere had replaced the states as the fundamental components of the *res publica americana.*[27]

Chief Justice Warren later was to call *Baker v. Carr* the most important decision rendered during his tenure in that office; and, had he chosen to do so, he could have called upon Felix Frankfurter to prove it. The case had far more basic implications than the narrow round of its decision—a direction to a federal district court to hear a complaint on legislative misapportionment— might indicate. For in undertaking to examine the consequences of Tennessee's failure to follow its own constitution and reapportion its legislature every ten years on the basis of the latest census figures, the Court turned its back on the venerable doctrine of "the political question." It was a doctrine of abstention, not of jurisdiction, and rested on the proposition that there were some things that courts were singularly unfitted to do—supervise foreign relations, fix the dates of duration of hostilities, determine the status of Indian tribes, and determine whether a state had a republican form of government.

Indeed, the latter category was the seedbed for the doctrine and went back to *Luther v. Borden* in 1849, when the Court refused to enter the Dorr Rebellion by deciding which of the two contending factions was the legitimate government of Rhode Island. A dozen cases had included within the category controversies regarding the relationship between population and representation. They had done so, however, without the concurrence of Hugo Black, who as early as 1946 had seen the issue as falling within his view of a constrained but more sharply focused judicial power—explicit, quantified, predictable.[28]

But Felix Frankfurter did not see things that way at all. A variety of reasons—the very Jewishness which he denied, his deep sense of history, his view of the judicial process, a deep allegiance to a fundamental federalism, and a corresponding apprehension of unitary homogenization—came together to make *Baker v. Carr* run deeply against his inner grain. Moreover, they came together at a time when his personal relationships on the bench were not without their difficulties.

Several irascible passes at arms with the Chief Justice had been duly noted in the public press, and something of the same note tinctured a eulogy on the passing of Learned Hand—that the great judge was perhaps fortunate to have served on an appellate tribunal where his influence had been limited to one third rather than on the Supreme Court, where it would have fallen to one ninth.

To be sure, the Chief Justice had his own problems. The John Birch Society had called for a massive letterwriting campaign to force his impeachment and then established an essay contest with a prize of one thousand dollars for the best grounds. First prize went to Eddie Rase, of U.C.L.A., notwithstanding Warren's apocryphal suggestion that Mrs. Warren would be an easy winner. And, also from the Chief Justice's native California, a retired Marine colonel in the employ of Project Alert suggested that Warren be not impeached but hanged.

While the Chief Justice bore his defamation with outer fortitude and impassivity and was fairness itself in both court and conference room, another Frankfurter reference suggested an escalation of institutional friction. For in his eulogy Frankfurter

noted how the *gaudium certaminis* (joy of battle) was utterly
absent from Hand's temperament, and the comment was capable
of extension to his own court's internal proceedings and perhaps
to his own participation in them. Indeed, something of a parallel
reference came from his great antagonist at yet another testimonial dinner. For when Robert M. Hutchins, speaking for the
Fund for the Republic, deplored the current atmosphere of conformity, Black responded that controversy was still very much
alive in his own area of activity—"It's a grand fight. The Supreme Court does disagree. I hope it always will."[29]

And disagree it did in the kaleidoscopic array of opinions that
Baker v. Carr provoked on March 26, 1962, when the Court
concluded that the relationship between population and representation should lie within the judicial power of the United
States. And after sixteen years Black and Frankfurter exchanged
places. Back in 1946 Frankfurter had successfully restrained his
Court from entering "this political thicket" over Black's objection that the constitutionally guaranteed right to vote at all necessarily carried the right to have that vote counted with
approximately equal weight.[30]

It was truly remarkable that Black was silent in a case that
epitomized so much of his constitutional philosophy, which
otherwise provoked such an array of judicial views. Yet, in a
sense he did not have to submit an opinion. One could deduce
what he thought—albeit in the opposition—from the long, forceful and eloquent opinion with which Felix Frankfurter went
down fighting, and fighting hard:

> The Court today reverses a uniform course of decision
> established by a dozen cases . . . a massive repudiation
> of the experience of our whole past . . . asserting [a] de-
> structively novel judicial power . . . Disregard of inher-
> ent limits in the effective exercise of the Court's "judicial
> power" not only presages the futility of judicial interven-
> tion in the essentially political conflict of forces . . .
> [but] may well impair the Court's position as the ultimate
> organ of "the Supreme Law of the Land." . . .[31]

The dissent was his judicial testament. Within a week of its delivery he collapsed following a speech he had given for the seventy-fifth anniversary of the Interstate Commerce Commission. He never sat on the Court again.

The Last Hurrah

In something of an ultimate paradox, the thesis perhaps closest to Frankfurter's heart was engrossed on the constitutional text within a few weeks after he had been stricken from the bench. Moreover, it was done by the very colleague who had once been the protagonist of what Frankfurter decried as the corruptive antithesis and by means of the footnote jurisprudence that had also drawn his censure.

For, as was noted by several observers, in matters touching church and state Felix Frankfurter was something of an absolutist himself. For his reading of the First Amendment provisions on establishment and free exercise of religion was not quite Voltairean but not too far removed from an Enlightenment *écrasez l'infâme* that would have barred any religious coloration from all areas of public activity. It was a doctrine that had been gingerly asserted and applied and wound its way from the parochial-school transportation permitted in *Everson* to the on-premises instruction allowed in *Zorach*.

Through it all, Black's constitutional ideas in fact if not in form crept ever closer to Frankfurter's, and the nexus between them became complete in *Engel v. Vitale,* which outlawed the prayer to be said by voluntary participants at the beginning of each school day:

> Almighty God, we acknowledge our dependence upon Thee and beg Thy blessings upon us, our parents, our teachers, and our country.[32]

With the exception of the dissenting Potter Stewart, Black spoke for the entire Court in pronouncing the prayer an inherently religious exercise that lay beyond the Board of Regents of the State of New York to compose or prescribe. It was a good opinion, considering the little room he had for maneuver. The findings of the lower court had explicitly established the absence of coercion—unlike the schoolchildren in the flag-salute cases, pupils were free to be silent or leave—and thereby foreclosed the far easier ground of decision based on a constraint of the free exercise of religion. And, as Justice Douglas' concurrence showed, there were formidable historical difficulties—"I cannot say that to authorize this prayer is to establish a religion in the strictly historic meaning of the words."[33]

All in all, however, the proscription was a plausible and persuasive effort whose linchpin was a footnote worthy to rank with *Carolene Products* 4:

> There is of course nothing in the decision reached here that is inconsistent with the fact that school children and others are officially encouraged to express love for our country by reciting historical documents, such as the Declaration of Independence, which contains references to the Deity, or by singing officially espoused anthems which include the composer's profession of faith in a Supreme Being or with the fact that there are many manifestations in our public life of belief in God. Such patriotic or ceremonial exercises bear no true resemblance to the unquestioned religious exercises that the State of New York has sponsored in this instance.[34]

Black read his opinion on decision day in a low and impressive voice and added the impromptu observation that "the prayer of each man must be his own." Not that it did him much good in the storm of protest that followed. Criticisms ran from almost all shades of American opinion in a range from Reinhold Niebuhr's scholarly remonstrance to Ida Mae Adams' letter to *The New York Times* suggesting that the Supreme Court crier's daily call that God save the honorable Court be amplified to include "and in your wisdom show it the error of its ways."[35]

There were some contrasts and anomalies. American Catholics who had strenuously resisted the reading of the King James Bible in the public schools rallied *en masse* to the defense of the syncretistic Regents' Prayer. Not all of them did. In contrast to his predecessor's failure to throw the moral power of the Presidency behind the desegregation decisions of the Supreme Court, John F. Kennedy defended the outlawing of school prayer with the observation that the option of praying at home remained open.

And there remained the possibility that Black had reached and expounded the *Engel* opinion as he did as a consequence of the absence of the stricken Frankfurter. For, while Frankfurter doubtless saw his lot on the Court as an increasing sequence of provocative exasperations, there was another side to the coin. Here his strenuous efforts to have his own way—the biting dissents, the unending concurrences, the barbed interpolations in opinion reading, the schoolmasterish interrogation of counsel— must have been frequently counterproductive.

Indeed, it was supposed that Frankfurter's insistent pushing of Learned Hand for appointment to the Supreme Court was the very reason behind the great judge's failure to be appointed. And along much the same line was the reproof Mrs. Frankfurter was overheard administering to her husband, as they left the White House, for treating the President of the United States like a student in one of his Harvard seminars.[36]

Perhaps the temperamental contrast between Black and Frankfurter was never more apparent than in their treatment during oral argument. Black, the crack trial lawyer and superb appellate advocate, "never badgered counsel. He asked fewer questions . . . than many of the justices and those he asked were always courteously put, in the fashion of a judge who wants to be exactly clear what position a lawyer is taking rather than that of a law professor trying to trap a student."[37]

And perhaps also it was because Felix Frankfurter was the advocate *manqué* that he behaved as he did. "He fought long, hard, and loud . . ." ran a Black reminiscence of the conference room. "[He was] forceful, insistent, eloquent and persuasive." And in an interview with Professor Fred Rodell of the

Yale Law School, Chief Justice Warren, without mentioning a name, said much the same thing in recalling that not a single voice had been raised in the Supreme Court conferences over a time period that corresponded to Frankfurter's retirement.

Frankfurter retired on August 28, 1962, when his physical condition made it apparent that it would be impossible for him to shoulder a full work load when Court would resume the following fall. Though gone, he was far from forgotten; retirement did not abate the *gaudium certaminis* of his own spirit, and one of his last public acts was to reenter the constitutional lists via the *Harvard Law Review* ("when I retired from active service with the Court, I did not retire from the Court's problem") in an article which was a formidable attack on Black's theory of the incorporation of the First Amendment in the Fourteenth.[38]

Black bore Frankfurter's final literary effort with characteristic equanimity—"He is spending his last days to prove he is right and I am wrong. I admire him for it!" Perhaps the recollection of the snappish exchanges duly recorded in the Frankfurter diaries took something off the final hospital parting wherein Frankfurter asserted that never a cross word had passed between them—"He really believes *that*."[39]

Black published a response of sorts in the same volume. It was not a conventional rejoinder; rather it was a eulogy, for before Volume 78 of the *Harvard Law Review* had run its course Felix Frankfurter was gone, dying on Washington's Birthday of 1965, and Black summed up their extraordinary love-hate relationship in a moving personal tribute. And one thing was certain: neither the Supreme Court nor Hugo Black was ever the same again.[40]

CHAPTER EIGHTEEN

The Court That Never Was

Changing of the Guard IV

Frankfurter's successor was Arthur Goldberg, incumbent Secretary of Labor and sometime general counsel of the United Steelworkers. It was a succession that offered material for a wide range of reflections. Most obvious, perhaps, was the way it reflected the temper of the Kennedy administration and the kind of Court the young President would mold as a reasonably predictable pattern of appointments came his way over the two terms that the Twenty-second Amendment allowed him.

There were other reflections. For the history-minded there was the contrast between the matter-of-fact public acceptance of the activist and Jewish Justice Goldberg in 1962 and the storm over the activist and Jewish Justice Brandeis a half century earlier, or even the rumblings attending the activist and Jewish Justice Frankfurter in 1939. And a sociologist might read significance in the third successive Jewish incumbency in the "scholar's seat," which had numbered Story and Holmes as well as Cardozo and Frankfurter among its holders, and whose passage from its initial

373

New England affiliation reflected the advent of an equally authentic if more complex American pluralism.

Goldberg was in fact the second Kennedy Justice. The administration's initial appointment had come in mid-spring of 1962 with the replacement of the ill and exhausted Charles E. Whittaker by Assistant Attorney General Byron R. White, whose nickname, "Whizzer," and Phi Beta Kappa key combined to suggest that Camelot hallmark blending physical verve and intellectual excellence. And the White appointment also embodied the changing times in a collection of its own special landmarks. For White had served the Court before, under Chief Justice Vinson, and thereby became the first clerk to be appointed. And he was also the first Coloradan and the first All-American. ("From triple threat to bench" reported *Time*.)[1]

White and Goldberg were only a beginning, of course. But coming so close together and involving a marked community of intelligence and temperament, the two appointments prompted speculation on the future direction of the Court. With Frankfurter retired and the Black bloc of B.B.D. & W. intact, a consensus saw the Court moving with quickened steps along the path to which it had already set its foot. "There is a new Court," Alexander Bickel wrote in *The New Republic*. "It will be some time before it finds itself. . . ."[2]

He was right on both counts. For, notwithstanding the consensus, and symptomatic of identity crisis, the two Kennedy Justices parted company in five of the first fifteen cases. Yet the arrival of a new order was still unmistakable. Now the Court met at 10 A.M., instead of noon, a change unthinkable under Felix Frankfurter with his scrupulous concern for tradition. A little more time, and the pages would be out of knickers and into long pants; a little longer yet, and "Decision Monday," itself a product of an age of leisurely reading and writing, would fall casualty to the urgencies of new times and new media, with opinions being delivered as they became ready.

The Revolution Continued

But the big things were changing too, and on March 16 four venerable precedents fell at a single sitting of the Court. The most spectacular crash occurred in *Gideon v. Wainwright,* which was soon to be the subject of a book, *Gideon's Trumpet,* and in which the author's flyleaf dedication ("For Mr. Justice Black, who first heard the sound of the trumpet . . .") could serve as the epigraph for the resounding vindication it afforded Black's tenacity and constitutional faith.[3]

For in terms of time the foremost article of that faith could be seen as that dedication to the adversary process and a reading with insistent literalism of the capitalized provision of the Sixth Amendment granting the accused in all criminal prosecutions the right to have the "Assistance of Counsel for his defense."

Back in 1938 Black had written *Johnson v. Zerbst,* establishing that right in federal courts as a virtual absolute, but this counterpart effort on the state side seemed singularly unsuccessful. Four years later, he had been rebuffed in *Betts v. Brady.* There, in an early assertion of his incorporation theory, he insisted that the Sixth Amendment bound the states as well as the nation. Nonetheless he made the point in season and out of season in a variety of modes. There were acute observers who saw his famous 1940 "sunrise confession" opinion in *Chambers v. Florida* as resting on the right to a lawyer rather than incommunicado interrogation, and there were also uncritical enthusiasts who failed to note that his insistence that a trial be a fair fight carried the equal insistence that it be a hard one.[4]

But these subtleties were all overshadowed by the gracious gesture with which Chief Justice Warren gave Black the task of transforming his *Betts v. Brady* dissent into the form of ruling law and thereby reversing the old doctrine that, capital cases aside, states were under no obligation to furnish counsel to indigent defendants. And Black responded with an effort that matched his eloquence in *Chambers*—"From the very beginning, our state and national constitutions and laws have laid great

emphasis on . . . safeguards designed to assure fair trials. . . .
This noble ideal cannot be realized if a poor man charged with a
crime has to face his accusers without a lawyer to assist him." He
wrote for a Court that was unanimous as to result. Some concurring opinions, however, took issue, not with his eloquence, but
with his logic. And Justice Harlan in particular was critical of
the mode in which some difficult historical material was brushed
away and suggested that the precedents being reversed should get
"a more respectful burial than has been accorded."5

But there was no pretense about maintaining continuity with
the past in the other reversals of March 16. Back to back with
Gideon were two other cases enlarging the federal judicial protectorate over the criminally accused. *Fay v. Noia* established the
right of lateral access to the federal courts by abolishing exhaus-
tion of state appeals as a precondition of habeas corpus; *Draper
v. Washington* required state courts to furnish indigent prisoners
adequate trial records for appeal. And then to complete the reversing quartet, the protectorate over urban electorates was also
reiterated and extended. After four previously unsuccessful challenges in the Supreme Court, *Gray v. Sanders* finally overturned
Georgia's county-unit system, the minifederalist apparatus that
had long held urban Atlanta in thrall to the rural outlands.6

The reversing quartet, so emblematic, in both tone and content, of judicial revolution, would have been even more symbolic
had it included cases expounding the constitutional dimensions
of the other protectorates, the racial minorities and the moral and
religious dissidents. But if the quartet lacked such cases, the term
did not, and most appropriately it carried them as opening and
closing episodes.

Constituting a dramatic enough prelude, *Meredith v. Fair* enmeshed the Court and the Kennedy administration in a unique
and tragic sequence. At initial issue was the action of a single
federal appellate judge who four times had stayed the order of
his colleagues admitting James H. Meredith to the University of
Mississippi. Shortly before the term opened, Black resolved the
impasse between the Fifth Circuit Court of Appeals and its recalcitrant judge by staying the stay. He did so on his own motion,

which was sufficient legal authority. But he also noted, "I have submitted [the order] to each of my Brethren, and I am authorized to state that each of them agrees that the case is properly before the Court, that I have power to act, and that under the circumstances I should exercise that power as I have done here."[7]

Unimpressed by this judicial *sortie en masse,* Governor Ross Barnett personally refused Meredith's application for admission, and the political crisis accordingly followed the judicial one. The President undertook a solemn television appeal in public, his Attorney General brother negotiated desperately in private, but, in terms of peaceful resolution of the crisis, all to no avail. Violence erupted on a massive scale at Oxford, Mississippi, with widespread property damage, personal injuries and two deaths. But the power and prestige of the Presidency had been laid behind the judicial order, and it was enforced.

Bad as things were, *Meredith* carried the implication that delay and temporization had only to make them worse. At the very time of the Oxford riots and a decade after the arguments in *Brown II, The New York Times* reported that the South Carolina school board, which had been a respondent in that case, had yet to take a single step to carry out the Supreme Court's decree. Perhaps some concerned second thoughts as to the infirmities in the *Brown* formula underlay the very vehemence with which the Court declared "deliberate speed" inapplicable to desegregation of recreational facilities in a case coming up from Memphis. And in the same case, in what was technically an *obiter dictum,* there was also asserted the warning that the *Brown III* formula did not countenance "indefinite delay" in school desegregation.[8]

Yet there were considerations and considerations. As far back as January 1954, the black majority of the county served by the South Carolina school board was seen by Felix Frankfurter as "one illustration of the complexities of our problem." Still another one emerged two weeks after the reversing quartet, when *Goss v. Knoxville* voided a freedom-of-choice plan because of its tendency to perpetuate a segregated school system; along with it was also voided the concept of a color-blind Constitution.[9]

If *Meredith* was the overture, the coda of the first term of the
Kennedy Court might be perceived in *Schempp v.

School Dis-
trict,* which was delivered on the closing day and provided a
counterpart reiteration of special jurisdiction over religious and
moral dissidents. It thereby manifested that on the church-and-
state front, as on the racial one, the changing Court showed little
disposition to take a single backward step. Notwithstanding the
storm of the preceding summer, *Schempp* now enlarged the proscription of officially composed prayers in public schools to include the reading of the Scriptures themselves.[10]

To be sure, some peripheral concessions were made on the
religious front. The spokesman for the Court was not a member
of the libertarian bloc of B.B.D. & W., but Tom Clark, the very
Justice who had undertaken the previous summer to defend the
Regents' Prayer decision in an unprecedented public speech.
And while the thrust of Clark's opinion embodied the uncompro-
mising secularism of Felix Frankfurter, not only were the accents
of his delivery mild, patient and persuasive, but the delivery carried its own tribute to Scripture—"It certainly may be said that
the Bible is worthy of study for its literary and historic qualities."
And to Clark's tribute Black added his own, in part because of
the shortness of time to prepare some formal remarks. That summer, in presiding over a meeting of federal appellate judges, he
brought with him one of the several Bibles in his own library
and, in lieu of an opening speech for the convocation, read several passages from it to the assembled jurists, including his favorite reading from First Corinthians on the transcendence of
charity.[11]

The Silver Ascendancy

While the two Kennedy Justices did differ with each other,
they also stood solidly together in a still wider area of agreement
with a consequence that suggested still another name for the
reconstituted Court on which they served. In noting that there
was indeed a new majority, *The New Republic* also suggested its
label—"A Hugo Black majority, one might call it, for in the

second half of Justice Black's third decade of service, the Court is overturning many a precedent that was entered on the books over his dissent."[12]

And to much the same effect was a spate of contemporary tributes both in and out of the law. The *American University Law Review* ran a symposium on his judicial attitudes and values. The prestigious *Harvard Law Review* not only dedicated its February 1963 issue to his twenty-fifth year on the Court, but included his portrait as an almost unprecedented frontispiece. In a braver and in its way more significant tribute (for *Time* noted that Black was "no more welcome in racist Alabama than· he would have been in fiery Salem") the *Alabama Law Review* carried the article "Justice Black and His Law Clerks." Irving Dilliard, onetime editor of the editorial page of the *St. Louis Post-Dispatch,* and now a Princeton professor, published *One Man's Stand for Freedom,* an annotated collection of opinions running from *Johnson v. Zerbst* to *Meredith v. Fair*—"This is a book about and by a man who possesses the quality of courage to a degree rarely found today in the United States."[13]

But most significant of all was his appearance at the summit of American iconography, the cover of *Time.* It was the second time he had been there. Back in his Senate investigating days he had made an appearance there, but the circumstances and contexts of the two illustrations were about as unalike as the black-and-white picture of the inquisitorial Senator (hand cupped at ear so as not to miss an incriminating word) differed from the full-color portrait of the robed and benign Justice. The contrast in stories matched that of the pictures. The 1935 narration ("Investigation by Headline") was done in an arch and sniping style; that of 1964 ("The Limits That Create Liberty & The Liberty That Creates Limits") was gracious, sober, purposeful, and it paid a particular tribute to the Justice who "inspired and dominated" the Supreme Court.[14]

Unhappily, the new majority seemed flawed, and the fault showed itself with painful conspicuousness in a division between Black and Douglas toward the close of the 1963 term in the Colorado water division case of *Arizona v. California.* The break was all the more obvious because the year had started on the more characteristic note of solidarity of continuing their strict-constructionist dissent to the Court's adoption (rather than congressional enactment) of new rules of procedure pursuant to the statutory formula. There was not such solidarity, however, when Douglas read his dissenting opinion in the Colorado water case the following spring. On the contrary, most observers commented upon the sharpness of the attack, both written and oral, on the position set out in Black's majority opinion. ("The present case . . . will, I think, be marked as the baldest attempt by judges in modern times to spin their own philosophy into the fabric of the law in derogation of the will of the legislature.") Moreover, few were willing to ascribe the fission to differing perceptions of the statute involved. In a typical observation, Milton Viorst, writing in *The New York Times*, asserted that that divergence was rooted in Black's disapproval of Douglas' fourth marriage, and the *Times* itself saw a "cooling of relations" between the two.[15]

It was not a new prophecy by any means. Back in 1947 Wesley McCune in his *Nine Young Men* suggested that the partnership was on the downgrade, and Arthur Schlesinger, Jr., had apprehended much the same thing in his famous *Fortune* article published almost a decade later. As things turned out, the prophecy of 1963 had about the same validity as the earlier ones, and the partnership that had persisted already through three changes of the guard was to continue unabated. Indeed, the split in the Colorado waters case was about as significant in terms of permanency of attitude as Douglas' solitary dissent that winter in *Dennis v. Denver and Rio Grande*. Here for "the first time within the memory of the Court observers . . . he dissented from a negligence decision favoring a worker." He would not soon do so again.[16]

An Oration in the Capitol

Doubtless the very *élan* that the nascent Kennedy Court brought to its task exacerbated all the more the simmering and pervasive hostility that the judicial revolution had inevitably brought in its train. Remarkable, however, was a new note emerging in the chorus of criticism, for it was one that came, not from the Court's enemies, but from its friends. In a sense this new and higher criticism was the inevitable consequence of the dialectic of judicial revolution, which had to presume nonexistent continuities, draw attenuated conclusions from irrelevant premises, and even speak in silences. It was also the product of the Warren Fabianism that persistently linked the most soaring of constitutional data to what was actually gradgrind statutory interpretations. And, it also drew on the cryptic "certiorari denied," the faceless "per curiams," the Constitution-amending footnotes, and the sequences of assertion, dissent, and counterdissent.

All in all this cluster of sibylline techniques produced an inevitable obscurantism, whereby—certainly as far as Shepherd's *Citations* was concerned—*Plessy v. Ferguson* had only been distinguished but never overruled and continued in much of its pristine glory as good constitutional law. And hence the understandable remonstrance of a leading lay exegete of the Court, which he captioned "Information, Please" and where he reiterated complaints of law professors against "opinions that do not opine." And to much the same effect was a commentary of *The New Republic* on the judicial veto of the Georgia county-unit system; here was combined praise for the result with criticism of a rationale that "shed not one ray of light on the apportionment problem in general and fails even to state a tenable principle upon which to base its own decision."[17]

Criticism of the new Court from the old enemies continued also. At one level the unremitting hatred was exemplified by the "Impeach Earl Warren" pamphlets discovered in the lockers of Earl Warren High School, of Downey, California. On a somewhat higher plane than the pamphlets were a cluster of constitutional amendments—with three state ratifications by April 1963, and sixteen by year's end—proposing, among other things, a super-court of appeals styled the "Court of the Union" and composed of the chief justices of the several states.[18]

Warren publicly criticized the amendments, but he tactfully refrained from pointing out their Achilles' heel: how an unconstitutionally apportioned legislature could validly ratify any amendment, least of all one cementing its own unconstitutional status. The Chief Justice seemed somewhat more forthright in other responses. He condemned as out of order a proposal of South Carolina's Representative Robert T. Ashmore that "In God We Trust" be emblazoned behind the dais of the Supreme Court itself. He was even more blunt in fact if not in form in delivering what was obviously a rejoinder to the charge made by the Chief Justice of Alabama before the Council of State Chief Justices: that the Supreme Court was remaking the Constitution and using the First Amendment for the "systematic destruction of state sovereignty." In a nice states'-rights touch, Warren waited until he stood on native ground and then told the California Bar Association that Supreme Court intervention would be minimal if the state courts protected human rights more vigilantly.[19]

Following the Chief Justice's lead and adding an element of his own, Justice Goldberg passed over from defense to attack at the annual American Bar Association meeting, as he denounced opposition to the Court's decisions as opposition to the "law itself" and called on both lawyers and judges to put aside their personal views and rally behind the Court. In Aspen, Colorado, Justice Brennan said much the same thing, albeit in a somewhat softer tone, as he spoke out against the general lack of understanding of what the Court was about and called for "principled criticism" to replace the obviously unprincipled variety.[20]

Yet, none of the speeches seemed to do much good in terms of calming public hostility. A few months after his own effort Warren was still greeted with the usual pickets when he arrived for a speaking engagement at the Association of the Bar of the City of New York, and a shower of placards and handbills as well. And unquestionably it was the long sequence of experiences such as this, when added to the billboards calling for his impeachment and the incessant hate mail, that underlay the most impassioned address of his public career.

It was an address that denounced the forces of hatred "eating their way into the bloodstream of the national life." He delivered it on November 25, 1963, in the rotunda of the Capitol, and the Chief Justice spoke on the shortest of notice. The Supreme Court did not sit that Monday, however, for the funeral rites of a President forced the hurried cancellation of the judicial calendar.[21]

The cold, stark and unforgettable weekend must have had a particular impact on the members of the Court. The last social affair in the White House under the Presidency of John Kennedy was the annual reception for the Justices. It was duly held on November 20, just before the President's departure for Texas and three days before the bronze casket was returned to Washington. For the Court, as for the country, the events of that weekend marked the end of an era in several ways.

At the moment the most obvious judicial impact was the Chief Justice's service on the commission that bore his name and was charged with investigation of the whole tragedy. It was a duty that provided for a continuing nexus to Dallas and invested the news coming out of that city with a relevance it might not have had under other circumstances. Thus, the Supreme Court was involved obliquely in a wire-service dispatch near the year's end concerning a bail-bond hearing for a certain Jack Ruby. For among the circumstances that the dispatch thought worthy of mention was the fact that matters were discussed in the presence of a poster calling for the impeachment of Earl Warren.

The Black Term

Notwithstanding his Kennedy eulogy, pickets as usual greeted the Chief Justice when he spoke in New York at the New School for Social Research, and doubtless the pickets felt that they had much to picket about. One particularly strong element in their concern was the rising tide of pornography, for which the Kennedy-fortified Court had been denounced by a group of respected clergymen who held that the Court had virtually promoted degeneracy by overturning state bans on Henry Miller's *Tropic of Cancer* and the French movie *The Lovers*.

Remarkably enough, the Court had reached its result by applying the complex Brennan formula in theory and the Black formula in fact. Certainly the end result was but a step away from the absolute permissiveness that Black saw as a necessary consequence of the letter of the First Amendment. And much the same situation followed from the Court's judgment in *New York Times v. Sullivan*. Here a double denial of Black's First Amendment views as a thesis was followed by their application as an operative fact. Or, at least, there were those who said that making proof of actual knowledge of falsity the precondition of a public official's recovery for defamation demanded a procedural and philosophical impossibility and thereby confirmed in deed the very dogma that Black denied in theory.[22]

Sullivan came out of racially troubled Birmingham and was an admirable illustration of the interacting elements underlying the judicial revolution. Its real subject matter was not so much newspaper comment as the round of demonstration, protest and repression in all matters of race relations. Not that Black had overmuch firsthand knowledge on recent events there, for ten years after *Brown II* the fallout of the case still kept him from a public appearance in his home town, and indeed his law-school class did not invite him to the fiftieth anniversary of their graduation. On the other hand, the decennial anniversary did afford the opportunity to excise its most famous phrase from the vocabulary of operative law, and he took it with apparent relish in *Griffin v. County School Board*—"The time for mere 'deliberate speed' has run out."[23]

His comment was in one plane pure *obiter dictum*. *Griffin* had nothing to do with time, but rather with the right of one Virginia county to close its public schools while those elsewhere remained open. But it was crucially symbolic in more fundamental reality both for itself and for the ever-growing complexities of the new round of civil-rights cases. Thus, the last round of James Meredith's troubled entry into the University of Mississippi confronted Black with a choice of means and ends as his disposition to summary resolution of some long-protracted points collided with the insistence that a defendant held the right of trial by jury in all criminal matters. With the asserted contempt of Governor Ross Barnett as the subject matter, however, Black missed by one vote writing into law his long-time view that jury trials were as appropriate to contempt of judges as they were for any other crime.

Five of his colleagues disagreed, however, and Governor Barnett was left to face the members of the Fifth Federal Circuit Court of Appeals rather than a jury of local laymen, who doubtless would have been far more sympathetic to his position. "The list of dissenters," noted *The New Republic*, "should make interesting reading in Jackson, Mississippi. They include none other than Chief Justice Warren, whom the segregationists . . . attack as being singularly intent on the subjugation of the Government, and Justices Black, Douglas and Goldberg, also vividly advertised as activist." Yet, even in defeat, a portion of Black's influence was manifest, for the majority opinion radically softened the ancient rigor of the contempt power by holding that sentences imposed under its authority could not constitutionally exceed those imposed for petty offenses.[24]

On balance, however, as critics and admirers agreed, the 1964 term bore Black's hallmark in any number of particulars, with his economic views being engrained in constitutional interpretation every bit as deeply as his political ones. Indeed, ranking with his opinion at the preceding term in *Ferguson v. Skrupa,* which professed indifference as to whether a legislature took Adam Smith or John Maynard Keynes as its mentor, was the Court's contemporary decision in *Continental Can.* For here the antitrust latitudinarianism of *du Pont I* was neatly converted to the hard gospel of *du Pont II* in a proscription of a merger involving glass and metal processors.[25]

Political considerations were also particularly dominant, however, and on the issue of congressional apportionment with *Wesberry v. Sanders* affording the opportunity to turn his 1946 dissent to *Colegrove v. Green* into ruling law. It was not quite the literalism of some other views, for he extrapolated a requirement of equally populated congressional districts from the provision of Article I of the Constitution that Representatives "shall be . . . chosen . . . by the People of the several states."[26]

But literalist absolutism, however, could be read into *Escobedo v. Illinois,* which extended the right to counsel in the courtroom back to the police station. As in so many other cases, a colleague, here Justice Goldberg, wrote the opinion of the Court, but the views he expressed were ones that Hugo Black had long championed. And, as in so many other cases also, the expressed opinion fell short of the true sweep of the Black perception. For had Justice Black really gotten his way, the police-station rights of the criminally accused would have included not only the immediate right to a lawyer but a freedom from self-incrimination by means of lineups, fingerprinting and blood samples.[27]

The Referenda

The views were not particularly popular as a variety of data indicated. Historically, the history of judicial pay raises had been something of a barometer of what the country thought of the Court, and here the Justices received a raise of $4,500 per annum, while all the other federal judges were getting almost twice that amount. Indeed, the Senate had been meanly disposed to hold the Court's raise to $2,500, and the final salaries wound up well short of the $60,000 per year which a presidential commission had recommended.

Another historic element of congressional criticism appeared in the deluge of bills to undo the Court's decisions by statutory revision or constitutional amendment. Already the House of Representatives had passed the Tuck Bill, which proposed to strip the Court of jurisdiction in apportionment controversies and a similar majority—though short of the constitutionally required margin—had been indicated for the Becker amendment, which proposed to override the school-prayer decisions by changing the Constitution to that effect.

Hence, it came as a matter of particular significance that Senator Barry Goldwater chose the author of the amendment to be his running mate on the Republican ticket in a national election that was to be as nearly a national referendum on the Supreme Court as the Senator could make it. In what was virtually his own hallmark speech of his campaign, Goldwater asserted that law and order had been sacrificed "just to give criminals a sporting chance to go free" and made and remade a campaign promise to "redress constitutional interpretations in favor of the public."[28]

Formally, it was a kind of half debate, for, in a tactic at once adroit and lofty, Lyndon Johnson refused to bring the Court into the campaign at all. This did not mean that the issues went undiscussed. The pages of *The New York Times* provided a mirror of the ongoing controversy, as Arthur Krock and Anthony Lewis proceeded from identity in analysis to opposite poles in appraisal over the Court's increasing disposition to remold the nation's social and political institutions. There were other levels of encounter. Retired Justice Whittaker, soon to resign that status and join General Motors, charged his former colleagues with usurping the right of local self-government. And, on a literally parochial plane, a Monsignor Haverty in a speech before the Catholic Youth Association denounced the Court as "the greatest evil in the country today."[29]

The Court did not want for defenders. In a kind of inverted ecumenism, the head of the Rabbinical Council of America deplored Monsignor Haverty's criticism, and at the professional level of the law itself, an increasing number of distinguished attorneys spoke out in support. CBS added its argument with a discreetly sympathetic television presentation of *Gideon's Trumpet*. In New York, Representative Emanuel Celler and Mayor Robert F. Wagner insisted that the anti-Court polemics could only undermine the very law and order that the polemicists sought. And from the same state, its soon-to-be Senator added his voice to the defense of the Court which his dead brother had helped to mold.

The Turn of the Tide

If Lyndon Johnson's enormous victory on November 3, 1964, might be accounted, among other things, a vindication of the Supreme Court, it was by no means the end of the controversy. Rather, polemics seemed to take a new and invigorated turn with J. Edgar Hoover's postelection characterization of certain Justices as "bleeding hearts." But there was also a new and obvious sense of security in Justice Goldberg's spirited attack on what he called the "myths" of the Court's detractors—that the Court had usurped power; that it went out of its way to decide issues better left alone; that it considered itself infallible; that it was split between liberals and conservatives; or that judicial review was undemocratic.[30]

And the new judicial security was especially evident in the way the Court disposed of the apportionment controversy on the last day of the 1964–1965 term. The case was *Reynolds v. Sims,* up from Black's Alabama; and, like *Baker v. Carr* before it, it involved the long failure of the state legislature to undertake redistricting, notwithstanding significant population shifts. The Court's answer was at once massive and dispositive: every house of every state legislature must be redistricted on the basis of population alone. Spectators in the courtroom, Anthony Lewis reported, "felt as if they were at a second American Constitutional Convention."[31]

The late Felix Frankfurter would have agreed, though hardly in approval. Whether the Court should sit as a continuing constitutional convention was one question. And quite another was the issue of whether judicial power ("Aye, there's the rub") was capable of recognizing "geography, economics, urban-rural conflict, and all the other nonlegal factors that throughout our history entered into political districting." But the Chief Justice saw things differently. "Legislators represent the people, not trees or acres. Legislators are elected by votes, not farms, or cities, or economic interests . . . [Accordingly] we hold . . . seats in both houses of a bicameral state legislature must be apportioned on a population basis." And, more than this, the new rules were placed in effect, not with deliberate speed, but with precise directions and timetables for implementation.[32]

In so many ways the apportionment decision could have served as the hallmark of what might have been the Kennedy Court. Yet it was scarcely printed in the reports when one of the charter members abruptly left the bench. At the time, the resignation of Arthur Goldberg to accept the ambassadorship to the United Nations and his replacement by Abe Fortas seemed to involve little change in personal constitutional philosophy and none in the institutional attitudes of the new Court.

Abe Fortas duly added his new title to the list of distinguished accomplishments in *Who's Who in the South and Southwest*— Yale law professor, Undersecretary of the Interior, and more lately, Washington lawyer "and presidential adviser." He also sent in his new business address substituting the Supreme Court for "c/o White House, 1600 Pennsylvania Avenue, Washington, D.C." The new listing thereby rectified some questionable references in the old. But the question of judgment would recur again with profound consequences for Court and country.[33]

CHAPTER NINETEEN

The Great Change

Time *Marches On*

The story that had accompanied Black's second appearance
on the cover of *Time* noted that in some ways he had become the
"restrainer of the ebullient Justice Goldberg" and then commented on the defense of property rights, which had become an
important element in his latest opinions. Both matters had their
immediate roots in the sit-in cases that had begun on February 1,
1960, when four black freshmen from North Carolina Agricultural and Technical College sought lunch-counter service from
the Greensboro Woolworth.[1]

The request for food was a spontaneous beginning of direct
action, the protest of a new generation and a new generation of
protest. Radically differing from the patient litigation of the
N.A.A.C.P., it was itself urgent, massive and highly conspicuous.
It sought to open, not compose, controversy, to rally public—or
at least, congressional—opinion, and (as one observer noted) to
spread the social cost of discrimination by bringing discomfort to
an otherwise complacent and satisfied majority. And it brought
discomfort in abundance to the Supreme Court.

The sit-in cases came in successive waves, and their progress in the Court was marked by a variety of characteristics. Most obvious was the diversity of rationalizations to which the Court resorted in overturning the local convictions: lack of evidence; freedom of assembly; abatement by federal statute; and so on. The sequence was also marked by the disintegration of an initial judicial unanimity, an impatience in the dissents, and the obvious apprehension of the majority opinions.

Something of a critical point of inflection came on June 22, 1964, and Black's several opinions that day served as a litmus of judicial difficulties. He spoke for the Court in reversing the sit-in convictions in *Barr v. Columbia,* where there was no evidence of the peace disturbance charged, and in *Robinson v. Florida,* where the state statute requiring separate rest rooms was found to involve state coercion to discriminate. In *Bell v. Maryland,* however, he spoke in dissent for himself and two others. For *Bell* involved a trespass conviction, where no state authority had prompted the discrimination involved and no federal law prohibited it.[2]

One difficulty of the case was suggested by the long interval that separated the June day of its decision from the argument of the preceding October. Another was apparent in the 6–3 decision and the diversity of theories underlying the reversal. William Brennan in the opinion of the Court gingerly skirted the basic constitutional issue and remanded the case to the Maryland courts for consideration in the light of recently passed state legislation. Douglas, however, seeking to meet the core point head on, would have reversed the conviction outright on the ground of the corporate character of the complaining witness. And so would Justice Goldberg, who saw that result compelled by the legislative history of the Fourteenth Amendment.

The legislative history of the amendment, as Black's *Adamson* opinion suggested, was almost a special preserve of the senior Justice, and a line from his dissent was especially aimed at the Goldberg thesis—"there is nothing whatever in the material cited to support the proposition that the 14th Amendment, without congressional legislation, prohibits owners of restaurants

. . . to refuse service to Negroes." His disagreement with the corporate theory of Douglas was more oblique, but nonetheless implicit in the proposition with which he set out his view of the fundamental constitutional issue: the Fourteenth Amendment of itself "does not compel either a black man or a white man running his own private business to trade with anyone against his will."[3]

However, there was another note, which would repeatedly run through his sit-in opinions concerning groups who would take law into their own hands, and a rule that he would reiterate again and again: "Whatever power it may allow the states or grant to the Congress to regulate the use of private property, the Constitution does not confer upon any group the right to substitute rule by force for rule by law." It was present when he once more dissented to the dismissal of another round of sit-in convictions for actions that had preceded the Civil Rights Act of 1964 but were declared abated by the passage of that statute.[4]

With *Cox v. Louisiana,* it was also present in his dissent, and now the temper and tone of his language underwent obvious escalation—"minority groups, I venture to suggest, are the ones who have always suffered and always will suffer most when street multitudes are allowed to substitute their pressure for the less glamorous but more dependable processes of the law." Characteristically, he agreed with the majority on dismissing charges of peace disturbance and obstructing public ways, but the core offense—mass picketing of a Baton Rouge courthouse where students were being held for trial—was another thing again. And something of the same apprehension seemed to tincture Justice Goldberg's majority opinion—"We emphatically reject the notion . . . that the First and Fourteenth Amendments afford the same kind of freedom to those who would communicate ideas by . . . patrolling, marching, and picketing on streets and highways, as those amendments afford to . . . pure speech."[5]

But all this was prologue to the library stand-in litigated in *Brown v. Louisiana.* Here Justice Fortas upheld the action as constitutionally protected "monuments of protest" against a segregated bookmobile system. Black, however, saw no such thing. Rather, he insisted, it was "high time to challenge the assumption . . . that the groups who think they have been mistreated or that actually have been mistreated have a constitutional right to use the public's streets, buildings and property to protest whatever, wherever, whenever, they want, without regard to whom their conduct may disturb." In print he said that he was "deeply troubled" with respect to groups who would read the decision "as I do"—"a license to invade the tranquility and beauty of our libraries whenever they have a quarrel with some state policy that may or may not exist." But, even surpassing this, was his oral delivery—"Justice Black Blisters 5 to 4 Ruling." A reporter for the *Washington Post* described it as one of the most bitter and heated in recent memory, with Black shaking his finger at the courtroom audience in accompaniment of oral comments "that made his strongly worded dissent seem pale by comparison."[6]

And then in late 1966, some six months later, came the Court's turnabout in *Adderly v. Florida*. The facts were not too dissimilar to those of earlier cases, here the mass picketing of the Tallahassee jail by Florida A. & M. students was to protest the incarceration there of their fellow students following an effort to desegregate the local theaters. Douglas turned in a strongly worded vindication of the student action, and three of the Justices agreed with him. But it was Black who spoke for a majority of five: "The state, no less than a private owner of property, has power to preserve the property under its control for the use to which it is lawfully dedicated." It was a major premise, and it drew the fire of both his old partner on the Court and the N.A.A.C.P. as well.[7]

The Preferred Priority

In a footnote comment, Jack Greenberg of the N.A.A.C.P. probed the major premise: "Justice Black's analogy to the power of a private owner over property, as Justice Douglas pointed out in dissent, ignored the fact that the right of assembly and petition for redress of grievances does not run to private proprietors but to restrain the state in its dealings with its citizens. The inappropriate reference to private property was apparently an attempt to inject into the majority opinion one of the central themes of the sit-in dissents."[8]

But Mr. Greenberg and the *Time* cover story to the contrary, Black's concern with property rights was not wholly occasioned by the sit-in cases. Rather, a concern had been surfacing in his philosophy for some time. Thus, in 1962 at his famous public interview at the American Jewish Congress convention, he had explicitly noted that "we have a system of property in this country which is also protected by the Constitution." But there could be no question that the sit-ins were critical in fusing several sensitive strands of thought.[9]

One was his concern for the small storekeeper, where, as noted, he not only was his father's son but showed much the same emotional response as his old friend and onetime haberdasher, Harry Truman. ("If anyone came to my store and tried to stop business, I'd throw him out.") Indeed, the small businessman's point of view was particularly evident in the flash point that developed between him and Justice Goldberg in the sit-in cases. For as *Time* commented, Goldberg's view of the Supreme Court as a kind of "national schoolmaster" operated as a kind of Frankfurterism in reverse moving Black to new postures of judicial restraint.[10]

Indeed there had been some subtle back-up from Frankfurter himself. As early as February 1962, when the Reverend Fred Shuttlesworth was involved in one of his several appeals to the Supreme Court, Frankfurter commended Black for his "conciliatory efforts . . . to satisfy the human appeal in the Shuttlesworth situation" and observed that "you and I are in agreement that it will not advance the cause of constitutional equality for Negroes for the Court to be taking short cuts, to discriminate as partisans in favor of Negroes or even to appear to do so." And when the cases of late 1964 were argued, the now retired Justice Frankfurter wrote his senior active colleague:

The Great Change 395

And, so I would not dream of telling you of my pride in you for dissenting yesterday. I am not even surprised, my dear Hugo, for while I [was] even still in action around the table, my ear was active, and I took in every word you said the first time the "sit-in" problem came before the conference. That is why I say I am not surprised to read what you wrote. But I can express my great respect for the powerful way in which you did it, particularly the part dealing with the impact of the Act of 1964 on the problems before the Court.[11]

And there was another element: Black's perception of the right of privacy.

The Bombshell

"I like my privacy as well as the next man," Black said in his dissent in *Griswold v. Connecticut* on June 7, 1965. "Unlike my brethren, I am simply unable to find a constitutional right to it." True as far as it went, but the statement needed clarification. Black did perceive a constitutional right to privacy essentially derivative to that of property as a passage from his American Jewish Congress interview indicated: "I would feel a little badly if somebody were to try to come into my house and tell me that he had a constitutional right to come in there because he wanted to make a speech against the Supreme Court."[12]

But Justice Douglas, speaking for the Court on the issue of whether a state might make the use of contraceptives by married couples a criminal act, saw the right of privacy—marital privacy —as primary rather than derivative. He did not find it in any of the specific provisions of the Bill of Rights now carried into the Fourteenth Amendment. Rather, the right emerged from the "penumbral emanations" of the First, Third, Fourth, Fifth and Ninth Amendments. And Justice Goldberg concurred in an unprecedented citation of the Ninth Amendment alone, on which he and two others would rest the reversal. Justices White and

Harlan also submitted separate concurrences. And Black, in dissent, spoke for himself and Potter Stewart in a formula that might well have been the overlay by which his instinctual puritanism responded to the majority's new morality.[13]

His words provoked a variety of reactions. Charles J. Bloch, of the Macon bar, wrote *The New York Times* and inquired if Black would now be criticized for his conservatism. (Twenty-seven years earlier, Henry Ware Allen wrote the paper along the same line.) The current *New Republic,* more in sorrow than in anger, noted the turnabout of "the Court's great literalist, at whose bidding the Bill of Rights and Fourteenth Amendment have in the past meant many an admirable thing." And most significant of all was the nonplussed reaction of the law reviews, who responded almost as if they could not believe their ears.[14]

The polite incredulity was understandable enough. The law reviews, like so many before them—the Klan, the Bourbon establishment, the Senate inner club, the nuclear New Dealers— had simply cast Black in their own image of him, here the hero-judge fearlessly recasting the law. But here, as before, Black was incapable of being caught in a neatly packaged and predictable formula, even though the law reviews had ceaselessly sought to do so over Black's three decades on the Court.

There was something of a remarkably parallel sequence over those years in Black's increasing impress on American law and the influence of the law reviews in the same area. Time was when that influence was a matter of low estate. In ironic contrast to Stone's publicized doubt of Black's legal ability was Chief Justice Hughes's early misgivings as to Stone and the capabilities of a man whose legal experience was substantially concerned with the writing efforts of law students. Indeed, the very man Black replaced on the Court, Justice Van Devanter, used to question the wisdom of reference to the law reviews in the Supreme Court opinions, and Justice Butler supposedly never concurred in an opinion that cited one.

But by 1965 things were very different in the respectful deference shown the reviews in the Supreme Court reports almost as a matter of course. By then, citations of law reviews constituted almost half the references in Supreme Court opinions to secondary material. Even more remarkable was "the curious phenomenon—the deference paid by Supreme Court Justices to the works of the novices in their trade, the law students." For almost one fifth of the references were to student notes.[15]

There was a reason for this:

> Nothing in any other professional group [David Riesman, himself a former law review editor, noted] remotely resembles this guild of students, who, working even harder than their fellows, manage to cooperate sufficiently to meet the chronic emergency of a periodical. Indeed this cooperation often develops into an island of teamwork in a sea of ruthless rivalry. This teamwork [and the selection for it] is . . . based on impersonal and objective criteria in the sense that it ignores social, class, and ethnic lines . . . it attracts people who can stand a certain amount of impersonality and who are trained to be objective . . . The law reviews put pressure upon the profession, and the profession on the society.[16]

The reviews also put pressure of various types on the Supreme Court, and perhaps the only true deference they paid it was to exempt the Justices from the rewriting that the "brashly serious-minded" student editors administered to their professor and practitioner contributors. The student editors had another sanction, and this, as Felix Frankfurter once noted, was the frequent and joyous duty of reversing the Supreme Court "in an infallible judgment of 165 words." And even more formidable was their affirmance; for, as Oliver Wendell Holmes once noted, he did not mind the boys at Harvard saying he was wrong but found insufferable their saying he was right.[17]

Remarkably enough, the young editors did not say that Black was wrong or even that he was right in his Connecticut contraception dissent. The *Harvard Law Review,* oldest and most prestigious of them all (and indeed where an article by Louis D. Brandeis and Samuel D. Warren on the right of privacy was the fountainhead of the whole discussion), did review the case at length. The shade of Justice Holmes perhaps bridled as the *Review* magisterially approved the Goldberg concurrence ("Mr. Justice Goldberg's discussion of the history of the Ninth Amendment shows that this was indeed its intended meaning") and relegated Goldberg's senior colleague to a footnote—"But see Mr. Justice Black's dissent, in which it is argued that the amendment was designed to protect 'state powers.' "[18]

The *Yale Law Journal,* on which Hugo L. Black, Jr., had served as editor, did not even issue a case note in the matter, while the *Brooklyn Law Review* suggested that the Black position was really underlain by the vagueness of the majority. The *Mississippi Law Journal* resorted to the lexicon of Felix Frankfurter to indicate that a better balancing of interests was required. And, perhaps most perceptive of all, the *University of Chicago Law Review* repeated a point that Professor Paul Freund had made a few years earlier: that the incorporation theory of *Adamson* set limits as well as horizons for Black and foreclosed his looking outside the first eight Amendments.[19]

Coonskin Caps and Old New Dealers

Something of the same process was going on in the hitherto occult and mysterious world of antitrust, where Black was having better success in imposing on judicial discretion the clarity and the limitations that he sought to apply to the constitutional text itself. Indeed, there was a notable parallelism between his reaction to the "rule of reason" with which the Supreme Court had tempered the literal strictures of the Sherman Anti-Trust Act and to the larger jurisdiction that the Court had obtained over economic legislation through the use of the due-process clause.[20]

More than matching his criticism of judicial vetoes imposed in the name of due process was his hostility to the rule of reason, with "its incredibly complicated and prolonged economic investigations . . . so often wholly fruitless. . . ." And for a substitute he proposed essentially the same sanction that he suggested in constitutional interpretation: the plain letter of the law. The antitrust absolutisms did not pass without challenge. "In justice," wrote an otherwise admiring Charles Curtis, "this is unlike Black." And Columbia's Milton Handler was more explicit:

> The vice of this view . . . is that it moves in the direction of treating antitrust in terms of absolutes. To be sure, the businessman would like more certain guidance to his vulnerability under the antitrust laws. But does he . . . want certainty at the expense of the unqualified prohibition of a wide variety of normal and useful business arrangements? The very nature of the conflict which antitrust seeks to control makes it inevitable that its legality will depend on a subtle weighing of various economic facts.[21]

The criticism had little effect as the Black doctrine continued to burgeon following its renaissance in *du Pont II* in the early Warren Court. Another critical mutation came in *U.S. v. Philadelphia National Bank,* in which the opinion of Justice Brennan expressed thoughts long held by Justice Black. Here, on an ambiguous salient of statutory law, and over the objection of what Justice Harlan would later call "the numbers game," the calculus of antitrust underwent a radical simplification into long, or even short, division. For now the levels of illegal economic concentration were determined, not by an arcane weighing of a host of intangibles but rather by the allocation of a relevant market into participant shares.[22]

On June 1, 1966, the hard-line formulation received its most vigorous application in *U.S. v. Von's Grocery Company.* Appropriately, Black spoke for the Court and banned the defendant's acquisition of the Shipping Bag Food Stores on the ground that the resulting increase in corporate concentration—7.5 percent of the Los Angeles grocery market—would violate the antitrust laws. Predictably enough, the decision brought a swirl of criticism. There was a touch of specialist hauteur ("Mr. Justice Black's notion of concentration, to say the least, is novel") in Professor Handler's insistence that the restatement of antitrust principles in absolutist terms ran counter to the history, philosophy, purpose and language of the statutes involved. And on a less scholarly note, *Fortune* delivered a hard-hitting editorial, "Anti-Trust in a Coonskin Cap," which insisted that the test of competition was one of quality, not amount, and by any true index of price or choice, there was far more of it in the concentrated supermarkets of Los Angeles than ever existed in Clay County when William La Fayette Black opened his Ashland store.[23]

Yet, for all the pristine populism in antitrust, there was a subtle change of attitude toward corporate enterprise. It was notable both for itself and for the responsive commentary—or lack of commentary—thereby produced, particularly on the Black-Douglas partnership. That partnership, remarkably enough, could be said to have its beginnings in Black's *Connecticut General* dissent arguing that a corporation was a nonperson insofar as the protection of the Fourteenth Amendment was concerned. "I was then Chairman of the SEC," Douglas recalled, "with no thought of ever being a judge. But the dissent so moved me that I wrote him a congratulatory letter." Twelve years later he spoke for himself and Black in dissenting from *Wheeling Steel v. Glander,* which restated the historic doctrine on constitutional personality.[24]

Yet, when another facet of the same doctrine was presented, Black declined to follow Douglas' suggestion that a lunch counter maintained by an individual proprietor stood on a footing essentially different from one maintained by a corporation, particularly a large national corporation. His position was given an unintentional but luminous underscoring by the defense of an adoring niece, who wrapped the name of just such an enterprise in the syntax of country storekeeping. ("I see in Justice Black's dissent, deep concern for the operators of McCrory's in Rock Hill, South Carolina, and Gus Blass & Co. in Little Rock, Arkansas. These establishments did not make the rules forbidding service to Negroes. . . .")[25]

Hazel Black Davis, however, had distinguished company for her position in declining to grant the Douglas distinction. After a fashion the most distinguished authority on the modern corporation itself took something of the same position. Or such was the import of Adolph A. Berle's vocabulary when the distinguished author of *The Modern Corporation and Private Property* delivered the prestigious Carpentier Lecture for 1967 at the University of Pennsylvania. Entitled *The Three Faces of Power,* the Berle lectures covered any number of related points, and the most insistent was the thesis that the Supreme Court now sat as a revolutionary committee. He also chose to review what he called "the Black-Douglas doctrine" from *Connecticut General* to *Wheeling Steel* into the sit-in case of *Bell v. Maryland.* His conclusion was that as a "matter of history, of sociology, and even verbal interpretation, the Black-Douglas argument is unanswerable." But he omitted to say that the founder of the doctrine declined to carry it into what he himself saw as both its highest application and its inexorable conclusion—the sit-in protests at corporately owned lunch counters.[26]

The Old and the New

Berle's ambiguity—indeed, ambivalence—was symbolic in its way, for it suggested that the old New Dealers no more had Black in their pocket than the Klan or the Bourbon establishment before them. And this was even more the case in that vaguely bounded but institutionally existent body known as the modern intellectual establishment and particularly its liberal-left component. Sometimes its response to Black was typographically muffled, as with *Harvard Law Review*'s footnote presentation regarding his contraception dissent or with the parenthetic treatment by Yale's Professor Thomas I. Emerson when Black at last wrote his sit-in position into law—"(The reach of the *Adderly* decision is by no means clear. It could mean a total withdrawal from Justice Roberts' [and Justice Black's] position in the *Hague* case)." Sometimes the criticism was more forthright, as when Harvard's Professor Louis L. Jaffe suggested that Black's constitutional philosophy was essentially a resourceful manipulation of the specifics of the Bill of Rights, but with a "moral assurance so great that he is not led to question his mental processes." And sometimes there was a mixture of respectful doubt and positive awe, as in Fred Graham's interview for *The New York Times* on the occasion of Black's eightieth birthday.[27]

Here the reporter's notes matched the photograph of the taut, alert face in describing the remarkable vigor of mind and body. (Graham remarked especially on the "strong hands and thick wrists.") Graham also cautiously recorded that "there are those who say" that Black was breaking from "the forward-looking philosophy he had held as the leader of the Court." Noting that breaks with past position—flag salutes, the Fourth Amendment, double jeopardy—were not exactly novel in the Justice's history, Graham seemed to imply that something new was emerging. And here the reporter proposed that the latest round of Black dissents, twenty-eight at the last term and high for the Justice, went back to the library stand-in case, wherein the dissenter had "blistered the Court."[28]

The vigor that Graham captured in the interview was especially manifest in a Southern tour that the Blacks took at the close of the 1966 term. It was the first public appearance he had made in his native state since *Brown II* of 1954, and even older memories were evoked as he retraced much of the route he had driven by Overland Whippet in the senatorial campaign forty years before—Ashland, Harlan, Sylacauga and Tuscaloosa, where the Phi Beta Kappa key he had won sixty-three years before was duly awarded. ("Hugo was a ball of fire," Mrs. Black recalled. "He had twinkled, sparkled, scintillated, effervesced, charmed, endeared, and re-endeared himself to relatives, old friends, and strangers—Alabamians all!")[29]

And the nuances of the Graham article were also borne out by a second development of the tour, for there could be no doubt that some of the cordiality of the homecoming had been facilitated by the new role of great dissenter. But it was also true that Alabama had changed far more than he had changed, and an index of how far both had come emerged in what became a *de facto* civic dinner in Birmingham. It was held at the Jewish coun-

try club, a not insignificant social datum, and perhaps the shades
of Felix Frankfurter and some old Klansmen listened with some
—but not much—surprise as Black compressed his old Populist
rhetoric, a defense of *Brown,* and his evolved judicial philosophy
in a few sentences:

> When I first came to the Court I had grave doubts about
> judicial review. Grave doubts. But I am now convinced
> that if we are to have the form of free government and
> free society which the Constitution intends, the Court
> must function as it has . . . I yield to no man in my love
> of the South. But I also love all my country . . . The
> American dream calls for a society in which every indi-
> vidual shall live as a free man . . . We look forward to
> a world in which men everywhere shall be entitled to walk
> upright, to enjoy full individual freedom, and to live in
> peace.[30]

One dissent, which doubtless did more than all the others to
ensure the welcome, came in *South Carolina v. Katzenbach.*
Splitting from every other colleague on the Court, Black reverted
to the lexicon of his 1935 filibuster to denounce the "conquered
province" of the Reconstruction. The theory was now reasserted,
as he saw it, in that provision of the Voting Rights Act of 1965
requiring Southern states to have the Attorney General's approval before enacting new voter-qualification statutes. And cut
from much the same cloth was his counterpart dissent to *Harper
v. Virginia,* where over his strong objection the Court, speaking
through his long-time partner, struck down the poll tax ("to
introduce wealth or the payment of a fee as a measure of a
voter's qualifications is to introduce an irrelevant factor").[31]

Dissents such as these plus the position on the sit-ins led to the
theory, particularly popular among law students, that the Justice
was really two men. Consciously or otherwise, following
Mencken's analysis of Holmes, the theorists insisted there was an
"Alabama Black," a backsliding recidivist, of the current opinions, and there was the fearless civil libertarian of yesteryear.

Nor were the law students alone in this position. As the year 1966 closed out, *The New York Times* reflected on what was the favorite datum on the supposedly changing Black—the state of the Black-Douglas relationship. Here the division in the poll-tax case was duly noted. So was *U.S. v. Hoffa,* where Black supplied the critically necessary vote to sustain an informer-procured conviction over claims of an unconstitutionally invaded right of privacy. And particular significance was attached to the written passages and oral comments attending their two opinions in *Fortson v. Morris,* which sustained the right of the Georgia legislature to elect the state's governor in the absence of a popular majority, one-man-one-vote to the contrary notwithstanding. Here the *Times* set particular store by the observation of Black in reading the opinion of the Court—"Our business is not to write laws to fit the times. Our task is to interpret the Constitution." It also singled out the bitter passage of Douglas in referring to "the great and glorious constitutional history of Georgia" in a dissent that spoke for the remainder of the old B.B.D. & W. bloc plus the new Justice Fortas.[32]

Yet, those who postulated the theory of the two Blacks could have well reflected on the comment of Harvard's Paul Freund: "I don't think Black is changing, but there are members of the Supreme Court who are trying to move past his position. What he's doing now is blocking that." And Freund also suggested another aspect of the situation: "People's ideas are taken up by the oncoming generation and moved forward. Suddenly the one disowning them is the one who started it all."[33]

And even this wise comment did not completely encompass the subject. On two fronts Black was still well in the van of the judicial revolution that had commenced with his accession to the Court. On the vexed question of pornography, he stood his ground in dissenting from *Ginsburg v. U.S.* and its famous premise ("the leer of the sensualist") that the mode of distribution was relevant to the constitutional protection of the material distributed. On freedom from self-incrimination he was perhaps even more literalist as he concurred with the Court in *Miranda v.*

Arizona that the privilege—with an affirmative statement of its availability and nature—was demanded from the first moment of police custody. More significantly, he dissented in *Schmerber v. California* from the holding that it did not cover blood samples taken involuntarily from suspected drunken drivers.[34]

Two other, not unrelated incidents should have set at rest the two-Blacks theory, and they came within twenty-four hours of each other in early June of 1967. On June 12, a unanimous Court struck down an antimiscegenation statute in a case felicitously styled *Loving v. Virginia*.[35] And a day later Lyndon Johnson announced his intention of nominating Thurgood Marshall to the Supreme Court. Both announcements were taken in stride by a public opinion whose only characteristic seemed to be its utter placidity. Too much so, perhaps, for all parties commenting on Marshall's appointment insisted that their support or opposition, as the case might be, was not occasioned by the nominee's race.

Nonetheless, there was an extended hearing, and this was followed by extended debate. When all was over, Marshall had cleared the test of confirmation with only eleven votes being cast against him. It was five fewer than were registered against Black. There was another and far closer connection to Black. In the most dispositive answer of all to the two-Blacks theory, the one-time general counsel of the National Association for the Advancement of Colored People chose to take the initial oath of his new office at the hands of Justice Hugo Black. The occasion provided its own set of paradoxes. Most obvious was the one whereby a former member of the Ku Klux Klan who had taken that organization's oath (to "most zealously and valiantly shield and defend white supremacy") from the Imperial Wizard himself now raised his right hand once more to swear in the first black member of the Supreme Court.[36]

Thirty years earlier, almost to the day, Walter White, then Executive Director of the N.A.A.C.P., had talked long and earnestly with the senior Senator from Alabama and Supreme Court Justice-designate and had believed the assurances of fair play from the bench. Yet even though White was the prophet vindicated on one count, he never could have foreseen what was in its way the ultimate irony of the Marshall inaugural. For the Alabama Baptist whose opinion had banished prayer from the public school gave, as a memento to the black colleague he had inaugurated—a Bible.[87]

CHAPTER TWENTY

The Lengthening Shadows

Arrivals and Departures

The judicial revolution that bore Warren's name and Black's stamp was also shaped by some critically important and largely unappreciated contributions made by Justice Tom C. Clark. One was *Schempp,* on the Bible and the schools. Another was *Mapp,* which entailed state-court exclusion of illegally seized evidence. As Black's gentle teasing indicated—"The trouble with Tom Clark is that he doesn't read enough"—the Texas Justice was generally disposed to accept the landmarks his fathers had set rather than probe their foundations. Not always, however; Clark was revisionist enough to publicly express remorse for his essentially peripheral connection with the Nisei relocations and the Nuremberg trials. Generally, however, he had to be accounted both traditional and conservative, and his replacement by Thurgood Marshall could be seen only as reinforcing the revolutionary ascendancy.[1]

Obviously it meant far more than had Lyndon Johnson's earlier replacement of Arthur Goldberg with Abe Fortas, in which one liberal activist replaced another. Assertedly, however, the two Johnson appointments did have one element in common: both, it was said, were the premeditated consequences of presidential actions intended to create vacancies on the Court—the appointment of one sitting Justice's son as Attorney General and the appeal to another's long labor-negotiating experience (and Jewish heritage) to become U.N. ambassador and forge a lasting peace in the Middle East.

Ironically enough, however, the political tincturing thus introduced not only caused Black's fourth changing of the guard to be remarkably different from those that had gone before, but would introduce a flawed component producing an end result quite different from the one intended. Nothing of the mutational sequence that lay ahead, however, was suggested by the second factor of the equation, which emerged on June 21, 1968, with Warren's announcement of his intended retirement upon the nomination and qualification of his successor.

The announcement touched off an immediate round of speculation and controversy. One topic concerned the constitutional innovator who proposed to match his recess appointment to the Court by placing a counterpart condition upon his departure from it. More immediately relevant was the politically controversial situation of an outgoing President deciding the lifetime succession to the highest judicial office in the country just a few months before the election at which his own successor would be chosen.

Political controversy, moreover, was supposedly honeycombed with personalities. Washington rumor, fortified by the personal credence of the prestigious James "Scotty" Reston of *The New York Times,* had it that a "deep, personal hostility" to Vice-President Richard Nixon, now the front-running candidate for the Presidency, united Lyndon Johnson and Earl Warren in an unspoken concert to deny him the appointment of a Chief Justice in the event of electoral victory.[2]

The importance of that appointment to the Nixon program and platform had been suggested a full year before the balloting. In November 1967, writing for the *Reader's Digest,* Mr. Nixon fired the opening gun of his campaign in an article charging that recent Supreme Court decisions "weakened law and encouraged criminals." Variously stressed, the theme would appear constantly in the next twelve months. One mode of address was the criticism of decisions that freed proven murderers—"And I say, my friends, that some . . . decisions . . . have gone too far in weakening the peace forces as against the criminal forces of this country." Another was the assertion of what would otherwise be the most obvious and taken-for-granted fact of political life—but which nonetheless usually brought down the house—the promise to appoint a new Attorney General.[3]

But most of all was the mode in which the venerable vocabulary of the Jefferson-Hamilton duel in the Washington cabinet was once more abroad in the land, now in the promise to appoint judges who would construe the Constitution "strictly and fairly." "I told Hugo when we read that in the paper," Justice Douglas later recalled, " 'He's talking about you and me.' Hugo laughed and said 'I don't think so.' "[4]

Paralleling the out-and-out campaign rhetoric directed against the Court on the hustings was the slightly more disguised variety loosed in the halls of Congress. Some clustered around the significantly named Omnibus Crime Control and Safe Streets Act of 1968. But even more emerged in the Senate hearings—the first ever attended by a nominee—on Johnson's appointment of Abe Fortas as Warren's successor. For here Fortas became both target and surrogate victim of the key cases of the judicial revolution.

Like Banquo's ghost, the elusive and intangible aura of race and *Brown II* seemed to lie below and beyond a variety of questions and comments. It combined with sex and crime in protestations on the latest criminal decisions whose fruit was suggested by the subsequent crimes of the rapist freed in *Mallory*. "Mallory, Mallory," intoned Senator Strom Thurmond to Fortas, "let that name ring in your ears." And sex alone was salient in the special showing of *Flaming Creatures*, which was held for the Senators and staff as a sample of the material the nominee had held entitled to First Amendment protection.[5]

But perhaps the high point of the abortive proceedings—the

harassed Fortas broke them off in a refusal to return—came in a virtual line-by-line reading of recent pronouncements of senior Justice Black ("It is history and language . . . which influences me . . . not reasonableness") accompanied by solicitous inquiry of the nominee's agreement or disagreement. And here the harassed witness, all the while avowing "the greatest veneration for Mr. Justice Black" wearily dodged from pillar to post.[6]

There were reports that the veneration was not reciprocated. One observer noted that Fortas had joined the Court just in time to supply the key vote and write the official opinion upholding the library stand-in case of *Brown v. Louisiana*. And perhaps the ultralibertarian accents of that opinion stressing that First Amendment rights were not confined to verbal expressions provoked in turn the incandescence of Black's dissent. On a more workaday level of the law, Fortas deflected Black's drive for a judge-made sequence of uniform rules in federal matters when he changed his vote to hold that a Small Business Administration loan was governed by Texas law and thereby sent the senior Associate Justice into dissent.[7]

Moreover, there was no question that a large number of Senators had no veneration for Mr. Justice Fortas but regarded him as part of the effort of a lame-duck President to name the Chief Justice of the United States and another Associate Justice too—supposedly Homer Throneberry of Texas. More importantly, they announced their intention to filibuster until Christmas to prevent it. They did not have to fight it out that long; on October 1, the nomination aborted when a motion to end debate failed well short of the majority needed.

The key element in the failure was the changed position of the Senate minority leader, Everett McKinley Dirksen, who, with Maryland's Governor Spiro T. Agnew, had been a formidable source of bipartisan support for the nomination. Dirksen had been even more than this, for he had strongly defended the President against charges of cronyism and ridiculed what he called a new doctrine that would require an incumbent President to make appointments from among his political enemies.

All this, however, antedated the grass-roots response to the pioneering criminal-law decisions emanating from the Warren Court. One came in *Witherspoon v. Illinois,* where, on June 3, 1968, over Black's bitter dissent and with Fortas voting with the majority, the Court reduced to life imprisonment the death penalty of the murderer of a Chicago policeman by reason of the peremptory challenge of jurors opposing capital punishment. And still another was provided by the gingerly police interrogation, widely reported as to be well within the bounds of *Miranda,* of a drifter named Richard Speck, who had killed eight student nurses in Chicago.[8]

The two crimes plus the forthcoming election, in which Dirksen was to seek his fourth six-year term, were seen by some to be decisive, and the Senate minority leader subtly shifted his position. ("Hell, Dirksen . . . can turn himself around, and no one can lay a glove on him," went one report.) With the shift went the last hope to break the filibuster and confirm the nomination. And thus to the victims of *Mallory, Witherspoon* and *Speck* might be added the name of Abe Fortas in his failure to achieve the office of Chief Justice of the United States.[9]

A Judicial Testament

The catechism on which Fortas had suffered his passage-by-passage interrogation before the Senate Judiciary was the Carpentier Lecture, which Black had given just a few months earlier at Columbia University. The lectureship had been established in 1903 under an endowment calling for "speakers of preeminent ability" and enjoining that the event be made "so honorable that nobody, however great or distinguished, would willingly choose to decline [an] invitation." And in glittering succession, from the inaugural undertaking of James Lord Bryce to Adolph Berle the year before, the two conditions had been more than fulfilled.[10]

But Black's acceptance was another thing again. As the unclaimed Phi Beta Kappa key suggested, an itch to impress others with public intellectual credentials was not one of the driving forces of his nature. Moreover, and notwithstanding a disposition to accede to testimonial tributes of organizations of which he approved, public speeches were seldom given by him. The Madison Lecture and the American Jewish Congress public colloquy thereby represented highly uncharacteristic events, and far closer to the mark was Justice Harlan's observation a few years earlier that Black had "scrupulously eschewed extrajudicial announcement of his own views upon any of the great issues of our times." Hence, it took not only the high honor of the lecture, but the blackened eye of the dean of the Columbia Law School —an injury inflicted by a tennis ball driven by Mrs. Black—to induce the Justice to capitulate and accept the long-tendered invitation.[11]

On March 20, 1968, he made the first of his three appearances, and his theme made for both contrast and comparison. It was a world apart from the inaugural lecture of James Bryce, who combined a Copernican faith in law as an inductive and deductive science and a gently teasing comment on the divided American constitutional design of forty-five state legislatures and one national one—"all constantly making legislative experiments in the pure scientific spirit." It was very close to Berle's warning of the year before, that the Supreme Court was now sitting as a revolutionary committee.[12]

But his three lectures were every bit as much testament as polemic. Still extraordinarily vigorous at eighty-two, Black sentimentally combined an old man's nostalgic backward glance at the "long journey from a frontier farmhouse in the hills of Clay County, Alabama, to the United States Supreme Court" with a dedication to the women in his life. He specified the names, observing that there were some ladies who might get ideas from a more general dedication ("My mother, my wife Josephine, my wife Elizabeth, and my daughter, Josephine"). There was also an excursus through the lives and times of the men who had been the heroes of his wide reading: Trajan, John Lilburne, John Wilkes, James Madison and Benjamin Franklin. In fact, there was an especial appropriateness in citing the assertion of the octogenarian Franklin ("nearing the end of his glorious career") that the American constitutional design was symbolized by a rising, not a setting, sun.[13]

Yet, beneath the reiteration of Franklin's optimism lay an admonition that was essentially a reprise of the note Berle had sounded the preceding year. Developing that theme, Black now paraphrased Lord Acton on the context of the Court's new jurisprudence—"Power corrupts and unrestricted power will tempt Supreme Court Justices just as history tells us it has tempted other judges." And in this context he suggested his colleagues' most insidious temptation—"a completely honest belief that unless they do act the nation will suffer." He then came to his key proposition:

> Judges take an oath to support the Constitution as it is, not as they think it should be. I cannot subscribe to the doctrine that consistent with that oath a judge can arrogate to himself a power to "adapt" the Constitution to new times.[14]

All else was essentially commentary. Conceding that he had occasionally reversed himself—the flag-salute cases were an obvious example—Black categorically denied that he had changed his constitutional philosophy ("at least not in the last forty years"). In a parallel line of review, he sketched the judicial démarche concerning due process of law from *Palko* of his first term on the Court through his long-term and unavailing effort ("I assume I am still trying") to secure wholesale application of the Bill of Rights to state action. Here he seemed to finally concede that half a loaf was better than none, for he approved the process of selective incorporation of one provision at a time on the grounds that this at least kept judges "from roaming at will."[15]

After asserting his basic theme on the constraints of the judicial oath ("I should support the Constitution as written, not as revised by the Supreme Court from time to time"), he reiterated the absolute constitutional right "without any ifs, ands, buts or whereases" to think, speak, or write free of government constraint. But he also insisted that this carried no privilege "to picket, demonstrate, or march, usually accompanied by singing, shouting, or loud praying . . . in and around other people's property, even including their *homes.*" He closed on a note of religious fervor:

> My experiences with and for our government have filled my heart with gratitude and devotion to the Constitution, which made my public life possible. That Constitution is my legal bible; its plan of government is my plan and its destiny my destiny. I cherish every word of it from the first to the last, and I personally deplore even the slightest deviations from its least important commands.[16]

Codicils and Commentaries

If *A Constitutional Faith* was Black's juridical testament, a codicil of sorts was entered to it the following fall with the taping of the CBS news special. Indeed, the telecast was more than codicil, although it did restate and elaborate some points made on the lecture platform. It was also a popularized version, almost a vulgate, of the Carpentier Lecture. And even though the actual transmission was not effected until after Election Day, the program also constituted his special contribution to the great debate on the role and function of the Supreme Court.

The program opened with Black not only reaffirming a constitutional faith in absolutes but reading its text from the dog-eared copy of the great document that he always carried in his right-hand coat pocket. Almost in passing he noted that most Americans did not seem to understand the Constitution, commented on his mail from those who did not ("Some of them tell me to go to Russia. Go *back* to Russia"), and suggested Plato, Socrates and Walter Lippmann as possessing the potential to have been great judges. He also gave his views on a random array of other topics as he condemned judicial efforts to keep the Constitution up to date, regretted the missed opportunity of "deliberate speed," and appraised old friends, associates, and adversaries—Franklin Roosevelt ("he was magnificent"), Harry Truman ("Oh, I was very fond of Harry"), John W. Davis ("a great man to discuss the law") and Robert H. Jackson ("always magnificent").[17]

It was past the halfway point when Eric Sevareid, without mentioning Richard Nixon's name, brought up the "public clamor about the Court" and "the notion that its decisions have somehow restricted police and aided criminal elements." Black responded with the same staccato thrusts that were the heart of his coast-to-coast radio broadcast thirty-one years earlier: "Well, the Court didn't do it. . . . The Constitution-makers did it. They were the ones who put in no man should be compelled to convict himself." And then he drove his point home by agreeing with Martin Agronsky that these constraints certainly did make it more difficult for the police to convict criminals:

> Certainly. Why shouldn't they? What were they written for? Why did they write the Bill of Rights? They practically all relate to the ways cases should be tried. And practically all of them make it more difficult to convict people of crimes.[18]

On this theme Black was in close and obvious rapport with his interrogators, whose tone and turns of phrase showed them to be from that vaguely bounded persuasion known as liberal intellectual. If the group had ever considered Black one of their own, the contraception dissent would have given them initial pause, and not inconsiderable shock. ("Some who oppose my views," Black noted at Columbia, ". . . have expressed a sort of sympathy and sorrow because of the naïveté or ignorance, which alone in their judgment could account for views with which they so violently disagree.")[19]

If any doubts remained, the television interview ended them. On obviously delicate ground, Sevareid seemed to walk on eggs as he recalled Black's dissent to the library stand-in case in the light of a possibly inherent right to use public places as a forum to protest oppression, and the dialogue quickly moved to the demonstrators at the recent Democratic convention. Here the Justice indicated that his future view of the young people would depend on what came out of the tangled evidence. His tone and vocabulary, however, were not without some significant implications of their own:

> Daley says they did so-and-so, and the other side says they're just a group of young idealists singing sweet songs of mercy and love, and I don't know. That's what the press seemed to think and the television, that they were just young budding idealists who should not be noticed.[20]

With this prelude, Black went on to insist that the right of assembly did not include the right to use other people's property:

> AGRONSKY: You mean, even government property?
> BLACK: Why, certainly, that's not theirs.
> AGRONSKY: You can't assemble in mid-air.
> BLACK: That's not theirs.
> SEVAREID: Well, whose is it—is government property—
> BLACK: It belongs to the government as a whole. Just exactly as a corporation's property belongs to the corporation as a whole. And just as an individual owns it. Now the government would be in a very bad fix, I think, if the Constitution provided that the Congress was without power to keep people from coming into the Library of Congress and spending the day there, demonstrating or singing because they wanted to protest the government. I don't think they could. They've got a right to talk where they have a right to be, under valid laws.[21]

And at this point Agronsky changed the subject from demonstrations to obscenity.

Changing of the Guard V

Deferred until well after Election Day, Black's telecast went without effect on the course of current events, and Richard Nixon captured the Presidency by a narrow margin. No less an authority than Richard Rovere insisted in *The New Yorker* that "Mr. Nixon's attacks on the Court undoubtedly helped him

win. . . ." He took office with Chief Justice Warren's retirement
still pending; Nixon had asked the Chief Justice to serve through
the current term of Court and thereby deferred his choice until
later in the year. On May 5, 1969, an article in *The New York
Times* speculated on the new President's opportunity to change
the "tone and direction" of the Supreme Court with his appointment. Before the day was over that opportunity had, in effect,
doubled—a bombshell article in *Life* opened the last act of the
Fortas tragedy by disclosing a web of extrajudicial relationships
between the junior Justice and a convicted stock manipulator.[22]

It was an almost classic tragedy of the good man undone by a
single flaw, and here Fortas' obvious reluctance to go on the
Court in the first place—"at great financial sacrifice, I must
say"—suggested an apprehension of both his own weakness and
some shattering ending ahead. The drama continued down to the
very last moment with rumor, counterrumor, visits of the Attorney General to the Chief Justice, and all the while the anguished
Fortas weighed his course. "I spent two nights with him," William Douglas recalled, "practically all night, talking to him,
urging him not to resign, because he hadn't done anything which
was unethical." Fortas agreed, but he nonetheless submitted his
resignation. There were varying acknowledgements. The Chief
Justice praised his departing colleague's intelligence and compas-
sion; the President's curt acknowledgment had not a word to
spare.[23]

Almost before the week was out, the President named Judge
Warren Earl Burger, of the Federal Court of Appeals of the
District of Columbia, to the office for which the disgraced Fortas
had been nominated just a year earlier. This time Senate confirmation was prompt and overwhelming. The Warren era
accordingly came to an end on June 23, 1969, as the outgoing
Chief Justice swore in his successor. It was a warm and pleasant
affair graced by Mr. Nixon's presence and generous remarks,
"not as President of the United States, but as a member of the
bar [of] this Court." The retiring Warren responded in like vein,
stressing the continuity of the Court and noting that the 180
years of its existence had been spanned by the service of seven

members, "the last of whom is our senior Justice, Mr. Justice Black."[24]

Notwithstanding the surface geniality, the changing of the guard involved an almost unparalleled sequence of bitter and turbulent confrontations before it had run its course. Two nominations went unsuccessfully to the Senate, which rejected Judge Clement F. Haynsworth, of the Fourth Circuit, and Judge G. Harrold Carswell, of the Fifth. Indeed, the whole 1970 term of the Court came and went with the seat of Abe Fortas unfilled. Finally, yet another federal circuit judge, Harry A. Blackmun, of the Eighth Circuit, managed to clear the Senate, and the Court once more stood restored to full strength.

It was a very different Court from the one that existed just two years before, and Eric Sevareid summed up the transition in a telecast comment to Justice Douglas: "You know, the whole Court situation would be somewhat—considerably—different if Justice Fortas hadn't resigned. . . ."[25]

The Commentators

While the difficulties of Abe Fortas dominated the popular press, much of the literature of the law involved a continuing commentary on the pronouncements, judicial and otherwise, of Justice Black. In an ironic exemplification of permissiveness of comment, Professor Glendon Schubert of Toronto's York University publicly described the Black telecast as a distressing exchange between the "well-informed, sensitive and liberal" commentators and a "rigid, crochety, dogmatic old man." The judgment was formally delivered at Boston University's Gaspar Bacon Lecture, and in something of a battle of endowed oratory, Schubert extended his criticism to Black's Carpentier Lecture as well. But particularly resorted to were Black's eighteen dissents in the 1968–1969 term. The number was once more the high for any member of the Court, and the Bacon lecturer singled out several for particular quotation.[26]

One was the bristling prose of *Tinker v. Des Moines Indepen-*

dent School District, responding to the Court's grant of a right to wear black armbands in protest of the Vietnam war with references to contemporary "break-ins, sit-ins, lie-ins, and smash-ins" and to subjecting "all the public schools in the country to the whims and caprices of their loudest-mouthed but maybe not their brightest students." Another was the disagreement with the Court's veto of Wisconsin's prejudgment law in *Sniadach v. Family Finance* as "plain judicial usurpation of state legislative powers to decide what the state law shall be." And a third was Black's characterization of *Harrison v. U.S.* as making it far more difficult to protect society "against those who have made it impossible to live today in safety."[27]

Professor Schubert concluded that Black's backsliding from liberal orthodoxy could be accounted for in terms of "a socio-psychological explanation of cultural obsolence and . . . a biological explanation of psychophysiological senescence." But he stood almost as alone in conclusion as he did in vocabulary. Indeed, he himself quoted a representative of the dominant contrary view that the seeming backslider was really a psychological constant in a changing world and might even have been "the only one of the justices who had reacted, rightly or wrongly, to the real world of the sixties."[28]

And in one mode or another something of the same deference of tone seemed to tincture most of the intellectual attacks on Black's various theses. It appeared in Jerome Barron's disturbing insistence that the new absolutisms in the current technological milieu would inhibit, not free, communications. It appeared in C. Peter Magrath's caveat that some restraint was necessary, not to save the people from pornography, but to save pornography from the people. It appeared in Wallace Mendelson's comprehensive attack on Black's judicial tactics, all the while asserting that Black was one of the great men of his generation. And it appeared in the biggest blockbuster of them all—Alexander Bickel's Holmes Lectures of 1969.[29]

Published under the title *The Supreme Court and the Idea of Progress,* the lectures dispassionately and almost bloodlessly dissected the record of the Warren Court and found both substance and style deficient in terms of rationality, coherence and consistency. Yet, particularly touching was the special treatment reserved for Justice Black—"magnificent in old age and wedded to the sacred text of the Constitution." To be sure, the lecturer noted Black's past "self-assertive subjectivism" and the increasing frequency of Black defections ("if that is the right word") toward the end of the Warren era. But he also explicitly differentiated the senior associate from his rationalist colleagues on the Court—"another classification is needed for Mr. Justice Black."[30]

And still another form of deference came from still another quarter and, by accident or design, responded to Professor Schubert's assertion of senescence. (Indeed, one reviewer suggested that the Bacon lecturer seemed to be personally offended by Black's judicial positions.) This came from the Court, which had its own extraconstitutional instrument for the retirement of superannuated members, an instrument that in times past had been manifested by the unofficial committees that had waited upon Justices Robert C. Grier and Stephen J. Field. But there was no committee now. Indeed, quite the opposite was indicated by the action of Chief Justice Burger on the occasion of Black's 84th birthday on February 27, 1970. Noting that the observance of such occasions was not commonly undertaken in the course of the Court's work, the Chief Justice went on to propose that "our brother, Justice Black, is a very uncommon man" and, after appropriate good wishes, pointed out that he was "authorized by the Court to say that this is unanimous; there are no dissents."[31]

The Burger-Black rapport, and perhaps the most appreciated deference of all, was involved in a Birmingham visit undertaken at the close of the 1970 term. Invitations to the South were coming more frequently now; Black had been invited to dedicate the new law-school building at the University of Georgia in late 1967, and in the summer of 1968 Black had returned to Alabama for the meetings of the state and Birmingham bar associations. And the following summer he came back once more to the convention of the Alabama Bar Association, this time in the company of the Chief Justice of the United States.

It turned out to be a very special homecoming. Reportedly his presence caused the eight-dollar tickets to the convention's grand banquet at the Parliament House Hotel to be scalped for thirty-five dollars, with a large demand unfulfilled. But the five hundred diners who did manage to attend got a memorable evening for their ticket whatever its price. They heard the governor of Alabama salute the guest of honor as a distinguished native son and the Chief Justice of the United States praise him as "a man of old-fashioned virtues."[32]

And then came the great moment as the venerable guest "hesitatingly rose" and the applauding audience rose also, with the handclapping lifted into a sustained and cheering tumult. There were a few sour notes in the great moment. A passing cab driver noted that "the old scalawag" had done more harm to the white race than any other man he could think of. And two of the guests at the banquet were observed to keep their seats. Yet, one observer saw virtue in adversity:

> You know why those two guys didn't stand up with the rest of us? Because they couldn't bear the thought that their grandchildren would be studying about Mr. Justice Black in years to come and be saying that he was the greatest American jurist since John Marshall.[33]

CHAPTER TWENTY-ONE

The Living Constitution

Four Score and Five

On February 27, 1971, Black celebrated his eighty-fifth birthday with a meeting of his former law clerks and one of his rare conferences with the press. Many of the clerks were now aging men themselves; one of them noted the sad evidence that time was taking its inevitable physical toll. The beloved tennis was now a thing of the past, and so was the bridge. Yet if sight and hearing were diminishing, the flame of the spirit burned as brightly as ever; and the self-description as "a crotchety, stodgy old fellow"—almost a word-for-word repetition of Professor Schubert's description—seemed not so much an admission against interest as a strong argument that he was not. If anything, a gentle mellowness was tempering the fierce pride: "Although I would not say everything or do everything that I had in the past . . . each time I've done it because it was the right thing to do then. So I have no cause for regret." Still elusive as quicksilver, he denied any plans to retire or not to retire—"I'll let life take its way as it goes."[1]

The only case he referred to in the press conference was

Brown III, and here he once again reiterated his second thoughts on the infirmity of "deliberate speed" and indicated that he had gone along with the phrase against his better judgment, because of the critical necessity of judicial unanimity. And the signs were that he had just done so again in the recent *Charlotte-Mecklenburg* proceeding. While he joined the Court's validation of a massive busing plan, oral argument had been punctuated by his own sharp remarks from the bench on the effort "to change the arrangement of people's lives all over this nation" and a brisk criticism of the N.A.A.C.P. counsel's attack on neighborhood schools. And, unusually enough, his remarks stirred the apprehension of a liberal paper ("Signs of Split on Bias") and the even more unusual applause ("Black Is Beautiful") of its local conservative competitor.[2]

The divergent reactions of the two papers were a small part of the complex mosaic of his recent opinions that reflected the ongoing American dilemma. Appropriately, it had fallen on him to finally excise "deliberate speed" in a square injunction ("at once—now") to a school district rather than by *obiter dictum* in some irrelevant case. And appropriately he joined the Court's judgment in *Jones v. Mayer,* holding that the Civil Rights Act of 1966 had been legislatively directed against, and intended to supply a private remedy for, private acts of discrimination in the sale of real estate. The conclusion was heatedly assailed as the *locus classicus* of law-office history, for it burst like a bombshell over Professor Fairman's massive study to the opposite effect in the Holmes Devise history of the Supreme Court. "Either one must bow to that determination," wrote Fairman of *Jones v. Mayer,* "and revise what has been written about the Thirty-ninth Congress, or else examine the opinion critically for what it might be worth as an interpretation of history."[3]

But there were other elements in the mosaic. Black's was the decisive voice and vote in *Palmer v. Thompson,* which permitted Jackson, Mississippi, to close its swimming pools rather than continue operation on a desegregated but uneconomic basis. ("Neither the Fourteenth Amendment nor any act of Congress purports to impose an affirmative duty on a state to operate swimming pools.") And he had been on the winning and losing sides of decisions involving referenda saturated with racial implications. He was among the four dissenters to the judicial nullification of the California election nullifying the state's fair-housing statute. On the other hand and praising the referendum type as the essence of democracy, he wrote the opinion of the Court upholding the right of municipalities to vote out low-income-housing projects despite vigorous appeals against the highly selective impact of such exclusionary action upon the poor in general and blacks in particular.[4]

Equally pluralistic were his criminal opinions. Concern both for the great discontinuities of the times and for constitutional literalism was especially evident in *Berger v. New York*. Here, protesting that the Founding Fathers knew all about eavesdropping and insisting that the constraints of the Fourth Amendment protected papers and not spoken words, he penned a dissent against the Court's limitation on electronic surveillance. It sounded like a congressional speech in favor of the Safe Streets Act: "Crimes, horrid crimes are with us . . . ." And he could be particularly irate with his colleagues themselves, as the time he blisteringly objected to the reversal of a conviction on a procedural point—"here is a gross and wholly indefensible miscarriage of justice . . . calculated to make many good people believe our court actually enjoys frustrating justice by unnecessarily turning professional criminals loose to prey upon society with impunity."[5]

On the other hand, his literalism persisted in a dissent to *U.S. v. 37 Photographs,* wherein the Court denied the government's power to forbid an individual citizen to carry pornography into the country. Remarkably enough, the opinion of the Court drew heavily on a Senate debate in a different age and almost a different country, with Senator Black one of the participants. Yet neither the majority nor his own dissent mentioned the fact. Nor did he make further mention of books that would shock the morals of a man who had not been in church for forty years. But there was a thread of continuity; the Senator had expressed his antipathy toward letting customs clerks determine what Americans could read, and the Justice said the same thing.[6]

The literalism, however, persisted only so far. Notwithstanding the pornography dissent and the reiteration of the now famous " 'no law abridging' means *no law abridging,*" Black was very much the Alabama Baptist in disassociating himself from Justice Harlan's opinion upholding the constitutional right of a draft protester to exhibit to children that four-letter verb that, just a few years earlier, Norman Mailer had been forbidden to spell and, even contemporaneously, Mae West insisted she could not be paid to speak.[7]

There was also a middle ground, and doubtless the shade of Chief Justice Stone looked down approvingly as Black blended the new and the old by delicately pruning, manipulating and engrafting new meanings into old words. Thus, rescuing the District of Columbia antiabortion statute from an assertedly unconstitutional vagueness, Black reversed a district judge on the authority of Noah Webster (that "health" includes "mental attitudes"). But he also shifted the burden of proof from prosecution to defense and thereby created a "most liberal abortion statute" and a thoroughly constitutional one at that. And in something of a counterpart *tour de force*—over the protest of an otherwise admiring newspaper ("Ducking the First Amendment"), he passed over claims that the statutory draft exemption for "religious" reasons unconstitutionally discriminated against other ethical convictions and read the statute as protecting conscientious objectors of every stripe.[8]

Indeed, the new caution and mellowness in his opinions was reflected in the views he expressed at the birthday press conference—that the work of the Court went misunderstood, that it was not more contentious than ever, that it was manned by fine people ("honest men who did the best they could") and that possibly there were times when the opposing point of view was the better one. ("When you get to my age you find it difficult to know if you were right or they were right.")[9]

There was one organization that had no doubt as to who was

right, and this was the American Jewish Congress, which had established an annual percentage score on each member of the Supreme Court in terms of favorable recognition of asserted constitutional rights. Black's batting average for his eighty-fifth year stood at .585, down sharply from a lifetime figure of .735. In lineal terms the averages were even more illuminating. When compilation of these constitutional box scores began in 1957, Black was at the top of the Court. In 1963 and 1964 he had fallen to third place; in 1965 and 1966 to fifth; in 1967 to seventh; in 1968 to last. But by 1970 he had moved back to fifth place, and the American Jewish Congress review noted that his voting pattern was closer to the liberal bloc than it had been for years. And perhaps the burgeoning reassociation with William Douglas was the closest thing to a homecoming that an exile might ever have.

The Teetering Balance

If the shade of Harlan Stone looked down disapprovingly on Black's novel technique of subtly amendatory interpretation instead of total nullification of a statute, that of Felix Frankfurter saw in Black's dissents the vindication of the warnings delivered three decades earlier on "each temporary majority on this Court —and none is very long— . . . translating its own notions of policy into Decisions." And in the denaturalization of *Rogers v. Belli,* Black sounded exactly the same note, insisting that adjudicated constitutional rights "should not be blown around by every passing wind that changes the composition of this Court . . . the Court's construction . . . proceeds on the premise that a majority of this Court can change the Constitution day by day, month by month, year by year. . . ."[10]

The precise issue concerned the power of Congress to forfeit the citizenship of one born abroad as distinguished from one described in the Fourteenth Amendment as "born or naturalized" in the United States. In *Belli,* by a 5-to-4 decision, the Court upheld that power. It also distinguished—or overruled, some would say—a 5-to-4 decision that Black had written in *Afroyim v. Rusk*, affirming the contrary doctrine. But *Afroyim* had itself overruled the 5-to-4 decision in *Perez v. Brownell*, asserting a plenary congressional power in the matter.[11]

And this unstable equilibrium was especially exemplified on December 21, 1970, when Black's single vote managed to void both a section of a statute of Congress and the laws of the fifty states. It was not without its ironic overtones. Back in 1935, on the occasion of a Supreme Court decision voiding the Agricultural Adjustment Act by the narrowest of margins, Senator Black asserted that the United States was now ruled by five men. Thirty-five years later, the extraordinary knife-edge balance of the Court and the play of Justice Black's evolved philosophy brought the speaker within the ambit of his own earlier words and provided an even sharper focus for them.

The occasion was *Oregon v. Mitchell*, which with three other consolidated cases undertook to prove the validity of the Voting Rights Act of 1970 and its dramatic enfranchisement of eighteen-year-olds, whatever their state laws might say on the subject. Less obvious, but of almost equal constitutional moment, was the statute's bans on literacy tests of any type and on long state residential requirements as a precondition of voting in presidential elections. There were grave reservations as to the constitutionality of these provisions, and these were echoed by the President when he signed the bill into law. And the grave doubt expressed in the two political branches of government was underscored by a special provision of accelerated judicial review.[12]

Hence, within four months of passage, the consolidated voting-rights cases had been argued, and the decision was in hand before the year 1970 was out. And an extraordinary decision it was, unparalleled in almost a century and a half. As it turned out, a single Justice held the decisive vote on an otherwise evenly decided Court, which was no novelty. What was almost without precedent was his casting that vote on opposite sides of two propositions that every one of his colleagues saw as organically inseparable.

Nothing quite like it had occurred since *Ogden v. Saunders* in 1837. There again the Court, save for one Justice, split down the middle on two points that all Justices save that one saw as opposite sides of the same coin. The first was whether states could pass *in futuro* insolvency laws. The other was whether such laws could have any out-of-state effect. And here Justice William Johnson agreed with three of his colleagues that the Constitution did not bar a properly drawn state statute and then crossed over to the side of the three initial dissenters ("who viewed all such statutes as void") so as to permit the validated statute to operate only in the courts of the enacting state.[13]

In 1970 the same pattern emerged as another unlikely pair of propositions were shaped by the act of one man. There was, of course, no opinion of the Court in the matter. Instead, the extraordinary pattern of dissent and concurrence was summed up in Black's own "view of the cases":

> . . . I believe Congress can fix the age of voters in national elections . . . but cannot set the voting age in state and local elections . . . my brothers DOUGLAS, BRENNAN, WHITE and MARSHALL join me in concluding that Congress can enfranchise 18-year-old citizens in national elections, but dissent from the judgment that Congress can*not* extend the franchise to 18-year-old citizens in state and local elections . . . my brothers THE CHIEF JUSTICE, HARLAN, STEWART, and BLACKMUN join me in concluding that Congress cannot interfere with the age for voters set by States for state and local elections. They, however, dissent from the judgment that Congress can control voter qualifications in federal elections.[14]

Thus the word of a single man established the law of the land. Remarkably, there was little uproar or outcry. One conservative columnist, deploring "the catastrophic affront to orderly and sensible government," called on Congress to repeal the act which had started all the trouble in the first place. Otherwise criticism ran along the line taken by James Kilpatrick, who, writing more in sorrow than in anger, turned out an effort called "Sad Day for Mr. Justice Black" and regretted that the champion of plain words and plain meaning had extrapolated the congressional power over the "manner of elections" to an authority to prescribe the qualifications of voters.[15]

The eighteen-year-old-voter case had many roots. There was the obvious mutation of the one-man, one-vote doctrine of *Baker v. Carr*. There was the accelerating political integration of the country thanks to the new media and the rising mobility of population. There was the surfacing of a new youth orientation in the American culture. But most of all, unquestionably, was the impact of the most unpopular war in the nation's history and its by-product of teen-agers conscripted for jungle fighting half a world away.

And in leaving its mark otherwise on the Court, the war would give Hugo Black a great judicial exit.

The Paper and The Papers

"Despite talk of increasing conservatism," the 1971 American Jewish Congress report noted in a reference to Black, "he never wavered on issues affecting freedom of expression and particularly political expression." In part, no doubt, the tribute was prompted by Black's concurring opinion in the celebrated case of the Pentagon Papers, otherwise known as *New York Times v. U.S.*, which provided an almost incredibly appropriate medium for his last judicial utterance. A novelist could not have drawn it better, for the mix of facts—a secret history of the Vietnam war purloined by a Pentagon adviser and turned over to the press for publication—combined the tumult of pressing events, high drama and momentous questions of constitutional law, and combined them in the area of constitutional law closest to Black's heart.[16]

The case got to the Supreme Court in the form of urgent appeals from lower courts in New York and Washington, and it got there with breakneck speed. Scarcely a fortnight was needed to make the transit from initial injunction to the final Supreme Court decree. And more than this, the action of the Court on June 30, 1971, made the special summer session part of that sequence of extraordinary summer proceedings—the Nazi saboteurs and World War II, the Rosenbergs and the cold war, Little Rock and the civil-rights revolution. Unlike all the special proceedings before it, however, the central issue in the Pentagon Papers case had a simplicity so stark that perhaps the major difficulty was really the mode in which the basic question had gone unresolved so long—did the national courts have the authority, without (or perhaps even with) specific congressional sanction, to prohibit the publication of information whose secrecy was deemed critical to the national interest? Or perhaps the question might be put in terms of the content of two constitutional phrases, "judicial power" of the Third Article and "make no law" of the First Amendment.

On these points, the Court responded with a constellation of opinions whose total lucidity resembled nothing quite so much as a cobwebbed windshield. At one extreme lay the Chief Justice's view, largely shared by Justice Blackmun, that the issue was no more complex than the obligation to return stolen property ("that duty I had thought—perhaps naïvely—was to report forthwith to the responsible public officers. This duty rests on taxi drivers, Justices, and the *New York Times*"). In the ruling center stood Justices White and Stewart, who concluded that, in the absence of a strong showing that publication would produce a "direct, immediate, and irreparable" injury, disclosure by publication would not be enjoined. At the other pole were Black and Douglas who in separate opinions expressed shock that the Court had been so much as asked to rule on the point.[17]

Black's opinion included any number of other points. He let it be known what he thought of the Vietnam war, although this was hardly a secret to the millions of viewers who had seen the 1968 telecast. ("We've had only one war that I thoroughly approved. And that was the war against Hitler. And that's the only one.") But now, in what was technically an *obiter dictum,* he made explicit what had previously been implied:

And paramount among the responsibilities of a free press
is the duty to prevent any part of the government from
deceiving the people and sending them off to distant lands
to die of foreign fevers and foreign shot and shell.[18]

But not *obiter dictum,* and in his view of things the heart of
the case, was that portion of the argument of the Solicitor General that was addressed specifically to him and that he appropriately quoted in his opinion by way of declaration of his own
constitutional faith:

> Now, Mr. Justice [Black], your construction of . . . [the
> First Amendment] is well known, and I certainly respect
> it. You say no law means no law, and that should be ob-
> vious. I can only say, Mr. Justice, that to me it is equally
> obvious that "no law" does not mean "no law," and I
> would seek to persuade the Court that that is true . . .
> There are other parts of the Constitution that grant power
> and responsibilities to the Executive and . . . the 1st
> Amendment was not intended to make it impossible for
> the Executive to function or to protect the security of the
> United States.[19]

And with the thesis and counterthesis thus set out, he commented with fire and vigor on the choices he saw presented:

> In other words, we are asked to hold that despite the 1st
> Amendment's emphatic command, the Executive Branch,
> the Congress, and the Judiciary can make laws enjoining
> the publication of current news and abridging freedom of
> the press in the name of "national security." The Govern-
> ment does not even attempt to rely on an act of Congress.
> Instead it makes the bold and dangerously far-reaching
> contention that the courts should take it upon themselves
> to "make" a law abridging freedom of the press in the
> name of equity, presidential power, and national secu-
> rity.[20]

There were any number of sources to which he could have
resorted for a responsive quotation. His own record was brim-

ming with pertinent observations on judges making law—whether in contempt or antitrust or economic regulation—and his views on inherent presidential powers had been set out in the steel-seizure case. Instead of quoting himself, however, he chose to quote a colleague who had retired from the Court thirty years before and almost to the day:

> The greater the importance of safeguarding the community from incitement to the overthrow of our institutions . . . the more imperative is the need to preserve inviolate the constitutional rights of free speech, free press and free assembly. . . . Therein lies the security of the Republic, the very foundation of constitutional government.[21]

The quotation was the last thing Mr. Justice Black was to deliver from the bench, and had he deliberately chosen a judicial epigraph, it is doubtful that he would have changed a thing, for the brief passage admirably caught the heart of his constitutional faith.

And it also captured the paradox of Hugo Black, for the last official words of the Justice were supplied by the very man whom the vote of the Senator had deemed unfit for the Court—Charles Evans Hughes.

The Greening of America

Through a Glass Darkly

A few weeks before the Pentagon Papers decision, Black had attended the dedication of the Lyndon Johnson Library in Austin. His appearance elicited the concern of friends, for his strength was obviously running low and there was need to husband it against the work that lay ahead. Nonetheless his last extrajudicial public appearance had its felicitous side, and his venerable presence on the platform that May day of 1971 bore a striking witness to the extraordinary reach of his career. Thirty-four years earlier, almost to the day, Senator Hugo Black had hailed young Lyndon Johnson's victory in a special congressional election as a proof of popular support of Franklin Roosevelt's Court-packing plan. And on May 22, 1971, Justice Hugo Black remained involved in the highest affairs of state as the Johnson Presidency was being encased in its archival reliquary and handed over to the verdict of American history.

The Black niche in that history was already secure in a variety of facets, and a small card on his desk bearing the years, months and days of the Supreme Court service of John Marshall and

Stephen J. Field indicated that within just a few short months his own unprecedented term there would add yet another laurel to his record. Yet, there was a question in his mind whether the distinction would ever come. He even insured against it. At the close of the 1970 term he delivered to Elizabeth a signed but undated letter of retirement against the possibility that some physical disability might leave him both unfit for judicial service and incapable of formally leaving it.[1]

His forehandedness was not without justification. On August 28, 1971, the wire services carried the story of his admission to Bethesda Naval Hospital. There were no details, and the continued absence of medical reports suggested that all was not well. Rather, the silence made it more and more apparent that he would not be back for the opening of the Court in October. Any suspicion that he had simply been an old man clinging to office to set a record was dispelled on September 17, when his letter of retirement, now dated by himself, went forward to the President. Accepting it with regret, Mr. Nixon drew on his own experience as an attorney at the bar of the Supreme Court to recall Black's dogged pursuit of truth and went on to observe that such were the Justice's "independence, tenacity and integrity of mind, that his imprint on the Court and our nation will be indelible."[2]

The action had not come a moment too soon. A stroke followed the next day, and the enormous vitality seemed at last to have met its match. Yet even as he lay disabled, the events he had helped set in motion were producing his monument. A particularly significant development came from his native Alabama, where the legislature followed the President's lead in framing its own tributes, the lower house doing so on the resolution of the first black to serve there since the Reconstruction.

And then came the ultimate irony in a life filled with paradox. His constitutionally irrevocable pension benefits under the judicial retirement act of 1937—for which, all unknowing, he had voted on his fifty-first birthday and which had been a source of difficulty to constitutional purists—were to last barely a week. He died at the beginning of Saturday, September 25, 1971, with death being attributed to the stroke of the preceding Sunday and a resulting inflammation of the arteries. Nor did death come singly. In another room on the same hospital corridor, fatally stricken, lay Justice John Harlan, his distant cousin, warm personal friend and ongoing intellectual antagonist, who had continued the Frankfurter duel—now finally at an end.

A brief lying-in-state was held at a Washington funeral home, with callers receiving counterparts of the small copy of the Constitution the dead Justice had carried in his coat pocket. The funeral itself was held at the National Cathedral on Monday, September 27, with Woodrow Wilson's grandson, Dean Francis Sayre, presiding. In attendance were the great and the near-great, headed by the President and Attorney General in a front pew. The ritual was ecumenism itself—"Rock of Ages" and "Swing Low, Sweet Chariot," the 23rd and 121st Psalms, readings from the underlined portions of books in his library—Aeschylus, Cicero, Jefferson—and selections from his own opinions. Dean Sayre read the thirteenth chapter of First Corinthians (Black always substituted "love" for "charity" in his own rendition), and Doctor Howlett of All Souls Unitarian Church preached the eulogy with certain passages stirring up particular reflections in some hearers (". . . he had little patience with the so-called 'strict constructionists' "). There was a brief graveside service with a reprise of First Corinthians, chapter 13, and a prayerful hope that the dead man's "toughness of fiber, the simplicity, the honesty of mien, and the warm understanding" might live on in the lives of others.

All across the nation the newspapers (those which had survived the hydraulic merger forces that Black had fought so strenuously) united in a eulogy very different from the sentiments that the great majority had expressed during another September a quarter-century earlier. And flags were half-masted in response to a presidential order during the religious tribute, in which a Unitarian eulogy over a deceased Baptist in an Episcopal cathedral caught something of the complexity of the living man. Two final touches caught it even better. The coffin was plain, knotty pine—that splintery, springy and tenacious tree of his Alabama hills. And inside the coffin, in the coat pocket of the dead Justice, was a copy of the Constitution he had carried in his life.[3]

A Constitutional Faith

There were some other rites to be undertaken. As the Chief Justice opened the October 1971 term, noting with obvious sadness "the absence of our beloved colleague the late Justice Hugo Black" and suggesting that Black's outstanding quality had been "his unbounded faith in the people and the political processes of a free people under the American Constitution," Douglas added a terse and moving statement, which closed by commemorating Black's commitment to the "society of the dialogue."[4]

The same day proceedings in the House of Representatives echoed much the same themes. They came from a diversity of speakers including a black from California, a Jesuit from Massachusetts and—what would have pleased him most of all—the Representative from Scottsboro, who placed in the record the eulogy of the *Montgomery* (Alabama) *Journal*. Two days later the Senate mourned its distinguished former member with Senators Edward M. Kennedy, Thomas J. McIntyre and Frank E. Moss taking the floor.

All this was prelude, however, to the classic rite held April 18, 1972, the memorial service of the bar of the Supreme Court, which was in its way a set piece as structured as any requiem in the Roman liturgy. The famous man was praised and the maxim *de mortuis nil nisi bonum* honored in the roll call and quotation of the great opinions—the Pentagon Papers, the steel seizure, the Sunrise Confessions, *Gideon, Adamson.*[5]

There were omissions. *Korematsu* went unmentioned, and so did the Connecticut contraception dissent. Far more infelicitous in view of a double applicability was the failure to cite or quote *San Antonio Parkway*. It was almost the *locus classicus* of the Black opinions in both strength and weakness, for it had power, clarity and simplicity. It also had a parade of horribles. And best of all, it came in dissent, protesting the refusal of the Court to let nature lovers state the ecological case against a throughway:

> The San Antonio Park has . . . many acres of open space covered with trees, flowers, and running brooks. It is a lovely place for people to retreat from the frantic pace of bustling urban life to enjoy the simple pleasures of open space, quiet solitude, and clean air. It is a refuge for young and old alike—the kind of a park where a family man can take his wife and children or lovers can while away a sunny afternoon together. After today's decision, the people of San Antonio and the birds and animals that make their home in the park will share their quiet retreat with an ugly, smelly stream of traffic pouring down a super six-lane "north Expressway." Trees, shrubs, and flowers will be mown down. The cars will spew forth air and noise pollution contaminating those acres not buried under concrete. Mothers will grow anxious and desert the park lest their children be crushed beneath the massive wheels of interstate trucks.[6]

But the opinion also had a relevance to an extraordinary, popular and controversial book, *The Greening of America,* which had been written by his former law clerk and was itself the subject of comment in the memorial proceedings. Black was mentioned in the book and it was not the first time his name had appeared in the author's writings. For Charles Reich had written the tribute "Mr. Justice Black and the Living Constitution" that had hailed Black's seventy-seventh birthday and the completion of his first quarter century on the Court.[7]

In it Professor Reich insisted that there could be no such thing as a constitution with a static meaning, that constancy required changes, and that integrity required movement "in the same direction and at the same rate as the rest of society." Reich further noted the paradox that Black's devotion to an unchanging Bill of Rights in a changing world involved a process whereby Black "has changed" and "is changing."[8]

Black declined a large part of the honor, and a part of his

Griswold dissent seemed almost addressed in specific reply to his young friend:

> I realize that many good and able men have eloquently spoken and written, sometimes in rhapsodical strains, about the duty of this Court to keep the Constitution in tune with the times. The idea is that the Constitution must be changed from time to time and that this Court is charged with a duty to make these changes. For myself I must with all deference reject that philosophy. The Constitution makers knew the need for change and provided for it. Amendments suggested by the people's representative can be submitted. . . . That method of change was good enough for our Fathers, and being somewhat old-fashioned, I must add it is good enough for me.[9]

Professor Reich took no specific issue with the reprimand, if indeed reprimand it was. Rather, affection for his mentor seemed to continue undiminished. Or so the preface of *The Greening of America* indicated; there, in pleading a debt to long talks with "good and generous friends," the name of Hugo L. Black led all the rest. There were other names. In the literary sources first mention went to Karl Marx and Herbert Marcuse, with a gracious but unnecessary acknowledgment of intellectual dependence shown far better in extensive quotations throughout the text. And in style as in content, the book resembled its sources—obscure, rambling, apocalyptic, and marked by alienation, hatred and anger. But there was far more to the work than redistillation of the old and new radicals. There was also a sequence of piercing flashes of insight, which in a famous division of Consciousness I, II, and III sketched the successive perceptions of the American mind in historical evolution. And scoring formidable hits again and again on the shortcomings of contemporary institutions, there went up an intense and moving *cri de coeur* against the mindlessness and anonymity that marked so much of the current world.

Even more remarkable was the response, for Charles Reich had manifestly touched a universal nerve. The book went through printing after printing, as judges and housewives, farm workers and teachers, academicans and professionals all acclaimed it for affording a new insight into the world about them, for spanning the generation gap, and for giving a glimpse of what the future might be. And it was to this new spirit that eighty-four-year-old Black's dissent in *San Antonio Parkway* had prophetically appealed.

And at the last of the funeral rites, Louis Oberdorfer, distinguished government official and sometime Black law clerk, mentioned the work of his colleague in that office. Appropriately enough he did so in a reference to an equivalent of sorts to the counterdissent, that new genre of judicial writing which had been among Black's contributions to the literature of the law.

For, as the readings in the National Cathedral services suggested, Black was not only a great reader but an underliner and marginal annotator as well. Oberdorfer had chosen, as part of his remarks at the obsequies at the Supreme Court bar, the annotation in Black's copy of *Greening*. It was a singularly apt passage; it dealt with the author's obvious disagreement with the traditional thesis "that the American dream is still possible and that success is determined by character, morality, hard work and self-denial." That thesis summed up the ethos of the frontier farmhouse in the hills of Clay County. Eight decades later, the Justice who had lived to see men walk on the moon believed it. For in a marginal notation to *Greening,* he entered a terse declaration of what was at once a counterdissent to the author's protest and a steely epigraph of his own constitutional faith: "I still do."[10]

Notes

PROLOGUE

1. Durr, "Hugo Black: A Personal Appraisal," *Georgia Law Review,* 6 (1971), 1 (hereinafter cited as Durr); Gerhart, *American Advocate: Robert H. Jackson* (1958), 274 (hereinafter cited as Gerhart).
2. Durr, 8–9; Memo to files by Justice Frankfurter, January 25, 1961, in Frankfurter Papers, Library of Congress; Letter to S. Sidney Ulmer, October 10, 1970; Ulmer, "Bricolage and Assorted Thoughts on Working in the Papers of Supreme Court Justices," *The Journal of Politics,* 35 (1973), 289. See also Cooper, "Mr. Justice Hugo L. Black of Alabama," *The Alabama Lawyer,* 33 (1967), 19; Freund, "Mr. Justice Black and the Judicial Function," *UCLA Law Review,* 14 (1967), 473.
3. Black, "Felix Frankfurter," *Harvard Law Review,* 78 (1965), 1521; Hugo Black, Jr., *My Father* (1975), 127.
4. Quoted in Childers, "Hugo Black, Always an Alabamian," *Birmingham News,* January 31, 1937.
5. Lerner, "Hugo Black—A Personal History," *Nation,* 145 (1937), 367; Schlesinger, *The Politics of Upheaval* (1960), 323 (hereinafter cited as Schlesinger).
6. Wright, "Hugo L. Black: A Great Man and a Great American," *Texas Law Review,* 50 (1971), 3.
7. The description is that of Huey Long in Schlesinger 323.
8. Smith v. California, 361 U.S. at 157 (1959); Irwin v. Gavit, 268 U.S. at 168 (1925).
9. *Nation,* 132 (1931), 262; *New Republic,* 66 (1931), 87; Wilson, *Patriotic Gore* (Galaxie Ed., 1966), 771. On the range of terms see Yarbrough, "Mr. Justice Black and Legal Positivism," *Virginia*

Law Review, 57 (1971), 375; and White, "The Rise and Fall of Justice Holmes," *Chicago Law Review,* 39 (1971), 53.

10. See Mencken, "Mr. Justice Holmes," in Cooke, ed., *The Vintage Mencken* (New York, 1955), 189; Letter from Mencken to Maury Maverick September 12, 1938, in Henderson, *Maury Maverick: A Political Biography* (1970), 178. "The 'tough' legal . . . critic and the craftsman and reformer in the law . . . did not always live on good terms with each other"—Lerner, *The Mind and Faith of Justice Holmes* (Boston, 1943), 47.

11. Chambers v. Florida, 309 U.S. at 241 (1940); Beard, *The Republic* (1943), 238–39; Korematsu v. U.S., 323 U.S. at 219 (1944).

12. *St. Louis Post-Dispatch,* May 19, 1960; "It seemed entirely fitting that Hugo Black of Alabama and Harry Truman of Missouri—politicians whose political style and heritage were strikingly Populist—should lead the New Deal reform battles"—Woodward, *The Burden of Southern History* (1968), 142; Berger v. N.Y., 388 U.S. at 73 (1967).

13. Andrew Jackson quoted in "Vacancies on the Court," 109 *New Republic* (1971), 357, and in Bickel, *The Morality of Consent* (1975), 9.

14. The Holmes assertion is from Max Lowenthal's letter to Felix Frankfurter, November 21, 1952, Frankfurter Papers, LC.

15. *New York Times,* March 9, 1931.

16. *New York Times,* December 4, 1968; "Text of Historic TV Interview of Justice Black," *Congressional Quarterly Report,* 29 (1969), 8 (hereinafter cited as TV Transcript).

17. Williams, *Hugo L. Black: A Study in the Judicial Process* (1950) (hereinafter cited as Black TV Transcript).

18. Engel v. Vitale, 370 U.S. at 435, n. 21 (1962).

19. TV Transcript, 9.

20. *Ibid.*

21. Graham, *The Self-Inflicted Wound* (1970), 15; White, *The Making of a President—1968* (1969), 346; Graham, 10.

22. Brown v. Board of Education, 347 U.S. 483 (1954).

23. *New York Times,* October 13, 1968.

CHAPTER ONE

1. *New York Times,* October 1, 1937.

2. *Life,* October 12, 1937; Interview with Mr. Claude Hamilton, August 9, 1973.

3. *New York Times,* August 15, 1937, and December 12, 1926; Letter to Franklin Roosevelt, May 18, 1938 in Freedman, ed., *Roosevelt and Frankfurter* (1937), 457 (hereinafter cited as Freedman).

4. *Literary Digest,* May 29, 1937.

5. Moley, *The First New Deal* (1966), 287.

6. Black, "Inside a Senate Investigation," *Harper's,* 172 (1936), 286.
7. *Literary Digest,* August 21, 1937.
8. *Congressional Record,* 81 (1937), 9099.
9. *Ibid.,* 9102; Farley, *Jim Farley's Story* (1948), 98 (hereinafter cited as Farley).
10. *New York Times,* August 13, 1937.
11. *Time,* August 23, 1937.
12. Letter to R. W. Washburn, August 16, 1937 (copy), in Borah Papers, Library of Congress (hereinafter cited as Borah Papers, LC).
13. *Ibid.*
14. White, *A Man Called White* (1948), 177.
15. Van der Veer (Hamilton), "Hugo Black and the K.K.K.," *American Heritage,* April 1968.
16. Letter from Irving Brant to Felix Frankfurter, September 23, 1937, Frankfurter Papers, LC (the letter together with others of Mr. Brant is quoted herein with his kind permission); *Congressional Record* 81 (1937), 9098.
17. Letter to Jess Hawley, August 16, 1937, in Borah Papers, LC; Letter to Franklin Roosevelt, September 1, 1937, Freedman, 406; *Chicago Times,* August 22, 1937.
18. Raymond Clapper quoted in Frank, *Mr. Justice Black, The Man and His Opinions* (1949) (hereinafter cited as Frank), 102.
19. Catledge, *My Life and Times* (1971), 107; Ickes, *The Secret Diary of Harold Ickes,* Vol. II (1954) (hereinafter cited as Ickes), 196.
20. Berman memorandum, March 22, 1956; Ickes, 215; Whalen, *The Founding Father* (1964), 200.

CHAPTER TWO

1. *Congressional Record,* 81 (1937), 9412.
2. Memorandum of interview, March 22, 1956, Daniel Berman Papers, Chevy Chase, Md. The author is deeply grateful to Mrs. Aline Berman for access to her late husband's papers. Affidavit of W. R. Vest, September 15, 1937, in *Pittsburgh Post-Gazette,* September 18, 1937.
3. Lilienthal, *The Journals of David Lilienthal,* Vol. I (1964), 9 (hereinafter cited as Lilienthal).
4. *Pittsburgh Post-Gazette,* September 18, 1937.
5. *Literary Digest,* September 27, 1937; for whatever it is worth, the author believes the second hypothesis. Interestingly, it was Paul Block who obtained Henry Wallace's "Dear Guru" letters (Markowitz, *The Rise and Fall of the People's Century* [1973], 338–39) and offered $5,000 for information on any Roosevelt cabinet member committing an indictable offense (Ickes, Vol. II, 292).
6. *Pittsburgh Post-Gazette,* September 13, 16, 1937.
7. *New York Times,* September 13, 1937; Williams, 59.
8. *Pittsburgh Post-Gazette,* September 15, 16, 17, 18, 1937.

9. *Newsweek,* September 27, 1937; *New York Times,* August 18, September 14, 23, October 4, 1937.
10. *Pittsburgh Post-Gazette,* September 15, 1937; *Nation,* 165 (1937), 367–69.
11. *Newsweek,* September 20, 1937.
12. *Nation,* September 25, 1937, 145; Frank, 103; *Congressional Record,* 131 (1937), 9216–9219; *New York Times,* September 14, 15, 18, 1937.
13. Letters from F. L. Stork, November 8, 1937, C. C. Burlingham, October 6, 1937, and Grenville Clark, September 16, 1937, in Borah Papers.
14. Telegrams to Robert G. Taylor, September 27, 1937, and *Christian Science Monitor,* October 3, 1937, and letter to Isaac Levy, October 14, 1937, *ibid.*
15. *Nation,* 145 (1937), 312; 389th Press Conference, in Rosenman, ed., *The Public Papers and Addresses of Franklin D. Roosevelt* (1938–50), Vol. 6, 108.
16. *Pittsburgh Post-Gazette,* September 15, 18, 1937.
17. *Newsweek,* September 20, 1937; *New Republic,* 42 (1937), 213.
18. Durr, 15; *Newsweek,* October 11, 1937.
19. *Congressional Record,* 129 (1935), 6533.
20. Farley, 98–99; "With respect to Mr. James Farley, I have run across him a good many times in New York, but always in the presence of others and we never discussed his ideas about that radio speech of Justice Black"—Letter of Claude A. Hamilton to the author, July 6, 1973.
21. Durr, 18.
22. *New York Times,* September 26, 1971.
23. The entire address is reprinted in Williams, 27–30.
24. *Newsweek,* October 11, 1937; *New Republic,* 42 (1937), 387; Letter to Robert Gray Taylor, October 4, 1937; Moore, *Senator Josiah William Bailey of North Carolina* (1968), 142.
25. H. Williams, *Huey Long* (1969), 703.
26. Goldman, *Rendezvous with Destiny* (1966), 43.
27. Farley, 108; High, "Mr. Roosevelt and the Future," *Harper's,* 45 (1937), 175; Ashurst, Manuscript Diary, University of Arizona, p. 573 (entry of May 18, 1937).
28. Letter to Felix Frankfurter, September 23, 1937, Frankfurter Papers, LC.
29. Ickes, Vol. II, 145; "Bishop Sheil later told friends that the Cardinal had affirmed his own confidence in Justice Black's fairness and integrity"—Tully, *FDR Was My Boss* (1949), 241.
30. *Life,* October 18, 1937; Roseman, *Working with Roosevelt* (1952), 166.
31. Interview with Mr. Jerome Cooper, May 30, 1972. The character of press comment on Black's appointment was indicated by *Newsweek*'s description of Mr. Cooper as "Birmingham Jew and Harvard Law School graduate"—*Newsweek,* October 11, 1937.

32. Letter to Black, August 18, 1937, in Mason, *Harlan Fiske Stone* (1956), 467 (hereinafter cited as Mason); Ashurst, 351; Pusey, *Charles Evans Hughes*, Vol. II (1951), 773–74 (hereinafter cited as Pusey). An appropriate counterpart involved Mrs. Black. Somewhat remarkably (but typifying the Blacks' unpretentious domestic life), she and Hughes had never met prior to her husband's appointment to the Court. Their first encounter was cordiality itself, and in parting Mrs. Black observed in her quietly exuberant way, "Mr. Chief Justice, I always knew you were beautiful." Next morning a warmly inscribed photograph of the Olympianly bearded Hughes was delivered to her by special messenger—Interview with Claude Hamilton, August 9, 1973.

33. Douglas, *Go East, Young Man,* xiv–xv (1974); Cooper interview, note 31 *supra.*

34. *Time,* October 11, 1937.

35. Ex Parte Leavitt, 302 U.S. 633 (1937); *New York Times,* October 5, 1937.

36. Letter to author, May 22, 1973; *New York Times,* November 2, 1937; Letter to John Bankhead, October 3, 1937; Moore, note 24 *supra,* 142.

CHAPTER THREE

1. Frank, 40; Memorandum of interview, June 20, 1956, Berman Papers, Berman Residence, Chevy Chase, Maryland (hereinafter cited as Berman Interview).

2. *Greenville Advocate,* May 4, 1892, quoted in Rogers, *The One-Gallus Rebellion—Agrarians in Alabama 1865–1896* (1970), 206; also see generally Francis S. Hackney, *From Populism to Progressivism in Alabama 1890–1910* (1969).

3. Transcript, Ku Klux Klan Klorero, September 2, 1926, reprinted in *Pittsburgh Post-Gazette,* September 16, 1937.

4. Georgia v. Evans, 316 U.S. 159 (1942).

5. *Pittsburgh Post-Gazette,* September 15, 1937.

6. Berman Interview, June 1956; see Hugo Black, Jr., *My Father* (1975), 4–5; Interview with Mrs. Hugo L. Black, December 4, 1972.

7. Cooper, "Mr. Justice Hugo L. Black: Footnotes to a Great Case," *Alabama Law Review,* 24 (1972), 2; Black, *A Constitutional Faith,* Dedication Page.

8. Black, "Reminiscences," *Alabama Law Review,* 18 (1965), 3; Durr, 3. The episode is remarkably like Justice Story's severance of association with Marblehead Academy.

9. Black, "Reminiscences," *loc. cit.,* 4; Black, *A Constitutional Faith;* Berman Interview, June 1956.

10. Carmer, *Stars Fell on Alabama* (1934) (hereinafter cited as Carmer); Black, "Reminiscences," *loc cit.,* 6.

11. *Ibid.,* 9, 10.
12. Meador, *Mr. Justice Black and His Books* (1974), 8.
13. Sherman, "Justice Black as a Police Judge," *St. Louis Post-Dispatch,* June 17, 1946.
14. Leighton, "Birmingham, Alabama," *Harper's,* 175 (1937), 225.
15. Frank, 16.
16. Leighton, *op. cit. supra,* 233; Lerner, "Hugo Black—A Personal History," *Nation,* 145 (1937), 367; Letter of Justice Douglas to the author, July 14, 1975.
17. Frank, 139.
18. Hamilton, *Hugo Black: The Alabama Years* (1972), 37 (hereinafter cited as Hamilton).
19. *Ibid.,* 43.
20. Chambers v. Florida, 309 U.S. 227 (1940).
21. Durr, 3.
22. *Chicago Times,* August 20, 1937.
23. Hamilton, 91.
24. *Ibid.,* 89, 90, 91.
25. *Ibid.,* 93.

CHAPTER FOUR

1. Radio address, October 1, 1937, Williams, 28. Among those not speaking, I must set down the name of Mr. James Esdale, former Grand Dragon of the Alabama Klan, whom I met in his Birmingham office on May 30, 1972, thanks to the kindness of Professor Virginia Hamilton, author of *Hugo Black: The Alabama Years.* Clear-eyed (indeed, piercing-eyed), trim, and extraordinarily vital, the octogenarian Mr. Esdale responded to my first question, "I took an oath not to reveal certain matters. Would you have me break that oath?"
2. Berman Interview, June 1956; *Ibid.,* March 1956.
3. Lerner, "Hugo Black—A Personal History," *Nation,* October 9, 1937.
4. Smith v. DeLaye, 193 Alabama 500, 68 Southern 993 (1918). One of the offenders was the *Cincinnati Enquirer* (February 10, 1915), where the advertiser of "Sandy River" and "Magnolia" boasted: "This department is on the job; all goods carefully packed and sealed in plain packages without revealing markings."
5. Hamilton, 66–67.
6. The defendants included Frank Boykin, future congressional colleague of Black.
7. Cash, *The Mind of the South* (1941), 335 (hereinafter cited as Cash).
8. Letter from W. E. Bayette to Charles Evans Hughes, September 27, 1937 (copy), Brandeis Papers, University of Louisville.

Notes 447

9. Durr, 5; Interview of 1967, posthumously published, *New York Times*, September 26, 1971.
10. Interview with Senator John Sparkman, May 23, 1972. Senator Sparkman served as Black's chairman for Morgan County in the 1926 Democratic primary.
11. Cash, 336–37.
12. Lerner, note 3 *supra.*
13. Posthumously published interview, note 9 *supra.*
14. Berman Interview, March and June, 1956.
15. Posthumously published interview, note 9 *supra.*
16. Berman Interview, March 1956.
17. Hamilton, 105.
18. *Pittsburgh Post-Gazette*, September 17, 1937; for the significance of "ITSUB" see Miller, "The Ku Klux Klan," in Katz and Kutler, eds., *New Perspectives on the American Past—1877 to the Present* (1969), 228.
19. *Birmingham Post*, August 15, 1937; Interview with Mr. Esdale, May 31, 1972.
20. Hamilton, 125.
21. Alexander, *The Ku Klux Klan in the Southwest* (1965), 247.
22. Letter from William Bankhead to Kenneth Romney, August 18, 1936; Hamilton, 134.
23. Hamilton, 135.
24. *Pittsburgh Post-Gazette*, September 15, 16, 17, 1937.
25. *Ibid.*, September 15, 1937.
26. *Ibid.*, September 17, 1937.

CHAPTER FIVE

1. Letter from R. L. Heflin to Thomas Heflin, August 12, 1926; Hamilton, 134.
2. *Birmingham Post*, May 8, 1929; Adickes v. S. H. Kress & Co., 398 U.S. at 144 (1970).
3. Frank, 45; Cash, 146–47.
4. *Congressional Record*, 69 (1928), 4088.
5. Ashurst, *A Many Colored Toga* (1962), 288 (hereinafter cited as Ashurst).
6. *Congressional Record*, 69 (1928), 8815.
7. H. L. Mencken, "Al," *A Carnival of Buncombe* (1956), 150.
8. Davis, *Uncle Hugo* (1965), 22 (hereinafter cited as Davis).
9. Hamilton, 155.
10. Letter from John T. Heflin to Thomas Heflin, May 24, 1928; Hamilton, 152; *Ibid.*, 154.
11. Hamilton, 155.
12. Carmer, *Stars Fell on Alabama* (1934), 30.
13. Hamilton, 157; Berman Interview, March 1956.

14. Reagan, "Race as a Factor in the Presidential Election of 1928 in Alabama," *The Alabama Review,* 19 (1966), 14; Green, *The Man Bilbo* (1963), 77.
15. *Congressional Record,* 69 (1928), 10091.
16. *Congressional Record,* 72 (1929), 5418; *Ibid.,* 4469.
17. Letter from William Bankhead to John Bankhead, January 8, 1930; Hamilton, 185.
18. Letter from William Bankhead to John Bankhead, April 25, 1930; Hamilton, 186; *Ibid.,* 188.
19. Letter from O. H. Stevenson to Hugo Black, July 11, 1930; Hamilton, 186; *Birmingham News,* October 11, 1930; Hamilton, 188; Ashurst, 287.
20. Hamilton, 190.
21. *Ibid.; Congressional Record,* 75 (1932), 8938; Ashurst, 310.
22. Ashurst, 255.
23. Hamilton, 207.
24. Myers and Newton, eds., *The Hoover Administration* (1936), 470.
25. Herbert Hoover, *Memoirs,* Vol. III (1952), 378.
26. Hamilton, 208.
27. *Ibid.,* 212.
28. *Congressional Record,* 76 (1932), 4706–4707.
29. Hamilton, 217. See also Schlesinger, Vol. 1, 226, and generally, Schwartz, *The Interregnum of Despair* (1970).

CHAPTER SIX

1. Telegram from Hugo Black to Franklin Roosevelt, Black File, Roosevelt Library, Hyde Park, N.Y.
2. Ashurst, 333; White House Staff Memorandum, March 10, 1933; Black File, Roosevelt Library.
3. Moley, *The First New Deal* (1966), 287; Studs Terkel, *Hard Times* (1970), 250, 252.
4. Perkins, *The Roosevelt I Knew* (1946), 192.
5. *Congressional Record,* 77 (1933), 5284; Black TV Transcript, 10; *New York Times,* November 2, 1937.
6. Robinson, *The Roosevelt Leadership* (1955), 112.
7. Frank, 91.
8. *Time,* August 26, 1935.
9. Telegram from Black to Marvin McIntyre, July 25, 1933, Black File, Roosevelt Library; Hamilton, 247.
10. Hamilton, 229.
11. See Johnson, "Senator Black and the American Merchant Marine," 12 *University of Southern California Law Review,* 12 (1967), 318.
12. *Time,* March 5, 1934.
13. Jurney v. McCracken, 294 U.S. 125 (1935).
14. Frank, xi.

15. Schlesinger, *The Politics of Upheaval* (1960).
16. Hamilton, 247, 249, 250; Interview with Virginia Foster Durr, September 3, 1973.
17. Ickes, Vol. I, 555.
18. Blum, *From the Morgenthau Diaries* (1959), 317; Cooper, "Mr. Justice Hugo La Fayette Black of Alabama," *The Alabama Lawyer,* 33 (1972), 19.
19. Farley, *Behind the Ballots* (1938), 294.
20. Black, "Inside a Senate Investigation," *Harper's* (1936).
21. Hearst v. Black, 87 F.2d at 70 (1938).

CHAPTER SEVEN

1. Tully, *FDR Was My Boss* (1949), 80.
2. Schlesinger, *The Politics of Upheaval* (1960), 322.
3. Butler v. United States, 297 U.S. 1 (1936); Schlesinger, Vol. 3, 480.
4. *Congressional Record,* 79 (1935).
5. See Frankfurter, "Congressional Control over the Business of the Supreme Court," Kurland, ed., *Felix Frankfurter on the Supreme Court* (1970), 358.
6. Morehead v. Tipaldo, 298 U.S. 587 (1936).
7. *Congressional Record,* 80 (1936).
8. Lilienthal, *Journals,* Vol. I (1964), 64.
9. White, *A Man Called White* (1948), 177.
10. Letter from Franklin Roosevelt to Hugo Black, February 6, 1937; Hamilton, 262.
11. Hamilton, 263.
12. West Coast Hotel Co. v. Parrish, 300 U.S. 379 (1937).
13. Ashurst, 368; Lilienthal, note 8 *supra.*
14. Letter to Franklin Roosevelt, May 27, 1935; Leonard, *A Search for a Judicial Philosophy* (1971), 165.
15. Perkins, *The Roosevelt I Knew* (1949), 256.
16. Letter from Edgar Borah to R. M. Washburn, August 16, 1937, Borah Papers, LC.
17. Tindall, *The Emergence of the New South* (1967), 267.
18. *Ibid.*
19. Hamilton, 271.
20. *Congressional Record,* 81 (1937), 7950.
21. Frank, "Hugo Black," in Friedman and Israel, *The Justices of the United States Supreme Court,* Vol. 3 (1969), 2322.
22. Hugo Black, Jr., *My Father* (1975), 46.

CHAPTER EIGHT

1. FTC v. Standard Education Society, 302 U.S. 112 (1937); 86 F(2) at 692 (1936).

2. Connecticut General Life Insurance Co. v. Johnson, 303 U.S. 77 (1938); *New York Times,* February 1, 1938; McCart v. Indianapolis Water Co., 302 U.S. at 441 (1938); Indiana ex rel. Anderson v. Brand, 303 U.S. at 109 (1938).
3. Palko v. Connecticut, 302 U.S. 319 (1937).
4. *Congressional Record,* 79 (1935), 6526; Letter from H. L. Mencken to Maury Maverick, June 18, 1939, Henderson, *Maury Maverick, A Political Biography.*
5. Letter from Oliver Wendell Holmes to Lewis Einstein, October 14, 1917, Joseph P. Peabody, ed., *The Holmes–Einstein Letters* (New York, 1964), 15.
6. Patterson v. Alabama, 302 U.S. 733 (1937); two of Patterson's previous convictions had previously been reversed. Powell v. Alabama, 287 U.S. 45 (1932) (right to counsel) and Patterson v. Alabama, 294 U.S. 600 (1935) (jury exclusion); Belfrage, "Dixie Detour," *Harper's,* 175 (1937), 377.
7. Erie Railroad v. Thompson, 304 U.S. 64 (1938); U.S. v. Carolene Products Co., 304 U.S. 144 (1938).
8. Letter from Felix Frankfurter to Franklin Roosevelt, April 27, 1938, Freedman, 456.
9. 1 Stat. 92 (1789).
10. Swift v. Tyson, 16 Peters 1 (1842).
11. Southern Pacific v. Jensen, 244 U.S. at 222 (1917).
12. Willing v. Binenstock, 302 U.S. at 275 (1937).
13. New York Life Ins. Co. v. Gamer, 303 U.S. 161 (1938). Some scholars do not see Black's opinion overruling *Swift v. Tyson.* See Arthur John Keeffe, "In Praise of Joseph Story, *Swift v. Tyson,* and the True National Common Law," *The American University Law Review,* 18 (1969), 316. See also Mason, 478 n.
14. Guaranty Trust Co. v. York, 326 U.S. at 101 (1945) (Frankfurter); Great Northern v. Sunburst Oil, 287 U.S. at 365 (1932) (Cardozo); Black, "Erie Railroad v. Tompkins," *Missouri Bar Journal,* 13 (1942), 175.
15. *Congressional Record,* 79 (1935), 757.
16. 304 U.S. at 152–154 n. 4.
17. *Ibid.* at 155.
18. *Time,* May 23, 1938.
19. *Ibid.;* Letter from Felix Frankfurter to Franklin Roosevelt, June 9, 1937, Freedman, 401–2.
20. Helvering v. Gerhardt, 304 U.S. 405 (1938); South Carolina Highway Department v. Barnwell Brothers, 303 U.S. 177 (1938); Mason, 492 n.
21. See Mason, 334–35 n.
22. *St. Louis Post-Dispatch,* January 22, 1938; Childs, "The Supreme Court Today," *Harper's,* 176 (1938), 582.
23. Mason, 474; Childs, *Witness to Power* (1975), 37–40.
24. Mason, 475 n.

CHAPTER NINE

1. Letter from Harold J. Laski to Franklin Roosevelt, March 27, 1939, Freedman, 490.
2. Beauharnais v. Illinois, 343 U.S. at 286 (1945).
3. Letter from William Douglas to Felix Frankfurter, April 6, 1934, in Frankfurter Papers, Library of Congress, and quoted with the kind permission of Mr. Justice Douglas.
4. Letter from Irving Brant to the author, March 21, 1973.
5. Memorandum from Frankfurter to Black, November 13, 1943; Howard, *Justice Frank Murphy* (1968), 431 (hereinafter cited as Howard); William Holdsworth, *History of English Law* (3rd ed., 1917), Vol. X, 1852.
6. Frankfurter, "The Zeitgeist and the Judiciary," in Kurland, ed., *Felix Frankfurter on the Supreme Court* (1970), 1.
7. Letter from Harlan Stone to Felix Frankfurter, February 8, 1938, in Mason, 469; Frankfurter to Grenville Clark, December 16, 1937, in Frankfurter Papers, LC; Frankfurter to Black, in Mason, 471–72 n.
8. Schubert, *The Constitutional Polity* (1970), 129.
9. Letter from Irving Brant to Franklin Roosevelt, December 28, 1941, in Mason, 428.
10. Lash, ed., *From the Diaries of Felix Frankfurter* (1975), 283; Black, *My Father* (1975), 234.
11. Lash, *op. cit. supra*, 125; Atkinson, "Justice Sherman Minton," *Northwestern Law Review*, 69 (1974), 724.
12. NLRB v. Fansteel, Metallurgical Corp., 306 U.S. 240 (1939).
13. NLRB v. Fainblatt, 306 U.S. 601; 306 U.S. at 610 (McReynolds dissenting); Memorandum from Black to Stone, March 16, 1939, Mason, 622.
14. U.S. v. Darby, 312 U.S. 100; Mason, 556; Memorandum from Black to Stone, January 25, 1941; Mason, 554.
15. Letter from Harlan Stone to Sterling Carr, March 26, 1941, Mason, 556.
16. Johnson v. Zerbst, 304 U.S. 458 (1938).
17. Pierre v. Louisiana, 306 U.S. 351 (1939); Smith v. Texas, 311 U.S. 128 (1940); *Ibid.* at 235.
18. Chambers v. Florida, 309 U.S. 227 (1940); *Ibid.* at 235.
19. Reich, "Justice Black and the Living Constitution," *Harvard Law Review*, 76 (1966), 83; Black TV Transcript, 14.
20. Williams, 34, 132; Charles Beard, *The Republic* (1943), 237–39.
21. *The New Republic*, March 18, 1940.
22. Hague v. CIO, 307 U.S. 496 (1939).
23. Mason, 576 n.; Letter from Harlan Stone to Sterling Carr, November 25, 1941; Mason, 580.
24. Thornhill v. Alabama, 310 U.S. 88 (1940).‑

25. Milk Wagon Drivers Union v. Lake Valley Company, 311 U.S. 91 (1940).
26. Milk Wagon Drivers Union v. Meadmoor Dairy, 312 U.S. 287 (1941); *Ibid.* at 293.
27. *Ibid.* at 301–2.
28. Times Mirror Co. v. Superior Court of California, and Bridges v. California, 314 U.S. 252 (1941).
29. 314 U.S. at 271.
30. *Ibid.* at 282.

CHAPTER TEN

1. *Time,* July 13, 1942.
2. Ex Parte Quirin, 317 U.S. 1 (1942).
3. Black TV Transcript, 13; Berman Interview, March 22, 1956; Meador, *Mr. Justice Black and His Books* (1974), 94; Ickes diaries, May 19, 1940.
4. Cramer v. United States, 325 U.S. 1 (1945); Note to Chief Justice Stone, March 25, 1944, in Mason, 693; Viereck v. United States, 318 U.S. 236 (1945).
5. 320 U.S. 81 (1943).
6. Korematsu v. United States, 323 U.S. 214 (1944); Note to Black, November 9, 1944, in Mason, 677; Note to Black, November 9, 1944, in Frankfurter Papers, LC; 323 U.S.
7. Dilliard, *One Man's Stand for Freedom* (1963), 113; Berman Interview, March 1956; *New York Times,* September 26, 1971.
8. DeFunis v. Odegaard, 94 Supreme Court at 1717, n. 20 (1974).
9. Note to Justice Stone, January 29, 1946, in Mason, 668.
10. In re Yamashita, 327 U.S. 1 (1946).
11. Ex Parte Kamato, 317 U.S. 69 (1942); Duncan v. Kahanamoko, 327 U.S. 304 (1946); *Ibid.* at 318.
12. Schneiderman v. United States, 320 U.S. 118 (1943); Baumgartner v. United States, 322 U.S. 665 (1944). In a subsequent successful denaturalization of a Bundist, Black did contribute a concurring opinion, Knauer v. United States, 328 U.S. at 674 (1946).
13. Minersville School District v. Gobitis.
14. Jones v. Opelika, 319 U.S. 103 (1943); Hamilton 134–35.
15. United States v. Local 807 I.B.T., 315 U.S. 521 (1942); Byrnes, *All in One Lifetime* (1958), 11–12.
16. West Virginia Board of Education v. Barnette, 319 U.S. 624 (1943); *Ibid* at 644.
17. Note to Black, April 1, 1943, Mason, 601; Mason, 607; Letter from C. C. Burlingham to Harlan Stone, January 18, 1944, in Mason, 609. Indeed, had Burlingham known of Black's change of position in Martin v. Struthers, 319 U.S. 141 (1943)—where he began by defending an anti-doorbell-ringing (really anti-Witness) ordinance

and ended by outlawing it—the condemnation might have been more severe.

18. 319 U.S. at 646.
19. Letter from Felix Frankfurter to C. C. Burlingham, March 6, 1937, Frankfurter Papers, LC; Smith v. Allwright, 321 U.S. 649 (1944); Note to Stone, January 17, 1944, in Mason, 615.
20. Grovey v. Townsend, 295 U.S. 45 (1935); U.S. v. Classic, 313 U.S. 299 (1941).
21. 321 U.S. at 669.
22. U.S. v. Southeastern Underwriters, 322 U.S. 533 (1945).
23. Fashion Originators Guild v. FTC, 321 U.S. 457 (1941); Associated Press v. U.S., 326 U.S. 1 (1945).
24. Allen-Bradley Co. v. Local No. 3, I.B.E.W., 325 U.S. at 809 (1945).
25. Paul v. Virginia, 8 Wallace 168 (1869); *Congressional Record,* 79 (1935), 6533.
26. Ickes, Vol. III, 177.
27. Letter from Harlan Stone to E. W. Patterson, June 16, 1941, in Mason, 618.
28. Note to Stone, May 16, 1944, in Mason, 618.
29. 322 U.S. at 595; Note to Frankfurter, May 16, 1944, in Mason, 624 n.

CHAPTER ELEVEN

1. United States v. Southeastern Underwriters, 322 U.S. 533 (1944); *Ibid.* at 595; 50 Stat. 33.
2. 61 Stat. 34 (1947); Jewell Ridge Coal Corp. v. Local 6167 UMW, 325 U.S. 161 (1945).
3. Telephone interview with Clark M. Clifford, April 6, 1972, arranged through the good offices of Christian Peper, Esquire, of the St. Louis bar; search of the Truman Library failed to uncover Mr. Clifford's Madison memorandum.
4. FPC v. Hope Natural Gas Co., 320 U.S. 591 (1944); *Ibid.* at 625; *Ibid.* at 619.
5. Mercoid Corp. v. Midcontinent Investment Co., 320 U.S. 661 (1944); *Ibid.* at 678; *Ibid.* at 673.
6. Braun v. Gerdes, 321 U.S. 178 (1944); *Ibid.* at 193.
7. Mahnich v. Southern Steamship Co., 321 U.S. 96 (1944).
8. Smith v. Allwright, 321 U.S. 649 (1944); *Ibid.* at 669.
9. Jackson, "Decisional Law and Stare Decisis," *A.B.A. Journal,* 30 (1944), 334.
10. Letters of March 30, and September 1, 1937, Freedman, 392 and 408.
11. West Coast Hotel v. Parrish, 300 U.S. 379 (1937); *U. of Penn. Law Review,* 103 (1954), 295.
12. Gerhart, 254.

13. *Birmingham News,* April 4, 1945.
14. Harper, 319.
15. Letter from "Eddy" to "Dear Felix" April 12, 1945, on University of Texas Law School stationery, Frankfurter Papers, LC. Professor Charles Alan Wright has identified the writer as Edmund Morgan, Harvard's Royall Professor, on temporary assignment in Austin.
16. Berman Interview, June 2, 1956.
17. Tennessee Coal and Iron Railroad Co. v. Muscoda Local 123, 321 U.S. 590.
18. "An old law partner got me to join . . . then I joined the Moose"— Berman Interview, March 22, 1956. For a closer description see that of "General H. Lee Randolph" in Hugo Black, Jr., *My Father* (1975), 33–36, 56, 190.
19. Note to Conference, May 5, 1945, in Mason, 642.
20. Note, March 27, 1944, in Mason, 641.
21. Gerhart, 252.
22. Schlesinger, *The Politics of Upheaval* (1960), 313. Note from Vieva Fisher to Justice Louis Brandeis, September 25, 1937, Brandeis Papers, University of Louisville, Louisville, Kentucky.
23. Bonham's Case 8 Eng. Reports 1187 (1610).
24. Note to the Court, June 11, 1945, Mason, 643; Note from Black to Harlan Stone, June 11, 1945; *Ibid.*
25. *Ibid.* at 645–47; 325 U.S. 897 (1945).
26. Note to Black, June 9, 1945, Frankfurter Papers, LC.
27. Burton Diaries, Library of Congress, entry of October 10, 1946.
28. *Ibid.*
29. Mason, 716; Burton Diaries, *supra,* April 26, 1946; Fleeson, "Supreme Court Feud," *Washington Star,* May 16, 1946.
30. Gerhart, 286.
31. Burton Diaries, entry of April 30, 1946.
32. Undated and uncaptioned memorandum, Frankfurter Papers, LC.
33. *Ibid.,* Gerhart, 288, but see Kurland, "Robert H. Jackson," in Friedman and Israel, eds., *The Justices of the Supreme Court,* Vol IV (1969), 2562–63.
34. Gerhart, 260.
35. *Ibid.* at 260, 494 n. 85.
36. *Ibid.* at 257, 493 n. 82.
37. Cooper, *Sincerely Your Friend* (1973); Kurland, *supra,* 2569.
38. Gerhart, 262–63.
39. *Ibid.* at 264–65.
40. Note from Frankfurter to Black, September 30, 1950, Frankfurter Papers, LC; Letter from Jackson to Frankfurter, June 19, 1956, in Atkinson, "Justice Sherman Minton," *Northwestern University Law Review,* 69 (1974), 723.
41. Harper, 319; Undated memorandum, Frankfurter Papers, LC; "The Supreme Court 1947," *Fortune,* January 1947.

42. Gerhart, 251, 492 n. 69.
43. Letter from Black to Frankfurter, October 9, 1950, in Frankfurter Papers, LC; Black, "Mr. Justice Frankfurter," *Harvard Law Review,* 78 (1965), 1521; Black TV Transcript, 11; Cooper, note 37 *supra.*
44. Schlesinger, note 41 *supra,* 77.

CHAPTER TWELVE

1. Letter to Frankfurter, March 16, 1939, Frankfurter Papers, LC.
2. *PM* quoted in Gerhart, 245; Memorandum, October 16, 1945, Howard 397; Memorandum of Arthur Krock, January 8, 1947, Gerhart, 274; Note to Murphy, October 17, 1945, Howard, 397.
3. Note to Black, November 13, 1943, Frankfurter Papers, LC, and partially quoted, Howard, 430–32.
4. *Ibid.;* Adamson v. California, 332 U.S. at 90.
5. United States v. United Mine Workers, 330 U.S. 258 (1947).
6. *Time,* March 17, 1947.
7. SEC v. Chenery Corporation, 318 U.S. 80 (1943).
8. 318 U.S. at 97.
9. Note to Reed, January 29, 1943, Howard, 416.
10. Note to Black, May 20, 1946, Frankfurter Papers, LC; Note to Frankfurter, June 18, 1947, Howard, 419; Note to Frankfurter, June 18, 1947, Harper, 325; SEC v. Chenery Corporation, 332 U.S. 209 (1947).
11. "Mr. Justice Brandeis and the Constitution," *Harvard Law Review* (1931), 45, 53, reprinted in Kurland, 247, 255–56; *Congressional Record,* 81 (1934), 1294.
12. Note to Stone, May 25, 1942 in Mason, 595; House Report, 1st Sess., 80th Congress (1947).
13. 7 Peters 243 (1833).
14. Hurtado v. California, 110 U.S. 516 (1884); Twining v. New Jersey, 211 U.S. 78 (1908); Palko v. Connecticut, 302 U.S. 319 (1937).
15. 302 U.S. at 329.
16. Chambers v. Florida, 309 U.S. at 235 n. (1940).
17. Note to Black, October 31, 1939, Howard, 428. Professor Howard evidently questions the correctness of the dating, for he qualifies his citation with the caveat "if accurately dated."
18. Powell v. Alabama, 287 U.S. 45 (1932); 316 U.S. 455 (1942); 316 U.S. at 474.
19. Note to Black, November 13, 1943, note 3 *supra.*
20. "Mr. Justice Brandeis and the Constitution," note 11 *supra,* 58.
21. Note to Black, note 3 *supra.*
22. Adamson v. California, 332 U.S. 46 (1947); Black TV Transcript, 13.
23. 332 U.S. at 74.
24. 332 U.S. at 64; "Does the 14th Amendment incorporate the Bill of

Rights? The Original Understanding," *Stanford Law Review*, 2 (1949), 5 at 162.

25. See Alfred J. Kelly, "Clio and the Court: An Illicit Love Affair," in Philip B. Kurland, ed., *The Supreme Court Review: 1965* (1965), 119; Paul L. Murphy, "Time to Reclaim: The Current Challenge of American Constitutional History," *American Historical Review*, Vol. LXIX (1963), 64; Leonard W. Levy, "The Right Against Self-Incrimination: History and Judicial History," *Political Science Quarterly*, Vol. LXXXIV (1969), 1; 332 U.S. at 67 and 324 U.S. at 416–17.

26. Quoted in Levy, note 25 *supra*, 13.

27. 330 U.S. 1 (1947).

28. Letter to Grenville Clark, March 6, 1937, Frankfurter Papers, LC.

29. "Mr. Justice Frankfurter," *Harvard Law Review*, 78 (1965), 1521.

30. 208 U.S. 510 (1925); "Can the Supreme Court Guarantee Toleration?" reprinted in Kurland, 174.

31. Note to Rutledge, January 22, 1944, Howard 345 n.; 330 U.S. at 15; Letter from Irving Brant to Wiley Rutledge, March 11, 1947, in Fowler, 70; *Ibid.*, 79.

32. Undated note from Frankfurter to Murphy, 1947, in Howard, 450.

33. McCollum v. Board of Education, 333 U.S. 203 (1948); Fowler, 349.

34. See Fowler, 339–40.

35. 333 U.S. at 231 and 216.

36. Zorach v. Clausen, 343 U.S. 306 (1952); 343 U.S. at 313; Kurland, "The Regents Prayer Case," *Supreme Court Review*, 16 (1962).

37. 343 U.S. at 318.

38. Berman Interview, March 22, 1956.

39. Meador, *Mr. Justice Black and His Books* (1974), 55; Hugo Black, Jr., *My Father* (1975), 104.

40. West Virginia State Board of Education v. Barnette, 319 U.S. at 646 (1943).

41. Letter from Frank Murphy to Bishop William Murphy, May 10, 1948, Howard, 452; *Ibid.*

42. See Graves v. New York, ex rel. O'Keefe, 306 U.S. at 489 (1939) and New York v. United States, 366 U.S. 572 (1946).

43. Howard, 435.

44. *Ibid.*

45. *Ibid.*

46. Davis v. U.S., 328 U.S. 582 (1946); Zap v. U.S., 328 U.S. 624 (1946); Goldstein v. U.S., 316 U.S. 124 (1941); Goldman v. U.S., 316 U.S. 129 (1948); Johnson v. U.S., 333 U.S. 10 (1948).

47. Harris v. U.S., 331 U.S. 145 (1948); Tropiano v. U.S., 334 U.S. 699 (1948).

48. U.S. v. Rabinowitz, 339 U.S. 56 (1950).

49. 46 Wolf v. Colorado, 338 U.S. 25 (1949).

50. 338 U.S. at 29 (1949).

CHAPTER THIRTEEN

1. *Time,* February 17, 1947.
2. Berea College v. Kentucky, 211 U.S. at 69 (1908); Korematsu v. United States, 323 U.S. at 233 (1944); Note to Douglas, January 6, 1949, Howard, 459.
3. Israel, "Wiley Rutledge," in Friedman and Israel, eds., *The Justices of the Supreme Court,* Vol. IV (1969), 2598.
4. *Time,* September 26, 1949; Harper, 305.
5. Morrison, *W. J. Cash, Southern Prophet* (1967), 247 n.
6. Rodell, "The Supreme Court Is Standing Pat," *New Republic,* December 19, 1949.
7. U.S. v. Lovett, 328 U.S. at 318 (1946).
8. Christoffel v. U.S., 338 U.S. 84 (1949).
9. Eisler v. U.S., 338 U.S. at 194 (1949); O'Brian, *National Security and Industrial Freedom* (Cambridge, 1955), 24–26.
10. American Communications Association v. Douds, 339 U.S. 382 (1950); *Time,* May 15, 1950; De Jonge v. Oregon, 299 U.S. at 365 (1937).
11. Dennis v. U.S., 341 U.S. 494 (1951); Garner v. Board of Public Works, 341 U.S. 716 (1951); *Time,* June 11, 1951.
12. *New Republic,* June 18, 1951; 341 U.S. at 494 (1951).
13. Joint Anti-Fascist Refugee Committee v. McGrath, 341 U.S. at 145 (1951); Blau v. U.S., 340 U.S. 332 (1950); *Time,* December 15, 1950.
14. Edgar Gressman, "The Supreme Court," *New Republic,* September 3, 1951; Letter to Franklin Roosevelt, May 17, 1938, Freedman, 457; Hugo Black, Jr., *My Father,* 102, 179 (1975).
15. *New York Times,* December 8, 1942; Montgomery, *Hail to the Chiefs* (1970), 86–87; Letter to Hazel Davis, July 29, 1950, Davis, 55.
16. Letter to Hazel Davis, March 14, 1952; *New York Times,* December 11, 1952; See Josephine Black, "I Was a Yeomanette CPO," *Junior League,* May 1937.
17. Black TV Transcript, 10.
18. *Ibid.*
19. Schmidt, *Henry Wallace: Quixotic Crusade* (1960), 79; Taylor v. Birmingham, 340 U.S. 832 (1950).
20. Shelley v. Kraemer, 334 U.S. 1 (1948).
21. U.S. v. Alpers, 338 U.S. 680 (1950); P.U.C. v. Pollak, 343 U.S. 431 (1932).
22. Kovacs v. Cooper, 336 U.S. at 102 (1949); *Ibid.* at 90.
23. Rochin v. California, 342 U.S. 165 (1952).
24. *Ibid.* at 176–77.
25. Beauharnais v. Illinois, 343 U.S. 250 (1952); *Ibid.* at 260; Letter

from James Beauharnais, December 4, 1953, copy in Frankfurter Papers, LC; 343 U.S. at 275.
26. Feiner v. New York, 340 U.S. 315 (1951); Beard v. Alexandria, 341 U.S. 622 (1951); Adler v. Board of Education, 342 U.S. 485 (1952); Sacher v. United States, 343 U.S. 1 (1932).
27. Youngstown Sheet and Tube v. Sawyer, 343 U.S. 579 (1952).
28. *Ibid.* at 589; *Ibid.*
29. *Time,* June 9, 1952.
30. Blackman, *Presidential Seizures in Labor Disputes* (1967), 62; Douglas TV Transcript, 15.
31. U.S. v. Rosenberg, 345 U.S. 1003 (1953).
32. *Time,* June 22, 1953; Douglas, *Go East Young Man* (1974), 23.
33. 346 U.S. 324 (1953); Berman Interview, June 29, 1956; and see Nizer, *The Implosion Conspiracy* (1973), 461–72.

CHAPTER FOURTEEN

1. Weaver, *Warren: The Man, the Court, the Era* (1967), 198–99.
2. *Saturday Review,* August 29, 1964.
3. Myrdal, *An American Dilemma* (1944), 579 (hereinafter cited as Myrdal).
4. Myrdal, *An American Dilemma,* XXV (Anniversary Edition, 1962); Morgan, *A Time to Speak* (1964), 48; Myrdal, 469.
5. *Congressional Record,* 79 (1935), 6533.
6. *Supra;* Letter from White to Max Lowenthal, August 20, 1937, in Frankfurter Papers, LC.
7. Chambers v. Florida, 309 U.S. 227, 241 (1940).
8. Reich, "Mr. Justice Black and the Living Constitution," *Harvard Law Review,* 76 (1963), 673, 679.
9. Civil Rights Cases, 109 U.S. 3 (1883); Plessy v. Ferguson, 163 U.S. 537, 559 (1896).
10. Roberts v. City of Boston, 59 Mass. 198 (1844); *Congressional Globe,* 39th Cong., 1st Sess. 776 (1866); 163 U.S. at 551.
11. McLaurin v. Regents, 339 U.S. 637 (1950); Henderson v. United States, 339 U.S. 816 (1950); Sweatt v. Painter, 339 U.S. 629, 634 (1950).
12. Brown v. Board, 98 F.Supp. 797 (1951); Briggs v. Elliott, 98 F.Supp. 529 (1952); Belton v. Gebhart, 32 Del ch. 343 (1952); Bolling v. Sharpe; 344 U.S. 873 (1952).
13. Lash, ed., *From the Frankfurter Diaries* (1975), 334–35; Taylor v. Birmingham, 340 U.S. 832 (1950); Schmidt, *Henry Wallace: Quixotic Crusade* (1960), 79.
14. *New Republic,* June 23, 1952.
15. *Ibid.,* June 12, 1950.
16. "To Secure These Rights," Friedman, ed., *The Civil Rights Reader* (1967), 18.

17. *New Republic,* June 23, 1952.
18. District of Columbia v. J. R. Thompson Co., 346 U.S. 100.
19. *New Republic,* July 27, 1952.
20. MacKenzie, "Thurgood Marshall," in Friedman and Israel, eds., *The Justices of the Supreme Court,* Vol. III (1969), 3073; see also Harbaugh, *Lawyer's Lawyer* (1973), 505.
21. Brown v. Board, 345 U.S. 972 (1953).
22. Baker, *Felix Frankfurter* (1969), 306; Kelly, "The School Desegregation Case," in Garraty, ed., *Quarrels That Have Shaped the Constitution,* 264.
23. Kelly, *supra.*
24. Brown v. Board, 347 U.S. 483, 489, 492 (1954).
25. *Ibid.* at 495.
26. *Ibid.*
27. Bolling v. Sharpe, 347 U.S. 497, 500 (1954).
28. Scath v. Sandford, 19 Harvard 1 40 (1857).
29. 349 U.S. 294, 301 (1955).
30. *Ibid.* at 300.
31. Murphy and Pritchett, *Courts, Judges, and Politics* (1961), 344, 614.
32. *New York Times,* May 23, 1954; Letter to C. C. Burlingham, May 28, 1954.
33. Frankfurter letter, *supra.* " 'I had lunch with Justice Frankfurter the day he was going to [Chief Justice Vinson's] funeral,' Alexander Bickel recalled . . . 'He kept murmuring "an act of Providence, an act of Providence" from which I concluded he feared a divided vote on *Brown,* with himself . . . casting the deciding vote.' "—Lash, ed., *From the Diaries of Felix Frankfurter* (1975), 83. Contrariwise was Justice Clark's view: "I still give more credit to Vinson—his opinions in *Shelley v. Kraemer* and *Sweatt* changed the climate. Indeed *Sweatt* cut the pattern."—Letter to the author, February 27, 1975, and quoted with the kind permission of the Justice.
34. Brown v. Board, 72 S.Ct. 1070 (1952).
35. Barrows v. Jackson, 346 U.S. 249 (1953).
36. Note to Black, November 13, 1943, in Frankfurter Papers, LC.
37. 332 U.S. at 74 (1947).
38. Harper v. Virginia Bd. of Elections, 383 U.S. 663, 669, 677 n. 7 (1966); Black TV Transcript, 12.
39. Adamson v. California, 332 U.S. at 62; see also Green v. United States, 356 U.S. 165, 192 (1958).
40. Note to Conference, December 5, 1953, Frankfurter Papers, LC; the clerk was the late Alexander Mordecai Bickel, Sterling Professor at the Yale Law School.
41. Note to Justice Clark, June 4, 1953, Frankfurter Papers, LC.
42. Note to Conference, January 13, 1954, Frankfurter Papers, LC.
43. Ulmer, "Earl Warren and the Brown Decision," *Journal of Politics,* 33 (1971), 693.
44. *New York Times,* December 7, 1971.

45. Bickel, *The Supreme Court and the Idea of Progress* (1970), 7; *New York Times,* December 10, 1971.
46. Ulmer, *supra,* 697 n. 94.
47. Letter from Frankfurter to C. C. Burlingham, November 12, 1958.
48. Virginia v. West Virginia, 222 U.S. 17, 20 (1911).
49. Ulmer, 690, 699.
50. Bickel, note 45 *supra,* 33; Letter to Walter Lippmann, August 8, 1957, Frankfurter Papers, LC; Black TV Transcript, 14.
51. Letter to Mark DeWolfe Home, May 5, 1958, Frankfurter Papers, LC.
52. Letters to Charles Fairman, August 31, 1954, and Grenville Clark, December 16, 1937, Frankfurter Papers, LC.
53. Note to Black, November 13, 1943, Frankfurter Papers, LC.
54. Holmes, *The Common Law* (1881), 1.
55. Jackson, *The Supreme Court in the American System of Government* (1955), 57–58.
56. Ickes, Vol. II (1954), 615.
57. Frank, 138.
58. *Birmingham News,* April 4, 1945.
59. Letter to Felix Frankfurter, May 18, 1954, Frankfurter Papers, LC.
60. Letter to Jerome A. Cooper, Nov. 3, 1961, in Cooper, "Mr. Justice Black," *Alabama Law Review,* 24 (1971), 4; Douglas, *Go West Young Man,* 458 (1974).
61. Letter to Hazel Black Davis, March 14, 1952, in Davis, 130; Hugo Black, Jr., *My Father* (1975), 208.
62. Letter to Max Lowenthal, August 20, 1937, Frankfurter Papers, LC.

CHAPTER FIFTEEN

1. Myrdal, 1065–70; and see Miller, "Toward a Concept of Constitutional Duty," *The Supreme Court Review* (1968), 199.
2. See, for example, Mayor of Baltimore v. Dawson, 350 U.S. 877 (1955) (beaches and bathhouses); Holmes v. Atlanta, 350 U.S. 879 (1955) (golf courses); *New Republic,* June 20, 1955.
3. Irvine v. California, 347 U.S. 128 (1954); *Ibid.* at 132.
4. *Ibid.* at 142.
5. Barsky v. Board of Regents, 347 U.S. 442 (1954).
6. Rice v. Sioux City Cemetery, 349 U.S. 70 (1955); Peters v. Hobby, 349 U.S. 331 (1955); *Ibid.* at 350.
7. Pennsylvania v. Nelson, 350 U.S. 497 (1956); *Time,* April 16, 1956; Slowchower v. Board of Higher Education, 350 U.S. 551 (1956); *Time,* April 23, 1956; Cole v. Young, 351 U.S. 536 (1956); Black v. Cutter Laboratories, 351 U.S. 292 (1956).
8. *Time,* June 25, 1956; *Business Week,* June 9, 1956; *New York Times,* June 15, 1956; Berman Interview, June 20, 1956; *New York Times,* March 12, 1956.

9. *Time,* June 25, 1956.
10. Railways Dept., AFL v. Hanson, 351 U.S. 225 (1956).
11. Kurland, "Robert H. Jackson," in Friedman and Israel, *The Justices of the Supreme Court,* Vol. IV (1969), 2569.
12. *New York Times,* October 5, 1956.
13. *Time,* July 14, 1957.
14. Katcher, *Earl Warren* (1967), 355.
15. *Congressional Record,* 118 (1972), 2702.

CHAPTER SIXTEEN

1. Schware v. Board of Bar Examiners, 353 U.S. 232 (1957); Konigsberg v. State Bar of California, 353 U.S. 252 (1957).
2. Jencks v. U.S., 353 U.S. 657 (1957); Katcher, *Earl Warren* (1967), 364; 353 U.S. at 681–82
3. Service v. Dulles, 354 U.S. 363 (1957); Yates v. U.S. 354 U.S. 298 (1957); *Ibid.* at 349.
4. Watkins v. U.S., 354 U.S. 178 (1957); Sweezy v. N.H., 354 U.S. 234 (1957); 354 U.S. at 195.
5. Letter from Felix Frankfurter to Bruce Bliven, July 24, 1954, in Frankfurter Papers, LC.
6. Mallory v. U.S., 354 U.S. 449 (1957).
7. McNabb v. U.S., 318 U.S. 332 (1943). Mallory was killed by a Philadelphia policeman following a robbery and rape, *St. Louis Post-Dispatch,* July 13, 1972.
8. Paul Wilkes, "Matter Investigated, Case Closed," *New York Times,* April 19, 1970. Senator Strom Thurmond quoted in Clark, *Crime in America* (1970), 328.
9. U.S. v. Du Pont de Nemours, 351 U.S. 377 (1956) (hereinafter Du Pont I); U.S. v. Du Pont de Nemours, 353 U.S. 586 (1957) (hereinafter Du Pont II).
10. *Time,* June 20, 1957.
11. Davis, 41.
12. Letter to Justice Clark, November 30, 1972, in Frankfurter Papers, LC.
13. *Time,* August 5, 1957.
14. Hand, *The Bill of Rights* (1964), 50.
15. *New York Times,* March 17, 1958.
16. Letter to Senator Thomas Hennings, May 5, 1958, Kemper, *Decade of Fear* (1965), 170 n. 10.
17. Letter of August 12, 1958, signed by Hubert Humphrey and nine other Senators, Murphy, *Congress and the Court* (1962), 201.
18. Murphy, 223.
19. *Congressional Record,* 104 (1958), 18693.
20. Burton Diary, September 18, 1958, Library of Congress.
21. Transcript, Cooper v. Aaron, 94.

22. Cooper v. Aaron, 358 U.S. 1 (1958). See Miller, "Toward a Concept of Constitutional Duty," *The Supreme Court Review* (1968), 20.
23. Letter to C. C. Burlingham, November 12, 1958, Frankfurter Papers, LC.
24. *Ibid.*
25. N.A.A.C.P. v. Alabama, 357 U.S. 449 (1958); Greene v. McElroy, 360 U.S. 474 (1959); Abbate v. U.S., 359 U.S. 187 (1959); Bartkus v. Illinois, 359 U.S. 121 (1959); Palermo v. U.S., 360 U.S. 343 (1959); Barenblatt v. U.S., 360 U.S. 109 (1959); Uphaus v. Wyman, 360 U.S. 72 (1959).
26. 360 U.S. at 134; *New York Times,* November 9, 1958.
27. *New Republic,* June 22, 1959.
28. Curtis, *Law as Large as Life* (1959), 43, 57, 60.

CHAPTER SEVENTEEN

1. *New Republic,* June 22, 1959; Kingsley v. Board of Regents, 360 U.S. 384 (1959).
2. Hannegan v. Esquire, Inc., 327 U.S. 146 (1946); Alpert, "Judicial Censorship of Obscene Literature," *Harvard Law Review,* 52 (1938), 40.
3. Butler v. Michigan, 352 U.S. 380 (1957); Regina v. Hinklin, 3 Q.B. 360 (1868); 352 U.S. at 383.
4. Roth v. U.S., 354 U.S. 476 (1957); Alberts v. California, 364 U.S. 476 (1957); 354 U.S. at 487.
5. Doubleday Co. v. New York, 335 U.S. 848 (1948); and see generally, Kalven, "Metaphysics of the Law of Obscenity," *Supreme Court Review* (1960), 1.
6. Potter Stewart in Jacobellis v. Ohio, 378 U.S. at 197 (1964).
7. 361 U.S. at 384.
8. *Ibid.* at 147.
9. Black, "The Bill of Rights," *New York University Law Review,* 35 (1960), 865; *Ibid.* at 867.
10. *Ibid.* at 877–78.
11. "Mr. Justice Black," *New Republic,* March 14, 1960.
12. Pollak, "Language and Its Legal Interpreters," *New Republic,* May 2, 1960.
13. Charles L. Black, Jr., "Mr. Justice Black, The Supreme Court," *Harper's,* February 1961.
14. *Ibid.* at 65.
15. *Ibid.* at 68.
16. *Ibid.* at 65 and 68.
17. "Justice Black and the First Amendment Absolutes," *New York University Law Review,* 37 (1962).
18. *Ibid.* at 553.

19. See, for example, Gompers v. United States, 233 U.S. 604, 610 (1914); Hughes, *The Supreme Court of the United States* (1926), 36.
20. Uphaus v. Wyman, 364 U.S. 388 (1960), and 361 U.S. 72 (1959); *New Republic*, August 18, 1960; 364 U.S. at 400.
21. See Dillard, ed., *One Man's Stand for Freedom* (1963), 379, and Mr. Dilliard's characterization of the passage as one of Black's "most memorable dissents," 377.
22. Konigsberg v. State Bar, 366 U.S. 36 (1961); *Ibid.* at 67.
23. Communist Party v. Subversive Activities Control Board, 367 U.S. 1; *Ibid.* at 164; Scales v. United States, 367 U.S. 3, 203 (1961); *Ibid.* at 270.
24. Mapp v. Ohio, 367 U.S. 643 (1961); *Ibid.* at 666.
25. *Ibid.* at 666.
26. Gomillion v. Lightfoot, 364 U.S. 339 (1960); Baker v. Carr.
27. Baker v. Carr, 364 U.S. 186, 898 (1962).
28. Luther v. Borden, 10 Howard 98 (1849).
29. "Learned Hand," *Harvard Law Review*, 70 (1960), 850; *New York Times*, June 18, 1960. Of possible significance also is a note in the Frankfurter Papers: "Felix—I strongly hope nothing will happen that causes you to leave the Court—not on account of this case—but simply because I hope you stay, Hugo." To which Frankfurter appended: "This note was passed to me by Black in conference on Friday, March 1, 1957, when some hypothetical digression was made regarding service on the Court."
30. Colegrove v. Green, 328 U.S. 549 (1946).
31. 369 U.S. at 266–67 (1968).
32. Engel v. Vitale, 370 U.S. at 422 (1962).
33. *Ibid.* at 442.
34. *Ibid.* at 435, n. 21.
35. *New York Times*, June 26, 1962.
36. See Lash, *From the Diaries of Felix Frankfurter* (1975), 239.
37. Wright, "Hugo L. Black: A Great Man and Great American," *Texas Law Review*, 50 (1971), 2.
38. Frankfurter, "Memorandum on Incorporation of the Bill of Rights into the Fourteenth Amendment," *Harvard Law Review*, 78 (1965), 746; Black, *supra*, n. 36.
39. Letter of Elizabeth Black to the author, June 4, 1974. See also Lash, note 36 *supra*, 174, 175, 177, 209, 283, 331, 343.
40. Black, "Mr. Justice Frankfurter," *Harvard Law Review*, 78 (1965), 1521.

CHAPTER EIGHTEEN

1. *Time*, April 16, 1962.
2. *New Republic*, March 16, 1963.

3. Gideon v. Wainwright, 372 U.S. 335 (1963); Lewis, *Gideon's Trumpet,* inscription in Justice Black's copy, Black Collection, Supreme Court Library.
4. Johnson v. Zerbst, 304 U.S. 458 (1938); Betts v. Brady, 316 U.S. 455 (1942).
5. 372 U.S. at 344; *Ibid.* at 349.
6. Fay v. Noia, 372 U.S. 391 (1963); Draper v. Washington, 37 U.S.; Grey v. Sanders, 376 U.S. 1 (1964).
7. Meredith v. Fair, 371 U.S. 19 (1962).
8. Watson v. Memphis, 373 U.S. 526 (1963).
9. Memorandum to the Court, January 1954, Frankfurter Papers, LC; Goss v. Knoxville Board of Education, 373 U.S. 683 (1963).
10. School District of Abington Township v. Schempp, 374 U.S. 203 (1963).
11. *Ibid.* at 225; Interview with Elizabeth Black, December 4, 1973.
12. *New Republic,* July 11, 1964.
13. Symposium, *American University Law Review,* 10 (1961), 1; *Harvard Law Review,* 76 (1963), 673; *Time,* October 8, 1964; Daniel J. Meador, *Alabama Law Review,* 15 (1962), 57; Dilliard, ed., *One Man's Stand for Freedom* (1963), xi.
14. *Time,* October 9, 1935; October 9, 1964.
15. 374 U.S. 365; Arizona v. California, 373 U.S. 546, 628 (1963); *New York Times,* June 4, 1963.
16. McCune, *Nine Young Men* (1947), 123–27; Schlesinger, "The Supreme Court 1947," *Fortune,* January (1947); Dennis v. Denver and Rio Grande, 375 U.S. 208 (1964).
17. *New Republic,* December 4, 1961; *Ibid.,* April 6, 1963.
18. *New York Times,* April 14, May 1, 1963.
19. *Ibid.,* September 26, 1963.
20. *Ibid.,* August 30, 1963.
21. *Ibid.,* November 25, 1963.
22. Jacobellis v. Ohio, 378 U.S. 184 (1964); New York Times v. Sullivan, 376 U.S. 254 (1964).
23. Griffin v. County School Board, 377 U.S. 218 (1964).
24. *New Republic,* April 18, 1964.
25. Ferguson v. Skrupa, 372 U.S. 727 (1963); 378 U.S. 441 (1964).
26. Wesberry v. Sanders, 376 U.S. 1 (1964).
27. See, for example, Breithaupt v. Abram, 352 U.S. 432 (1957).
28. *New York Times,* September 16, 1964.
29. *Ibid.,* November 8, 1964.
30. *Ibid.*
31. Reynolds v. Sims, 377 U.S. 533 (1964); "Earl Warren," Friedman and Israel, eds., *The Justices of the Supreme Court,* Vol IV (1969), 2745.
32. See 377 U.S. 21, 562.
33. See Shogan, *A Question of Judgment* (1972).

CHAPTER NINETEEN

1. *Time,* October 9, 1964.
2. Barr v. Columbia, 378 U.S. 146 (1964); Robinson v. Florida, 378 U.S. 153 (1964); Bell v. Maryland, 378 U.S. 226 (1964). Reportedly Black worked on his opinion for twelve hours straight, finishing at 3:50 A.M. and mailing it the next morning: "I'm going to be satisfied with this one"—Davis, 75.
3. 378 U.S. at 338 and 343.
4. *Ibid.* at 346; Hanson v. City of Rock Hill, 379 U.S. 306 (1964).
5. Cox v. Louisiana, 379 U.S. 536, 559 (1965); *Ibid.* at 555 and 583.
6. Brown v. Louisiana, 383 U.S. 131 (1966); *Ibid.* at 162 and 167; *Washington Post,* February 24, 1966, quoted in Howard, "Mr. Justice Black, the Negro Protest Movement, and the Rule of Law," *Virginia Law Review,* 53 (1967), 1045 (hereinafter cited as A. Howard).
7. Adderly v. Florida, 385 U.S. 39 (1966); *Ibid.* at 47.
8. Greenberg, "The Supreme Court, Civil Rights, and Civil Dissonance," *Yale Law Journal,* 77 (1968), 1520, 1576 n. 75.
9. "Justice Black and the Absolutes," Dilliard, ed., *One Man's Stand for Freedom* (1963), 477 (hereinafter cited as Dilliard).
10. *St. Louis Post-Dispatch,* March 19, 1960; *Time,* October 9, 1964.
11. Notes to Black, February 19, 1962, and December 15, 1964; Griswold v. Connecticut, 381 U.S. 479, 510.
12. Dilliard, 477.
13. 381 U.S. at 484.
14. *New York Times,* June 21, 1965, November 2, 1937; *New Republic,* June 19, 1965.
15. Bernstein, "The Supreme Court and Secondary Source Material," *Georgetown Law Journal,* 57 (1968), 55.
16. Riesman, "Toward an Anthropological Science of Law and the Legal Profession," in *Individualism Reconsidered and Other Essays* (1954), 452.
17. *Ibid.;* Frankfurter, "The Zeitgeist and the Judiciary," Kurland, 1.
18. "The Supreme Court—1965 Term," *Harvard Law Review,* 79 (1965), 163.
19. *University of Chicago Law Review,* 33 (1965), 814 n. 83; Freund, "Mr. Justice Black and the Judicial Function," *UCLA Law Review,* 14 (1967), 467.
20. U.S. v. Standard Oil Co., 221 U.S. 1 (1911).
21. Curtis, *Law as Large as Life* (1959), 23; Handler, "Antitrust," *The Record of the Bar of the City of New York,* October 1968.
22. U.S. v. Philadelphia National Bank, 374 U.S. 321 (1963).
23. *U.S. v. Von's Grocery Company,* 384 U.S. 270 (1966); Handler, 19th Annual Antitrust Review, *Yale Law Journal,* 76 (1966), 92, 113; *Fortune,* November 1966.

24. *Hugo La Fayette Black,* House Document 92-236 (1972); Wheeling Steel Company v. Glander, 337 U.S. 562 (1949).
25. Davis, 83.
26. Berle, *The Three Faces of Power* (1967), 35.
27. The *Nation,* December 26, 1966; Jaffe, *Was Brandeis an Activist?* (1966).
28. *New York Times,* February 28, 1966.
29. Cooper, "Mr. Justice Hugo LaFayette Black of Alabama," *The Alabama Lawyer* (1970), 20 n. 6; "Mr. Justice Hugo L. Black: Footnotes to a Great Case," *Alabama Law Review,* 24 (1972), 5.
30. *Ibid.,* 5.
31. South Carolina v. Katzenbach, 383 U.S. 301 (1966); Harper v. Virginia, 383 U.S. 663 (1966); *Congressional Record,* 79 (1935), 6525; Howard, 1047; Hoffa v. U.S., 385 U.S. 293 (1966); Fortson v. Morris, 385 U.S. 231 (1966).
32. See A. Howard, 1047–1048; *New York Times,* December 14, 1966.
33. *Ibid.*
34. Ginsburg v. U.S., 383 U.S. 663 (1968); Miranda v. Arizona, 384 U.S. 436 (1966); Schmerber v. California, 384 U.S. 757 (1966).
35. Loving v. Virginia, 388 U.S. 1 (1967).
36. *Pittsburgh Post-Gazette,* September 18, 1937.
37. "I am happy to present this Bible to the Honorable Thurgood Marshall on the date I administered the oath of office to him as Associate Justice of the United States, September 1, 1967." I am grateful to Mr. Justice Marshal for supplying me with a photocopy of the inscription.

CHAPTER TWENTY

1. *Congressional Record,* 118 (1972), 2702.
2. *New York Times,* June 23, 1968.
3. Graham, *The Self-Inflicted Wound* (1970).
4. *New York Times,* October 4, 1968; Douglas TV Transcript, 14.
5. Hearings on the Nomination of Abe Fortas to be Chief Justice of the United States, Senate Judiciary Committee, 90th Cong., 2d Sess., 168.
6. *Ibid.,* 272.
7. See Shogan, *A Question of Judgment* (1972), 132–34, wherein it is asserted that Black denounced a draft of the Fortas opinion as "the worst piece of work he had seen in that field in a dozen years." Perhaps the purported quotation suggests the salutary purpose of the hearsay rule. Black was fully capable of attacking an idea in such terms, but any such personal implication was uncharacteristic.
8. Witherspoon v. Illinois, 391 U.S. 510 (1968).
9. Neil McNeil, *Dirksen: Portrait of a Public Man* (Cleveland, 1972), 332. See also 332–36.

10. Black, *A Constitutional Faith* (1968).
11. Harlan, "Mr. Justice Black," *Harvard Law Review*, 81 (1968), 2.
12. *New York Times*, October 11, 1904; Berle, *The Three Faces of Power* (1967), 3.
13. Black, *A Constitutional Faith* (1968), 65, 22.
14. *Ibid.*
15. *Ibid.*
16. *Ibid.*
17. Black TV Transcript, 3, 5, 10.
18. *Ibid.*, 11.
19. Black, *A Constitutional Faith*.
20. Black TV Transcript, 8.
21. *Ibid.*
22. "Letter from Washington," *The New Yorker*, March 25, 1972.
23. Fortas Hearings, *supra*, 168; Douglas TV Transcript, 4.
24. "Retirement of Mr. Chief Justice Warren," 395 U.S. vii (1969).
25. Douglas TV Transcript, 4.
26. Schubert, *The Constitutional Polity* (1970).
27. Tinker v. Des Moines Independent Community School District, 393 U.S. 503, 525 (1969); Sniadach v. Family Finance, 395 U.S. 337, 345 (1969); Harrison v. U.S., 392 U.S. 219 (1968).
28. Schubert, *op. cit.*
29. Barron, "Acess to the Press: A First Amendment Right," *Harvard Law Review*, 80 (1967), 1641; Magrath, "The Grapes of Roth," *The Supreme Court Review—1966–67* (1966); Mendelson, "Hugo Black and Judicial Discretion," *Political Science Quarterly*, 85 (1970), 17; Bickel, *The Supreme Court and the Idea of Progress* (1970).
30. Bickel, *ibid.*, 14.
31. *American Journal of Legal History*, 15 (1971), 244; *New York Times*, February 27, 1971.
32. *New York Times*, July 19, 1970.
33. *Ibid.*

CHAPTER TWENTY-ONE

1. Cooper, "Mr. Justice Hugo L. Black: Footnote to a Great Case," *Alabama Law Review*, 24 (1972), 7; *St. Louis Post-Dispatch*, February 26, 1971.
2. *New York Times*, February 28, 1971. *St. Louis Post-Dispatch*, February 26, 1971; Swann v. Charlotte-Mecklenburg Board of Education, 402 U.S. 1 (1971); *St. Louis Globe Democrat*, October 15, 1970.
3. Alexander v. Holmes, 396 U.S. 19 (1969); Jones v. Alfred H. Mayer Real Estate Co., 392 U.S. 409 (1968); Fairman, *Reconstruction and Reunion* (Vol. VII, Holmes Devise History), *History of the Supreme Court of the United States* (1972).

468   *Notes*

4. Palmer v. Thompson, 403 U.S. 217 (1971); Reitman v. Mulkey, 387 U.S. 369 (1971); James v. Valtierra, 402 U.S. 137.
5. Berger v. New York, 388 U.S. 41, 73 (1967); Whiteley v. Warden, 401 U.S. 560, 576 (1970).
6. U.S. v. 37 Photographs, 402 U.S. 367 (1971).
7. Cohen v. California, 403 U.S. 15 (1971); cf. A Book Named "John Clelland's Memoirs of a Woman of Pleasure" v. Attorney General of Massachusetts, 383 U.S. 413 (1966).
8. U.S. v. Vuitch, 402 U.S. 62 (1971); *St. Louis Post-Dispatch,* June 16, 1970, commenting on Welsh v. U.S., 398 U.S. 333 (1970).
9. *St. Louis Post-Dispatch,* February 26, 1971.
10. Memo to Black, November 13, 1943, in Frankfurter Papers, LC.
11. Rogers v. Belli, 401 U.S. 815 (1971); Afroyim v. Rusk, 387 U.S. 253 (1967); Perez v. Brownell, 356 U.S. 44 (1948).
12. Oregon v. Mitchell, 400 U.S. 112 (1970).
13. Ogden v. Saunders, 12 Wheaton 212 (1827).
14. 400 U.S. at 118 (1971).
15. *St. Louis Globe-Democrat,* January 5, 1971.
16. Release, American Jewish Congress, October 12, 1971; New York Times v. United States, 403 U.S. 713 (1971).
17. *Ibid.* at 751.
18. Black TV Transcript; 403 U.S. at 717.
19. *Ibid.* at 717–18.
20. *Ibid.* at 720–21.
21. *Ibid.* at 720.

EPILOGUE

1. Interview with Elizabeth Black, December 1, 1972.
2. *New York Times,* September 26, 1971.
3. See *Hugo La Fayette Black,* House Document 92-236 (1972).
4. *Ibid.,* 1, 3.
5. Proceedings in the Supreme Court in Memory of Justice Hugo L. Black, 405 U.S. ix (1972).
6. San Antonio Conservation Committee v. Texas Highway Dept., 400 U.S. 968; see also "Children and Lovers," *St. Louis Post-Dispatch,* December 27, 1970.
7. Reich, "Justice Hugo Black and the Living Constitution," *Harvard Law Review,* 76 (1962), 673.
8. *Ibid.,* 750.
9. Griswold v. Connecticut, 381 U.S. at 522 (1965).
10. Reich, *The Greening of America,* noted at 405 U.S. xiii (1972).

Bibliography

Agee, James, and Jones, Walker, *Let Us Now Praise Famous Men,* Boston: Houghton Mifflin, 1960.

Alexander, Charles C., *The Ku Klux Klan in the Southwest.* Lexington, Ky.: University of Kentucky Press, 1965.

Allen, Robert S., and Shannon, William, *The Truman Merry-Go-Round.* New York: Vanguard Press, 1950.

Ashurst, Henry F., *A Many-Colored Toga: The Diary of Henry Fountain Ashurst,* ed. George Sparks. Tucson: University of Arizona Press, 1962.

Atkinson, David N., "Justice Sherman Minton, and Behavior Patterns Inside the Supreme Court," *Northwestern University Law Review,* LXIX, No. 5 (Nov.-Dec., 1974), pp. 716–36.

Barth, Alan, *Prophets with Honor.* New York: Knopf, 1974.

Beard, Charles A., *The Republic.* New York: The Viking Press, 1943.

Belfrage, Cedric, "Dixie Detour," *Harper's,* September 1937, pp. 371–80.

Berle, Adolph A., *The Three Faces of Power,* 1st ed. New York: Harcourt, Brace and World, 1967.

Berman, Daniel, *It Is So Ordered: The Supreme Court Rules on Segregation.* New York: Norton, 1966.

Bernstein, Neil N., "The Supreme Court and Secondary Source Material," *Georgetown Law Journal,* LVII, No. 1 (Oct. 1968), pp. 55–80.

Bickel, Alexander, "The New Court," *New Republic,* March 16, 1963, pp. 15–17.

———, *The Supreme Court and the Idea of Progress.* New York: Harper & Row, 1970.

Bishop, Joseph W., Jr., *Obiter Dicta.* New York: Atheneum, 1971.

469

Black, Charles L., *The People and the Court: Judicial Review in a Democracy.* New York: Macmillan, 1967.

Black, Hugo L., "The Bill of Rights," *New York University Law Review,* XXXVII, No. 4 (June 1962), pp. 865–81.

———, *A Constitutional Faith.* New York: Knopf, 1968.

———, "Erie Railroad v. Tompkins," *Missouri Bar Journal,* XIII, No. 8 (Oct. 1942), pp. 173–76.

———, "Inside a Senate Investigation," *Harper's,* February 1936, pp. 275–86.

———, "Justice Black and the First Amendment Absolutes: A Public Interview," *New York University Law Review,* XXXVII, No. 4 (April 1960), pp. 549–63.

———, "Mr. Justice Frankfurter," *Harvard Law Review,* LXXVIII, No. 8 (June 1965), pp. 1521–22.

———, Papers, Library of Congress.

———, "Reminiscences," *Alabama Law Review,* XVIII, No. 1 (Fall, 1963), pp. 3–11.

———, "There Is a South of Union and Freedom," *Georgia Law Review,* II, No. 1 (Fall, 1967), pp. 10–15.

Black, Hugo L., Jr., *My Father, A Remembrance.* New York: Random House, 1975.

Black, Josephine, "I Was a Yeomanette CPO," *Junior League,* May 1937.

Blackman, John L., Jr., *Presidential Seizures in Labor Disputes.* Cambridge: Harvard University Press, 1967.

Brennan, William J., Jr., "Inside View of the High Court," *New York Times Magazine,* October 6, 1963, pp. 35, 100, 102, 103.

Blum, John Morton, *From the Morgenthau Diaries.* Boston: Houghton Mifflin, 1959–67, 3 vols.

Byrnes, James F., *All in One Lifetime.* New York: Harper, 1958.

Cahn, Edmond, ed., *The Crest Rights.* New York: Macmillan, 1963.

Carmer, Carl, *Stars Fell on Alabama.* New York: Blue Ribbon Books, 1934.

Carter, Dan T., *Scottsboro, A Tragedy of the American South.* Baton Rouge: Louisiana State University Press, 1969.

Cash, W. J., *The Mind of the South.* New York: Knopf, 1950.

Catledge, Turner, *My Life and The Times.* New York: Harper & Row, 1971.

Chalmers, David M., *Hooded Americanism.* Garden City: Doubleday, 1965.

Childers, James Saxon, "Hugo Black, Always an Alabamian," *Birmingham News,* January 31, 1937.

Childs, Marquis, "Justice Black's Dissents and the Inner Workings of the Supreme Court," *St. Louis Post-Dispatch,* January 23, 1938.
————, "The Supreme Court Today," *Harper's,* May 1938, pp. 581–88.
————, *Witness to Power,* New York: McGraw-Hill (1975).
Clark, Charles L., Jr., "The Unfinished Business of the Supreme Court," *University of Washington Law Review,* Vol. 46, No. 1 (Oct. 1970), pp. 3–45.
Clark, Ramsey, *Crime in America.* New York: Simon and Schuster, 1970.
Clark, Thomas D., and Kirwan, Albert D., *The South Since Appomattox.* New York: Oxford University Press, 1967.
Clayton, James E., *The Making of Justice.* New York: Dutton, 1964.
Cooke, Alistair, ed., *The Vintage Mencken.* New York: Vintage (Random House), 1955.
Cooper, Jerome A., "Mr. Justice Hugo Black: A Free Man," *Alabama Law Review,* XVII (1965), pp. 191–200.
————, "Mr. Justice Hugo La Fayette Black of Alabama," *The Alabama bama Law Review,* XXIV, No. 1 (Fall, 1972), pp. 1–9.
————, "Mr. Justice Hugo La Fayette Black of Alabama," *The Alabama Lawyer,* XXXIII, No. 1 (Jan. 1972), pp. 17–22.
————, *"Sincerely Your Friend": Letters of Mr. Justice Hugo L. Black to Jerome A. Cooper.* Tuscaloosa: University of Alabama Press, 1973.
Countryman, Vern, ed., *Douglas of the Supreme Court.* Garden City: Doubleday, 1959.
Cox, Archibald, *The Warren Court.* Cambridge: Harvard University Press, 1968.
Cronan, E. David, "A Southern Progressive Looks at the New Deal," *Journal of Southern History,* XXIV, No. 2 (May 1958), pp. 151–76.
Curtis, Charles P., *The Law as Large as Life: A Natural Law for Today and the Supreme Court as Its Prophet.* New York: Simon and Schuster, 1959.
————, *Lions Under the Throne.* Boston: Houghton Mifflin, 1947.
Cushman, Robert, "Ex Parte Quirin et al—The Nazi Saboteurs Case," *Cornell Law Quarterly,* XXVIII, No. 1 (Nov. 1942), pp. 54–65.
————, "Incorporation: Due Process and the Bill of Rights," *Cornell Law Quarterly,* LI, No. 3 (Spring, 1966), pp. 467–501.
Davis, Helen Black, *Uncle Hugo.* Amarillo: privately published, 1965.
Decker, Raymond G., "Justice Hugo L. Black: The Balancer of Absolutes," *California Law Review,* XLIX, No. 6 (Nov. 1971), pp. 1335–55.
Dilliard, Irving, ed., *One Man's Stand for Freedom, Mr. Justice Black and the Bill of Rights.* New York: Knopf, 1963.

Dorsen, Norman, "Mr. Justice Black and Mr. Justice Harlan," *New York University Law Review*, XLVI, No. 4 (Oct. 1971), pp. 649–52.

Durr, Clifford J., "Hugo L. Black: A Personal Appraisal," *Georgia Law Review*, VI, No. 1 (Fall, 1971), pp. 1–13.

Emerson, Thomas I., *Toward a General Theory of the First Amendment*. New York: Random House, 1963.

Fairman, Charles, and Morrison, Stanley, "Does the Fourteenth Amendment Incorporate the Bill of Rights? The Original Understanding," *Stanford Law Review*, II, No. 1 (Dec. 1949), pp. 5–139.

Farley, James A., *Behind the Ballots*. New York: Harcourt, Brace, 1938.

———, *Jim Farley's Story*. New York: Whittlesey House, 1948.

Frank, John P., "Hugo L. Black: He Has Joined the Giants," *American Bar Association Journal*, Vol. 58 (Jan. 1972), pp. 21–25.

———, *Marble Palace: The Supreme Court in American Life*. New York: Knopf, 1958.

———, *The Warren Court*. New York: Macmillan, 1964.

Frankfurter, Felix, "Memorandum on 'Incorporation of the Bill of Rights into the Fourteenth Amendment,'" *Harvard Law Review*, LXXVIII, No. 4 (Feb. 1965), pp. 746–83.

———, Papers, Library of Congress.

Freedman, Max, ed., *Roosevelt and Frankfurter: Their Correspondence 1928–1945*. Boston: Little, Brown, 1967.

Freeland, Richard M., *The Truman Doctrine and the Origins of McCarthyism*. New York: Knopf, 1971.

Freund, Paul A., "Mr. Justice Black and the Judicial Function," *UCLA Law Review*, XIV, No. 2 (Jan. 1967), pp. 467–74.

———, *On Understanding the Supreme Court*. Boston: Little, Brown, 1951.

Friedman, Leon, and Israel, Fred, eds., *The Justices of the Supreme Court of the United States*. New York: Chelsea House, 1969, 4 vols.

Gerhart, Eugene C., *America's Advocate: Robert H. Jackson*. Indianapolis: Bobbs-Merrill, 1958.

Goldman, Eric, *Rendezvous with Destiny*. New York: Knopf, 1966.

Graham, Fred, *The Self-Inflicted Wound*. New York: Macmillan, 1970.

Green, Adwin Wigfall, *The Man Bilbo*. Baton Rouge: Louisiana State University Press, 1963.

Greenberg, Jack, "The Supreme Court, Civil Rights and Civil Dissonance," *Yale Law Journal*, Vol. 77, No. 8 (July 1968), pp. 1520–44.

Grossman, Edgar, "The Supreme Court," *New Republic*, September 3, 1951, pp. 10–13.

Hackney, Francis S., *From Populism to Progressivism in Alabama, 1890–1910*. Princeton: Princeton University Press, 1969.

Hamilton, Virginia V., "Hugo Black and the K.K.K.," *American Heritage*, XIX, No. 3 (April 1968), pp. 60–65, 108–111.
———, *Hugo Black: The Alabama Years*. Baton Rouge: Louisiana State University Press, 1972.
Hand, Learned, *The Bill of Rights*. Cambridge: Harvard University Press, 1958.
Handler, Milton, "Antitrust," *The Record of the Bar of the City of New York*, October 1960.
Harlan, John M., "Mr. Justice Black—Remarks of a Colleague," *Harvard Law Review*, LXXXI, No. 1 (Nov. 1967), pp. 1–3.
Harper, Fowler V., *Justice Rutledge and the Bright Constellation*. Indianapolis: Bobbs-Merrill, 1965.
Harris, Richard, "The New Justice," *The New Yorker*, March 25, 1972, pp. 44–105.
Hartman, Susan, *Truman and the 80th Congress*. Columbia, Mo.: University of Missouri Press, 1971.
Hegman, Ira, "The Chief Justice, Racial Segregation, and the Friendly Critics," *California Law Review*, XL, No. 1 (March 1961), pp. 104–25.
Henderson, Richard B., *Maury Maverick: A Political Biography*. Austin: University of Texas Press, 1970.
High, Stanley, "Mr. Roosevelt and the Future," *Harper's*, September 1937, pp. 337–46.
Hofstadter, Richard, *Anti-Intellectualism in American Life*. New York: Knopf, 1963.
Hogan, Harry J., "The Supreme Court and the Crisis in Liberalism," *The Journal of Politics*, XXXIII, No. 2 (May 1971), pp. 257–92.
Hook, Sidney, *The Paradoxes of Freedom*. Berkeley: University of California Press, 1962.
Hoover, Herbert C., *Memoirs*. New York: Macmillan, 1951–52, 3 vols.
Howard, A. E. Dick, "Mr. Justice Black, the Negro Protest Movement and the Rule of Law," *Virginia Law Review*, LIII, No. 5 (June 1967), pp. 1030–84.
Hunt, Morton, *The Mugging*. New York: Atheneum, 1962.
Ickes, Harold L., *The Secret Diary of Harold Ickes*. New York: Simon and Schuster, 1953, 3 vols.
Jackson, Kenneth T., *The Ku Klux Klan in the City, 1915–1930*. New York: Oxford University Press, 1967.
Jackson, Robert H., "Decisional Law and Stare Decisis," *American Bar Association Journal*, June 1944, pp. 334–35.
Jaffe, Louis, *English and American Judges as Lawmakers*. New York: Oxford, 1969.

Johnson, Nicholas, "Senator Black and the American Merchant Marine," *University of Southern California Law Review,* XIV, No. 2 (Jan. 1967), pp. 399–427.

Kalven, Harry, Jr., and Steffen, Roscoe T., "The Bar Admission Cases: An Unfinished Debate Between Justice Frankfurter and Justice Black," *Law in Transition,* XXI, No. 3 (Fall, 1961), pp. 155–96.

———, "The Metaphysics of the Law of Obscenity," *The Supreme Court Review,* 1960, pp. 1–45.

Katcher, Leo, *Earl Warren, A Political Biography.* New York: McGraw-Hill, 1967.

Katz, Stanley, and Kutler, Stanley, eds., *New Perspectives on the American Past,* 2nd ed. Boston: Little, Brown, 1969, 2 vols.

Keeffe, Arthur John, "In Praise of Joseph Story, *Swift v. Tyson,* and the True National Common Law," *The American University Law Review,* XVIII, No. 2 (March 1969), pp. 316–75.

———, "Justice Black Leaves His Mark," *American Bar Association Journal,* January 1912, pp. 63–65.

Kluger, Richard, *Simple Justice.* New York: Knopf, 1975.

Konefsky, Samuel J., *Chief Justice Stone and the Supreme Court.* New York: Macmillan, 1945.

Kristol, Irving, "Pornography, Obscenity and the Case for Censorship," *New York Times Magazine,* March 28, 1971, pp. 24–25, 112–16.

Krueger, Thomas A., *And Promises to Keep: The Southern Conference for Human Welfare.* Nashville: Vanderbilt University Press, 1967.

Kurland, Philip, *The Constitution and The Warren Court.* Chicago: University of Chicago Press, 1970.

———, "Equal in Origin and Equal in Title to the Legislative and Executive Branches of the Government," *Harvard Law Review,* LXVIII, No. 1 (Nov. 1968), pp. 145–76.

———, *Supreme Court Review,* Chicago: University of Chicago Law School, 1960–74.

Lasch, Christopher, *The New Radicalism in America 1889–1963.* New York: Knopf, 1965.

Lash, Joseph P., ed., *From the Diaries of Felix Frankfurter.* New York: Norton, 1975.

Leighton, George R., "Birmingham, Alabama," *Harper's,* August 1937, pp. 225–42.

Lerner, Max, *America as a Civilization.* New York: Simon and Schuster, 1957, 2 vols.

———, "Hugo Black: A Personal History," *Nation,* October 9, 1937, pp. 367–69.

Lewis, Anthony, "Explanation, Please," *New Republic,* December 4, 1961, pp. 9–10.

Liebman, Lance, "Swing Man on the Supreme Court," *New York Times Magazine*, October 8, 1972, pp. 16–17, 94, 95, 98, 100.

Lilienthal, David, *Journals*. New York: Harper & Row, 1964–69, 4 vols.

Losos, Joseph O., "The Supreme Court and Its Critics: Is the Court Moving Left?" *The Review of Politics*, XXI, No. 3 (July 1, 1959), pp. 495–510.

Lowe, David, *KKK: Invisible Empire*. New York: Norton, 1967.

Magrath, C. Peter, "The Obscenity Cases: The Grapes of Roth," *Supreme Court Review*, 1966, pp. 7–78.

Mason, Alpheus Thomas, *Harlan Fiske Stone, Pillar of the Law*. New York: Viking, 1956.

Mayer, Martin, *The Lawyers*. New York: Harper & Row, 1967.

McBride, Patrick, "Mr. Justice Black and His Qualified Absolutes," *Loyola University of Los Angeles Law Review*, II (April 1969), pp. 37–70.

McCloskey, Robert, "Reflections on the Warren Court," *Virginia Law Review*, LI, No. 7 (Nov. 1965), pp. 1229–70.

McGovney, Dudley O., "Is Hugo L. Black a Supreme Court Justice?" *California Law Review*, XXVI, No. 1 (Nov. 1937), pp. 1–32.

Meador, Daniel J., "Justice Black and His Law Clerks," *Alabama Law Review*, XV, No. 1 (Fall, 1962), pp. 57–63.

Meiklejohn, Alexander, *Free Speech and Its Relationship to Self-Government, 1941*. New York: Harper, 1960.

Memorial Addresses and Other Tributes in the Congress of the United States on the Life and Contributions of Hugo La Fayette Black. Washington: Government Printing Office, 1972.

Mencken, Henry L., *A Carnival of Buncombe*. Baltimore: Johns Hopkins University Press, 1956.

Mendelson, Wallace, "Hugo Black and Judicial Discretion," *Political Science Quarterly*, March 1970, pp. 17–19.

———, *Justices Black and Frankfurter, Conflict on the Court*. Chicago: University of Chicago Press, 1961.

Meyers, William, and Newton, Walter, eds., *The Hoover Administration*, Vol. 1. New York: Scribner, 1936.

Miller, Arthur S., "On Affirmative Thrust to the Powers of Law," *George Washington Law Review*, XXX, No. 3 (March 1962), pp. 399–428.

———, and Scheflin, Alan W., "The Power of the Supreme Court in the Age of the Positive State," *Duke Law Journal*, 1967, No. 2 (April 1967), pp. 273–320; 1967, No. 3 (June 1967), pp. 522–51.

Miller, Charles A., *The Supreme Court and the Uses of History*. Cambridge: Harvard University Press, 1969.

Mishkin, Paul J., "The High Court, The Writ and Due Process of Law," *Harvard Law Review*, LXXIX, No. 1 (Nov. 1965), pp. 56–102.

Moley, Raymond, *After Seven Years*. New York and London: Harper and Cross, 1939.

———, *The First New Deal*. New York: Harcourt, Brace & World, 1966.

———, "An Inquisitor Came to Glory," *Newsweek*, October 11, 1937, p. 44.

Montgomery, Ruth, *Hail to the Chiefs*. New York: Coward-McCann, 1970.

Moore, John R., *Senator Josiah William Bailey of North Carolina*. Durham, N.C.: Duke University Press, 1968.

Morgan, Charles, Jr., *A Time to Speak*. New York: Harper & Row, 1964.

Morrison, Joseph L., *W. J. Cash, Southern Prophet*. New York: Knopf, 1967.

Muggeridge, Malcolm, *Tread Softly for You Are Treading on My Jokes*. London: Collins, 1966.

Murphy, Paul L., *The Constitution in Crisis Times*. New York: Harper & Row, 1972.

Murphy, Walter F., *Congress and the Court*. Chicago: University of Chicago Press, 1962.

Myrdal, Gunnar, *An American Dilemma: The Negro Problem and Modern Democracy*. New York: Harper, 1944.

Neale, A. D., *The Antitrust Laws of the United States of America*. Cambridge, England: Cambridge University Press, 1960, p. 200.

Neary, John, "Up, Uppity, and Away," *Esquire*, May 1971, pp. 109–11, 188–96.

Nichols, Egbert Ray, and Baccus, Joseph, eds., *Selected Articles on Minimum Wages and Maximum Hours*. New York: H. W. Wilson, Pi Kappa Delta, 1937.

Nizer, Louis, *The Implosion Conspiracy*. Garden City: Doubleday, 1973.

Nock, Albert Jay, "The State of the Union—The Picking of Hugo Black," *American Mercury*, XLII, No. 166 (Oct. 1937), pp. 229–33.

Norris, Harold, *Mr. Justice Murphy and the Bill of Rights*. Dobbs Ferry, N.Y.: Oceana Publications, 1965.

O'Brian, John Lord, *National Security and Industrial Freedom*. Cambridge: Harvard University Press, 1955.

Patterson, James T., *Congressional Conservation and the New Deal*. Lexington: University of Kentucky Press, 1967.

Peltason, Jack Walter, *Fifty-eight Lonely Men: Southern Federal Judges and School Desegregation*, 1st ed. New York: Harcourt, Brace & World, 1961.

Perkins, Frances, *The Roosevelt I Knew*. New York: Viking, 1946.

Petersen, William, "The Incarceration of Japanese Americans," *National Review*, XXIV, No. 48 (Dec. 8, 1972), pp. 1349–50, 1367–69.

Pritchett, C. Herman, *The Roosevelt Court*. New York: Macmillan, 1948.

Reagan, Hugh D., "Race as a Factor in the Presidential Election of 1928 in Alabama," *Alabama Review*, XIX, No. 1 (Jan. 1966), pp. 1–19.

Reich, Charles A., *The Greening of America*. New York: Random House, 1970.

Rodell, Fred, "The Supreme Court Is Standing Pat," *New Republic*, December 19, 1949, pp. 11–13.

Rogers, William W., *The One-Gallused Rebellion—Agrarians in Alabama*. Baton Rouge: Louisiana State University Press, 1970.

Schlesinger, Arthur M., Jr., *The Age of Roosevelt, Vol. 1, Crisis of the Old Order, 1919–1933*. Boston: Houghton Mifflin, 1957.

———, *The Age of Roosevelt, Vol. 2, The Coming of the New Deal*. Boston: Houghton Mifflin, 1959.

———, *The Age of Roosevelt, Vol. 3, The Politics of Upheaval*. Boston: Houghton Mifflin, 1960.

———, "The Supreme Court, 1947," *Fortune*, Vol. XXXV, No. 1 (Jan. 1947), pp. 73–79, 201–2, 204–12.

Schmidt, Karl, *Henry Wallace: Quixotic Crusade*. Syracuse: Syracuse University Press, 1960.

Schubert, Glendon, *The Constitutional Politics*. Boston: Boston University Press, 1970.

Shogan, Robert, *A Question of Judgment*. Indianapolis: Bobbs-Merrill, 1972.

Steele, L. M., "Nine Men in Black Who Think White," *New York Times Magazine*, October 13, 1968.

Strickland, Stephen Parks, ed., *Hugo Black and the Supreme Court: A Symposium*. Indianapolis: Bobbs-Merrill, 1967.

Terkel, Studs, *Hard Times*. New York: Pantheon (Random House), 1970.

Tindall, George Brown, *The Emergence of the New South*. Baton Rouge: Louisiana State University Press, 1967.

Tully, Grace, *FDR Was My Boss*. Chicago: Peoples Book Club, 1949.

"TV Interview of Justice Black, Text of," *Congressional Quarterly Report*, XXVIII, Vol. 1 (Jan. 3, 1969), pp. 6–11.

Ulmer, Sidney, "Bricolage: Assorted Thoughts on Working in the Papers of Supreme Court Justices," *Journal of Politics*, XXXV, pp. 286–310.

———, "Earl Warren and the Brown Decision," *Journal of Politics*, XXXIII (1971), pp. 689–702.

———, "The Longitudinal Behavior of Hugo La Fayette Black: Parabolic Support for Civil Liberties, 1937–1971," *Florida State University Law Review,* I, No. 1 (Winter, 1973).

White, G. Edward, "The Rise and Fall of Justice Holmes," *Chicago Law Review,* XXXIX, No. 1 (Fall, 1971), pp. 51–77.

White, Theodore Harold, *The Making of a President—1968.* New York: Atheneum, 1969.

White, Walter, *A Man Called White.* New York: Viking, 1948.

Wilkes, Paul, "Matter Investigated, Case Closed," *New York Times Magazine,* April 19, 1970.

Williams, Charlotte, *Hugo Black, A Study in the Judicial Process.* Baltimore: Johns Hopkins University Press, 1950.

Williams, T. Harry, *Huey Long.* New York: Knopf, 1969.

Wilson, Edmund, *Patriotic Gore.* New York: Galaxie, 1966.

Woodward, C. Vann, *The Burden of Southern History.* Baton Rouge: Louisiana State University Press, 1960, 1968.

Wright, Charles Alan, "Hugo L. Black: A Great Man and A Great American," *Texas Law Review,* L, No. 1 (Dec. 1971), pp. 1–5.

Yarbrough, Tinsley, "Justices Black and Douglas: The Judicial Function and the Scope of Constitutional Liberties," *Duke Law Journal,* Vol. 1913, No. 2 (Jan. 1973), pp. 441–86.

———, "Mr. Justice Black and Legal Positivism," *Virginia Law Review,* LVII, No. 3 (1971), pp. 375–407.

Index

Ashland, Ala. 89, 90, 400, 402
Ashland Academy, 41, 89
Ashurst, Henry, 51, 55, 76, 78,
    138–39, 140, 141, 148, 169
Association of the Bar of the City
    of New York, 383
Atomic Energy Act of 1946, 293

Bailey, Josiah W., 74, 80
Baker v. Carr, 366–68, 388
Bankhead family, 24
Bankhead, John H., 67, 116, 118,
    120, 121, 135, 139, 140–41,
    143
Bankhead, William B., 168
Barkley, Alben, 47, 127, 231, 232,
    286
Barnett, Ross, 377, 385
Barr v. Columbia, 391
Barron, Jerome, 419
Barron v. Baltimore, 260
Barrows v. Jackson, 314
Barsky, Joseph, 331–32
Barsky v. Board of Regents, 331–
    332
Bartkus v. Illinois, 352
Baruch, Bernard M., 145
Baumgartner v. U.S., 215
Beard, Charles, 29, 154, 203
Beauharnais v. Illinois, 289
Bell v. Maryland, 391, 401
Berger v. New York, 424
Berle, Adolph A., 401, 412
Bessemer jail, 99–100
Bethune, Mary McLeod, 202
Betts v. Brady, 375
Bickel, Alexander M., 321, 358,
    374, 419–20
Bilbo, Theodore, 232
Bill of Rights, 23, 29, 205, 218,
    258, 259–61, 262, 263, 269,
    401
Bingham, Hiram, 127
Bingham, John A., 315
Birmingham, Ala., 22, 90, 92–94
Birmingham Medical College, 90
Black, Charles L., 359

Black, Elizabeth DeMerritte, 344,
    403, 412, 434
Black, Hugo L.,
    birth, antecedents and upbring-
        ing, 85–86, 88–89, 106–07
    family, 101, 106–07, 283–84,
        352
    education, 89–92
    admission to bar, 92
    early law practice, 94, 95
    prosecuting attorney, 98–99, 107
    police judgeship, 97
    Army service, 19, 100
    Ku Klux Klan, 62–63, 64, 71,
        105–06, 110, 113–14, 182
    marriage, 101
    Prohibition prosecutor, 107–08
    Father Coyle murder case, 103–
        105
    senatorial campaign (1926),
        117–121
    first Senate term, 127–45
    congressional investigator, 23,
        151–60, 341
    election of 1928, 133, 135
    senatorial reelection, 139–42
    election of 1932, 144
    second Senate term, 146–72
    and New Deal, 23, 166
    and NRA, 148–51
    airmail controversy, 153–54
    and Merchant Marine, 152–53
    and public-utility holding-com-
        pany regulation, 154–57
    seizure of telegrams, 159–60,
        162, 171
    and election of 1936, 158, 165–
        166
    Chairman, Senate Labor Com-
        mittee, 56, 168
    Court-packing plan, 162–69
    and Wage and Hour Act, 169–
        172, 237–40
    Presidential possibilities, 166,
        172
    appointment to Supreme Court,
        50–58
    radio broadcast, 37, 43

About the Author

A native of St. Louis, Mr. Dunne is a graduate of Georgetown University and St. Louis University Law School. During World War II, he served on a destroyer in the Pacific. He joined the legal staff of the Federal Reserve Bank of St. Louis in 1949 and became General Counsel in 1963; in 1967 he was appointed to the position of Vice-President. Formerly Visiting Professor of Law at the University of Missouri, he is now Professor of Law at St. Louis University. He is the author of *Monetary Decisions of the Supreme Court* and *Justice Joseph Story and the Rise of the Supreme Court*. Mr. Dunne is married to the former Nancy O'Neill, and they have six children.